Jordanians, Palestinians,
and the Hashemite Kingdom
in the Middle East Peace Process

For Ambassador Molloy,
with Warmest Regards

5/12/99

Jordanians, Palestinians, &The Hashemite Kingdom
in the
Middle East
Peace Process

Adnan Abu-Odeh

UNITED STATES INSTITUTE OF PEACE PRESS
Washington, D.C.

The views expressed in this book are those of the author alone. They do not necessarily reflect views of the United States Institute of Peace.

United States Institute of Peace
1200 17th Street NW
Washington, DC 20036

First published 1999

Printed in the United States of America

The paper used in this publication meets the minimum requirements of American National Standards for Information Sciences—Permanence of Paper for Printed Library Materials, ANSI Z39.48-1984.

Library of Congress Cataloging-in-Publication Data
Abu-Odeh, Adnan.
    Jordanians, Palestinians, and the Hashemite Kingdom in the Middle East peace process / Adnan Abu-Odeh.
        p. cm.
    Includes bibliographical references and index.
    ISBN 1-878379-89-5 (hardback). — ISBN 1-878379-88-7 (paperback)
    1. Jordan—Foreign relations—Palestine. 2. Palestine—Foreign relations—Jordan. 3. Palestinian Arabs—Politics and government. 4. Jordan—Politics and government. 5. Nationalism—Jordan. 6. Nationalism—Palestine. I. Title.
    DS154.16.P19A28 1999
    327.569505694—dc21   99-35751
                                                                        CIP

This book is dedicated to all who believe that sharing is not only a social value but also a cardinal pillar of peace-making and peace-maintaining

Contents

Foreword

K ing Hussein's funeral in February 1999 attracted statesmen from around the world. Arab leaders stood alongside Israelis; President Clinton and an ailing President Yeltsin were present; and so was Palestinian leader Yassir Arafat, a long-time rival of the Hashemite monarch. The presence of these statesmen was not only a tribute to a long-ruling monarch whose statesmanship was widely appreciated. It was also testimony to the wide range of friendly relations that Jordan as a state has been able to knit with countries near and far.

With a small population and few natural resources, Jordan has had to count on its human resources and its geostrategic position to gain stature and support on the world scene. King Hussein was masterful at keeping his throne in the face of multiple threats, ruling his country in a generally benign, patriarchal fashion, and convincing many in the Middle East region and abroad that a stable and well-governed Jordan was in their interest.

While many observers and writers have reflected on Jordan's strategic role and King Hussein's special qualities, few have looked inside the kingdom to examine the distinctive feature of the country, the fact that it is an amalgam of two closely related, but different, populations, the original Transjordanian inhabitants, and the more recent Palestinian arrivals. To an outsider, this distinction may seem to be a minor one. After all, both groups speak the same language, practice the same religion, and have the same general appearance. But they do not have the same history, nor do they have the same political identity.

Adnan Abu-Odeh is uniquely qualified to address the delicate matter of Jordanian-Palestinian relations and how they have been shaped by the evolution of the conflict with Israel. He is a Palestinian from Nablus, but identifies himself today as a Palestinian-Jordanian. During the traumatic days of 1970 when King Hussein ordered his army to drive the Palestine Liberation Organization out of Amman, Abu-Odeh was one of the few Palestinians to remain in the king's camp. As minister of information, adviser at the Royal Court, and Jordan's ambassador to the United Nations, Abu-Odeh represented Jordan over the next two decades, while always remaining aware of his Palestinian origins.

An entire generation of Western scholars and journalists came to know Adnan Abu-Odeh as one of the Jordanian officials who could help explain Arab politics generally, and the details of Jordan's circumstances in particular. His special quality was frankness, psychological insight, an analytical mind, and a sense of humor. These are all qualities that come through in his book, *Jordanians, Palestinians, and the Hashemite Kingdom in the Middle East Peace Process*. With the ascension of King Abdullah II to the throne, Abu-Odeh has returned to the Royal Palace as adviser to the new monarch, which makes the views he expresses in this book of particular importance as Jordan begins a new political era.

The themes found in this insightful study involve an intertwining of the histories of three peoples, Zionists (later Israelis), Palestinians (those who lived west of the Jordan River during the British mandate), and Transjordanians (those, mostly of tribal origin, who lived east of the Jordan River during the British mandate). Nationalist sentiment developed among each of these groups early in the twentieth century. But when the British era came to an end in 1948, two states were provided for these three peoples. Thus began the entangling of Palestinian and Transjordanian political identities.

Abu-Odeh reviews this early history with the eye of an insider, someone whose own life was affected by these events. And yet he tells the story with a degree of objectivity that is rare in such accounts. He sees things with a discriminating eye, and some of his interpretations are novel, but one never feels that he is grinding a political axe. He is trying to explain and to help his readers understand. Of course, he has a point of view. He believes that Palestinians and Transjordanians are fated to live together on the East Bank and should do so cooperatively. He worries about exclusivist ideologies, whether of the Zionist, Palestinian, or Transjordanian variety.

Some of the most insightful moments in this book come in the latter chapters, as Abu-Odeh tells the story of the troubled relationship between Jordan and the PLO. The 1967 war changed so much for Jordan and for the Palestinians. King Hussein lost the West Bank and East Jerusalem. The PLO, under Arafat's leadership, emerged as a competitor for the loyalty of Palestinians everywhere, including in the Hashemite Kingdom. During my first trip to Amman in early 1970, it was impossible to travel around the city without a PLO escort. The PLO was close to running a state within a state, and eventually King Hussein was impelled to act in September. "Black September," as Palestinians termed the military crackdown ordered by the king, scarred relations between the two peoples for years to come.

Throughout much of the 1970s and 1980s, King Hussein was seen by Israelis and Americans as the likely negotiator for the West Bank. The PLO disputed this claim, and the Israelis were never able to produce an offer that was sufficiently attractive to make it worthwhile for Jordan to risk Arab ire by negotiating on behalf of the Palestinians. Indeed, from 1974 onward, all Arab states, including Jordan, formally subscribed to the notion that the PLO was "the sole legitimate representative of the Palestinian people."

A turning point in the story of Jordan's relations with the Palestinians came in 1987–88 with the *intifada,* or uprising. During this youth revolt against the Israeli occupation, it became clear that few Palestinians in the West Bank and Gaza who had grown up under Israeli occupation had any sense that Jordan spoke on their behalf. Indeed, even the PLO had to work hard to be acceptable to this new generation of activists. Toward the end of August 1988, King Hussein drew the inevitable conclusion. He publicly announced that Jordan would no longer make any legal or political claim to the West Bank. Henceforth, Israel should address itself to the Palestinians and their representative, the PLO, for any negotiations concerning that territory. The kingdom that had been constructed by Hussein's grandfather would return to the modest dimensions of the Transjordan first envisaged by Winston Churchill at the Cairo Conference in 1921.

This change in the legal definition of Jordan raised questions about the status of Palestinians residing in Jordan. They had citizenship and political rights, but some Transjordanians looked at them as foreigners, and in some state institutions, especially the army, it was rare to find Palestinians at senior levels. Abu-Odeh is frank in addressing the problems that arose in this period as Transjordanians and Palestinian-Jordanians tried to work out their new relationship.

Throughout these domestic struggles, the Hashemites had the historical advantage of being a supranational symbol. Neither Transjordanian nor Palestinian by origin, King Abdullah and his offspring, as descendants of the Prophet Muhammad, could claim the loyalty of diverse tribes and of Arabs and Muslims of various origins. Indeed, Abdullah had originally hoped to expand his small kingdom to both the north (Syria) and west (Palestine) and thought of himself as a pan-Arabist. With time, his grandson, King Hussein, saw his role in more modest terms, but he never ceased to present himself as an Arab patriot, even if his geographical base of power might be limited.

Now Jordan has to face the future without its founding leaders and without the West Bank. King Abdullah II will not be able to avoid the issues raised in this book. Many have already noted that his wife, and Jordan's new queen, is Palestinian. Perhaps this provides a hint, as does Abu-Odeh's return to the Royal Palace, that Jordan's new king intends to make of Jordan a modern state open to all of its citizens, Transjordanians and Palestinians alike. And then, if the peace process regains momentum, one might even imagine Israel, a new Palestinian state, and Jordan showing how in this small region three peoples can live in peace and without the debilitating constraints of narrow-minded ethnic and national identities. But that is for the future, a future that Adnan Abu-Odeh, if I know him, is thinking about with his usual creativity.

William B. Quandt
University of Virginia

Preface

The end of the Cold War and the demise of the Soviet Union, among other factors, have had a positive impact on peacemaking in the Middle East. During the Cold War era, the rivalry between the two superpowers dominated the world scene. Regional problems, including the Arab-Israeli conflict, were seen in the context of this larger rivalry. Threats to national and regional security springing from ethnic, religious, or national differences were perceived to be minor, and the Arab-Israeli conflict was seen simply as the result of a Jewish state being surrounded by hostile Arab states.

With the end of the Cold War, however, these "minor" issues have become the primary threats to security and stability in many areas of the world. The Balkan War represents just one example. In the Middle East, the peace process since the Oslo Declaration of Principles (DOP) in 1993 has scored tangible accomplishments on both the Israeli-Palestinian and the Israeli-Jordanian fronts. The concerned parties, along with the United States (as facilitator) and the world at large, have focused their attention on the intentions and capabilities of Israeli, Palestinian, and Jordanian leaders—on what they have already achieved and on what hurdles they might face as the peace process continues. However, the strength of the opposition to the peace process has by no means diminished. The assassination of Prime Minister Yitzhak Rabin of Israel in November 1995 was an early indication of the difficulties and dangers of trying to make peace in the region, and in the years since then Israeli, Palestinian, and Jordanian leaders have developed increasingly divergent opinions on how the peace process should advance.

This book looks at the relationships between Transjordanians and Palestinians within Jordan. These relationships, greatly affected by the DOP and the Israeli-Jordan Treaty of Peace of 1994, still represent an unresolved issue in Jordan's political makeup. In the last few years, they have become the focus of debate between activists in the Transjordanian and Palestinian-Jordanian communities—a debate that has been widely covered by the Jordanian press. King Hussein himself became embroiled as an arbiter in the debate in November 1995; at his death in February 1999 (shortly before this book went to press), the views of the opposing sides were as far apart as ever. The arguments used by each side indicate that despite the Jordanian-Israeli peace treaty, the peace process in Jordan itself has a long way to go before the refugee problem is satisfactorily solved.

This book examines the origins and development of the symbiotic relationship between Transjordanians and Palestinians, tracing the dynamics that have been triggered over the years and discussing the validity of each side's apprehensions. Finally, it suggests a broad outline for establishing a practical relationship that will help cement the long overdue peace in the Middle East rather than threaten what has already been accomplished.

*   *   *

This book is not meant to be another book on the history of Jordan and Palestine, although the first eight chapters are mostly a historical narrative, while the other three chapters are mostly analytical. The focus in the book is on the Transjordanian-Palestinian dynamic, which could not be traced clearly in isolation from specific historical events that generated and sustained this dynamic throughout the last eight decades in this century.

Inevitably, this book devotes considerable attention to the Hashemite kings of Jordan, who, more than any other individuals, have shaped the development of Jordan and its people. No individual, however, no matter how powerful he or she might be, can dictate so complex and potent a relationship as that between Transjordanians and Palestinian-Jordanians. Thus, although King Hussein exercised unparalleled influence over his kingdom for more than forty years, his passing has altered neither the driving forces nor the defining characteristics of the Transjordanian-Palestinian relationship as it emerged after the fedayeen episode in Jordan between 1968 and 1971. In terms of that relationship, therefore, the new king faces the same challenges as those that confronted his father.

*   *   *

On the eve of World War I, the territory of today's Hashemite Kingdom of Jordan was part of the Ottoman Empire. Administratively, it was part of the province of Damascus. After the war, the territories west and east of the Jordan River came under British domination. On July 24, 1922, the League of Nations conferred upon Britain a mandate over Palestine including the territory east of the Jordan (Transjordan). Britain, however, was able to obtain approval from the League of Nations for excluding Transjordan from the provisions of the Palestine mandate relating to the Jewish national home, thus separating the two entities, Palestine and the Emirate of Transjordan. Thereafter, the people of the latter came to be known as Transjordanians. In 1946, when the Emirate of Transjordan obtained its independence from Britain, it became the Hashemite Kingdom of Jordan. Its people came to be known as Jordanians. In 1950, when the eastern part of Palestine was united with the Hashemite Kingdom, the former was named the West Bank of Jordan and the latter the East Bank. Both banks combined formed the new Hashemite Kingdom of Jordan, and the people on both banks became Jordanians.

This brief historical review is intended to help explain why, especially in the chapters that focus on current debates about national identities, this book uses the following terms:

Transjordanians: Jordanian nationals of Transjordanian origin.

Palestinians: The Arab people of Mandatory Palestine.

Palestinian-Jordanians: Palestinians who became Jordanian nationals after the unity of the West and East Banks in 1950.

Jordanians: Jordanian nationals irrespective of their origin.

Acknowledgments

I would like to thank the United States Institute of Peace for the fellowship it offered me for 1995–96, during which year much of this book was written. I would like to thank my colleagues at the Jennings Randolph Program for International Peace for their encouragement, especially Joe Klaits for his support and the intelligent critique he shared with me over the course of my writing. I am indebted to the editor, Dr. Nigel Quinney, for his patience and fine professionalism. I thank Dr. Ma'en Al-Nsour for being a great research assistant without whose generous help this book would never have been finished on time.

I am no less grateful to the Woodrow Wilson International Center for Scholars for granting me a six-month fellowship to finish my project. I especially thank Dr. Samuel F. Wells, Jr., the deputy director, for his generosity and encouragement.

Also, I wish to express my gratitude to the Center for Strategic and International Studies for hosting me for three months in Washington, D.C., during which time I was able to work on the last phase of my book and to finalize it for publication. In particular, I would like to thank Ambassador Richard Fairbanks for his guidance and support and Judith Kipper for her continuous encouragement and intelligent insight, which contributed greatly to the production of this book. I am also indebted to Dr. Murhaf Jweijati for his research assistance and patience when my project was undergoing some fundamental changes.

I would like to thank my son Sa'ad for exhibiting unusual patience in helping me prepare the final computerized drafts of the manuscript; without his assistance, I would have felt even more the paralysis in front of computers that typically afflicts people of my age. I would also like to thank my daughter Lama, whose relentless critical insights and unyielding challenges made the writing of this book even more pleasurable.

Finally, I would like to thank my wife, Khawla, for putting up with all my anxieties, obsessions, and unending demands with her usual grace and irony.

Jordanians, Palestinians, and the Hashemite Kingdom in the Middle East Peace Process

Jordan and Its Neighbors

Introduction

On the morning of September 15, 1970, I stood at attention before King Hussein in his suburban Amman residence and handed him a sealed report from the director general of Jordan's Intelligence Department (JGI). This was a most unusual practice; it had always been the director general's job to carry intelligence reports to the king. I was not aware then that this change in established practice was one signal of the secrecy that shrouded the formation of a military cabinet. Nor was I aware that I was about to become a member of that cabinet, which was being formed as part of the king's decision to crack down on the fedayeen organizations.

Having quickly read the report, the king said with a sober concern, "Brother Adnan, you are one of the few people in this country who are aware of the implications of the situation. If it continues any longer, I am afraid we shall lose Jordan *and* Palestine. Therefore, we [the royal 'we'] have decided to form a military cabinet to restore law and order to the country and put an end to this chaos. You will be the minister of information in this cabinet."

I understood everything the king had said except the last part about my appointment as a minister. It had never occurred to me that one day I would become a cabinet minister. In those days, a ministerial portfolio was the preserve of community leaders, notables, members of prominent tribes or clans, and sometimes senior officials. Neither my age nor my social status qualified me for such a senior post. I was only thirty-six years

3

old and a major in the JGI, and I came from a working-class Palestinian family. The king, looking me in the eyes, must have noticed my consternation, for he repeated the last sentence more slowly. Now my prompt answer consisted of a military salute and two words: "Yes, sir!"

On the afternoon of June 19, 1991, almost twenty-one years later, a Transjordanian nationalist and a member of Parliament (MP) sent a cable to the king asking him to change his mind regarding the selection of Taher al-Masri, a Palestinian-Jordanian, as prime minister and to terminate my own official functions because they had been rejected by the people. On that day, the king had commissioned al-Masri to form a new cabinet. I was the king's political adviser, a post I had then held for seven years. The nationalist MP concluded his cable by urging the king "to associate himself with Jordan and Jordanians before it is too late."

Reading the cable, I was disgusted but not surprised. Later that day I related the event to my wife, who is a Transjordanian herself, and she was shocked. She knew that since my "Yes, sir" to the king's order in 1970, I had been exposed to two attempts on my life and one abduction plot, all instigated by various factions of the Palestine Liberation Organization (PLO).

What made the difference between my wife's angry reaction and my cool one was the fact that I had already taken the first shock fifteen years earlier. Shortly after my return from a nine-month fellowship at Harvard University's Center for International Affairs in July 1976, I was appointed minister of information in a newly formed cabinet. With this appointment, I became the target of a systematic discrediting campaign launched through rumors. The main theme of the campaign was that I was a CIA agent imposed on King Hussein and that my nine months' fellowship at Harvard University had in fact consisted of a CIA training course. I investigated the source and the objective of this campaign. I was deeply shocked to find that it came from some of the Transjordanian elite, who had been motivated by the September 1970 showdown with the fedayeen. Up to that point, I had been aware of similar discrediting claims against me from the PLO, but those claims I could understand, since to the PLO I was a defector, a Palestinian siding with the opposing Transjordanian camp, and not a Palestinian-Jordanian standing for the restoration of law and order to his state. To be discredited now by Transjordanians was utterly incomprehensible until I discerned their motivation.

These newly revived Transjordanian nationalists had defined their objective as the safeguarding of Jordan against a potential Palestinian takeover.

Their premise was that Jordan was for Transjordanians, and Palestinian-Jordanians should be excluded from the government, especially from senior posts, because they were disloyal to Jordan. My patriotic record belied their premise, as did the patriotic record of every other Palestinian-Jordanian who had publicly defended the integrity of the country.

On that June evening in 1991, as my wife puffed out her frustration and anger in a rare emotional display, I kept asking myself, "What has happened over the last two decades?" I felt a pressing need for an answer, and I realized that in order to find one I would have to examine the roots and the course of the Transjordanian-Palestinian interaction since the rise of Palestine and Transjordan as two distinct entities following the breakup of the Ottoman Empire after World War I. I also realized that the Palestinian-Transjordanian interaction could not be understood unless it was examined within the broader triangular interaction among Transjordanians, Palestinians, and Israelis—an interaction triggered in the early 1920s and persisting to this day mainly due to the fact that the colonial map of the region, which was drawn after World War I without the consent of the local communities, produced three peoples and two countries. The examination of the implications of this flaw, its manifestations on the Jordanian scene as well as its bearing on the Middle East peace process, formed the genesis of this book.

1

The Origins of Palestinian and Transjordanian Nationalism

R ight after the end of World War I, the victorious Allies, now the heirs of the Ottoman Empire, introduced two systems into the eastern Mediterranean Arab region. The first was the nation-state system, and the second was a new international regime that gave some of the wartime allies a "mandate" to administer the former Ottoman colonies until they became full-fledged nation-states. In the eastern parts of the region, Arab and Kurdish populations were combined into a new Mesopotamian country named Iraq, which eventually was governed by a Hashemite prince. Iraq under King Faisal looked like an independent state, but it was in fact more of a British protectorate. Meanwhile, Syria and a greatly enlarged Lebanon were governed by France. And the new Arab entity that was to become Jordan was carved out of a Palestine that had been enlarged eastward and beyond the River Jordan by the British government and the Zionist leaders with the goal of building a national home for the Jews.

Under the terms of the Sykes-Picot Agreement of May 1916, Britain and France finalized the new political map of the area in 1920. Iraq, Jordan, and Palestine took the red-pink color in the atlas to indicate that they were dominated by the British, while Syria and Lebanon took the purple-blue color to indicate French domination. With the new map, the old parochial loyalties—to a tribe or a region, to a village, a town, or a district—were made even more complicated by a new loyalty to the centralized political authority the map now defined as a nascent nation-state. Just as the Arab identity had flourished during the last decade of the Ottoman rule as a result of the Young Turks' policy of "Turkishization," so new regional map–defined identities now began to materialize. Hence the Syrian Arab became distinguishable from the Lebanese Arab, the Iraqi Arab from the Jordanian Arab, and the Jordanian Arab from the Palestinian Arab. These newly emerging Arab identities sowed the seeds of a new state of mind: *wataniyah*, or regional nationalism.

PALESTINIAN NATIONALISM

When the mandate established the borders of Palestine on the new world map, the concept of *Filastin* (the Arabic word for Palestine) had already existed for a long time, not only in the minds of European consuls in Jerusalem—thanks to their biblical culture[1]—but also in the minds of the Palestinians themselves, especially the social elite. Several factors contributed to the further consolidation of this concept at the time the new borders were created and during the first decades of the new entity's existence. In his book *Palestinian Identity*, Rashid Khalidi, professor of history at the University of Chicago and himself of Palestinian origin, identifies four factors among others that contributed to the identification of the population of Palestine with the country in the years immediately before World War I. These factors are (1) the religious attachment to Palestine as a holy land on the part of Muslims, Christians, and Jews; (2) Ottoman administrative boundaries, which, from 1874 onward, made of Jerusalem, Bethlehem, Hebron, Beersheeba, Gaza, and Jaffa districts one separate unit administered independently from any other Ottoman province; (3) the external threat posed by the ambitions and constant efforts of the European powers (and later by Zionism) "to expand their influence and standing there throughout the nineteenth century," a fact that "naturally affected the self-view of the inhabitants of the country"; and (4) "the powerful local attachment to place," or "urban patriotism," a phenomenon of Islamic tradition.[2]

As to the religious factor, the fact that the country contained numerous holy shrines and religiously revered sites, both biblical and Muslim, contributed to the formation of a distinct social life among the population that lived in the midst of and around those sites. Much of their tradition and many of their customs revolved around the sanctified places. The major holy shrines like the Dome of the Rock, al-Aqsa Mosque, the Wailing Wall, the Church of the Holy Sepulcher in Jerusalem, the Nativity Church in Bethlehem, the Annunciation Church in Nazareth, and al-Haram al-Ibrahimi in Hebron all attracted visitors and pilgrims from local and distant communities that subscribed to one of the three monotheistic religions. For the indigenous people, these holy shrines were not only sacred sites to which to make pilgrimage but also venues for collective prayers on religious and national occasions. In addition, these places were spiritually captivating, and people visited them even when they had come to the area for business or social reasons rather than religious ones.

In addition to the major holy shrines, the Palestinians occasionally visited the tombs of *awliya'* (saints), and there they held customary religious festivities. In *The Emergence of the Palestinian Arab National Movement,* Yehoshua Porath notes:

> The outstanding event was the celebration of al-Nabi Musa, i.e., the annual pilgrimage to the mosque which, according to Moslem-Palestinian tradition, is located on the site of the tomb of Moses near Jericho. This celebration, which was apparently initiated in the days of Saladin [the twelfth-century Muslim sultan who expelled the Christian crusaders from Jerusalem], attracted celebrants from all over southern and central Palestine and even from the northern district of the country.[3]

The Muslim celebrations used to start at the Nabi Musa location and end at the courtyard of al-Aqsa Mosque on Good Friday, two days before Easter, when Christians from all over Palestine would also assemble in Jerusalem to celebrate; thus, both Muslim Palestinians and Christian Palestinians would rally side by side in Jerusalem for three to five days annually. Over the years, this annual rally gave them the sense of belonging to a common homeland—or more accurately, it provided a sense of unity within defined geographical boundaries. This was Filastin.

The Christian holy places spread over the land of Palestine. Jerusalem and Bethlehem in the center of Palestine, Nazareth and Cana of Galilee in the north, the lake of Galilee in the northeast, and the baptism location at the southern end of the River Jordan—all are Christian holy places. Visits or pilgrimages to those places must have given the region encompassed by them a conceptual unity: the Holy Land. Indeed, because of the symbolic significance of Jerusalem and the Holy Land for Christianity, the church gave an institutional expression to the notion of Palestine as a distinct territorial entity. Since the early years of the Byzantine Empire, when Christianity was embraced by the emperor, the title of the Greek Orthodox patriarch in the patriarchal anthem has not changed. The anthem says, "Many years to His Beatitude, His Divinity, and His All Holiness, our Father, and Patriarch of the Holy City of Jerusalem and all Palestine, Syria, Arabia beyond the Jordan, Cana of Galilee, and Holy Zion." Porath points out that "the jurisdiction of the Greek Orthodox Patriarchate of Jerusalem extended over Palestine and Trans-Jordan. It should be remembered that this patriarchate had existed without break since the Roman period."[4] Rashid Khalidi addresses the same conception and says that to Christians "the conception was firmly based on the biblical definition of the country [Palestine] as running from, 'Dan to Beersheeba.' It was reinforced by the boundaries of the jurisdiction of the Greek Orthodox and Latin Patriarchates and the Protestant Episcopate of Jerusalem, all three of which included the entirety of Palestine irrespective of the Ottoman administrative divisions, which changed from time to time."[5] The Christian regional consciousness of Palestine as a distinct area helps account for the fact that Christian Palestinian journalists warned vehemently against Zionism even before World War I. Muslims had a similar conception. According to Khalidi

> this sense of Palestine as a country went back to "Fada'il al-Quds" (or "merits of Jerusalem") literature, which described Jerusalem and holy sites and places of note throughout Palestine, including Hebron, Jericho, Bethlehem, Nablus, al-Ramla, Safad, Ascalon, Acre, Gaza, and Nasareth for pilgrims and visitors to Palestine and for the devout and inquisitive elsewhere. These place names suggest that a clear idea of the rough boundaries of Palestine as a sort of sacred— if not yet a national—space already existed in the minds of authors and readers of this Islamic devotional literature.[6]

In the context of external threat, Zionism was the most crucial factor in consolidating the concept of Filastin among the Arab population because it was tangibly manifested by the Jewish colonies in the late nineteenth century and early twentieth century. Ali Mahafthah, a contemporary Jordanian historian, reported that

> the Palestinian Arabs were sensitized to the threat of the Jewish immigration as early as the last quarter of the nineteenth century when this immigration became more organized. The first confrontation between the Palestinian peasants and the Jewish settlers took place in the early eighties of the last century. In June 24, 1891, a number of the notables of Jerusalem sent a petition to the

Sublime Porte in Istanbul expressing their concern and demanding the prohibition of Jewish immigration and Jewish land purchase in Filastin.[7]

The Arab perception of Zionism as a threat to Arab nationalism is best expressed in Najib Azuri's work. Back in 1905, in *Le Reveil de la nation arabe,* Azuri argued that

> two important phenomena, of the same nature yet opposed to one another, and which so far have caught the attention of no one, are stirring in Asiatic Turkey: they are the reawakening of the Arab nation and the latent effort of the Jews to reconstitute on a very grand scale the ancient monarchy of Israel. These two movements are destined to fight one another continually, until one of them defeats the other. Upon the final outcome of this struggle between two peoples representing two opposing principles will depend the fate of the whole world.[8]

The emergence of Arabic newspapers after the reimposition in 1908 of the 1876 Ottoman constitution contributed to heightening Palestinian awareness of the Zionist threat. The first Arabic newspaper in Palestine to warn against the Zionist threat was Haifa's *al-Karmil,* first issued in 1909. Like *al-Karmil, Filastin,* a Jaffa journal that was founded by the two Christian brothers al-Issa in 1911, waged a campaign against Zionism. Porath points out that the *Filastin* journal

> created a new factor unifying the various sanjaqs of Palestine. It is no accident that one of the principal instances in which the journal *Filastin* employed the term Filastin to denote the whole of western Palestine was in connection with the anti-Zionist stand. Thus at the end of the Ottoman period the concept of Filastin was already widespread among the educated Arab public denoting the whole of Palestine or the Jerusalem sanjaq alone.[9]

Another factor that contributed to the consolidation of the Palestinian identity was the relatively rapid development of civil society in Palestine under the British administration—a development that was fueled not least by widespread education. According to Shaul Mishall, the Palestinians' relatively high rate of urbanization "helped the growth of a relatively extensive labor force, especially in the large cities like Jerusalem, Jaffa, and Haifa by the 1940s. Thus the labor force was over 25,000 strong, and most of it was organized in more than thirty unions operating in the framework of the Federation of Trade Unions and Workers' Organizations established in 1942."[10]

British direct rule spurred the strengthening of Palestinian identity by generating, as almost everywhere else, a strong anticolonial sentiment. Moreover, the Palestinian people viewed the British not only as a colonial power but also as collaborators with the Zionist movement in plotting against the Palestinians. This sense of a dual enemy sharpened Palestinian nationalism and made the Palestinian struggle look somewhat different from that of the other Arab peoples. While the Palestinians had to fight against two enemies at the same time, other Arab peoples were engaged in a struggle with a single enemy. This engendered in the Palestinian people, especially after 1948, when they were scattered all over the area, a sense of self-pity and of particularity, like the disabled member of the family who always expects special treatment from the other members.

The 1936–39 Palestinian rebellion against both the British authorities and the Jewish settlements was the most effective single episode in consolidating Palestinian nationalism. Although the second half of the rebellion turned out almost to be a conflict among the insurgents themselves, it did provide the Palestinian people with a vivid collective memory of their armed struggle against their two enemies. Irrespective of the rebellion's failure, the fact that it happened and challenged two enemies at the same time was both a source of national pride and an inspiration for the Palestinians for many decades to come, even though they failed to reap the rewards of their three-year sacrifice due to the mufti Haj Amin al-Husseini's intransigent refusal to accept the recommendations of the Peel Commission of 1937 and the white paper of 1939. The former suggested the partition of Palestine into three areas: Arab, Jewish, and international. The Jewish state was to comprise 20 percent of Palestine and would include the coastal plain and the Galilee. Jerusalem, Bethlehem, and possibly Nazareth would remain under the British mandate. The rest would stay Arab and be united with Transjordan. The white paper, in contrast, recommended restricting Jewish immigration and Jewish land purchase and proposed a plan for an independent Palestine with an Arab majority after a transitional period of ten years. The mufti's rejection of both of these proposals deprived the Palestinians of an opportunity to legitimize their national identity in a state—or at least in a prospective state.

Another factor promoting Palestinian self-identity was the weak Arab performance, politically and militarily, in the Palestinian theater after the 1947 United Nations partition plan. The failure of the international community to devise and implement a "just" solution intensified the Palestinians' sense of persecution, which in turn strengthened their attachment to an identity, culture, and land that they felt they should struggle to preserve.

Finally, two external factors have fed a Palestinian sense of distinction. First, in the international arena, the Palestinian question has been an issue

of continuous debate among the member states of the United ▐
since 1947. And second, on the Arab scene, the priority of the Palest▐
question has been indisputable; no other Arab issue has occupied as m▐
of the Arabs' interest and concern since the end of World War II except▐
perhaps, the Algerian War of Independence.

THE MAKING OF THE TRANSJORDANIAN NATIONALITY

When Emir Abdullah, the second son of Sharif Hussein bin Ali, the leader
of the Arab revolt against the Turks, arrived in Amman on March 2, 1921,
the country was as it had been under the Ottomans: poor, backward, and
ungovernable. Transjordan had never been identified as a distinct entity
before Britain and France became the dominant imperialistic powers in
the area. In fact, Transjordan was part of Wilayat Dimashq (the Province
of Damascus) up until its occupation by the British. Then, according to
the 1916 Sykes-Picot Agreement, Transjordan fell under British domination, and seven months before Abdullah's arrival, Irbid, Salt, Amman, and
Kerak had their own local governments with one or two British officers
acting as advisers and overseers. The country was ravaged by utter neglect.
Its 250,000 estimated settled inhabitants were fragmented into four districts. The social organization was largely tribal, with marriage, discipline,
local defense, and the individual's sense of social identity determined by
tribal affiliation. Life was mainly pastoral. In spite of the country's meager
resources and its resulting poverty, Transjordanians were proud and hos-
pitable. The annual agricultural output depended on the region's unpre-
dictable rains, and the few existing towns served as venues for what little
trade there was. Health services were almost nonexistent, the educational
system was extremely backward, and illiteracy was high. The majority of
the population were Arabs; a minority were Muslim Circassians or
Chechens. There was a religious minority of Christians, most of whom
were Greek Orthodox. The bedouin tribes were still nomadic and were
contemptuous of villagers and townspeople. They always posed a threat to
the sedentary, especially to the agricultural community during the drought
seasons. Civil society was nonexistent.

The warm welcome of Emir Abdullah by the inhabitants of Amman,
the community leaders, and the tribal chiefs coincided with the Cairo Conference in March 1921, which was held at the request of Winston Churchill,
the new British colonial secretary, in order to discuss the British
government's policy in the Middle East. The conference was attended by

ils and their chief assistants. Among the partici-
'of Arabia) in his capacity as Churchill's adviser
itional period after the war, the British colonial
in essential component in its security plan for
i considered it an indispensable bridge be-
...u the Gulf "to keep the Middle Eastern countries
...itn a minimum expense through a line of air bases stretch-
...ii Egypt to Iraq."[11] This expressed Churchill's overriding goal.
Nevertheless, because of war fatigue and a shortage of resources, the British Colonial Office was not inclined to extend the direct rule that the British exerted over Palestine (where it had a pledge to meet relating to the Balfour Declaration) to Transjordan. Moreover, Britain thought that accommodating the Arab nationalists was a better policy than confronting them. Lord Curzon, the British foreign secretary, had no desire to follow the French example of brutality in the Middle East (namely, in Syria). Furthermore, the insurrection in Mesopotamia, then at its peak, brought home the case against direct rule and further encouraged an accommodation with Arab nationalists. Abandoning Transjordan to the French was also out of the question. Lord Curzon communicated the remaining possibility to the high commissioner (Herbert Samuel in Palestine) in a series of telegrams: "Our policy is for this area [that is, Transjordan] to be independent but in closest relation with Palestine."[12] Thus the concept of the role of Transjordan as a location preceded the concept of Transjordan as an independent nation-state. In fact, its prospective role made the state, rather than the contrary. As we will see, this historical fact has shaped strategic thinking in Jordan until today.

Now, the Balfour Declaration of 1917—which stated that the British government viewed "with favor the establishment in Palestine of a National Home for the Jewish people"—had been endorsed by the San Remo Conference and had been incorporated into the British mandate over Palestine. But when the League of Nations was in the process of offering the British Parliament the mandate over Palestine, Churchill, as David Fromkin argues in A Peace to End All Peace, was aware that "his temporary decision not to encourage—or even allow—the building of a Jewish national home in Transjordan ran counter to the provisions of the mandate, which was redrafted to provide that Britain was not obligated to pursue the Balfour Declaration policy east of the Jordan River."[13]

After the Cairo Conference, Churchill and Emir Abdullah met in Jerusalem, where they discussed the future of Transjordan. The discussions resulted in Churchill recognizing Emir Abdullah as the ruler of Transjordan, provided that the emir recognized the British mandate over Transjordan as part of the Palestine mandate, renounced his claim to the throne of Iraq in favor of his brother Faisal, and prevented any hostile acts against the French in Syria. Thus, Emir Abdullah became the de facto ruler of the Emirate of Transjordan in April 1921. On May 15, 1923, Transjordan was proclaimed an independent entity by the British, but the Transjordanian government was still bound to the mandate authority in Palestine.

With the creation of Transjordan by the British, the features of a new identity in the region were drawn. Like many other colonized countries, Transjordan fell under the influence of what Benedict Anderson, an authority on the growth of nationalism, calls the three institutions of power: the census, the map, and the museum. In his opinion, these "profoundly shaped the way in which the colonial state imagined its domination—the nature of the human beings it ruled, the geography of its domain, and the legitimacy of its ancestry."[14]

It is interesting to note, though, that the Transjordanian elite were aware of the implications of the Balfour Declaration and its potential impact on their prospective state in Transjordan. One of the earliest attempts to chart the future of Transjordanians after World War I and before the arrival of Emir Abdullah in Amman was the Um Qays conference. Um Qays is a small town at the northern tip of present Jordan. A number of representative chiefs and community leaders convened at Um Qays on September 2, 1920, to formulate their demands on the British government. These demands, along with the British response, were later known as the Um Qays Treaty. The major demand was for the formation of an "independent national Arab government" under the leadership of an Arab emir, provided that such a government could be completely disconnected from the government of Palestine. The connection with the British high commissioner in Palestine should be dictated strictly by the fact that he was the deputy of the king of England. Conscious of the implications of the Balfour Declaration, Transjordanian representatives obviously wanted to avoid any confusion of Transjordan and Palestine as one entity. In their view, such an impression could arise from the facts that both Palestine and Transjordan were under the same overlord (Great Britain) and that both of them lay within the jurisdiction of the high commissioner in Palestine.

To ensure that the two entities were separate, the Um Qays appeal noted that the River Jordan would be the demarcation line between Transjordan and Palestine. The conferees also requested that the "Zionist immigration" into the prospective Transjordanian entity be prohibited, as well as the sale of land to Zionists.[15]

Transjordan's map was drawn up by the colonial powers, Britain and France, to meet their strategic requirements. Transjordan's case was similar to that of many others where, to cite Winichakul Thongchai in *Siam Mapped*, the "map anticipated the spatial reality" for the sake of the colonizing power's strategic considerations. In retrospect, the Churchill-Abdullah accord, on the one hand, succeeded in reducing the area of the prospective Jewish national home. But on the other hand, it created on the Palestinian-Jewish scene a third player—Transjordanian nationalism, an actor that cannot be disregarded. One has to wonder if Churchill was aware of this implication of his agreement with Emir Abdullah. As for the emir, in view of his self-image as the epitome of the Great Arab Revolt and his ambitions at the time, one can argue that he must have been convinced that there would in fact be only two players: himself, as the representative of Arab nationalism, and Zionism. Transjordan to him was merely a home base from which he could salvage Syria from the French and extend his rule over Palestine, fulfilling his dream to unite Greater Syria. Upon his arrival at Ma'an (a town in southern Transjordan) in November 1920, he delivered a speech to an audience of Arabs of different regional origins in which he said, "I do not wish to see any among you identify themselves by geographic regions. All the Arab countries are the countries of every Arab."[16]

Immediately after reaching his agreement with Churchill in Jerusalem in March 1921, Abdullah set out to build the would-be Transjordanian state. April 11 of the same year witnessed the establishment of the first government. It was called the Council of Consultants because Jordan had not become an independent state yet. The council was composed of eight people and headed by a Lebanese Druz. Three of its members were Syrian, two were from Hejaz, and only one was a Transjordanian.

In 1928 Britain and Emir Abdullah concluded a formal agreement according to which the emir would continue to administer Transjordan on behalf of the British government. The agreement also stated that the British resident in Amman would be responsible for Transjordan's foreign policy and, to some extent, for its defense. Transjordanian officials and British advisers would devise the necessary legislation to facilitate the full discharge of Britain's international commitment, and the country would be guided by the resident in all important fiscal policies, especially those that might affect Britain, such as the budget, the currency, and custom duties. According to Anne Sinai and Allen Pollack, this agreement constituted "the establishment of a virtual protectorate, but in return Abdullah was promised that Britain would continue to offset budgetary deficits through grants or loans and to provide such armed force as Britain deemed necessary 'for the defense of the country and to assist His Highness the Emir in the preservation of peace and order.'"[17]

Following the agreement, an "organic law" was passed, establishing limited constitutional procedures for the newly forming hereditary emirate and granting Transjordan the status of an independent state. In addition, a nationality law established the borders of this new state. Of equal significance was a land settlement program carried out in the 1930s and early 1940s. This program gave the individual peasant a proprietary sense of security and made agriculture more attractive to the seminomads—indeed, it even appealed to the nomads themselves.

As already mentioned, Transjordan as an independent entity was originally created as part of a British security plan. This entity was supposed to be a secure land link between Iraq and the Suez Canal, a buffer zone to protect the process of building a Jewish national home in Palestine, a friendly neighbor to the French in Syria, and a deterrent against the traditional bedouin raids on the sedentary. Therefore, Emir Abdullah was in need of a security force to meet his domestic requirements and an army on which he could rely in fulfilling his pan-Arab ambitions. Hence the Arab Legion was established in 1923 and named al-Jaish al-Arabi (the Arab army) to symbolize Emir Abdullah's ambitions and reflect his intentions to build an Arab state that extended well beyond the borders of Transjordan. The core of the army consisted of Arab officers and soldiers of Syrian, Hejazi, Transjordanian, Palestinian, Lebanese, and Iraqi origins, most of whom had belonged to Faisal's army before it was dissolved when the French occupied Damascus in July 1920. From the beginning, the British government commanded and financed the Arab Legion, using it to halt raids by Arab nationalists on the French military patrols and outposts along the borders with Syria. The emir's failure to prevent this use of the legion aroused the anger and dismay of Arab nationalists and of the legion's Syrian officers, who were eager to see their country freed from French control. The British put enormous pressure on Emir Abdullah to oust the nationalists who were active both in the legion and in his civil service. When the emir gave in to this pressure, the legion became a Transjordanian institution commanded by the British. The legion increased its numbers by recruiting indigenous Transjordanians. In 1930, Major John Bagot

Glubb, a British officer who had served in the desert of southwestern Iraq, joined the Arab Legion and founded the Desert Patrol; this group consisted of bedouins whose main task was to provide protection for the oil pipeline extending from Kirkuk in Iraq to Haifa in Palestine. This unit was later transformed into the Desert Mechanized Force and was destined to play an important role in defending internal security. Through this force the bedouins, who had threatened the security of pilgrims and settled farmers before the establishment of the emirate, now became their protectors. Thus "the poachers had become gamekeepers: devoted clients of the state, proud to make their living in the profession of arms, and potentially good soldiers by any standard."[18]

By attending to the emir's security and by maintaining law and order in Transjordan, the Arab Legion was not only playing a role in building the political entity of the state but was also inadvertently active in building a sense of Transjordanian identity. In a country where tribal rivalry was the norm and repugnance for central authority was common, it was essential to establish some supratribal structures if a nation was to be built. Other institutions—most notably, the Department of Education—also fostered a nascent sense of national identity and allegiance. But the Arab Legion was, without doubt, the most effective of the supratribal structures, because it incorporated the Transjordanian tribes successfully into the state structure. In the legion, soldiers were identified by their stripes and not by their tribes.

Another important supratribal structure was the emir himself. He was not a Transjordanian, yet he was not perceived by the people as an intruder or an outsider. After all, he derived his legitimacy from the Great Arab Revolt that his father had waged against the Turks and, even more important, from his status in Islam as a descendant of the prophet Muhammad. Neither was he viewed as an insider or as just another tribal chief who was trying to impose his hegemony on the other tribes. To the tribal chiefs, he was not a peer with whom it was legitimate and appropriate to compete but a revered chief who deserved their loyalty and submission. In *Politics and Change in al-Karak, Jordan,* Peter Gubser relates a telling story about Emir Abdullah and a powerful chief from the influential Majali tribe:

> The Emir is reported to have asked Rafifan Pasha why the Majaly and al-Karak did not substantially contribute to the Arab revolt. Rafifan Pasha replied that the Ottomans had ruled justly, that he and al-Karak had on the whole enjoyed good relations with them despite the 1910 revolt, and that he had pledged his

loyalty to their government. But, he added, "now that they are gone and that we have an Arab prince, we are quite pleased at the turn of events." He then emphasized that he, his tribe, and al-Karak would be as loyal to Emir Abdullah and his government as they had been to the Ottomans.[19]

Indeed, it is impossible to imagine how Transjordanian society could have been governed by a central authority that did not enjoy the dynamics that Emir Abdullah had created at the time. However, the result of having these two institutions, the legion and the emir, working closely together to their mutual benefit was the establishment of a patriarchal political system side by side with the long-existing patriarchal social system. According to Naseer Aruri, the army turned out to be "an agent of political socialization in as much as it helped shape certain attitudes about the regime. It inculcated the spirit of uncritical obedience to and sacrifice for the monarch. Sons of bedouin soldiers were enrolled in army schools at the age of ten and recruited into the army upon graduating."[20]

Yet assembling the various components of a society is different from integrating them. While the state-building process in Transjordan continued, the process of building a distinct Transjordanian nationalism as a conscious venture by the state never took off.

Indeed, there is no serious evidence to support the idea that Transjordanian nationalism was of any concern to Emir Abdullah, his successive governments, or the British resident throughout the emir's reign from 1921 to 1951. As for Emir Abdullah and his governments, this attitude could be attributed to two factors. First, Abdullah's pan-Arab convictions and ambitions did not allow him to confine himself to a Transjordanian nationalism; he was in pursuit of his dream of a united Greater Syria. Though the seat of his rule was in Amman, Abdullah never lost sight of Damascus in the north and Jerusalem in the west. In fact, he made tremendous efforts to win the Palestinian elite and notables to his side in his arduous political rivalry with the mufti, the Palestinians' national leader. It was highly unlikely that he would gain the sympathy and support of the Palestinians if he was perceived by them as a proponent of another identity.

The British resident, in contrast, was mainly concerned with advising and supervising Emir Abdullah's administration, paying special attention to security and financial matters. Therefore, Transjordanian nationalism was not a British concern. On the contrary, one could argue, Britain was opposed to the emergence of a distinct regional nationalism in Transjordan because it could have hindered efforts to build and secure a Jewish national home in Palestine; strong national sentiments in Transjordan would automatically have led to mass repudiation of, and a possible uprising against, the British presence and interference in the country, and the British were not ready to deal with this, especially when they were fully occupied with the seething unrest in Palestine.

Another factor that impeded the rapid growth of Transjordanian nationalism was Emir Abdullah's policy throughout his thirty-year rule of excluding Transjordanians from the highest post in the government—the head of the Council of Consultants or, later, prime minister. The only Transjordanian to assume this high post during the emir's rule was a Circassian—in other words, a member of an ethnic Muslim minority. Conventional wisdom among Transjordanians holds that Emir Abdullah wanted to emphasize his pan-Arab objectives and convictions by appointing non-Tranjordanians to the highest office in the state, while Palestinians and others ascribe this phenomenon to the shortage of qualified people among Transjordanians. Each of the two explanations contains an element of truth, but not the whole truth.

I believe the exclusion was dictated also by the emir's need to avoid serious threats from existing social subgroups, which in this case were the Transjordanian tribes. Creating an imbalance among the tribes could have posed a serious threat to the tribal coalition that supported the throne. An appointment by Emir Abdullah of a prime minister from a certain tribe would have been viewed as an act of favoritism by all other Transjordanian tribes. The emir was in no position to create resentment among those who formed the backbone of the state. Indeed, the emir could legitimately fear that such resentment would permeate the army, since it was composed of tribesmen. In addition, in those days the senior posts in the administration were very limited in number, so Emir Abdullah did not have enough rewards at his disposal to placate any resentful tribes. The only way out of such a dilemma was to exclude Transjordanians from the post of prime minister and to appoint people without a tribal power base. Transjordan, we should remember, was and still is a tribal society where kin links play a substantial role not only in local day-to-day life but also in the relationship between state and citizen. Ernst Gellner eloquently argues that

> from the viewpoint of the central state, the major danger, as Plato recognized so long ago, is the acquisition, or retention, by the military or clerical office-holders of links with particular kin groups, whose interests are then liable to sway the officer from the stern path of duty. . . . The strategies adopted for countering this pervasive danger vary in detail, but can be generically characterized as "gelding." The idea is to break the kin link by depriving the

budding warrior/bureaucrat/cleric either of ancestry, or of posterity, or of both. The techniques used included the use of eunuchs, of priests . . . , of foreigners, whose kin links could be assumed to be safely distant. . . . Foreigners were often prominent in palace elite guards and in the financial secretaries of the empires.[21]

Besides, Emir Abdullah, who was born in Mecca, a relatively urban center in the midst of the desert, and was educated in Istanbul, another urbanized center where he later on resided as deputy for Mecca in the Ottoman parliament, was quite aware that the rule of law was the solid foundation for building a modern state. His enterprise of building the state of Transjordan, whose population then led a pastoral life, required an urbanized elite to help him achieve the task—an elite that had practiced administration under the rule of law. Such people came from cities in Hejaz, Syria, Lebanon, and Palestine, and many of them were senior officials in the outgoing Ottoman government. Ironically, these officials, who laid the foundations of the modern state of Transjordan, were the ones who provided the nascent Transjordanian nationalism with "the other."

As is well known, ruling monarchy has no room for national leaders other than the monarch. Because of the absence of national leaders, Transjordanian youth identified generally with the high-ranking officers in the army or the senior officials in the government. This fact is one of the many that account for the Transjordanian drive for education, since education was the surest way for a young man to be able to assume a senior post in the government or to join the army as an officer. More important, the lack of alternative national leaders sowed the seeds of the state-centered Transjordanian nationalism as it exists today.

Nevertheless, a rather active political life emerged after the 1928 agreement with Britain, thanks to the clauses that gave the emir's government a constitutional character. The agreement called for the enactment of an electoral law that would elect a legislative council for a three-year term. The council was elected in June 1928 and was composed of sixteen elected members and six executive councilors ex officio. According to the organic law, the executive council was responsible to the emir and not to the legislative council, whose meetings were chaired by the prime minister and which had no power to override the executive veto. In addition, whatever bills the legislative council passed were subject to the emir's approval and the British resident's consent. The electoral law reserved a limited number of seats for the subnational communities—the bedouins, the Christians, and the Circassians. The number of seats reserved for each group was greater than their proportional representation. This system perpetuated the existing cleavages and slowed down the process of national integration. Such a political formula understandably triggered an opposing reaction.

One form the reaction took was the Transjordanian National Congress. This ad hoc assembly of representatives of various sectors of Transjordanian society held its first meeting in July 1928 in Amman and came out with a national charter that stressed that the emirate of Transjordan was an independent state within its natural known boundaries. On August 15, 1928, its chairman, Hussein al-Tarawneh, sent a letter to the British resident in Amman in which he stated that the British government should view Jordan as being similar to the independent countries of Egypt and Iraq and not to the colonies of Africa. On this basis al-Tarawneh made three major demands. First, he requested that steps be taken to ensure the separation between the executive and the legislative authorities in the country. Second, he asserted the necessity of handing over the administrative responsibilities in Jordan to its own people. Chairman al-Tarawneh's third major demand was to set up a national government worthy of the confidence of the people of Jordan and of Emir Abdullah.

As they had at the Um Qays conference in 1920, Transjordanians in 1928 again diplayed a clear desire for independence. This desire was mixed with a strong wish to see the administration exclusively manned by Transjordanians. In retrospect, the precursors of a distinct Transjordanian identity appeared as early as 1923, when Transjordan had been carved out of the British mandate over Palestine. Such tribal chiefs as Mithqal al-Fayez, along with some of the intelligentsia among the town dwellers such as Mustafa Wahbi al-Tal, made it an issue of national priority to purge the administration of non-Transjordanians. "Transjordan is for Transjordanians" was the first slogan with which Transjordanians asserted their national identity. Indeed, asserting one's identity by pointing to or identifying "the other" is a classic mechanism for fostering nationalism. This slogan was expressed repeatedly during five of the six national conferences that were held in Amman in 1928, 1929, 1930, 1932, June 1933, and August 1933. Table 1 summarizes the Transjordanian national demands made at these conferences and shows how important being identified as a distinct nation was becoming.

As the table indicates, both "Transjordan's independence" and "supporting the Palestinian cause" were emphasized by all six national conferences. "Arab unity" was stressed only once, and "Transjordan for the Transjordanians"—a euphemism for excluding non-Transjordanians from the administration—was emphasized four times out of six. An analytical

Table 1. National Conferences in Transjordan, 1928–33

Conference	Transjordan's independence/ national government	Loyalty to Emir Abdullah	Resolution Supporting the Palestinian cause	Financial stability/ better economy	Arab unity	Transjordan for the Transjordanians
First conference, July 25, 1928	Yes	Yes	Yes			
Second conference, December 7, 1929	Yes	Yes	Yes	Yes		
Third conference, May 25, 1930	Yes		Yes	Yes	Yes	Yes
Fourth conference, March 15, 1932	Yes	Yes	Yes	Yes		Yes
Fifth conference, June 6, 1933	Yes		Yes	Yes		Yes
General conference, August 6, 1933	Yes	Yes	Yes	Yes		Yes

Source: Suleiman Mousa, *Emarat Sharqal-Urdun* [The Emirate of Transjordan]: *1921–46* (Amman: Royal Institute for Islamic Civilization Studies, 1990).

examination of these four demands reveals the political aspirations of the Transjordanian people during the early years of the country's formation. The main premise was the independence of Transjordan. Arab unity as an objective was inconsistent with that premise, and so was the appointment of non-Transjordanians to the senior official posts in the Transjordanian administration. This explains why Arab unity was supported only once, whereas "Transjordan for the Tranjordanians" was supported four times out of six. On the other hand, "supporting the Palestinian cause" received the same support as "Transjordan's independence." This is a clear indication not only of Transjordanian sympathy with the Palestinians but also of the Transjordanian conviction that Jordan and Palestine were two separate entities. Note that the conferees did not focus on Great Britain as an enemy. This was surely a pragmatic attitude dictated by the understanding that without Britain, which had created the map of the country, Jordan might not have materialized at all. Furthermore, the conferees were very much aware of Jordan's crippling financial situation and its dependence on Britain to meet the responsibilities of the emerging state. In fact, the conferees were anxious to ask Britain to increase its financial support to Transjordan and to reform the financial system of the country in a manner that reflected its independence.

From this analysis, one can argue that for the Transjordanians to become a distinct nation, they had to dissociate themselves from the Palestinians with whom they shared the same mandate.

What is also interesting about the conferences' resolutions was the repeated declaration of allegiance to Emir Abdullah and his heirs. Again this is a sign of realism on the part of Transjordanians, who viewed the monarchy as an indispensable element in guaranteeing the territorial integrity of the country and in preventing its disintegration or possible inclusion in the plans devised by the colonial power for Palestine.

The First National Congress of 1928 gave rise to the party of the Executive Committee of the National Congress. Other political parties were founded, but all were short-lived and had no real programs. Their endurance was linked to the willingness of their founders to remain in the party. Because of parochial loyalties and personal relationships, individuals would cluster around tribal chiefs and notables. This situation, which precluded organization and discouraged a mass enlistment in the parties, persisted until 1950, when the merger of the Arab part of Palestine (the West Bank) with Transjordan (the East Bank) drastically changed the political scene, as we will see later.

It is true that before the Jordanian-Palestinian unity, there was political opposition in Transjordan, but it did not amount to a serious popular struggle, political or otherwise, dedicated to acquiring independence. Because of this, the Jordanian people do not have a vibrant collective memory based on a popular struggle against colonization as do other Arab peoples, such as the Moroccans, the Algerians, the Tunisians, the Libyans, the Egyptians, the Sudanese, the Syrians, the Iraqis, and the Palestinians. The only anticolonial episode to gain a degree of popularity in the history of Jordan was the expulsion of the British general John Bagot Glubb and the Jordanization of the Arab Legion in 1956. But this salient episode, as we will see, was accomplished by King Hussein himself and not by a mass movement or popular struggle. Thus, it was compatible with Jordan's state-centered nationalism. In fact, Jordan should be considered one of colonial Britain's success stories because the elite who ruled the country under the control and supervision of the British government and in collaboration with its field officers remained the ruling elite after independence. This fact undoubtedly saved the country from violence and political dislocations and contributed to the perpetuation of Jordanian state-centered nationalism. Three major ingredients contributed to the formation of this state-centered nationalism. The first was the indirect rule of the country by the British; this indirectness placed Emir Abdullah, instead of the people, in confrontation with the colonial power. The second was Transjordanian tribal society, which relied on the emir in his capacity as the grand "tribal chief" to confront the British. The third ingredient consisted of the country's scarce resources, which made the people heavily dependent on government employment. This fact had a twofold influence: it made the intelligentsia and the tribesmen—who made their living working for the government and the army—docile when it came to confronting Great Britain, the major financial supporter of Jordan at the time; and it led the Transjordanians to perceive non-Transjordanians as intruders.

Since Jordan's inception as a nation-state, the government has been the country's main employer. Government employment in Jordan represents a field for competition, less between qualifications and more between families, clans, tribes, and even nationalities. This was the case in the 1920s and 1930s—as Transjordanian political discourse reflected—and this is the case now at the turn of the century.

2

The Struggle over Palestine
Hashemite Pan-Arabism versus Palestinian Nationalism

The Sykes-Picot Agreement and the Balfour Declaration[1] produced a recipe for instability in the southern part of Greater Syria, namely, two countries (Palestine and Transjordan) for three peoples (Palestinians, Transjordanians, and a growing Jewish community in Palestine). This situation, in its turn, triggered a triangular interaction that has persisted until today among the three peoples. This chapter analyzes this triangular interaction between 1921 and 1950, which with other regional (the Arab League) and international factors produced the Palestinian debacle in 1948, the rise of the state of Israel in the same year, and the unification of the eastern part of Palestine with the Hashemite Kingdom of Jordan in 1950. During this period the Palestinians were the lynchpin in the triangular interaction.

THE TRANSJORDANIAN-PALESTINIAN POLITICAL INTERACTION, 1921–50

With the establishment of international boundaries between Palestine and Transjordan, people on both sides of the divide began to learn that there were two distinct identities: Palestinian and Transjordanian. The Transjordanians set about building the state, while the Palestinians became preoccupied with preserving their national identity in the face of the Zionist threat and with wresting their freedom from the British. Nevertheless, social relations between Transjordanians and Palestinians continued to exist, and trade between them increased. In both countries, the new level of security and the modern British administration triggered development in every aspect of life. The increasing Jewish immigration from Europe into Palestine further developed the economy, though these benefits were confined to the Jewish community.

Since Transjordan and Palestine were administered under the same mandate, they were often treated by the British government as two complementary entities. The Palestinian currency, which was also the official currency of Transjordan, was not the only manifestation of this policy. Nor was the secondment of Palestinian civil servants to the administration in Transjordan. Palestine supported the Transjordanian budget both directly and indirectly. A. Konikoff's 1946 economic survey of Transjordan explained:

> The Trans-Jordan section of the Hejaz Railway [is] administered and maintained by Palestine[,] which, in addition, participated in the improvement of roads in Trans-Jordan, in the upkeep of certain medical services, etc. The High Commissioner, too, is paid solely by Palestine, although he holds a commission for both Palestine and Trans-Jordan. . . . [The capital and maintenance cost of the Trans-Jordan Frontier Force, which was formed in 1926,] was at first borne as to five-sixths by Palestine and one-sixth by Trans-Jordan whose share was met by the special grant from the British Exchequer. . . . This arrangement was not fair to Palestine and was accordingly superseded in 1930 by a new one, whereby the British Government undertook to contribute three-quarters of the current cost in respect of the Trans-Jordan Frontier Force, and the whole of the capital cost in Trans-Jordan.[2]

In the political and security spheres, the interaction between Transjordan and Palestine took place on three levels. The first was the official one, determined by the fact that both regions were under the same mandate. The British resident in Amman operated under the directives of the high commissioner in Palestine, and Palestinian officials were usually appointed to the administration in Transjordan as well. The Arab Legion was responsible for security during and after World War II in both Palestine and Transjordan. The Transjordan Frontier Force was stationed in Zarqa (Transjordan), while its commander reported to a senior British officer in Palestine, and this officer was in turn accountable to the high commissioner.

The second level of interaction was dictated by the emir's approach to the Palestinian question. To him the Palestinian problem was an Arab issue and concern, and he, more than anyone else, was qualified to solve it and consequently rule Palestine. After all, he was a Hashemite—the son of Sharif Hussein, who had led the Arab Revolt for the sake of Arab unity in Asia—and, most important, he was already ruling a country adjacent to Palestine. Abdullah's interest in Palestine was not brought about by the communal conflict between Arabs and Jews there; rather, it was due to his genuine ambition to annex the area to Transjordan and make it part of his domain as a prelude to establishing Greater Syria. In his March 1921 meeting with Churchill in Jerusalem, Abdullah had pressed for the unification of Transjordan and Palestine, but Churchill had rejected this request. Certainly, Emir Abdullah was aware of the implications of the Balfour Declaration. But his concept of a "Jewish national home"—he envisaged giving the Jews self-rule in part of Palestine within a larger Arab state under his rule—was different from the one held by either the British or the Jewish Agency (the body created by the Sixteenth Zionist Congress with the consent of the British in 1929 to oversee immigration of Jews to Palestine, organize their settlement, and administer their affairs).

Emir Abdullah welcomed no challenges to his authority in Palestine, and he watched with concern as Haj Amin al-Husseini, appointed grand mufti of Jerusalem in May 1921, was elected president of the Supreme Muslim Council in 1922.[3] As al-Husseini emerged as the most prominent Arab figure in Palestine and the spokesman for Palestinian nationalism, the emir came to view him as a rival to reckon with. The emir's role in Palestine was elevated when the Peel Commission proposed in 1937 uniting the Arab part of Palestine with Transjordan. This proposal was the first attempt to involve Transjordan as a country in solving the Palestinian-Jewish conflict. The emir's role was further boosted when Transjordan, together with the Palestinian Higher Arab Committee and other Arab countries, participated in the 1939 roundtable conference that was held in London to discuss the conflict in the area.

During the Palestinian rebellion against the Jewish community and the British government from 1936 to 1939, the Transjordan security establishment was given the task of arresting the Palestinian insurgents who fled to Transjordan and blocking the smuggling of weapons from Transjordan to Palestine. This security task reinforced Abdullah's claims that he was a significant player in the region and encouraged some Palestinian notables who did not accept the political leadership of the mufti to turn to Emir Abdullah. Rivalry among clan chiefs and big landowners in Palestine was as rampant as it was among tribal chiefs in Transjordan. To Transjordanians, Emir Abdullah, in his capacity as a supratribal leader, seemed ideally equipped to control this rivalry. To some Palestinian notables, the emir also appeared to provide the solution for their political rivalry. These notables, including Ragheb Nashashibi of Jerusalem, were moderates and saw in Abdullah a leader who, unlike the uncompromising mufti, was moderate, shrewd, and realistic enough to help solve the Arab-Jewish conflict in Palestine. They were also close to the British administration, and their belief that the British supported Emir Abdullah increased their interest in him. In the thirties these Palestinians did not find it antinational to ally with Emir Abdullah, the ruler of a neighboring country, against a militant Palestinian leader; pan-Arabism under a Hashemite was still a vibrant rallying cry at that time.

The third level of interaction between Transjordan and Palestine took place between the two peoples of these countries. The Palestinians looked on the Transjordanians as Arab brethren from whom they expected sympathy and support in their opposition to Zionism. The Transjordanians, in turn, perceived the Palestinians as fellow Arabs who deserved that support as they struggled to preserve their homeland and their identity on Palestinian soil. This support was expressed repeatedly by the national conventions in Transjordan (see chapter 1). Transjordanian citizens, unlike their government, supported the rebels with arms, money, and shelter. In the 1948 armed disputes between the Palestinians and the Jews, Transjordanians rushed to the aid of their Palestinian brethren, volunteering to fight on their side.

During the state-building process, from the establishment of Transjordan as an independent entity until its national independence in May 1946, Transjordanians were gratified to witness their distinct identity grow side by side with the development of their political structure. They started to reap the benefits of their country's statehood in the form of better standards of living. And the more solid their state became, the more they sympathized with the Palestinians, who had to fight for what the Transjordanians were achieving in a much easier way. In addition, the threat to the Palestinian identity strengthened the will of Transjordanians to preserve their own independent identity. (If a house in one's neighborhood is on fire, two impulses are awakened at the same time: one is to rush to help put out the fire, and the other is to revel in the fact that one's own house is safe.) Moreover, the Transjordanians had practiced making alliances in their communal conflicts before the establishment of the state, yet they were keen to preserve their tribal identities within the state even after its inception. All these experiences and values gave the Transjordanians a particular notion of Arab unity—that of alliance rather than merger. In other words, for Transjordan, it would have been much more acceptable to have a confederal relationship with another Arab country than to merge with it. And a federal relationship would have been tolerated only as long as the head of the state was a supracommunal, supratribal leader like Emir Abdullah. One can argue that Transjordanians were careful at this point not to weaken their identity by merging with the Palestinians or any other Arab people. They were well aware that the Palestinians were not only much larger in numbers but also more advanced in nearly all aspects of life. These facts were more constraints than stimuli to merger.

Abdullah, however, viewed Transjordan as a base from which to move into Palestine and Syria to realize his dream of a Greater Syria. This fact explains why he never paid serious attention to promoting Transjordanian nationalism even while he was engaged in state building.

Thus, it is fair to say that there were two relatively different attitudes in Transjordan toward Palestine: the emir's and the people's. The political system of Transjordan allowed the emir's position to prevail, while his people's position lay dormant for a long time to come.

In November 1945, a few months after the end of the war, an Anglo-American Inquiry Committee was appointed

> to examine the status of the Jews in the former Axis-occupied countries and to find out how many were impelled by their conditions to migrate. Britain, weakened by the War, found itself under growing pressure from the Jews and Arabs alike, and the Labor government decided, therefore, to invite the U.S. to participate in finding a solution. The report of the committee was published on May 1, 1946. President Truman welcomed its recommendations that the immigration and land laws of the 1939 White Paper were to be rescinded.[4]

The report also recommended that one hundred thousand Jews who had been persecuted by the Nazis and the Fascists should be allowed to immigrate to Palestine as rapidly as prevailing conditions would permit. Its third recommendation proposed establishing self-governments for the Arab and the Jewish communities in Palestine.

Arab leaders convened in May 1946 and decided to reject the committee's recommendations. This report was the first warning to the Arabs that the Palestinian question had become a hot issue.

After rejecting the Anglo-American recommendations, the council of the Arab League decided to take the necessary measures to counter the implementation of the recommendations. Realizing the seriousness of the developments, the Arab states' representatives created a committee consisting of the member states and Palestine; this committee was entrusted with examining the various political aspects of the Palestinian question in light of the rapid developments. Thus, the Palestinian problem became an Arab responsibility and was no longer exclusively Palestinian. The mufti found himself under the guardianship of the Arab League, where he had to promote and defend his case within the balance of powers among the Arab states.

EMIR/KING ABDULLAH'S ROAD TO PALESTINE

Abdullah's road to Palestine was not smooth. Until World War II, he had to deal with three actors: the Palestinians, the British Authority in Transjordan, and Palestine and the Jewish Agency. The three actors, however, were within the confines of Transjordan and Palestine.

After the end of the war, all kinds of activities—political, diplomatic, and military—surged in and over Palestine. The number of actors increased, and the stage expanded. There were a number of reasons for this, and two of the most important were the sympathy of the international community for the plight of the Jews in Europe after the Holocaust and Britain's decision to end its mandate in Palestine. When the United Nations was founded in 1945, it became a supreme arbiter to which international conflicts were brought to be debated and—so the founders of the world body hoped—resolved. The United States became more involved in the Palestinian question than any time before. The Arab League was also founded in the same period and became a regional player with which Abdullah had to deal in addition to the three prewar players. The new actor complicated the situation for Abdullah because it highlighted Arab rivalries.

In 1946 the Jewish armed organizations in Palestine launched terrorist attacks against the British troops and installations to pressure the British government into allowing the distressed European Jews to immigrate to Palestine and to accelerate British evacuation. On February 14, 1947, the British government announced its decision to refer the Palestinian problem to the United Nations, which, in turn, set up the UN Special Committee on Palestine (UNSCOP). This special committee visited the Middle East on an investigative mission and published its recommendations on August 31, 1947. According to these recommendations, Palestine was to be partitioned into an Arab state, a Jewish state, and the city of Jerusalem. The Palestinian Higher Arab Committee (HAC),[5] the president of which was the mufti, boycotted UNSCOP and rejected its recommendations. Constrained by HAC's position, the Arab states rejected the partition recommendations too.

The Palestinian moderate camp (the mufti's rivals) were disappointed by HAC's position, and so was King Abdullah. To them, this recent rejection was but another link in the mufti's incessant failures to grasp the realities in Palestine and on the international scene. On November 17, the king met for the first time with Golda Meir in her capacity as acting head of the political department of the Jewish Agency. In this meeting the king stressed his support for the partition of Palestine and emphasized his desire to incorporate the Arab part of Palestine into his kingdom.

On November 29, the UN General Assembly adopted the partition plan, which provided for the establishment of an Arab state and a Jewish state linked economically, as well as an international regime for Jerusalem *(corpus separatum)*.

The partition plan sparked a host of reactions. The most negative one was the Arab League's rejection of the plan. Once again moderate Palestinians were unhappy with HAC's and the Arab League's position. Yet in the midst of the overwhelming Arab rejectionist rhetoric, they were unable to voice their position of accepting the plan. They had no official spokesman of their own. Presumably, they were satisfied that King Abdullah was their spokesman. The king himself, who privately supported the plan, had to go along with the Arab League's decision, hoping that the Arab states would eventually discover for themselves what was possible and what was not and that then his own plans would fall in place.

Since the partition had been adopted internationally as the basis for the conflict resolution in Palestine, the incorporation of the Arab part into the Hashemite Kingdom of Jordan became King Abdullah's first priority. To attain his goal he had to secure the support of the three main actors: the British government, the Jewish Agency, and the Arab League. As for the fourth actor, the Palestinians, he had to deal with the mufti, since the Palestinian moderates were already on his side. The mufti and the Arab League by that time had become almost one actor to him. Neutralizing the Arab League was equivalent to neutralizing the mufti.

KING ABDULLAH'S DIPLOMACY TOWARD THE THREE MAJOR ACTORS
Great Britain

In the aftermath of the UN partition plan in November 1947, the British government's grand design

> called for a system of defensive alliances to be concluded individually with each of the important Arab states. Under the new treaties Egypt, Iraq and Trans-Jordan would be recognized as entirely independent and sovereign states.

Britain's avoidance of the pro-Zionist line in the U.N. was expected to make Palestine expendable. . . . [Foreign Minister] Bevin clearly intended to . . . preserve Britain's strategic interests there through the extension of Abdullah's kingdom to include parts of the country.[6]

Thus, British policy converged with King Abdullah's plans. Besides, the two parties were against the mufti's return to Palestine. But that was not sufficient for the king to proceed with his plans. He needed a clear British commitment. For that purpose, the king dispatched his prime minister, Tawfiq Abul-Huda, to London, where he met behind closed doors with Ernest Bevin, the British foreign minister, on February 7, 1948. Abul-Huda was accompanied by General Glubb, the British chief-of-staff of the Arab Legion.

In his approach to Bevin, Abul-Huda evoked the British-Jordanian treaty, which was concluded upon Transjordan's independence a year earlier. The treaty called on the two parties to consult each other whenever a critical situation threatened to arise. To Abul-Huda, such a situation was arising. He warned that upon the British evacuation, a vacuum of power in Palestine would emerge. The Jews, who had an organized administration, a police force, and an army, would easily overpower the disorganized, ill-equipped, and poorly trained Palestinians; ignore the UN partition plan; and seize the whole of Arab Palestine. In case the Jews abided by the partition plan, the mufti would return from his exile to rule Arab Palestine. Neither of these two alternatives would suit either Britain or Transjordan. Therefore, the Transjordanian government proposed to send the Arab Legion across the Jordan River on the expiration of the mandate in order to control and administer the part of Palestine allotted to the Arabs and contiguous with the boundaries of Transjordan. Abul-Huda proceeded to emphasize that Palestinian notables had sent petitions to the king asking him to send the Arab Legion to defend them against the Jews and the mufti's militia upon the British evacuation. Bevin approved of Abul-Huda's analysis and proposal. He warned, though, against the Arab Legion's invasion of the areas allotted to the Jews, but Abul-Huda reassured him that that would not happen.

Soon Abul-Huda's warning about the consequences of the imbalance of power between the Jewish military organizations and the Palestinians' military capabilities was proven true. The situation in Palestine deteriorated. Bloody confrontations increased between Jews and Palestinian Arabs. The British, bracing for evacuation, did little to curb the escalating military confrontations. The Arab Rescue Army—a military force consisting mainly of Palestinians as well as Arab volunteers trained in Syria—entered Palestine in January 1948. The Haganah (the largest Jewish military organization, created in the 1920s to defend Jewish settlements) set out to secure all the areas allotted to the Jewish state by the UN partition plan. The Haganah adopted an "aggressive defense" strategy, in accordance with which it occupied Jaffa, Haifa, and Tiberias. To secure an uninterrupted territorial base, the Haganah also occupied the corridors leading to the Jewish settlements and scores of Arab villages, evicting the populations of most of them and turning them into refugees. In April 1948, the Jewish Irgun and Stern gang fighters perpetrated the infamous massacre of the Palestinian village of Deir Yassin. In this same month Abdul-Qader al-Husseini, the commander of the mufti's Jaish al-Jihad al-Muqaddas (the Holy War Army), was killed in the battle of al-Qastal near Jerusalem. Moreover, it was during this month that the Arab Rescue Army proved to be lame, while the Jewish military force turned out to be much larger and stronger than thought before the eruption of hostilities. As a result, the tide of the fighting turned in favor of the Jews. Palestinian society witnessed an unprecedented chaos and panic and rapidly began to disintegrate. The Jews continued their aggression, and the Palestinians turned to the Arab states as their only hope for rescue.

The Jewish Agency

His awareness of international developments after World War II, especially the prevailing sympathy for European Jews, left King Abdullah more sure than ever before that the establishment of a Jewish state in Palestine was imminent. The UN partition plan confirmed his assessment. Therefore, any Arab strategy based on aborting the establishment of the Jewish state was destined to failure. What appeared realistic to Abdullah was to reconcile Jordan's and the Palestinians' interests with the interests of the Jewish state in the offing. His "partition and merger plan" was realistically optimal. After all, Jordan would have access to the sea and would be able to develop as a Mediterranean state in cooperation with the advanced Jewish state.

These were the constituents of Abdullah's proposition when he approached the Jewish Agency after the war. In November 1947, he communicated to the agency his support for the partition plan and solicited its support for his plan of merging the Arab part of Palestine with his kingdom. Like Britain, the Jewish Agency had two common denominators with King Abdullah—opposition to a Palestinian state and exclusion of the mufti from the future of Palestine. When the Palestinian defensive situation deteriorated in 1948, despite the existence of the Arab Rescue Army, and the Arab public witnessed the first flow of scared Palestinian refugees, the Arab cry for war to defend the Palestinians drowned any voice of reason. King Abdullah, pursuing his personal diplomacy, made a last try with the Jewish Agency, hoping to reach an agreement with its leaders that would be acceptable to the Arabs and would spare them military confrontations.

Abdullah made his last try in a meeting with Golda Meir on May 10, 1948. He stressed his support for a peaceful settlement and presented Meir with specific proposals for reaching a final solution. The gist of those proposals can be summed up in the following:

1. Palestine would remain undivided, with autonomy for the areas where Jews predominate.

2. This arrangement would last for one year, after which the country would be joined with Transjordan.

3. There would be one parliament in which the Jews would be allotted 50 percent of the seats.

4. There would be a cabinet in which the Jews would be represented (no mention of the percentage).

The king also asked Meir why the Jews were in such a hurry to proclaim their state. This remark should be viewed in the context of his proposal; he was certainly aware that the Jews were striving for much more than he was suggesting. Nevertheless, his proposal was designed to solicit the most Palestinian and Arab support possible in order to ensure a peaceful solution. He also hinted to the Jewish Agency that a Jewish state was not excluded and would materialize in due time. Obviously, Meir was not persuaded, and the king's failure to persuade her made the war between the Arabs and the Jews inevitable.

The Arab League

The Arab League Charter created a sort of loose Arab confederation. The requirement that the Arab League's resolutions were to be passed by consensus rather than by a majority of votes hindered its ability to take effective action on many Arab issues. The Palestinian question was one of them. This decision-making process often proved to be paralyzing or produced irrational or unrealistic resolutions. In this context, the Arab League was but another constraint on King Abdullah's realistic thinking and ambitious plans for Palestine. What made the Arab League even more of a hindrance to King Abdullah's plans was its choice of the mufti as the representative of the Palestinian people. That choice reflected an emotional Arab approach to an issue whose great complexity demanded a rational approach. It is true that the mufti was the most popular Palestinian leader, but it is equally true that his popularity was not matched by his political wisdom. He was known for his autocratic approach, militancy, lack of resilience, and rejectionist attitude, all of which contributed to the Palestinians missing some promising opportunities to solve their conflict with the Jews in a fairly acceptable manner before the war. These negative attributes for a leader were to display themselves in the Arab League and adversely to influence the collective Arab action toward Palestine. Furthermore, the Arab League's choice of Amin al-Husseini, who had just returned from exile in Nazi Germany, as the spokesman for the Palestinian cause was self-defeating. The mufti, who was still a national leader to his people, was to many states, both Arab and non-Arab, persona non grata due to his support for Hitler. Certainly King Abdullah was not happy to see the mufti reappear on the Palestinian political scene.

To undercut the mufti's policies in the Arab League, King Abdullah had to rely on Iraq, which would not forgive the mufti for supporting Rashid Aly al-Keilany.[7] (Al-Keilany had deposed the Iraqi regent Abdul-Illah in 1941 and supported the Nazis.)

Syria, Lebanon, Saudi Arabia, and Egypt were opposed to King Abdullah because of his ambitions in Palestine and Syria, hence the support of these states for the mufti. Nevertheless, these states would not take a stand that might antagonize two of the Arab League's seven members (Jordan and Iraq) and prompt them to withdraw. Most important, these states were aware of the strength of the Arab Legion and would not risk losing it as a reliable military force in case they had to fight in Palestine. The Israeli writer Zvi Elpeleg correctly argues that "the support which the Grand Mufti had from Egypt, Syria and Saudi Arabia emanated more from their opposition to King Abdullah's expansionist objective than from their sympathy for the Mufti."[8]

These two political games, played simultaneously on the stage of the Arab League from 1946 to 1949, shed enough light to explain why the Arab League's performance on the Palestinian question was confused, complicated, and in some instances irresponsible. It also indicates that the Arab League contributed inadvertently to the plight of the Palestinians.

In the meeting in the council of the Arab League in October 1947, for example, Jordan, supported by Iraq, succeeded in preempting two serious proposals of the HAC's representative, who acted upon the instructions of the mufti and was supported by the anti-Hashemite camp. The council's meeting was to discuss the ways and means to counter UNSCOP's partition plan. The first proposal was to form a Palestinian government immediately to be headed by the mufti. The second was to appoint the mufti's cousin, Abdul-Qader al-Husseini, as the chief commander of the Arab Rescue Army.

On April 10, 1948, the Political Committee of the Arab League convened in Cairo to discuss the deteriorating situation in Palestine. When the Jordanian delegation emphasized the king's final decision to intervene militarily to save the Palestinians, Syria and Lebanon called for the formation of an all-Arab expeditionary force to occupy Palestine upon the British withdrawal, instead of having the Arab states act unilaterally. Egypt conceded and, in an effort to obstruct the king's goals, made an additional demand: that the Arab League announce that the Palestinians would be granted the right to choose their form of government freely in a liberated Palestine.

While the Political Committee was still in session, King Abdullah sent a telegram in which he offered to undertake the rescue of Palestine. Further, in a statement made by the Hashemite royal court in Amman, Jordan asserted its special position regarding Palestine and announced that its actions would support this position. The court's statement declared that the Hashemite Kingdom and Palestine were a single entity, comprising a coast and a hinterland. The statement also asserted that in defense of its interests and for the preservation of national existence, the kingdom vigorously opposed partition and trusteeship.

The reply came from the secretary general of the Arab League:

> The Committee has decided at its meeting today to thank your Majesty for your magnanimity and the Arab zeal. It was also decided to delegate General Ismail Safwat Pasha [the chairman of the Arab Military Committee] to discuss with your majesty the necessary measures to be taken to liberate the besieged Arabs and to prevent more massacres from taking place as happened at Deir Yassin village and other localities. The Committee are of the unanimous opinion that the presence in Palestine of the Arab Legion makes it possible for the Legion to accomplish this important task with the required haste. The Political Committee adjures your Majesty to please allow the Transjordan Arab Legion to do this duty.[9]

The text of the secretary general's message was worded so that it would not give the king the impression that he was the sole savior of Palestine. The reference to the presence of the Arab Legion in Palestine was meant to remind him that he should have done the job of securing the Palestinians without asking permission from the Arab League; after all, some Arab Legion units were already deployed in the theater of the Jewish military activities, while the other Arab states had no troops whatsoever there. The secretary general's request that the king "please allow" the legion to perform this duty confirms this connotation.

Nevertheless, the king was encouraged by the message. It helped him win his first political encounter with the Arab League as a whole and his second political victory over the mufti. Now the king was perceived as a potential savior by the majority of Palestinians, who were terrified by the Jewish military organizations' targeting of Palestinian civilians. This perception of the king as savior was certainly a double-edged sword. On the one hand, it strengthened the king's position with regard to the mufti, but on the other hand, it placed on him the moral onus of living up to the Palestinians' expectations, especially after the Haganah had captured Jaffa, Haifa, and Tiberias. The king realized that his new role held paramount importance; successful containment of the Jewish aggression against the Palestinians would legitimize his claims to the Arab part of Palestine.

On April 29, 1948, the Political Committee decided in favor of full-scale intervention in Palestine, and King Abdullah was later named general commander of the all-Arab expeditionary force. Each contributing state (Egypt, Syria, Lebanon, Jordan, and Iraq) was allocated an operational zone in which it maintained an independent command. The Arab Legion and the Iraqi army were given the task of occupying and defending the central part of Palestine. King Abdullah insisted on concentrating the Arab Legion in the area of Jerusalem and Nablus, the territory contiguous with Transjordan.

As the deadline for Britain's evacuation on May 15, 1948, approached, the intensity of the violence between the Arabs and the Jews grew. The British government's efforts to go through an orderly transfer of authority to the UN commission were disrupted by an escalation of the Jewish offensive, especially in Jerusalem, and the consequent decision of the Arab states to intervene militarily with regular troops.

THE WAR

On May 14, 1948, Ben-Gurion proclaimed the establishment of the State of Israel. At exactly twelve o'clock, the Jordanian troops proceeded to their designated operational theater in Palestine. Around the same time, a Jewish offensive was launched on Jerusalem. With these events, the first

Arab-Israeli war ushered in a new era for the Middle East and certainly a new era for the Hashemite Kingdom of Jordan.

None of the interested parties knew how the military situation would develop. Indeed, hardly had the British evacuated Jerusalem on May 15 than a Jewish offensive was launched to seize all the Arab and mixed zones of the New City of Jerusalem (later known as West Jerusalem) in order to form an uninterrupted Jewish area all the way up to the walls of the Old City, which included the Jewish quarter. When the Arab defenders of the Old City started to run short of ammunition, they sent desperate appeals to King Abdullah for help. On May 17, the king decided to act, issuing orders to General Glubb to defend the remaining section of the city of Jerusalem. Units of the Arab Legion advanced into the Arab section on May 18, and on May 28 the defenders of the Jewish quarter surrendered to the Arab Legion. The success of the Arab Legion in defending the Old City not only brought overwhelming satisfaction to King Abdullah but also gave him merit in the Arab world for saving the holy places. It was also a severe political blow to the mufti, since his power base was in Jerusalem. In fact, when the Jewish quarter surrendered to the legion, many of the mufti's supporters joined King Abdullah's camp.

Obviously, the battle for Jerusalem threatened the UN plan for the whole city. The Israelis complained about the Jordanian intervention to the American secretary of state, blaming what had happened on Britain, since it was in control of the Arab Legion. Britain, which depended on American aid for economic recovery after World War II, had no choice but to reassure the Americans. In a secret message to his counterpart, Secretary Marshall, Bevin revealed that the British officers in the Arab Legion had been instructed to withdraw to Transjordan if the Arab Legion attacked the territories allotted to the Jewish State. To diffuse the mounting international pressure, Britain submitted to the UN Security Council a draft resolution for a cease-fire in Jerusalem. On May 29, the Security Council adopted the British resolution and commissioned Count Folk Bernadotte of Sweden, the UN mediator for Palestine, to oversee its implementation.

The first Arab-Israeli war went on intermittently from May 15, 1948, to January 4, 1949. It was interrupted by two truces; the first was limited in time, between June 11 and July 9, 1948, and the second was unlimited in time and started on July 18, 1948. Egypt announced its readiness to begin armistice negotiations on January 4, 1949, and three days later, on January 7, 1949, the cease-fire went into effect, marking the formal end of the first Arab-Israeli war.

When the UN mediator, Count Bernadotte, suggested a truce at the end of the first round of the war, Israel was the first to accept, followed by the Arab League. In this first round, the Arab forces had held on to the Arab zones they defended but had failed to retrieve the towns and villages that had been occupied by the Haganah before the British withdrawal. During this first round, the Arab Legion was able to defend the territory allocated to it, to destroy and occupy a couple of settlements in the Jerusalem and Hebron areas, and, most important, to capture the Jewish quarter in the Old City of Jerusalem. The legion came out of the first round as the only Arab army that performed well, especially in Jerusalem and its approaches, where it succeeded in defending the Old City and repelling all the intensive Jewish attacks to capture it, to establish contact with Mount Scopus, and to open the road between the coast and Jerusalem. The Arab Legion's defense of Jerusalem in Bab al-Wad, northwest of the Holy City, was considered a heroic act, and from this engagement the Arab Legion gained its widespread reputation as a brave, well-trained army to be reckoned with.

During the third week of the war, a clear stalemate prevailed on all fronts, and this led to the first truce. The Israeli forces were stretched to the limit and in dire need of time to rest, reorganize, and import arms from abroad. The Arabs did not make any tangible use of the truce.

At this point, Bernadotte proposed a plan for the peaceful settlement of the conflict. His suggestions, issued on June 27, 1948, did not refer to the partition plan, which provided for an independent Arab state in part of Palestine. He proposed that the whole of Palestine as defined in the original mandate, including Transjordan, might form a union comprising two members, one Arab and the other Jewish. The functions of the union would be to promote the territory's common economic interests and coordinate foreign policy for its common defense.

As for the borders, Bernadotte suggested the inclusion of all or part of the Negev in the Arab territory and all or part of West Galilee in the Jewish territory. Jerusalem, according to Bernadotte's plan, should be Arab, while Haifa should become a free seaport, and an airport should be built at Lydda. Both Israel and the Arab League, to King Abdullah's dissatisfaction, rejected this proposal. The warring parties also refused the extension of the truce, and the second round of hostilities flared up on July 10, 1948.

During this round, which came to an end eight days later, the Israelis achieved remarkable successes on the battlefield. All Arab armies lost ground. The greatest loss on the Jordanian front was the occupation of Lydda and

Ramleh by the Israelis on July 11 and 12. These two adjacent Palestinian towns were supposedly part of the Arab portion of Palestine. Their occupation reversed King Abdullah's popularity, despite the Arab Legion's success in repelling a massive Israeli offensive against the Old City only three days later. The fall of Lydda and Ramleh sparked demonstrations in the Palestinian city of Nablus and in the Jordanian city of Salt. In fact, had the legion attempted to defend the towns, its troops would have been cut off, and the road to Jerusalem would have been open to the Israeli army. The success of the legion in defending the Old City three days later was precisely due to the fact that its power had not been exhausted in defending Lydda and Ramleh. In retrospect, the legion had been faced with a choice: to defend either the Old City or Lydda and Ramleh. The retention of the Old City was certainly much more important than the retention of the two towns. Nevertheless, one can imagine how the general public viewed this episode, especially since it occurred during the Muslim fasting month. Refugees from the two towns poured into Ramallah and Nablus stripped of everything except their clothes and telling stories of Israeli atrocities against them.

This single episode became one of the most saddening and painful events in the collective Palestinian memory. These two towns were lost after the Arab armies had entered Palestine, in contrast to the loss of the other cities, which had happened while inexperienced and poorly equipped Palestinian insurgents were defending them. Thus, this defeat inflicted heavy psychological damage on the Palestinian masses.

It also sowed the first seeds of suspicion among Palestinians and Arabs alike about the intentions of the Arab governments. The Arab public accused the Arab governments of being treacherous and subservient to the British as well as responsible for what was later called the "Palestinian debacle."

Yet the most important aspect of this episode consisted of the demonstrations that took place in Nablus and Salt. These demonstrations, which erupted simultaneously but without any prior coordination, represented the first time that Palestinians and Jordanians, while under the same rule, had expressed their anger jointly. Their demand to oust General Glubb was their first common political goal, and it gave them the sense that they could unite to accomplish national goals. The Nablus and Salt demonstrations, indeed, were the harbinger of the popular unity that was to become so important to Jordan's coherence as a state—even more important than the unity of the official establishments, which occurred in 1950 when the West Bank and the East Bank were united.

When the second truce went into effect on July 18, 1948, the Syrian and Lebanese armies had lost to the Israelis almost all the Palestinian territories that were under their control. Only the Jordanians, the Iraqis, and the Egyptians still held Palestinian territories. The Jordanians continued to hold East Jerusalem and all the West Bank. The Iraqis were in control of the Jenin-Tulkarem-Kalkiliya Triangle on the West Bank, while the Egyptians held the Gaza Strip, most of the Negev, and an enclave to the southwest of Hebron. Israel, in contrast, not only retained its portion of land under the partition plan but also occupied all of Galilee, Lydda, Ramleh, and other territories to the south. Most important, when the second truce started, Israel was at its peak militarily, while the Arab armies were worn down by the war. The Arab Legion in particular was constrained by the British policy of rationing supplies and ammunition.

The sense of military superiority tempted the Israeli leaders to occupy more land and improve their defensive lines. To achieve this objective, Israel had to deal with Egypt, Jordan, and Iraq. But before the Israelis could set out to accomplish these expansionist goals, Bernadotte proposed a new plan for a permanent peaceful settlement. He submitted his recommendations on September 16, 1948, and was assassinated by four Jewish terrorists one day after his report was issued. Among other things, Bernadotte recommended giving the whole of Galilee to the Jews and the whole of the Negev to the Arabs, as well as attaching all the Arab parts of Palestine to Jordan. Jerusalem, according to the Bernadotte plan, was to have a special status under UN supervision. Furthermore, he recommended that the Arab refugees be granted the right to return to the cities, towns, and villages from which they had been driven and that those who opted not to return be adequately compensated. Both the United States and Great Britain supported the plan, while the Arabs and the Israelis rejected it on different grounds.

For the Arab League, acceptance of the plan would have constituted official recognition of the State of Israel, a step that no Arab country was willing to take under the current circumstances; Arab public anger and frustration over the poor military performance of their armies were at their height. The Israelis opposed the plan because they wanted to have the Negev.

In the aftermath of his reelection, President Harry Truman, acting under pressure exerted by the Jewish lobby, reversed the United States' position on Bernadotte's plan. With this rejection, the plan ceased to be a possible solution for the problem.

To break the stalemate, the General Assembly set up a conciliatory committee of representatives from the United States, France, and Turkey, whose task was to resume diplomatic efforts and to come up with new suggestions for a peaceful settlement.

INTER-ARAB CONTENTION TO REPLACE ARAB CONSENSUS

The Arab states that had lost the war with Israel, especially Egypt and Syria, were looking for another battle and another adversary against whom to score a victory, and King Abdullah seemed an excellent choice. For these two reasons, on September 22 the Arab League, led by Egypt, announced the establishment of the All-Palestine Government with its seat in Gaza. On October 1, 1948, the Palestine National Congress convened in Gaza. The mufti was elected president, and Ahmad Hilmi, a prominent Palestinian political figure and a banker, was appointed prime minister. From its inception, this government was set up to be subservient to Egypt. In fact, it was merely an Egyptian ploy designed to prevent Jordan's annexation of Palestinian territory. At the outset of his short career, Hilmi submitted a letter to the Egyptian foreign minister in which he said:

> The units of the Holy War Army that are deployed in Gaza, Iraq-Swaidan, and El-Faluja under the command of Colonel Abdul-Haq el-Farrawi who operates under the supervision of the Egyptian command, have as of December 1, 1948, come under the responsibility of the All-Palestine Government. We have issued the necessary instructions to their commanders to continue to operate according to the ongoing arrangements, i.e., militarily under the Egyptian command, while administratively under the defense ministry of the All-Palestine Government.[10]

With this new development, King Abdullah found himself more than ever before in a serious confrontation with the mufti, who now enjoyed the support of Egypt, Syria, Saudi Arabia, and Lebanon.

Except for Jordan, all member states of the Arab League, including Iraq, recognized the All-Palestine Government. King Abdullah had to act promptly on three fronts—British, Palestinian, and Israeli—in order to abort the Egyptian move and undermine the potential rejuvenation of the mufti's political influence.

Britain embarked on a diplomatic effort that resulted in nonrecognition of the All-Palestine Government by any state outside the Arab countries.

On the Palestinian front, where King Abdullah was in control of the largest Palestinian population, four Palestinian conferences were held between October 1948 and January 1949 at the behest of the king and with the help of some of the Palestinian notables and the Jordanian military governors of the West Bank.

The most significant of the four conferences was the Jericho Conference, held on December 1, 1948. This conference proclaimed the union of Transjordan and Palestine under King Abdullah and emphasized the territorial integrity of Palestine. The speakers at the conference expressed their distrust of the Higher Arab Committee, implying their rejection of the mufti's leadership and their refusal to recognize the All-Palestine Government in Gaza. The conferees also authorized King Abdullah to solve the Palestinian problem to the best of his ability. According to the Palestinian historian Aref el-Aref, one thousand delegates attended the conference, many of whom were pressured into doing so by the Jordanian government. El-Aref writes in *Nakbet Filastin wa al-Firdaws al-Mafqud* (The Debacle of Palestine and the Lost Paradise):

> One of the immediate ripples of the Jericho Conference was that the Palestinian community split into two parts: one part supported the resolutions and the other denounced them. The supporters maintained that those resolutions were absolutely right because Palestine could no longer sustain itself on its own, especially after its losses of people and property, its disintegration and loss of self-confidence and dignity. The opponents argued that it was unacceptable for a small group of the people to determine the destiny of the country without the consent of the other groups. The Palestinian people who were scattered over Palestine, Trans-Jordan, Syria, Lebanon, Egypt, and Iraq were not in a position to express their opinion freely and candidly. The Azhar jurisprudence joined the opponents and denounced the Jericho resolutions and declared anyone who supported them a nonbeliever.[11]

The Jericho resolutions were ratified by the government and Parliament of Transjordan on December 7 and 13, respectively.

The All-Palestine Government was destined to fade away in no time for a number of reasons, especially its failure to attain its main goal of aborting the merger of the West Bank with Jordan. But Gaza, its seat, continued to wait for a successor to the All-Palestine Government to fill the vacancy. In this sense, Gaza remained the concrete symbol of the Palestinian identity and as such served as the antithesis of the notion of settling the diaspora Palestinians in the host countries as a substitute for establishing a Palestinian state on Palestinian turf. Indeed, it was the purely Palestinian population of the Gaza Strip, indigenous and refugees, who preserved the embryo of the Palestinian identity—though sometimes in deep freeze—for almost five decades. Thus, there was a logic to the fact that the

Oslo Declaration of Principles in 1993, in establishing a framework for a peaceful settlement between the Palestinians and Israelis, asserted "Gaza first."

ISRAEL'S QUEST FOR MORE LAND BEFORE SIGNING ARMISTICE AGREEMENTS

When the second truce went into effect on July 18, 1948, Israel was strong enough to think of acquiring more territory in order to strengthen its defensive military strategy. There were three Arab parties to deal with: Egypt, Iraq, and Jordan. Syria and Lebanon were not involved, since Israel had already stripped them of almost all the Palestinian territory that they were supposed to defend.

Thus, in spite of the truce, Israel launched an offensive against the Egyptian troops on December 22, 1948, and succeeded in expelling them from the southeastern flank of the Negev; Israel failed, however, to occupy the Egyptian enclave in Faluja (in the Hebron district) and was not able to extend its control to the Red Sea. When Egypt appealed for help, not a single Arab state responded. On January 4, 1949, Egypt announced that it was ready to negotiate an armistice agreement with Israel. Three days later, a cease-fire decreed by the United Nations went into effect. The failure of the Arab states to help Egypt in its last military encounter with Israel made it obvious that they would not close ranks again against the "common enemy." This position sparked a war of recriminations among the Arab leaders and governments. The government of each of the countries bordering Israel went to the armistice negotiating table in Rhodes to pursue its own national interests, utterly disregarding any professed commitment to the "Palestinian cause." Egypt was the first to sign an agreement with Israel on February 24, 1949, followed by Lebanon on March 23, Jordan on April 3, and Syria on July 20.

Meanwhile, Israel turned to the Palestinian territories held by Jordan. Israel had used military force to acquire more territory from the Egyptians; with Jordan, it used military force in the south and coercive diplomacy in the center.

While the Jordanian and Israeli negotiating teams in Rhodes were in the midst of figuring out each other's positions, two Israeli brigades occupied Umm Rashrash (Eilat), creating a new situation that neither Transjordan, with the support of the British, nor the United Nations was able to change.

Having secured an outlet to the Red Sea, the Israelis shifted their focus to the central front, where the Arab Legion, together with Iraqi troops, was deployed.

Israel was well aware that King Abdullah's main objective was to extend his sovereignty over the West Bank. Because the military balance of power had shifted in favor of Israel after the second round of Arab-Israeli fighting, Transjordan's national security now had only two safeguards: the truce and the British-Transjordanian Treaty, which King Abdullah thought he would invoke if threatened by the Israeli army. Israel's coercive diplomacy with the king exploited both his ambitions to expand Transjordan and his worries about the possibility of losing everything if hostilities were resumed. The Israelis knew that the king's worries had reached a peak after Israel's operation against the Egyptian army in the Negev in late December 1948. Now Israel intended to increase his worries by moving some of its military units along the cease-fire line in the Triangle district and by delaying the negotiations in Rhodes.

To avoid expansionist surprises from the Israelis, who were in a remarkably strong position, King Abdullah opted to engage with them diplomatically. The Israelis suggested to him in October 1948 that he arrange for the withdrawal of the Iraqis. On February 2, 1949, he met with the Iraqi regent and asked him to withdraw the Iraqi troops from their first line of defense in the Triangle area and hand it over to the Arab Legion. On March 10, 1949, the day on which the Israelis occupied Umm Rashrash (Eilat) on the Gulf of Aqaba, the Iraqis told King Abdullah that they were prepared to hand over their positions in the Triangle to the Arab Legion within fifteen days. When the Israelis learned about the Iraqi offer, they began to press for the rectification of the Triangle lines, and a series of meetings were held between the Jordanians and the Israelis to discuss this issue.

After several meetings, the two parties reached an agreement that allowed Israel, upon the Iraqi withdrawal, to take four hundred square kilometers of fertile land owned by the populations of more than twenty villages without endangering its international position and without firing one bullet.

The Israeli troops occupied the Triangle on a Saturday following the withdrawal of the Iraqis. Palestinian radio broadcast a highly emotional commentary, calling the event "Black Saturday."

The Triangle agreement drew severe criticism from the Palestinians, the Arab public, and Arab governments. The Iraqis in particular denounced the agreement as perfidious both to the Palestinians and to the Iraqi forces, who, they said, were placed in mortal danger.

The Palestinians called this agreement the "Triangle Conspiracy." Like the loss of Lydda and Ramleh, the agreement became another burden for King Abdullah with regard to the Palestinian question.

Yet for the king himself, the Triangle deal was the lesser of two evils. He confided to Wells Stabler, the American chargé d'affaires in Amman, "that he felt that if he refused to sign the agreement, Israel would recommence hostilities and the whole area might be lost. It would in fact be better to sacrifice another fifteen villages with an additional estimated 15,000 refugees than to lose what little was left of Arab Palestine."[12]

Nevertheless, the Lydda and Ramleh episode and the Triangle agreement adversely influenced King Abdullah's image. Until the 1967 war, his performance in 1948–49 continued to be judged by the Arab public not by what he achieved (securing East Jerusalem and the largest chunk of what remained of Palestine) but by what he failed to achieve. King Abdullah's Arab partners in the war, who were looking for a scapegoat to cover up their failure, contributed enormously to developing this theme through their political discourse and their national media.

Unification of the Two Banks

THE PROCESS OF CONSOLIDATION

Having undercut the mufti's power base and arranged for the Iraqis to pull out, King Abdullah had to move on merging the expanded kingdom and ensuring its security.

On April 11, 1950, general parliamentary elections were held on the two banks of the kingdom. All Palestinians, including refugees, were given the right to vote. The number of seats in the Lower House of Deputies was increased from twenty to forty. Twenty deputies were elected from the West Bank, and the other twenty were elected from the East Bank. Most of the elected West Bank deputies were supporters of King Abdullah. There were also former followers of the mufti and deputies who represented the Ba'ath party, which advocated Arab unity under a republican regime, and others who were critics of King Abdullah. The elections were conducted fairly. The number of seats in the upper house was also doubled, going from ten to twenty. The king appointed twelve East Bankers and eight West Bankers, with Abul-Huda as president and Suleiman Tukan from Nablus (the West Bank) as his deputy. A new cabinet was formed of ten members—five East Bankers and five West Bankers—and Said al-Mufti, an East Banker, became the prime minister.

On April 24, Parliament convened for the first time to confirm the union between the East and West Banks of Jordan. (At the time only two countries—Iraq and Pakistan—officially recognized the union of the West Bank and the East Bank.) In his speech from the throne, King Abdullah said:

> My government considers that the resolution of the Arab League Political Committee of April 12 1948 no longer stands valid as the Arab states have agreed to the permanent armistice and have followed this with acceptance of the UN partition plan in contravention of the aforementioned resolution of the Political Committee.[1]

The resolution to which King Abdullah was referring stated that the Arab armies were entering Palestine strictly for the purpose of saving it; that this entry was a temporary measure free of any characteristics of occupation or partition of Palestine; and that following the liberation of Palestine, it would be handed back to its owners so that they might rule as they wished.

In a joint session, both houses of Parliament adopted the following resolution:

> Expressing the people's faith in the efforts spent by His Majesty [King Abdullah] toward attainment of natural aspirations and basing itself on the right of self-determination and the existing de facto position between Jordan and Palestine and their national, natural, and geographic unity and their common interests and living space, Parliament, which represents both sides of the Jordan, resolves this day and declares: First, its support for complete unity between the two sides of the Jordan and their union into one state, which is the Hashemite Kingdom of Jordan, at whose head reigns King Abdullah ibn al-Hussein, on a basis of constitutional representative government and equality of the rights and duties of all citizens. Second, its reaffirmation of its intent to preserve the full Arab rights in Palestine, to defend those rights by all lawful means in the exercise of its natural rights but without prejudicing the final settlement of Palestine's just case within the sphere of national aspiration, inter-Arab cooperation, and international justice.[2]

This resolution completed the process of welding the top level of administration of the West Bank with the already existing official institutions of Jordan. It paved the way for the merger of the two banks: the process of integrating the social, economic, and cultural lives of the two peoples within the same state and constructing a pan-Jordanian identity. This process would require a much longer time.

Some of the important aspects of the welding operation are highlighted here:

1. The name of the new state—the Hashemite Kingdom of Jordan—did not include the word *Palestine* or any of its derivatives. But it did include references to the ruling royal family and to Jordan.
2. When the welding took place, the military and security institutions were wholly Transjordanian—except, of course, for the British officers, the few Palestinians who had been recruited into the police force after the disbanding of the Holy War Army, and those who had been part of the Palestinian police under the British mandate. Throughout the merging process in the 1950s, when Palestinians began to join the army, the combat units still remained mostly Transjordanian. It took fifteen years for a few Palestinians to reach the highest ranks in the army, which remained mostly Transjordanian.
3. The capital of the state continued to be Amman.
4. All the cabinet ministers and the members of the upper house were appointed posts.
5. In the first upper house of the Parliament in the union—besides giving the East Bank twelve seats while the Palestinians were given only eight— the king appointed an East Banker as speaker.
6. These facts show that the king chose right from the beginning to keep the center of gravity on the East Bank, despite the fact that the Palestinians constituted two-thirds of the population of the new state. (The West Bank community resented the king's policy but failed to protest it. They consoled themselves with the idea that they were under the rule of a Hashemite and not a Transjordanian, and a Hashemite sovereign, after all, was a supranational authority.)
7. Palestinians of all political stripes ran in the first parliamentary elections. The Palestinian contenders thought it would be better for their cause if they participated actively in the political life of Jordan. They hoped to influence the decision-making process through the established Jordanian institutions. Their first and most salient slogan for their intended political action was stated during the election campaign: "Yes to the union, no to the peace with Israel." This platform, on which the Palestinian activists predicated their political partnership, eventually constrained King Abdullah's plan to reach a separate peace agreement with Israel, a fact that defined Jordanian-Israeli relations for almost half a century to come.

Was the union of the two banks a sound policy, or was it a quick fix? It is difficult to judge. However, on three separate occasions in the 1980s, during intimate meetings in which King Hussein betrayed his private feelings to his audience, I heard him say without any further elaboration, "I have inherited this situation. If it had been up to me I would have done it differently." One of the audiences was Palestinian, another was American, and the third was European.

After the elections and the formation of the first government of the two-bank state, King Abdullah accelerated his efforts to achieve a peace treaty with Israel.

The new lines drawn by the armistice left Jordan in dire need of an outlet to the Mediterranean. In addition, the country was full of refugees on both banks. The king had to tackle the latter problem, either by making it possible for the refugees to return to their homes, especially those of Lydda and Ramleh, or by absorbing them. And he had to solve both these problems and others before he could return to Greater Syria, his main goal. He saw no other solution but to conclude a comprehensive peace treaty with Israel; otherwise, all he would have accomplished was to increase the population of his poor country in return for a small piece of land that was already overpopulated by refugees and, most important, was cut off from its traditional trading partners in Egypt, Lebanon, and Syria. The only trading partner left for the West Bank was the East Bank, with which it now constituted one country. Transjordan would be in serious economic trouble unless the border with Israel was opened for free trade and economic cooperation. King Abdullah had always held that the Jews would help him develop Jordan; now he had to turn to Israel simply for normalization.

The Jordanian government embarked on a long process of secret negotiations with Israel. They continued from November 1949 until May 1951, and their primary objective was to explore the Israeli position and to reach a comprehensive peace treaty, if possible. The negotiations failed to achieve their goal, making the Jordanian exploratory efforts an exercise in futility. Five obstacles blocked the way for a Jordanian-Israeli peace treaty.

The first and greatest obstacle was Israel itself. It would not compromise on the two issues that most concerned King Abdullah and his government: the relinquishment of territory and the readmission of Palestinian refugees. Israel's compromise on these two issues was essential as a face-saving measure if Jordan was to conclude a separate treaty with Israel. The Israeli Labor government wanted a peace treaty with Jordan because such a treaty would break the circle of Arab states, allowing others to follow suit. Besides, Israel, like Jordan, was in a difficult economic situation as a result of the war. Demobilizing and cutting down on defense spending would help its economy recover. Yet the rivalry between Mapai, the ruling party, and the rightist Herut party, led by Menachem Begin, made it difficult for Ben-Gurion to look any less Zionist before his people, who were elated by their military victory and the establishment of the state. The Holocaust complex created the belief that Israel's security could not be founded on a paper guarantee such as a treaty but must rely on defensible borders and Israel's military deterrence.

The second obstacle was the discouraging attitude of the British and the Americans, who believed, in view of King Abdullah's experience with the Israelis over the Triangle, that he would fall under Israeli pressures and might eventually lose more territory. As Avi Shlaim put it, "their aim was to explore the possibilities of a comprehensive peace settlement through the Palestine Conciliation Commission that had been appointed by the UN for this purpose, and they accordingly advised the king not to forge too far ahead with separate talks until the commission's own attitude was clearer."[3]

The third obstacle consisted of the Jordanian people—Transjordanians and Palestinians alike—who, in view of the Arab military defeat and its unexpected tragic result, were angry and had no desire to make peace with Israel. The government felt their anger and resentment deeply and had to reckon with them.

The fourth obstacle was the Jordanian government itself; due to local and other Arab pressures, it chose to chart a middle course between King Abdullah's rush toward peace with Israel and the Arabs' and Jordanians' opposition to peace. This policy was reflected in how Abul-Huda and Samir Rifa'i (a prominent figure of the old guard) conducted the talks with the Israelis. Their consistent demands to partition the Negev between Israel and Jordan, to get access to the sea by annexing the Gaza Strip or to have access to Acre through Nazareth, to allow the return of the Lydda and Ramleh refugees, and to offer special compensation to the Arab refugees from West Jerusalem failed to receive any positive response from Israel. All that Israel offered was the release of some blocked Palestinian accounts in Israeli banks. And even this offer did not seem to be a serious one.

The fifth obstacle was the general mood of anger and belligerency that swept the Arab world. The unifying cry was for revenge in another round of war. This mood pressured the Arab governments into adopting a resolution on April 1, 1950, that prohibited any member state from negotiating a separate peace treaty or any military, political, or economic agreement with Israel; any state that did so would be considered to have forfeited its membership in the Arab League.

Jordanian and Israeli officials held twenty meetings. The most important one was held on May 5, 1949. Its purpose was to explore the possibility of coordinating Israel's and Jordan's positions in preparation for a session of the Lausanne Conference, to be held on May 29 at the request of the Palestinian Conciliation Commission. The commission's task, as assigned by the United Nations, was to develop the armistice agreements into peace treaties. This meeting, which was held at Shunneh (Transjordan), included the king and his prime minister, Abul-Huda, as well as the Israeli foreign minister, Moshe Sharett; Lieutenant-Colonel Moshe Dayan; and others. In this meeting, Abul-Huda asserted that the 1947 UN partition plan should be the basis of the final settlement. Sharett considered the UN plan irrelevant. To him, going back to it was tantamount to turning back time. It was at this early stage when Israel revoked the partition plan as a basis for peacemaking. It is noteworthy, though, that Israel and the Arab states had separately signed the Lausanne Protocol on May 12. In accordance with the protocol, the two sides accepted the UN partition plan as a basis for discussion with the commission.

The two sides agreed, however, that since they were the only parties in Jerusalem, they should be the ones to conduct the negotiations regarding its future. The king also reiterated his two major demands: to annex Gaza so that Jordan would have access to the Mediterranean and to resolve the refugee problem.

The Lausanne Conference (April 27 to September 14, 1949) failed to achieve its objective of converting the armistice agreements into peace treaties; the gap between the Arab and the Israeli positions proved unbridgeable. The collective Arab position was based on the borders of the UN partition plan, the internationalization of Jerusalem, and the return of the refugees, while the Israeli position was based on the armistice demarcation lines as final borders, no return of refugees, and no internationalization of Jerusalem.

TIGHTENING THE BOLTS OF MERGER

When the two banks became one country, the demographic structure of the kingdom changed dramatically. For every citizen of Transjordanian origin, there were now two of Palestinian origin. The Transjordanians numbered almost four hundred thousand, and the Palestinians numbered more than eight hundred thousand. But it was not demographics alone that gave the Transjordanian-Palestinian partnership its rough start. Half the Palestinians, the new citizens of the kingdom, were refugees; the other

half, though they were still in their own towns and villages, were in a
difficult economic situation. The mood that prevailed among the new
citizens was one of frustration, despair, uncertainty, and militancy. They
had just lost a war. The victor was at the peak of its military strength. The
armistice agreement had barely managed to save the West Bank from Israeli occupation. It was very difficult for a poor state like Jordan to face
this new beginning with hope for the future.

The first challenge was to establish security both along the armistice
lines, to avoid any new military confrontation with Israel, and internally,
to avoid any insurrection fueled by anger and despair. King Abdullah was
able to meet this first challenge.

The second challenge was to settle and integrate the refugees. Here the
United Nations offered help. The General Assembly passed a resolution
on December 8, 1949, that established the United Nations Relief and
Works Agency (UNRWA) to look after the Palestinian refugees. Its functions were to provide relief and work for the refugees and, according to
the United States, to contribute to the economic development of the country, "primarily through the use of water resources of the Jordan and its
tributaries for the irrigation of potentially arable land. The agency plans to
undertake a number of important development projects in Jordan, which,
it is hoped, will result in permanent settlement in the area of some refugees. The Jordan government has promised full cooperation."[4]

The third challenge was to achieve the smooth integration of the official
institutions. This was accomplished gradually. King Abdullah started by
dissolving the committees that had been appointed by the Higher Arab
Committee (HAC) to run the daily affairs of the Palestinian cities and towns
before the entry of the Arab Legion into its zone of operations. The Jordanian military governors took over the administration of these Palestinian
towns, ordering the inhabitants of the controlled areas to obey only their
instructions. The units of al-Jihad al-Muqaddas that were loyal to the mufti
were disbanded. In March 1949, the military governors were replaced by
civilian governors who were responsible to the Jordanian minister of the
interior in Amman. In December 1949, the West Bank officials were formally subordinated to the government in Amman, achieving administrative unification. Right after the official annexation in April 1950, a commission was established to integrate the legal systems of the East and West
Banks. Members of the Palestinian elite were appointed to senior posts in
the government. The policy of appointing only those Palestinians who were
loyal to the Hashemites was designed to tighten the bonds between the

West Bank and Amman. The Jordan dinar was made the sole legal currency in the kingdom on September 30, 1950, replacing the Palestinian pound.

A fourth challenge was to integrate the two peoples under one pan-Jordanian identity in the course of time. It was significant that the Transjordanians knew more about Palestine than the Palestinians did about Transjordan, simply because more Transjordanians had visited or stayed in Palestine before 1948 than vice versa. Both Muslim and Christian Transjordanians had visited Palestine for religious purposes. Some of the rich Transjordanians had sent their children to one of the numerous private secondary schools in Jerusalem. Some qualified Transjordanian students who had finished their secondary schooling in Transjordan were given scholarships to al-Kulliyah al-Arabiah (the Arab College) in Jerusalem. Still other Transjordanians visited Palestine for medical treatment or for pleasure. Units of the Arab Legion were stationed in various locations in Palestine; this exposed the Transjordanian officers and soldiers to some aspects of Palestinian social life. Trade, of course, was a two-way street; it, too, played a role in acquainting Transjordanians with Palestine. Besides, unskilled Transjordanian labor looked for jobs in Palestinian cities—Haifa in particular—during years of drought.

Thus, before 1948, the Transjordanians viewed the Palestinians in much the same way they saw the Syrians: they considered these people more sophisticated and modernized than themselves. Immediately after 1948, the Transjordanians looked at Palestinians with a blend of sympathy, compassion, and curiosity. But when King Abdullah was assassinated in 1951, this sympathetic outlook was transformed into one of apprehension and wariness. In this patriarchal society, the assassination of the king was viewed as an assault on the whole people, and it ignited resentment. A Transjordanian whose father had been a police officer serving in the early 1950s on the West Bank told me that his father, his colleagues, and their families looked at the Palestinians as troublemakers who should always be subdued by force. This perception may have been a reflection of instructions given by senior officers, but it also certainly reflected the effect that King Abdullah's assassination had on them personally.

In addition, conservative Transjordanians, especially the bedouins (many of whom had lost relatives in the battle for Jerusalem), looked at the Palestinians from a high moral ground; the bedouins, in particular, believed that the Arab Legion had gone to Palestine in 1948 to defend the Palestinians because they had failed to defend themselves. This sentiment found its clearest expression during a parliamentary session on November 11, 1952, when two Palestinian deputies launched into a harsh criticism of Abul-Huda, the prime minister. Two tribal deputies retaliated and "began to lob epithets at the Palestinian representatives, charging them with 'feminine' cowardice in the 1948 War. These outbursts solicited equally provocative ripostes from the West Bank MP, and the chamber turned to bedlam. Daggers were fingered and the police had to intervene."[5]

The Palestinians looked at Jordan as an occupying power, due to the heavy-handed policy of the army, the military governors, and later the civil administration—a policy these groups had to adopt to lay the foundation for security and maintain stability and order. Suleiman Mousa, a Transjordanian historian, wrote, "it must be admitted that the [Transjordanian] administration [in Palestine between 1948 and 1950] committed unjustified, painful, and regrettable mistakes. . . . For example, people who called on a governor's office without head covers were scolded."[6]

Palestinians, too, held a high moral ground, believing that Jordan, like the other Arab states, had failed them. Even though the Arab Legion had defended Jerusalem, it had failed to protect Lydda and Ramleh. In the armistice agreement, Jordan had given up the Triangle to the Israelis without a fight. Nevertheless, Palestinians were impressed by the training, discipline, and courage of the Arab Legion soldiers.

Bitter at their present plight and uncertain about their future, the Palestinians were highly suggestible. The Arab states, in dire need of a scapegoat on whom to blame their military defeat, pointed to King Abdullah as the leader mainly responsible for the Arab defeat. Many Palestinians, and the refugees in particular, believed that the king was responsible for their plight. Yet the West Bankers who remained free of Israeli occupation also looked at King Abdullah as a protector against Israeli aggression. As a result, the Palestinians developed an ambivalent attitude toward the king. This ambivalence, in my opinion, accounts for two salient phenomena that characterized the Palestinian-Transjordanian relationship until 1967. The first phenomenon was that the Palestinians never called for separation from the East Bank, even at the height of their anger and dissatisfaction with the government's policies. Separation would have left them without a protector from the Israelis. The second phenomenon was the relatively rapid Palestinian oscillation between opposition to the Hashemite regime and allegiance to it. For example, they overwhelmingly supported King Hussein when he dismissed General Glubb in March 1956, yet they took the extreme opposite position when the king sacked the pro-Nasser Nabulsi government in April 1957. Gradually the "protector" component in this ambivalence outweighed the anger and opposition. After the unification of the two banks, General Glubb accompanied King Abdullah on one of his tours to the front-line villages on the West Bank, and in *A Soldier with the Arabs,* he described the public's reception of the king:

> Kalkiliya [a West Bank town] had suffered particularly from the Rhodes armistice demarcation line. It was a little town on the coastal plain. . . . Three hundred yards west of the little town began the orange groves which seemed to stretch as far as one could see across the plains to the sea. These orange groves had all been planted by the people of Kalkiliya, or their fathers before them, and had been their only means of subsistence. Then had come the Rhodes armistice which had drawn the demarcation line between the houses of the little town and their groves. All the oranges had been taken over by the Jews, and the people of Kalkiliya were left sitting in their houses—destitute. . . . As soon as we drove into the edge of the little town, we were surrounded by a seething crowd. . . . In a sudden lull, a voice called out "O father of Talal [that is, King Abdullah], protect us." In an instant, the whole crowd took up the words in a thunderous chorus. "O father of Talal, protect us" [*Ya abu Talal hameena*].[7]

THE POLITICAL INTERACTION

By the time King Abdullah was assassinated, the process of Jordanian-Palestinian political integration was proceeding relatively smoothly. Once the Palestinians became engaged, an opposition voice started to be heard on foreign and domestic issues alike. On international issues, the West Bank opposed the government's relationship with Great Britain and its pro-British orientation. To them, Britain was a major accomplice in establishing the State of Israel. The British command of the Arab Legion was responsible for preventing the army from going into action against the Israelis, who so often breached the armistice agreement and crossed the designated armistice lines to kill Palestinians or destroy their homes in a disproportionate retaliation.

In general, the Palestinians criticized the British presence in Jordan and called for the removal of the British command of the Arab Legion. Gradually this developed into a more specific demand: the abrogation of the British-Jordanian Treaty.

The West Bank opposition also scathingly criticized King Abdullah's contacts with Israel and his attempts to conclude a peace agreement with Israel. The government was vehemently criticized for signing the armistice agreement that transferred Wadi Araba to Israel and left thousands of Palestinians landless. In general, the Palestinians opposed any form of political settlement with Israel.

A third area of tension and a target of political criticism from the West Bank opposition were the government's attempts to resettle the refugees in Jordan. King Abdullah wanted to absorb the refugees into Jordan because he saw in them an economic and political potential that would contribute to the country's development. Through the resettlement policy, the king would guarantee the flow of foreign assistance; this was especially important if he failed—as he actually already had—to reach a peace settlement with Israel. A peace agreement, in contrast, would enable the refugees to return to their homes, and the borders with Israel would be open for cooperation and free trade.

To the West Bank opposition, the refugee problem could be solved only by repatriation or the effacing of Israel. The opposition considered resettlement of the refugees to be merely a way of liquidating the Palestinian problem for the benefit of Israel; it represented the loss of the Palestinians' rights.

The process of integration, though, had started. When the West Bank and the East Bank merged into one country, it was only natural that West Bankers and Transjordanians became one people of one nationality. But King Abdullah chose to naturalize the Palestinian refugees as well, since their representatives participated in the Jericho Conference. If he had failed to do so, his strategy to preempt the All-Palestine Government would have been in jeopardy. So while the integration process involved the West Bank and the East Bank, the refugees on both banks were not excluded. The refugees, understandably, chose to maintain their particularity by refusing resettlement and insisting on living in refugee camps. Resettlement to them was tantamount to relinquishing their rights, especially to compensation. Many refugees who became better off economically chose to leave the camps over the years and were absorbed into the larger society; even so, in no way did they give up their rights. Thus, the absorption process never ceased, although the camps, which symbolized the refugees' rights, persisted. Today, the majority of Palestinian refugees in Jordan are the children or grandchildren of those who, fifty years ago, escaped or were evicted from their homeland. These second- and third-generation refugees were born, raised, and integrated economically in Jordan. The issue to them now is not one of absorption but of rejection, should the mounting calls of Transjordanian nationalists be heeded.

Resettlement and all other issues that the Palestinian opposition addressed became in no time the same issues that the Transjordanian opposition adopted. The common Transjordanian-Palestinian struggle for specific political issues constituted another unofficial melting pot, in addition to the socioeconomic one, in which the two peoples started to integrate into one pan-Jordanian identity.

On the domestic scene, the West Bankers resented their inadequate representation in the administration, the army, and the various security agencies. The Palestinians had accepted the unification of the two banks and condoned King Abdullah's decision to make the East Bank the center of gravity of the state. In return, they looked for equity. In the first years of unity, the West Bankers felt that the government disregarded equity in its domestic policies. The broadest consensus and largest protest ever against this inequity took place on July 26, 1952, when ten out of twenty of the Palestinian deputies held a meeting in Nablus, on the West Bank, from which they submitted a memorandum to the prime minister, denouncing "the government's inaction against Israeli border incursions; its continued recourse to 'despotic' Defense Regulations; its neglect of Jerusalem as a political, administrative, and spiritual center; its discouragement of Palestinian enlistment in the Arab Legion; its economic and commercial bias against the West Bank; and its discrimination against Palestinians in hiring, firing, and promotions. Six other MPs sent telegrams associating themselves with this petition, and two Palestinian ministers even sent polite messages apologizing for their absence."[8]

The West Bankers also accused the government of favoring the merchants of the East Bank over those of the West Bank in the issuance of import licenses. This type of protest is concrete evidence that the West Bankers were poised for integration and not separation.

All these issues, as well as others that were the subject of debate at the institutional and popular levels, needed a democratic forum in which to be heard. However, with Parliament frequently suspended, political parties usually outlawed, and the press typically content to echo the government line, this forum did not exist. Hence the West Bankers, supported by budding young intellectuals on the East Bank, consistently demanded legal reform in the political system. Such reform was almost impossible under King Abdullah's rule, and Jordan had to wait until King Talal acceded to the throne in 1951 before major constitutional reform could take place.

KING TALAL USHERS IN AN ERA OF CHANGE AND ADAPTATION

Jordan successfully survived the crisis of King Abdullah's assassination, thanks to several factors: the statesmanship displayed by the government and the seasoned ruling elite; the British-Jordanian Treaty, which deterred potential external players from interfering in the country's future; and the Arab Legion, which maintained law and order. The late Queen Zain, King Hussein's mother, also played an essential role in preventing Emir Naif, the younger son of King Abdullah, from acceding to the throne in the absence of her husband, Crown Prince Talal, who was in Switzerland under medical treatment at the time of the assassination.

On September 6, 1951, Prince Talal was proclaimed king of the Hashemite Kingdom of Jordan. His accession to the throne was received with sincere joy by the public on both the East and West Banks. Many believed that he harbored anti-British sentiments. The Palestinians held Talal's father, not Talal himself, responsible for their tragedy. Indeed, Talal was well known for his sympathy with the Palestinians. Thus his accession ushered in a new chapter in the Palestinians' attitude toward the state—certainly a favorable one.

Though the assassination of King Abdullah was a dreadful and ominous prologue to the process of integrating Transjordanians and Palestinians, it ironically helped this process to go more smoothly than it would have gone under King Abdullah's rule. On the domestic scene, King Abdullah's forceful governing hand and his patriarchal approach would have intensified the tension between the government and the Palestinians. King Talal embarked on a process of reform in order to cope with the changes resulting from the union of the two banks and King Abdullah's assassination. King Talal dissolved the upper house and reconstituted it with more Palestinians. A new constitution was promulgated on January 2, 1952; it recognized the basic freedoms of speech, press, and assembly and made the prime minister and his cabinet collectively accountable to the House of Deputies (Article 51). It also granted the House of Deputies the authority to dismiss a cabinet by a two-thirds vote of no confidence (Article 53). While the basic freedoms were contingent on the "limits of the law," the new constitution changed the basic assumptions of the old patriarchal order. Aruri argues that

> for the first time, it allowed the people and their representatives to participate in the political system and to exercise restraint on the hitherto unchallenged executive authority. The credit for this rather hasty democratization goes largely to the merger of the two banks, the disappearance of Abdullah from the political scene, and the initiative of a group of young, educated, urban deputies, who discovered the appropriate circumstances for exerting pressure to obtain constitutional change.[9]

Certainly King Talal's liberal inclinations contributed to this crucial constitutional change, although King Abdullah had first promised to revise the constitution in his speech from the throne to the joint session of Parliament on April 24, 1950. On September 20, 1951, and after a private audience with King Talal, the U.S. chief of mission in Amman, Gerald Drew, wrote to the State Department, "He [King Talal] is reliably reported to want to withdraw as much as possible from intervention in the internal political affairs of the country and to rule as a constitutional monarch. This would fit in with the constitutional changes proposed by the prime minister in his address to the Parliament in September."[10]

In *From Abdullah to Hussein*, Robert Satloff wrote, "By all accounts, Talal was wedded to the notion of reigning as a constitutional monarch, an idea that most likely grew as much out of his driving need to be what Abdullah was not as it did out of his liberal inclination."[11]

On the regional scene, King Talal and Abul-Huda adopted a policy of maintaining good relations with the Arab League and abandoning King Abdullah's Greater Syria scheme. To be on good terms with the Arab League implied giving up the idea of reaching a separate peace treaty with Israel. Drew sent a telegram to the State Department in which he said, "I was favorably impressed by the serene and statesmanlike attitude of the Prime Minister toward problems of future. He is determined to maintain Jordan's sovereignty and independence but not afraid to break with personal policies of late King such as his . . . hostility to Arab League and Egypt in particular, and Greater Syria scheme."[12]

As far as the United States and Great Britain were concerned, the death of King Abdullah and the resolution of the crisis following his death with the proclamation of Prince Talal as king of Jordan relieved them of the nightmare of the late king's quest for a separate peace treaty with Israel. This, they knew, would only arouse the hostility of the Arab states and would eventually destabilize the whole region.

For all these reasons, the accession of King Talal ushered in a new era of stability and political relief. The new, relatively liberal constitution attempted to accommodate the politicized Palestinians, who had become the majority in the state. Nevertheless, the situation was undeniably difficult. The annexation of the West Bank, which resulted in all Palestinians (West Bankers and refugees alike) becoming Jordanian citizens, had tripled the population of the country. At the same time, the area of arable land had increased by only one-third. Unemployment was rampant, and commercial contacts between the West Bank and the rest of the Arab world were disrupted as a result of the closing of the Jordanian-Israeli border.

The new government under King Talal had to address all these issues. King Abdullah had believed that these problems could be solved by reaching a peace treaty with Israel. When he failed, he turned to Great Britain and the United States to help him. His rationale for this request was the absorption of refugees who were to become Jordanian citizens and the significance of Jordan for maintaining stability in the Middle East. As early as April 1950, the U.S. Department of State recommended assisting Jordan in its economic development:

> The major problems which confront Jordan today and which are of primary concern to the U.S. are the establishment of peaceful and friendly relations between Israel and Jordan, and the successful absorption into the polity and economy of Jordan of Arab Palestine, its inhabitants, and the bulk of the refugees now located there. . . . There are, of course, urgent political reasons for assisting Jordan in her economic development so that the large refugee population may be absorbed. These homeless and jobless people constitute an unstable element in the Near East wherever they have gathered, and there is ample evidence that communists have found fertile ground for their propaganda among them. In order to eliminate this danger to the stability and to the western orientation of the area, the refugees must be settled and provided with the necessary means of livelihood.[13]

Assistant Secretary of State George C. McGhee, who was touring the area in March 1951, had said to King Abdullah that he "felt confident that Jordan, apart from aid in connection with the refugee problem, could count on economic assistance, possibly through the expanded Point IV program [the U.S. assistance program to Jordan]."[14]

The British government helped Jordan in many ways. Development assistance from 1950 until the end of 1956 totaled seven and a half million pounds in interest-free loans. The British had also contributed nearly sixty million pounds for the support of the Arab Legion. At the end of 1956, the British were still committed to the construction of the Aqaba Deep Water Port and the Desert Road from Aqaba to Amman. Total cost of these projects was estimated at four and a half million pounds, of which 630,000 pounds had already been spent.[15]

The most valuable assistance offered by the British was to make it easy for the Palestinian intelligentsia in general and for those who became Jordanians in particular to acquire jobs in the oil-producing Gulf countries in the 1950s. Through British influence in those countries before they attained their political independence, Palestinians were given priority in employment over other Arabs. These countries, especially Kuwait, were standing on the threshold of building a state, a process for which they had the money but not adequate personnel. The Palestinians were available to meet their needs. The experienced and skilled workers, civil servants, and professionals who arrived in the early 1950s constituted a sort of bridgehead for their relatives and friends. Kuwait in particular became the promised land to the Palestinians; it was the hope of almost every Palestinian with a secondary school or college education to get a job in Kuwait. Many of them joined the Kuwaiti Department of Education. In the 1960s, the Gulf states became not only a major employer of Palestinians but also a major source of hard currency for Jordan due to the remittances that the Palestinians sent home. Because the Gulf states refrained from naturalizing the Palestinians, most of their savings were invested in Jordan, and these savings contributed to the rapid economic development of that country. In the late 1970s, the remittances sent to Jordan by Jordanian expatriates in the Gulf states were estimated to amount to more than a billion dollars per annum.

We should emphasize that the Palestinians were, perhaps, a burden on Jordan's poor economy only in the first years of unification and partnership. By the late 1950s, it was obvious that the Palestinians were a blessing to the country. The United States and its allies, for example, assisted Jordan because they were convinced that by helping to resettle and integrate the Palestinians into the country's polity and economy, Jordan would be immune to the spread of communism and would eventually become stable. And the direct Palestinian contribution to the development of Jordan was not confined to the capital Palestinians brought in; perhaps even more important were their entrepreneurship and accumulated skills in trade, industry, and farming.

However, in one of his dispatches to the British Foreign Office in October 1950, Sir Alec Kirkbride, head of the British mission in Amman, wrote that the happy system of government that had obtained in the old Transjordan had become a thing of the past.[16] By this time, the unification of the two banks had already taken place, and Kirkbride, who had spent most of his diplomatic service in Jordan, could see the difference between a pre-1948 Transjordan and the Hashemite Kingdom composed of the two banks. Before 1948, Transjordan had been a tribal society, and the social system in general had been patriarchal, like most Arab societies. The Jordanians had been ruled indirectly by the British through Emir Abdullah, whose rule was also patriarchal. This compatibility between the social and political systems created a cohesive society and a stable country. The Transjordanians had their community leaders, but above all there was one recognized supratribal leader to whom they referred their problems and disputes. An established patriarchal system is based on the people's continuing need for the leader, especially in two areas: jobs and security. If the central authority provides both to the people, it will have full, benign control over them. If it fails to provide them with jobs, it will have to resort to tougher security measures to maintain its full control. The pre-1948 Transjordanian system provided its people with both.

Though the Palestinian social system was also patriarchal, it was less tribal, except among the bedouins in the Negev and the few bedouin tribes that had settled in Palestinian villages, where an individual's primary loyalty was to the family or to the *hamula* (which occupies a place midway between the tribe and the family in the social system). For most Palestinians, loyalty to the tribe had ceased to be important a long time ago as a result of urbanization or of a settled farming life free of bedouin raids. In contrast, life in Transjordan was mostly pastoral, and the sedentary continued to be threatened by the bedouins until the rise of the state. In addition, most Palestinian villages consisted of a number of *hamulas*, rather than one tribe, as was the case in most Transjordanian villages. In other words, in a Palestinian village or town there were more social units and consequently more chieftains than in a Transjordanian village of the same size. Thus, competition, especially over leadership, was wider and more intensive in Palestinian society. And because this competition occurred among smaller units, the determining factor was the wealth of the competitors, either in terms of land ownership or capital; in Transjordan, where the competition took place among larger units, the determining factor was the number of members of the tribe. That is why in Palestine it was not uncommon for an influential leader, especially in the cities, to come from a small family. A well-to-do chieftain in Palestine could rely on his wealth to attract many people to vote for or support him. Such cases were rare in Transjordan.

As for the political system in Palestine, it was not patriarchal, as it was in Transjordan. Palestine before 1948 was ruled directly by Great Britain, a foreign European power that had nothing to do with personal patriarchalism. After thirty years of direct British rule, the Palestinians were used to the rule of law in all aspects of public life, while in Transjordan a combination of law and tribal tradition was employed to settle communal and personal disputes. Because of this blend, kinship was an important factor in public administration. Inevitably, these differences between the societies of the East and West Banks produced different patterns of interaction with the state. The East Bank pattern was characterized by compliance, while the West Bank pattern was characterized by defiance.

Nevertheless, Palestinians, whose social system is no less patriarchal, started to adapt to the Transjordanian patriarchal political system. For obvious reasons, the Palestinians who settled in a Transjordanian social environment in the East Bank were faster than the West Bankers in adapting to this system.

The difference between the two patterns persisted until the 1967 war for two major reasons. First, the central authority in Amman, after failing to democratize the government, stuck to its political patriarchal approach because this system had proved its success for three decades in Transjordan before the unity with the West Bank and because it was in harmony with the social patriarchal system. Second, the Palestinian refugees until 1967 had the sense that their situation was temporary. This sense of transience was based on their own deep-seated national aspirations and was enshrined in the second passage of the Unity Resolution issued by Parliament, which emphasized "Arab rights in Palestine" and reaffirmed Jordan's intent "to defend those rights by all lawful means in the exercise of its natural rights but without prejudicing the final settlement of Palestine's just case within the sphere of national aspiration, inter-Arab cooperation, and international justice."

The Palestinians understood this resolution to mean that the Jordanians intended to act with the Arabs to liberate Palestine. This impression was deepened by the ambiguous Jordanian official discourse, which emphasized Jordan's determination to reinstate Palestinian rights. For example, Abul-Huda, in a speech that presented his government's program to Parliament on June 8, 1954, proclaimed that "the government stresses that there is no peace and that there are no negotiations with the Jews and that any attempt to change this policy will have no impact. The refugees are owners and allies of the land. The government will work to assure them of an honorable life and to preserve their rights in international organizations, until they regain their rights in full."[17]

The West Bank pattern of government interaction produced an impression among the ruling elite in Amman that the Palestinian was the "bad guy," a peevish troublemaker. In contrast, the Transjordanian involved in oppositional political action, even if it was violent, was viewed as the misguided "good guy." These impressions were perpetuated by the demonstrations in 1955 against the Baghdad Pact and in 1957 against the firing of the Nabulsi government (discussed in chapter 4). East Bankers participated actively in these two big confrontations between the opposition and the palace. In fact, the 1957 episode was inflamed essentially by the coup attempted exclusively by East Bank army officers. Thanks to the authority of kinship in judging people and events, the defiant Transjordanian was viewed by the ruling elite as someone who had been led astray by the bad guy. Sooner or later he would return to the fold. These prejudices shaped the behavior of the government toward members of the political opposition. It was always easier for an East Banker to obtain forgiveness than it was for his comrade from the West Bank. The central authority felt it had good reason for these discrepancies, for the West Bank, not surprisingly, proved to be not only the flash point for political opposition but also the chief source of the opposition's support.

4

King Hussein
A Young Monarch, a Fresh Approach

In 1953, King Talal abdicated for reasons of health in favor of his son, who, when he assumed his constitutional powers on May 2, 1953, was only seventeen years old. Unlike his father and grandfather, King Hussein was not known to the public. The West Bankers, in particular, had no preconceived notions about him. His father was popular, and his grandfather was, to say the least, controversial. This ambiguity was an advantage. It provided King Hussein with a grace period during which he could establish his approach to governance without serious distractions.

King Hussein was the third monarch to rule in a two-year period. The twenty months of his father's rule gave the then prime minister, Abul-Huda, the opportunity to rule almost single-handedly. King Talal's illness and his inclination to avoid intervention in the government's work allowed Abul-Huda's autocratic tendencies full sway.

Still, it was during Talal's rule that a more liberal constitution was enacted. The more important effect, perhaps, was that Abul-Huda's heavy hand rejuvenated the opposition and strengthened its two factions: the conservative opposition, whose base was in Amman and whose members usually were themselves palace officials, caught up in the competition for power; and the semi-liberal opposition,[1] whose broad base of support was on the West Bank. Because Abul-Huda was the visible autocratic ruler and not the king, it was easier and safer to vilify him and to mount demonstrations against his policies than it would have been to demonstrate against the king, who was held in high esteem.

By the time King Hussein assumed power, the political opposition was more vibrant and self-confident than it had ever been. The government was reeling under the pressure that the opposition, especially the conservatives, was exerting. Thus, King Hussein felt the need to look for a fresh approach to governance and a young team to work with him. He had a sort of missionary fervor for modernizing and building the country's political independence. He chose Fawzi al-Mulqi to be his first prime minister "because he was someone the king 'knew very well' and because he had a 'whole fresh approach' to popular participation in government that appealed to the king's youthful vigor."[2]

Al-Mulqi's cabinet reflected the king's wishes. The ministers were considered young and modern. Al-Mulqi opened his term by relaxing control on the press and releasing political prisoners. He initiated a legislative process that would lead to further constitutional reform and maintained the stability of inter-Arab relations. The country might have entered into a calm period, had it not been for Israel. Just after the armistice agreement, according to General Glubb, some Palestinians went back innocently and unarmed to their villages or orchards on the other side of the demarcation line. None in those early years crossed the armistice line in order to fight or injure the Jews. The majority crossed over in order to rescue some of their belongings or to look for missing relatives. Others went to plow their land or harvest some of the crops from their orchards. The Israelis, however, were ruthless. Many of these refugees "were shot on sight by Israeli posts or patrols, without even the formality of arrest or questioning. . . . The farmers had not realized that, owing to a line drawn on a map somewhere, half of their fields were no longer their own."[3]

Later, Israeli military units would cross the armistice line in order to punish a whole village on the West Bank if Israel perceived that an infiltration originating in that village had killed or injured some Israelis. One such event happened after al-Mulqi had been in office for five months. On October 14, 1953, an Israeli unit commanded by Ariel Sharon attacked and demolished the medium-sized village of Qibya on the West Bank. Thirty-nine houses were destroyed, more than fifty people were killed, and dozens more were wounded. The National Guard platoon defending the village was easily overcome because its members were poorly trained and ill equipped. In addition, the army failed to send reinforcements to the National Guard. "It was one of the most lethal nights in the long, numbing, and inconclusive border war that defined the Arab-Israeli conflict throughout much of the 1950s and 1960s."[4]

The event sparked off demonstrations on both banks of the kingdom. The opposition and the public at large were infuriated, and they called for retaliation against Israel and expulsion from the Arab Legion of all British officers, who were perceived to be responsible for the policy of nonretaliation. Al-Mulqi, like his predecessor Abul-Huda, was a target for both the conservative and the semi-liberal opposition. The conservatives criticized his relative liberalism and leniency on the domestic scene, and they took their criticisms directly to the king. The semi-liberal opposition also criticized the prime minister's leniency toward the Israelis' military retaliation against the front-line villages and took their protests to the streets. To the detriment of al-Mulqi's image, the infiltration-retribution cycle continued. The king felt the need for a firmer and more experienced prime minister.

In May 1954, when al-Mulqi had been in office for a year, the king turned to Abul-Huda, despite the impression the young king had given on his assumption of authority that he was to rely on a new breed of politicians. The commissioning of Abul-Huda as a prime minister not only provoked fierce opposition in and outside Parliament but also compromised the king's image among the liberal opposition as a young democratically oriented leader. According to Aruri, King Hussein was attempting "to play the role of an arbitrary figure in a parliamentary government carefully avoiding exclusive identification with either faction" of the opposition.[5]

Thus, in his first year as ruler (May 1953 to May 1954), King Hussein swung 180 degrees from the young liberal al-Mulqi to the old autocratic Abul-Huda. As we will see, this became the pattern of his rule, shifting from the conservative to the liberal and vice versa, according to the requirements of internal security and inter-Arab relations.

THE OPPOSITION

The political opposition fell into two categories: the conservatives and the semi-liberals. The latter were known as "progressives," "revolutionaries," or "nationalists" (al-quwa al-wataniyah), depending on the political context in which they identified themselves. The designation depended on which group or alliance was being referred to. If an alliance included the

National Socialists, the Ba'athists, the Arab Nationalists (al-qawmiyin al-carab), the communists, the Nasserites, the Social Syrian Nationalist party, the Muslim Brotherhood, and the Islamic Liberation party (Hizb al-tahrir), they would call themselves the nationalists. If the alliance included all of these groups except the Muslim Brotherhood and the Islamic Liberation party, they would call themselves the liberals or the progressive forces (al-quwa al-taqadumiya). If the alliance was among the communists, the Ba'athists, the Arab Nationalists, and the Nasserites, they would call themselves the revolutionaries (al-quwa al-thawriya). And if the alliance included the Ba'athists, the Arab Nationalists, and the Nasserites, they would call themselves the pan-Arabists (al-quwa al-qawmiya).

Members of the conservative opposition, including the Social Syrian Nationalists and the Muslim Brotherhood, were monarchists. They have always been loyalists. Even when they have criticized the king's policies, their criticism can be considered loyal opposition; they have usually placed the blame on the government, a tendency that has suited their "who's out/who's in" game. Though they were organized in quasi parties, they usually operated as individuals and cliques. The broad base of the conservative opposition was on the East Bank, but it included East Bankers and West Bankers alike. They would usually join forces against the other category if the latter's position on a certain issue seemed to threaten their individual or collective interests. They drew their strength from the king himself and from the resources of the government that were usually made available to them. The core of their agenda was essentially local, based on their commitment to the independence of the country and loyalty to the Hashemite monarchy. Inter-Arab as well as other international relations were viewed from this perspective. They were aware of the limitations of the state and the constraints on the decision maker, since many of the conservative leaders had assumed ministerial posts. Except for the Social Syrian Nationalists and the Muslim Brotherhood, the conservatives regarded the Palestinian question as a matter of borders (how to keep the armistice lines between Jordan and Israel quiet and stable); thus, their aim was to maintain the status quo until the time was right to solve the problem in its entirety.

Members of the semi-liberal opposition were republican in ideology, but in practice they were ambivalent. Under quiet, normal circumstances, they accepted the monarchy and interacted positively with it. On certain occasions, they would even cheer the king as the undisputed national leader—for example, when he dismissed General Glubb on March 1, 1956, and when he signed the United Arab Command Agreement on October

24, 1956. On other occasions, the king would be harshly criticized, even condemned as a monarch. Thus, their loyalty to the monarchy was conditional, in contrast to the unquestioned loyalty of the conservative opposition.

The broad base for the semi-liberal opposition was on the West Bank, but it included leaders and activists from the East Bank, mostly from the middle class and the intelligentsia. With the wave of mass education that swept Jordan in the 1950s, more Jordanians than ever before were able to go to college. Since there were no universities in Jordan at that time, most Jordanian students, whether from the West Bank or the East Bank, attended the available universities in Egypt, Syria, Lebanon, and Iraq. Many of these students became more politically aware during their university years, and some of them became Ba'athists, communists, Nasserites, or Arab Nationalists. When they returned home, they joined the already existing opposition parties. Just as the conservatives of the two banks were allied by their loyalty to the throne, so the political liberal activists of the two banks were connected by their ideologies. The political opposition gave subsidiary groups and parties a common perspective on public affairs, and it brought them together to respond to the government's policies or to initiate special national demands.

The agenda of the semi-liberal opposition was mostly pan-Arab. Its leaders exploited the constraints on the country to embarrass rather than help the government. They adopted political positions that were either congruent with the pan-Arabists in Cairo, Damascus, or Baghdad or inspired by them. They appealed to the latent anger of the Palestinians and to the pan-Arab aspirations of both West Bankers and East Bankers. They drew on the resources of Egypt, Syria, and Iraq. This is why the king and the conservatives viewed them as an extension of foreign powers in the country. To the semi-liberals, the Palestinian problem was a question of existence: Israel should be liquidated and Palestine liberated. They did not take the conservative opposition seriously and converged with them only on local issues; for example, in 1954 both criticized al-Mulqi for his leniency, though each had a different perspective on this issue.

However, there was no rigid division between the conservative and the semi-liberal opposition, or between the opposition at large and the palace. Today's member of the opposition might be a cabinet minister tomorrow, for example, while a conservative opposition leader might join the liberal opposition and vice versa. In particular, the ambivalent attitude of the liberal opposition toward the monarchy put the political leadership in Jordan in a state of flux.

THE APEX AND THE NADIR IN JORDAN'S DEMOCRATIZATION PROCESS

The Palestinian factor instigated and accelerated the gradual shift from the Jordanians' patriarchal political system to democracy. When the two banks were unified, King Abdullah was aware that he had to develop a political system that would appease and eventually absorb the more politicized and sophisticated Palestinians who were now becoming citizens of the expanded state of Jordan. In his speech from the throne on April 24, 1950, before the joint session of Parliament that resolved to unify the two banks, he "promised to revise the constitution to provide for ministerial responsibility and checks and balances."[6] Yet it was under King Talal that the new constitution was promulgated, and it was King Hussein who had to deal with the new constitution and the new laws. We might say that King Abdullah promised, King Talal enacted, and King Hussein implemented. King Hussein was the one who had to go through the democratic experience and its political implications.

The first snag in the democratization process was the semi-liberal opposition itself, whose leaders failed to understand the military limitations that the Arab Legion faced in combating the Israeli army. They kept criticizing al-Mulqi's realistic policy toward Israel in the infiltration-retaliation cycle as a lenient one. Some even failed to comprehend the ramifications of the Jordanian-Israeli confrontation. In this context, General Glubb wrote that Jordan

> was in no position at this stage to throw the gauntlet to Israel. But Egypt and Syria and certain private societies and individuals were desirous only to destroy Jordan, even if Israel were to be the instrument for her destruction. Israel was aware of these facts; but she also wanted to destroy Jordan. For if Jordan were to collapse, Israel could hope to advance her frontiers to the Jordan River or beyond. Consequently the Israeli government did not concern itself with the debate as to whether the Jordan government was organizing or preventing infiltration. If the infiltrations came from Jordan soil, then the reprisals would be directed against Jordan.[7]

On December 15, 1955, the king chose Hazza' al-Majali, an open-minded, educated young politician, to make another new thrust. The focus this time was on developing Jordan's regional role by joining the Baghdad Pact (a Western defense treaty against the potential aggression of the Soviet Union and the spread of communism in the Middle East), since the British-Jordanian Treaty was gradually becoming irrelevant due to regional and international changes. Nasserism, for example, which championed not only Arab unity and the liberation of Palestine but also the liquidation of Western (British and French) colonialism throughout the Middle East, had placed the whole region on a new track; this made any contractual defense relationship with Britain self-defeating. King Hussein tried in early 1955 to develop the relationship between Jordan and Great Britain into a more acceptable framework. He and his prime minister "requested the British government to consider the Arab Legion subsidy as a payment for the use by Britain military personnel of Jordanian bases. They demanded that the payment be made to and disbursed by the Jordan government, instead of the British commander of the Arab Legion. Such change was deemed more consistent with national dignity. . . . The British government was not responsive."[8]

Internationally, the Cold War was on the ascent, and so was the preoccupation with the potential spread of communism. The United States was the obvious leader of the free world. For King Hussein to depend on Great Britain was like depending on the dependent. Inspired by Nasserism, resentful of the British role in Palestine, and mindful of the repressive role of the security forces under General Glubb's command, the Jordanian public were against the British-Jordanian Treaty. Some called for its readjustment, and others for its abrogation.

When Jordan was approached by the British government to join the Baghdad Pact, Nasser had already inflamed Arab public opinion against it. Nasser warned against joining the pact, since it was controlled by Britain, which was perceived by the Arab public as an accomplice in the Palestinian tragedy. This sort of argument was especially convincing to the Palestinian majority of the population, for they considered Israel rather than the Soviet Union to be the enemy. The king and some of his counselors found the rewards for joining the pact enticing: Jordan would receive economic aid and modern weapons for its army. The British-Jordanian Treaty, already a target of the opposition and a headache for the king, would become irrelevant, and it would be easy to terminate it if Jordan joined the pact. Most important, accession to the Baghdad Pact would enhance Jordan's security, especially against any potential Israeli attempt to occupy the West Bank. When Jordan was approached, the prime minister was Said al-Mufti of the old guard. Neither the Turkish president Jalal Bayar's official visit in early November 1955 nor the visit in early December from General Gerald Templer, British chief of the imperial general staff, succeeded in winning over al-Mufti's government. Bayar was received with commercial strikes and hostile leaflets, and Templer's visit was met with demonstrations. In both cases Sawt al-Arab (The Arab Voice) Radio from Cairo played a role in inciting the Jordanians against the pact. Al-Mufti's government resigned on December 13, and the king, convinced of Jordan's interest in acceding to the pact, decided to appoint a new young face. Upon the formation of the cabinet on December 15, 1955, Hazza' al-Majali announced that negotiations with Britain to link Jordan to the Baghdad Pact would be conducted in good time. Two days later, the people took to the streets to protest the policy and demand al-Majali's resignation. The demonstrations flared up in almost every city and town in the kingdom and became violent; some civilians were killed, and more than one hundred were wounded. Two ministers, one from the West Bank and the other from the East Bank, threatened to resign if the prime minister did not announce that he was rejecting the pact. Under these pressures, al-Majali resigned only five days after forming his first cabinet.

From the viewpoint of the Jordanian political establishment, this episode was one of several in which objective national reasoning was defeated by sentimental pan-Arab manipulation. It was enough to spark resentment in the palace and among conservative politicians toward the national opposition led by the ideological parties. Al-Majali himself blamed the failure to join the pact on the Palestinians, accusing "the Palestinian ministers of suffering from a mental disorder and of laboring under an inclination to negatives which they doubtless have inherited as a principle of 'negation for negation's sake' from the days of the mandate in Palestine."[9]

From the Baghdad Pact episode King Hussein made the correct inference: the Jordanian national aspirations, which were cemented to the pan-Arab aspirations, made Jordan's connection to Great Britain a burden and a handicap. His own ambitions as a young leader to modernize, develop, and defend his country were also barred, though indirectly, by the British connection in the form of the British command of the Arab Legion and the British-Jordanian Treaty. Any major step he had to take, like the Baghdad Pact, had to be supported by a growing public opinion that was already aligned with the pan-Arab discourse of Cairo and Damascus. The Baghdad Pact episode was the most obvious and recent example of how a Jordanian public opinion made or supported by the pan-Arab propaganda launched from outside the country could hinder a major political thrust by the king. King Hussein was utterly aware of the Palestinian component in Jordanian public opinion. King Hussein himself became gradually dissatisfied with Glubb's policies, from those relating to the training of Jordanian officers and their promotion to the higher echelons as a prelude to Arabizing the Arab Legion (a burning desire of the king's), to those relating to defending the West Bank. To the king, Glubb looked like an obsolete general from a different era. He was, after all, the most visible post–World War II symbol of the resented British colonization of Jordan.

General Glubb became a common target for both the king and the people; why not use him to bridge the chasm between them that had been revealed by the Baghdad Pact demonstrations? To King Hussein as well as to the people, the enemy was the Glubb-led army, which was the strongest national institution; why should it look like an occupying power with its British command? The king intended to make a fresh thrust, but this time he planned to do it himself and not through the government, now under the leadership of another member of the old guard, Samir Rifa'i. This thrust was toward identifying with the sweeping Arab nationalism, whose distinct aims were *al-taharir* (becoming liberated) and attaining full political independence.

On March 1, 1956, less than three months after the defeat of the Baghdad Pact policy, the king dismissed General Glubb from his post. The king's move was received in Jordan with wild jubilation; in every city and town, people demonstrated their support in the streets, in the schools, and in editorials and telegrams dispatched to the palace. Indeed, the king was viewed as a national superhero. To capitalize on his accomplishment, the king dissolved the unpopular Parliament that had been installed through rigged elections under Abul-Huda in 1954 and scheduled new elections for October 21, 1956. Next, from October 2–4, 1956, he reached an agreement with Egypt and Syria on a unified command—which was a very popular step because it implied that the king had joined Nasser in the quest to realize the goals of pan-Arabism. During the election campaign, free discussion of political issues was allowed. And just as the king wanted to capitalize on his dismissal of General Glubb, so did the semi-liberal opposition. They called for the abrogation of the British-Jordanian Treaty and advocated closer ties with Egypt. The elections were held on time and were free. The ideological parties won twenty-one seats out of forty. The National Socialists, a party that was generally left of center, won eleven seats, the largest number for any single party. The king commissioned the party's leader, Sulaiman al-Nabulsi, though he failed in his own bid for Parliament, to form a new cabinet on October 27, 1956. Al-Nabulsi was a first-time prime minister, like al-Majali and al-Mulqi. His cabinet was an eleven-man coalition and included six members of his party, three independents, one Ba'athist, and one from the communist National Front. For the majority of the cabinet (nine out of twelve, including the prime minister) to come from organized political parties belonging or leaning to the left of the political spectrum represented a new chapter in Jordan's political history.

This was the thrust that the king made, as if he were telling the opposition who had defeated his attempt to join the Baghdad Pact, "Here we are, working together; let's see what we can do to promote the national interests of the country. Now my nationalist credentials are established: I have sacked General Glubb, dissolved the unpopular Parliament, and joined Egypt and Syria, your inspiring partners, in the unified command. So let's do it your way, but mind you, I am the king; I am the chief executive."

King Hussein would not have gone this far with the semi-liberal opposition if he had not been sure that the army was wholly on his side. He had Arabized it by dismissing the British command, in response to the demand from the Jordanian nationalist officers, made known to him through Major Abu-Nuwar. Abu-Nuwar was the king's aide-de-camp after the king graduated from Sandhurst in England. Through Abu-Nuwar, the king became aware of the Free Officers Movement, and he identified with their demands.

Barely had al-Nabulsi formed his cabinet when Israel, on October 29, launched its Sinai military offensive, followed by the Anglo-French military intervention in Egypt. This intervention, conducted in coordination with Israel, was sparked by Nasser's nationalization of the Suez Canal Company, in which Great Britain and France had large financial stakes. The tripartite aggression infuriated the whole region. In response to the Egyptian resistance; the Arab anger against Britain, France, and Israel; and the firm diplomatic intervention of the United States and the Soviet Union, the British and French military forces withdrew from Egypt in December 1956, and the Israelis withdrew later. While Great Britain and France failed to achieve their goal of regaining control of the Suez Canal Company, Israel came out of the campaign with substantive gains. Egypt agreed in November 1956 to accept UN forces as peacekeepers, and Israel accepted American and UN guarantees of freedom of passage through the Gulf of Aqaba, an international waterway.

Nasser, nevertheless, emerged from this episode a hero and the undisputed leader of pan-Arab nationalism. Egypt's stature rose still further in Arab public opinion. The Palestinians in particular were infatuated with Nasser and thought of him as a national savior.

These were the circumstances under which al-Nabulsi's government acted, and it did not lose time in fulfilling most of its pledges to the electorate. According to Aruri,

> the political parties and the press functioned freely. The country followed a strictly pro-Egyptian policy. The Anglo-Jordanian Treaty was abrogated on March 15, 1957, with no dissenting votes in either house of Parliament. An Arab Solidarity Agreement was signed with Egypt, Syria, and Saudi Arabia on January 20, 1957, stipulating that the three pledge an annual payment of 12.5 million Egyptian pounds [$36 million] to the government as a substitute for the British subsidy.[10]

The general mood of the Jordanian people under al-Nabulsi's government became anti-Western. Each political party in those days believed that it alone represented the absolute truth and therefore it alone should assume absolute authority. For this reason, the parties competed not over economic and social programs but over recruiting new members, especially from the army. In those days in the Middle East, the army was the shortest route to power. Every party wanted to reach power first and control the country without any partner. In those days the demands for pluralism, freedom of the press, and free expression by the liberal parties were but ploys to be used against the government.

When King Hussein made his 1956 move to oust General Glubb, he did not take into consideration two important facts. The first was that the conservative old guard would not genuinely support the king's inclination toward liberal pan-Arab policies, and the second was that the professional Arab Legion might become a politically oriented Arab army, because it was the major target of the liberal parties. Aruri argues that "with the departure of Glubb and a group of senior British officers, including Colonel Sir Patrick Coghill, director-general of Intelligence, the Arab Legion ceased to be an exclusive instrument of the monarchy. The senior vacancies were occupied by nationalist and Ba'athist officers, who were to challenge the monarchy later."[11]

Al-Nabulsi's government continued to come under pressure from the nationalist parties and Parliament. It responded to many of their requests, such as "purging the army and the bureaucracy" of some officers and senior officials perceived to be pro-British or antinationalist and breaking diplomatic relations with France for its repressive policy in Algeria. Yet the most important development was the relaxation of restrictions on the banned communist party and the opening of the country's doors to Tass, the Soviet news agency, and to delegations from communist countries.

For the king, as well as the old guard and conservatives like the Muslim Brotherhood, these policies were excessive. The king felt that the move he had made toward the nationalists was being misused by the government and Parliament and that the government was acting as if the country had become an Egyptian protectorate. He felt that the country was drifting into chaos and that he had to act before it was too late.

On February 2, 1957, the king issued an open letter to al-Nabulsi, drawing his attention to the foreign views and principles that had infiltrated Jordanian society, warning him against a new kind of imperialism (communism), and instructing him to leave no gap that might allow the propaganda of communism to ruin Jordan. As Aruri puts it, the king's letter "did not only carry appeal to the conservative sentiments in the country but was a wider plea to anti-communist sentiments abroad. The king had served notice that the honeymoon of the monarchy and nationalists might soon be over."[12]

Al-Nabulsi did not comply with the king's letter. Instead, he decided to exchange diplomatic representation with the Soviet Union. The king retaliated on April 10, 1957, by requesting al-Nabulsi to submit his resignation, which he did. This resignation provoked a public uprising, and rallies were held in some West Bank cities to support the outgoing government and demand its return. To appease the public, the king commissioned Fakhri al-Khalidi, a moderate West Banker from Jerusalem, to form a cabinet, but al-Khalidi failed. Then the king commissioned Abdul-Halim al-Nimr, a national figure from the East Bank who was a prominent member of al-Nabulsi's National Socialist Party, but he also failed. The country appeared to be on the verge of chaos, and on April 13, 1957, units of the army loyal to the king clashed with units commanded by progovernment officers in an army camp near Amman in what seemed to be a military coup attempt. In a daring move, the king himself rushed to the army camp in the midst of the clashes and controlled the situation. Two days later, a government was formed by al-Khalidi, and on April 16, Washington announced that in accordance with the Eisenhower Doctrine, the United States would offer Jordan financial assistance if the latter became the victim of aggression. In a declaration made by President Eisenhower in January 1957, the Eisenhower Doctrine established America's intent to support any Middle Eastern state militarily and economically against communist aggression. Demonstrations broke out on April 23, 1957, demanding the resignation of the new government and denouncing the Eisenhower Doctrine.

Under this public pressure, al-Khalidi's government resigned on April 24, and on April 25 the king commissioned Ibrahim Hashem, a member of the old guard, to form a cabinet. On the same day the American Sixth Fleet was dispatched to the eastern Mediterranean, and on April 29 the United States approved a grant of $10 million to Jordan. The American grant was the first payment of a subsidy that has become annual.

The new government declared martial law and enforced emergency regulations. The security forces were placed under army control; all political parties were dissolved; and the liberal, revolutionary-oriented ones went underground and remained illegal until 1992. Military courts were formed on both banks, and censorship was reinstated. Some of the opposition's deputies fled the country; others were arrested and lost their membership of Parliament. Several military and civilian individuals who had been involved in the confrontation received jail sentences, and many others were dismissed. In brief, the opposition was crushed, and the king's major thrust toward democratization, begun in May 1953, was reversed in two weeks in April 1957. The climax and the nadir of the shift from King Abdullah's patriarchal political system were reached under al-Nabulsi's government. The Palestinian-Jordanians contributed enormously to both.

From the three attempted thrusts King Hussein made and the manner in which he handled them and their implications, one can detect a certain pattern that might be summed up in this way: scrambling, descending, and plateauing. Each thrust was attempted through a relatively young first-time prime minister (the scrambling). Each thrust had a national objective that was aborted by the opposition (the descending), and after each aborted thrust there was recourse to the old guard (plateauing). In all of them the Palestinian factor was obvious.

After April 1957 and throughout the rest of his reign, the principles that constituted the king's plateau can be summarized in this way: the king is the helmsman, the Parliament is not supreme, the monarchy and Jordanian national interests are one and the same, and the opposition is allowed to function within this framework.

Not only did King Hussein come out of the experience with al-Nabulsi's government stronger, but also he mellowed politically. His successful approach to putting an end to the political turbulence that plagued the country and the courage he displayed in doing so were remarkable. Domestically he was looked upon as the undisputed leader whose governance was the guarantee of the country's stability. Regionally he was no longer perceived as an inexperienced king but as an astute Arab leader to be reckoned with. And internationally he impressed many world leaders and garnered respect.

However, the experience produced three residues destined to influence Jordanian political life in the years to come. The first was the comradeship in the political struggle that bound West Bankers and East Bankers. The issues that had been publicly addressed under the al-Nabulsi government transcended the regional concerns of each bank. Arab unity, rejection of the Eisenhower Doctrine, adherence to the principle of nonalignment with either the Western or the Eastern bloc, and hostility to Israel as a "usurper of Arab land" and a "spearhead for imperialism" were the slogans under which the political opposition united. These issues produced a political alliance among the activists of the two banks so that identification by party became more important than one's subidentity (Muslim, Christian, Transjordanian, Palestinian, and so on). They became instead Jordanian Muslim Brotherhood, Jordanian Ba'athists, Jordanian communists, and so forth.

The second residue was that the Jordanian polity was divided into two parts: the majority that supported the king, comprising businessmen, traditional community leaders, and the grass roots; and the minority, comprising the political opposition. Unlike the latter, the majority were inactive, counting on the government to be their spokesperson; this created the "silent majority" in Jordan. However, like the political opposition, they transcended the lines of *al-iqlimiya* (regionalism) in their support of the principle that "stability comes first."

The third residue was an inferred lesson that King Hussein kept to himself. This lesson was that political pluralism posed a threat to the constitution—or rather to the monarchy itself if it was not practiced within the confines of the national Jordanian interests. Indeed, for the king, this became the most important and troubling legacy of his experience with al-Nabulsi's government. According to the Lebanese historian Kamal Salibi,

> the continued success of the Jordanian experiment appeared to depend entirely on the personal safety of the monarch. It would take no more than one bullet to reverse the progress of the country beyond the possibility of redemption. To prevent this bullet from being fired, let alone reaching its target, constant security was required. And, as long as this remained necessary, the restoration of proper constitutional democracy to the country had to wait.[13]

DOMESTIC POLITICAL STAGNATION AND REGIONAL POLITICAL ISOLATION

As a result of the revolution in the whole political setup—or perhaps due to the preemptive palace coup against al-Nabulsi's government—Egypt and Syria did not fulfill their financial commitments to Jordan under the Arab solidarity agreement signed a few months earlier. Only Saudi Arabia lived up to its commitment to help Jordan make up for the loss of the British grant, which had come to an end with the termination of Britain's treaty with Jordan. In contrast, Egypt and Syria launched an intensive media campaign against the king and Jordan. Damascus became the Jordanian opposition's base, where a Jordanian revolutionary command was established. Jordanian exiles mounted a subversive terrorist campaign against Jordanian official installations and personnel. In response, the Jordanian government intensified its security measures in Amman, Irbid, and the West Bank. This led to numerous overreactions by the Jordanian secret police, who perpetrated acts of suppression against the opposition, especially against suspects from the West Bank and their families.

Since King Hussein's assumption of power in 1953, the threat to the country's security had been internal, supported by external forces. Now the external forces were looking for support from within Jordan. On the domestic front, the government had to keep the opposition under control. In a country where the government is the major employer and the political activists come mainly from the intelligentsia, it was easy under martial law for the government to control the opposition by firing the suspects from their governmental posts.

To further emasculate the opposition, the government sought to control the expatriates—scores of thousands of Jordanian workers and intelligentsia who had jobs outside the country, mostly in the Gulf oil-producing countries. These expatriates had already become a major source of hard currency for their country. Indeed, Jordan had already started to reap economic and political benefits from them. In the late 1950s, more than 95 percent of the Jordanian expatriates were of Palestinian origin. With uncertainty about their future, the Gulf states, especially Kuwait, provided them with hope. The government's instrument for controlling the expatriates was the travel permit. No Jordanian could travel outside the country without getting a travel permit from the Ministry of the Interior through the administrative governor's office in the individual's district. This measure was intended to prevent young people from collaborating with the Jordanian opposition in exile and their patrons. A newly employed person or an expatriate who returned to Jordan for, say, vacation could not leave the country again without getting a travel permit; the permit had to be shown to the security officer at the airport or border checkpoints. Any suspicion about the applicant's political affiliation or activity was sufficient to deny him or her the travel permit, and this essentially would mean the loss of a much-needed job. Many people lost their jobs or contracts under this security system. Understandably, such a measure was resented not only by the punished expatriates and their families but also by all the other expatriates who identified with them. From their point of view, the government, which had failed to provide them with jobs, was now depriving them of the jobs they had been able to get or were about to get. The same system was applied to students who attended universities outside the country. Many students had to drop their university studies because they were denied a travel permit, or refrained from coming back home during summer holidays.

In a nutshell, personal security was sacrificed in the name of national security. This development had a negative impact on the attitude of Palestinians toward the regime, since the majority of the Jordanian expatriates were either Palestinian refugees or West Bankers. In general, the government-public relationship was characterized by tension throughout the five-year period that followed the 1957 political turmoil. However, this period also produced another noticeable sociopolitical phenomenon. During the seven years between the unity of the two banks in 1950 and the crackdown on the opposition in 1957, the political leaders on the West Bank had begun to supersede the traditional community leaders. Now that the political leaders had been driven underground, put in prison, exiled, or scared away from resuming their political activity, they were once again replaced by the more traditional leaders in day-to-day life. Under the new suppressive security policy, the average citizen's need for an intermediary between him or her and the authorities increased. And the traditional leadership was ready as always to meet the citizen's needs. The government encouraged this trend. As a result, traditional leaders replaced the political opposition leaders, a fact that had an adverse impact on Jordan when in 1963 the Arab states, under the leadership of Egypt, floated the notion of establishing a Palestinian representative body. Jordan then, unlike Jordan in 1948, when King Abdullah thwarted the All-Palestine Government through credible Palestinian leaders, did not have the required Palestinian leaders to counter the Egyptian initiative. This fact, in my opinion, helped to determine the course of events in the area later on.

Regionally, the king began to put together an alliance of countries that supposedly were natural allies: the pro-Western Hashemite Iraq and the monarchic Saudi Arabia. Internationally, he moved to consolidate his new alliance with the United States. Naturally, Israel was satisfied with these changes in Jordan's Arab and international policies, since they meant that the threat of Nasserism had receded from the country that had the most extensive borders with Israel and that comprised the largest Palestinian community.

On February 1, 1958, while King Hussein was preoccupied with consolidating his regional and international alliances, Egypt and Syria decided to unite under Nasser in what came to be known as the United Arab Republic (UAR). King Hussein's reaction to this potential threat to Jordan's statehood came only two weeks later, when on February 14 Iraq and Jordan announced the Hashemite Confederation (or Arab Union). This federation between the two Hashemite-ruled countries failed to attract Saudi Arabia. While the Egyptian-Syrian unity was hailed by the Arab masses as a triumph of Arab nationalism, the Hashemite Confederation was viewed as opposed to Arab nationalism because Iraq was still a member of the Baghdad Pact, and Jordan, less than one year earlier, had resorted to the umbrella of the Eisenhower Doctrine to save itself from sweeping Nasserism. Neither union lasted long. The Hashemite Confederation lasted only five months. On July 14, 1958, a bloody military coup toppled the Hashemite regime in Iraq, and the country became a republic. The United Arab Republic lasted until September 28, 1961, when it broke up as a result of a military coup in Damascus. In the meantime, the United Arab Republic posed a real threat not only to Jordan but also to Lebanon; there the Muslim community, which leaned toward Nasser, was encouraged by Nasser's presence next door in Damascus and called for Lebanon to join the United Arab Republic. When the Hashemite Confederation broke up as a result of the military coup in Baghdad, Jordan's position was tremendously weakened, and so was Lebanon's. Kamal Salibi makes this comment on the new situation:

> To the masses of the Arab world, the violent end of the monarchic regime in Iraq seemed to have removed one of the major hurdles along the road to full Arab unity under President Nasser, whose leadership was commonly believed to represent the wave of the Arab future. These were the only remaining obstacles to be overcome: Lebanon and Jordan. Once these were removed, whatever remained of Arab resistance to the Nasserist wave would be easily mopped up.[14]

Never had King Hussein felt as helpless, isolated, and vulnerable as he did on the afternoon of July 14, 1958, when he learned that his cousin, King Faisal II, and his family had been massacred in a bloody military coup by Iraqi revolutionaries. Yet as shocking and destabilizing as it was, the Baghdad coup failed to paralyze King Hussein, who betrayed no sign of fear or panic in the face of the uncertainty that now shrouded the future of the Hashemite dynasty in Jordan and threatened the very existence of the country. Internally, he had to rely on a group of old-guard politicians and on the bedouin combat units of the army; externally, he had to seek the support of the United States and Great Britain, to deter hostile forces both at home and in the region.

On July 15 and before the king had officially announced his decision to request military assistance from friendly countries, Jordan turned to the United Nations for protection from the United Arab Republic, invoking Article 51 of the UN Charter.[15] On July 19, British paratroopers landed at Amman airport and were soon patrolling its streets. Aruri sums up the outcome of the United Nations' involvement:

> The UN intervention in Jordan, which restored a measure of stability to the regime, was viewed with relief by almost all those concerned. It facilitated the withdrawal of the British troops from Jordan and thus improved the position of King Hussein. It made an Israeli incursion into the West Bank less likely, and it relieved Nasser of the burden of having to go to the defense of the Palestinians in the event they were attacked by Israel.[16]

The king's policy came to fruition. Deterrence was achieved, and the British paratroopers were completely withdrawn on November 2, 1958.

THE POLICY SHIFT FROM REACTION TO COUNTERACTION

Having survived the demise of the Hashemite Confederation and its ripples and recovered from the trauma of the 1958 bloody Iraqi coup, King Hussein started a new strategy.

On the international scene, his strategy was to promote Jordan's case and elaborate on Jordan's attitudes toward a number of political and ideological world issues. The emphasis on Jordan's alliance with the West was one of them. Commitment to combat communism and block its expansion in the region was another. Obviously the king's strategy was to secure a broad base of Western sympathy for Jordan.

King Hussein's strategy on the Arab scene was to get out of the trench, seek alliances with like-minded regimes, and fight the systematic ideological campaign that had been launched by the Arab radical regimes against the Arab monarchies in general and Jordan in particular. His countercampaign addressed the same issues—Palestine, Arab unity, and the concept of national progress—but from an entirely different perspective.

King Hussein's version of Arab nationalism was based on the principles and goals of the Great Arab Revolt and the teachings of Islam. It was to cement Arab unity and solidarity, in contrast to the Nasserite version, which

Table 2. The Radicals versus the King: Differences in Ideology on the Major Issues

	The Issue			
	Palestine	Arab Unity	Progress	Alliances
The Radicals	Arab unity a prerequisite to the liberation of Palestine	Under one leadership	Socialism	Nonalignment
King Hussein	Arab cooperation in all fields to restore Palestinian rights	Loose federation among equals	A better life	Pro-Western (in 1964, Jordan tilted toward Nasser's pan-Arabism)

brought about Arab disunity and "hampered the Arabs in dealing with the greatest political problem confronting us: the Palestine question."[17] Hussein's concept of Arab unity was a sort of loose Arab federation similar to the Hashemite Confederation, in which every member state maintained its independence. Table 2 shows the positions of the radicals and the king.

It is noteworthy that neither camp raised the issue of democracy, political pluralism, or human rights in the competition to win the minds and hearts of the public. If anything, this means that neither democracy nor human rights were real public concerns at that time. Note, however, that Palestine was definitely an issue. For Jordan it was the major issue that lay at the heart of the king's new strategy on the domestic scene.

Among the many lessons that King Hussein inferred from his recent two-year experience on the interrelated domestic and Arab scenes was that the Palestinian-Jordanians constituted an opening in Jordan's defenses against the Arab revolutionary rising tide. That opening was to be blocked. Until 1959, Jordan's policy toward the Palestinian problem was able to win only the minds of a Palestinian minority and failed to win the hearts of the sentimental majority. The king thought that systematic conscious efforts were needed to accelerate the development of the pan-Jordanian identity. Such efforts would complement the socioeconomic integration process, which had already made enormous strides, and protect the Palestinian-Jordanians against going astray of the state's positions on the Palestinian question.

Such an aggressive strategy required an aggressive team to back it up, and there were no more aggressive political leaders at that time than Hazza' al-Majali and Wasfi al-Tal. Both were solid patriots, each coming from a prominent tribe or clan. Al-Majali was from the south, while al-Tal was from the north. Both were relatively young; had been classmates in secondary school; and were friends, university graduates, and highly cultured men. More important, both had firsthand experience in Arab politics with regard to the Palestinian question. Al-Majali had been a senior official in King Abdullah's court during the 1948 Palestinian episode, and al-Tal had been an operations officer with the Arab Rescue Army. Finally, and most important of all, both of them belonged to the first generation in Transjordan the state. In other words, Hazza' al-Majali and Wasfi al-Tal were raised not only as a Majali or a Tal but also as Transjordanians.

King Hussein chose Hazza' al-Majali to launch this new phase and commissioned him to form a new cabinet. Although technically al-Majali was not a first-timer, his first government in 1955 had lasted only one week. On May 6, 1959, Hazza' al-Majali formed a new government that on August 25 appointed Wasfi al-Tal as acting director of the General Directorate for Guidance and Information. In this capacity, al-Tal's task was to run the entire Jordanian information and publicity system, for in those days the Ministry of Information did not exist. With al-Majali as prime minister and al-Tal as his commissar, Jordan experienced a fresh wave of self-confidence. This confidence was related not to the security issue but to the sense of nationhood. It was obvious that the al-Majali–al-Tal team, unlike the old guard, had a new concept. The old guard defended the monarchy in order to defend the country or their own interests. The new team defended the independence of Jordan in order to defend the monarchy. Their means of defense were not confined to security measures and political maneuvers. They had to mobilize the people behind constructive substantive issues. They pledged to modernize the country and to fight corruption and favoritism. Promoting a pan-Arab message that differed from the revolutionary one prevalent at that time was the clearest manifestation of the new team's aggressive defense strategy. Al-Tal personally oversaw its implementation on a day-to-day basis. He lectured on the adopted message. To give his media campaign more opportunities to succeed, al-Tal recruited Jordanian individuals who were truly motivated and not merely professionals. At that time there were two motivated groups ready to combat Nasserite Arabism on ideological and political grounds. The first group was the Muslim Brotherhood, who regarded Nasser as communist-oriented and who resented his crackdown on their Egyptian leadership. The second group was the Social Syrian Nationalists, whose belief in the unity of the Syrian Nation conflicted with Nasser's Arab unity, and who had been repressed by Nasser's allies in Syria. Al-Tal recruited people from both

Palestinian and Transjordanian backgrounds to give a boost to the grow-ing pan-Jordanian identity.

The goal of this new policy was to defend the independence of monarchic Jordan within the framework of the two banks. Historically, it could be considered the first phase in consciously constructing pan-Jordanian na-tionalism; the essence of this nationalism at that time was the exclusion of Jordan from the Nasserite version of Arab unity.

Nevertheless, this new policy was misunderstood by both Palestinians and Transjordanian Arab nationalists; at present, it is being misinterpreted by the young advocates of Transjordanian nationalism. Those Palestinians who mostly supported Nasserism as a means to restore Palestine viewed the new Jordanian political discourse at the time as an attempt to obstruct their aspirations. Today's young advocates of Transjordanian nationalism consider al-Majali and al-Tal as the fathers of the rising Transjordanian nationalism that would exclude Jordanians of Palestinian origin.

When the Jordanian government inaugurated its campaign against Nasser, the Arab radical media was already dividing the Arab states into the "progressive camp," which consisted of Egypt, Syria, and Iraq (later to include Yemen and Algeria), and the "reactionary camp," which consisted mainly of the monarchies, especially Jordan and Saudi Arabia. These two countries took the brunt of the revolutionary media war against the "reac-tionary camp." Now, as Jordan's media launched a campaign against the revolutionary camp, Jordan became not only the recipient of the lion's share of verbal abuse and the prime target for sabotage from the "revolu-tionary camp" but also the visible leader of the "reactionary camp." Dur-ing these years, the respect and admiration of the Gulf Arab sheiks for King Hussein began to grow, even before their countries gained their indepen-dence. They looked at him as the courageous spokesman for the conserva-tive, patriarchal societies. In those days it took real courage to defy Nasser.

THE PERIOD OF TURMOIL AND DISORIENTATION IN THE ARAB WORLD

No period in modern Arab history witnessed as many abrupt changes as did the period from 1959 to 1963. A number of rulers were unseated, regimes were overturned, and alliances changed like shifting sand dunes. The ferocious media and subversive warfare between the so-called revolu-tionary and conservative camps in the Arab world persisted. Jordan's role as the self-appointed proponent of the conservative Arab camp had its negative repercussions. One of its horrifying casualties was the assassination of Prime Minister Hazza' al-Majali on August 29, 1960. On October 1, 1960, Jordan resumed its diplomatic relations with Iraq, and Wasfi al-Tal was appointed as an ambassador to Baghdad. The main reason for this move was the revival of the burning issue of the "Palestinian entity," first raised by Egypt in late March 1959 and adopted, though in a different version, by Iraq in December 1959. To Jordan, this issue meant not only the destabilization of the country but also its potential disintegration.

What made the situation worse was that Kassem was trying to outbid Nasser on the Palestinian entity issue to the detriment of Jordan's national unity. Al-Tal's mission was to try to establish a common ground between Jordan and Iraq based on their common rejection of Nasser's leadership over the Arab world; beyond that, al-Tal hoped to entice Kassem to drop his call for a Palestinian entity and give priority instead to a joint Jordanian-Iraqi effort to weaken Nasser and get him out of Syria.[18]

Kassem, who was already suffering from his political isolation, welcomed the conciliatory initiative from Jordan. He even went so far as to announce that any aggression against Jordan would be an aggression against Iraq.

King Hussein then turned to Saudi Arabia, hoping to cement the unwritten Jordanian-Saudi alliance. He met King Saud in July 1961, and together "the two monarchs pledged to provide more efforts to unite the Arab ranks, defend Arab rights, and work for a solution of all Arab internal problems within Arab family grounds."[19] One month later the two monarchs agreed to establish a joint military command.

On September 28, 1961, a Syrian military coup succeeded in separating that country from the UAR. Jordan, for obvious reasons, accorded hasty recognition to the new Syrian regime. Heartened by Nasser's diminishing influence, King Hussein turned his focus to developing the country in almost every sphere. To fulfill this mission, the king commissioned Wasfi al-Tal as prime minister in January 1962. The seeds of development that had been planted by al-Majali's government were already beginning to bloom. Kamal Salibi writes:

> With the capital provided by British and American financial aid since the mid-1950s, the potash, phosphate, and cement industries of Jordan were already undergoing development by the early 1960s, and an oil refinery—the first of its kind in the country—was under construction in the town of Zarqa, east of Amman. A network of modern highways . . . was taking shape to knit the various parts of the country together. . . . Substantial remittances from the many Jordanians working in the Gulf countries, most of them Palestinians, were helping to develop the national economy. In Amman and Jerusalem and

their suburbs, a boom in the construction industry provided opportunities for employment and work for skilled and unskilled laborers, mostly Palestinians, many of them from the refugee camps. Christians from all over the world came to visit the holy places in the West Bank, after which they toured the rich archaeological sites of the East Bank, most notably the fabulous ruins of Petra. The resulting prosperity in Jordan was reflected in the rapid growth of a new middle class of entrepreneurs, merchants, and professionals.[20]

Both al-Tal and the king recognized that combating Nasserism through the media, as Jordan had for the last two years, would not keep Jordan immune from this issue of the "Palestinian entity." As prime minister, al-Tal decided to develop new tactics under the king's guidance and with his full support. The new approach was reflected in a white paper, which was introduced to the Parliament by al-Tal himself during a vote-of-confidence session for his second government in December 1962:

> Our primary objective of national mobilization both in the military and the civil sectors . . . is to implement the plan which we view as the most appropriate for the restoration of Palestine. For the Palestinian cause, to us, is an issue of life or death. The government will present to your August council the "Palestine Plan" which aims at shifting our country to the center of power, effectiveness, and mobilization of Arab effort . . . in one front that will bring about victory for our cause.[21]

One does not have to sift through the rhetoric to understand the aims of al-Tal's new policy. The phrase "shifting our country to the center of power, effectiveness," and so on reveals that the major objective was to enable Jordan to replace Nasser as the leader of the Arab nation on the Palestinian question.

The Palestinian issue was the most crucial as far as Jordan was concerned in its confrontation with Nasserism, and the 1962 white paper based Jordan's position on the facts that Jordan accommodated the largest Palestinian community (two-thirds of the Palestinian people) on its territory; that the West Bank of Jordan was the largest part of Palestine and had been rescued by Jordan from the potential Israeli occupation in the 1948 war; and that Jordan's borders with Israel were the longest, exceeding 350 miles (600 kilometers) and making Jordan's territory, in particular the West Bank, both a potential springboard for Arab armies to liberate Palestine and a first-priority target for Israel to occupy. Hence Jordan should be the Arab center of gravity with regard to Israel.

It is noteworthy that Hazem Nusseibeh, who drafted the white paper, is from Jerusalem (of Palestinian origin) and that the other three contributors reflected a range of backgrounds: Wasfi al-Tal was of Transjordanian origin, Sharif Abdul-Hamid Sharaf was a Hashemite, and Akram Zueiter was from Nablus (of Palestinian origin and one of the most prominent Palestinian nationalists who struggled for the Palestinian cause and Arab unity under the British mandate). The fact that the four of them participated in writing the white paper obviously indicates that huge strides had been made in the integration of Transjordanians and Palestinians since the 1950 unification of the two banks. Yet it is also significant, as Nusseibeh reports in his book (subtitled *The Unity of the Jordanian and the Palestinian People*), that the original text of the white paper included a proposal to change the name of the country from the Hashemite Kingdom of Jordan to the United State of Palestine and Jordan after the liberation of Palestine: "The Palestine Plan as was issued by the Jordanian Foreign Ministry did not include the political proposal which provided for 'the framework of the United State of Palestine and Jordan,' as a future political framework after the liberation of Palestine."[22]

Al-Tal's government had no time to complete its mission. Soon the winds of change swept the Middle East. A pro-Nasser military coup toppled the imam (monarch) of Yemen, who started a war against the new regime to restore his throne. Saudi Arabia supported him, and so did Jordan. Nasser dispatched an expeditionary force to Yemen in support of the new regime.

In February 1963, Kassem in Iraq was toppled in a military coup whose leader was pan-Arabist. A month later, in March 1963, a Ba'athist coup in Damascus ended the rule of the secessionists. The leaders of Egypt, Syria, and Iraq convened in Cairo to discuss the unity of the three countries. A federal unity treaty was concluded on April 17, 1963. In Jordan, joyous popular celebrations in support of the new Arab union developed into bloody confrontations with the army. Jordan's workshop scene changed into a security-oriented one.

To cope with this deteriorating situation, the king dissolved the Parliament and for the first time appointed a Hashemite, Sharif Hussein bin Nasser, as prime minister. Meanwhile, the Agreement on the Federal Arab Unity of Egypt, Iraq, and Syria that had caused such euphoria never took effect.

ARAB UNITY OR ARAB COORDINATION?

Just as the 1963 military coups in Baghdad and Damascus changed the balance of power among Arab states, so did the failure of Cairo, Baghdad, and Damascus to implement a federal unity among themselves. This failure resulted in the resumption of media warfare. While these countries were engaged in exchanging recriminations, the Israelis reasserted themselves. By the end of 1963, Israel had unilaterally set out to divert the water of the River Jordan into the Negev.

Besides, the polarization within the Arab world took a new turn. The revolutionary-versus-reactionary polarization that had characterized the inter-Arab scene since 1957 and had been a source of serious concern to Jordan was now superseded by a polarization within the revolutionary camp itself. As of July 1963, Syria and Iraq began discussions to unite their two countries and exclude Egypt. This Syrian-Iraqi move automatically brought Jordan and Egypt closer, since the consolidation of Syrian and Iraqi political forces was a potential threat not only to Nasser's prestige but also to Jordan's national security. After all, the Palestinian intelligentsia were very active in the pan-Arab Ba'ath and Arab nationalist movements.

Meanwhile, on December 2, 1963, Nasser called for an Arab summit to draw up a common Arab strategy for counteracting Israel's plans to divert water from the River Jordan. King Hussein accepted the invitation that same day, not only because the issue concerned Jordan most but also because he wanted to consolidate forces with Nasser in an attempt to counterbalance the rising Iraqi-Syrian alliance. The Arab summit convened in Cairo on January 13, 1964. One of its resolutions entrusted the representative of Palestine in the Arab League with the task of continuing his contacts with the member states of the Arab League and with the Palestinian people in order to establish the foundations for organizing the Palestinian people; the goal was to liberate the Palestinian homeland and allow its self-determination. The summit and its resolutions constituted a turning point in the political history of the Arab world following World War II. Until the Gulf War in 1991, the Cairo summit (along with the summit later that year in Alexandria, Egypt) became the institution that epitomized pan-Arabism—or rather the unanimously accepted form of pan-Arab unity. This form of unity could be characterized as a loose confederal formula. It was a substitute for Nasser's original version of Arab unity, which was based on merging the Arab states under one political leadership. The disparity between the two versions was enormous, and from a historical point of view, this change in focus marked a considerable political retreat for Nasser, who was still the undisputed leader of the Arab masses and the embodiment of their pan-Arab sentiments. This retreat did not happen overnight; it occurred in response to numerous political setbacks, and it was aimed at maintaining Arab unity at a higher level. Recent attempts at establishing Arab unity had all failed: the Hashemite Confederation had broken up in July 1958; the Egyptian-Syrian unity had broken up in September 1961; and the recent attempts to forge a federal unity among Egypt, Syria, and Iraq had not materialized.

As far as Jordan was concerned, this new formula for Arab unity was heartening, since it was closer to King Hussein's version of federal unity among equals. With the establishment of this formula, Jordan was relieved once and for all of one of the two major perceived threats to its national security. But ironically, while the January 1964 Cairo summit eliminated one of the two, it also rejuvenated the other—namely, the issue of the "Palestine entity." Jordan would continue to struggle with this issue until October 26, 1994, when it concluded the peace treaty with Israel.

5

The Seeds of the Palestinian Entity and the Rise of the National Palestinian Leadership

On April 24, 1996, while Israel was celebrating the forty-eighth anniversary of its independence, the Palestine National Council convened in Gaza and voted to repeal the clauses in the 1964 PLO charter that called for the Palestinian armed struggle to destroy Israel and establish instead a Palestinian state on the whole territory of Mandatory Palestine (the area today made up of Israel and the West Bank and Gaza). The session was attended by 572 council members, many of whom came to Palestine from the diaspora for this purpose, and the vote on the repeal was 504 in favor to 54 opposed.

On the same day that the Palestine National Council adopted this historic resolution, the Syrian president, Hafez Assad, was engaged in negotiating a cease-fire in Lebanon with the U.S. secretary of state, Warren Christopher. Israel had been striking back in Lebanon fiercely and disproportionately for the Katyusha rocket attacks on northern Israel instigated by the Lebanese Hizballah guerrillas.[1]

Forty-eight years earlier, the Palestine National Congress had convened in the same city, issuing on October 1, 1948, a declaration of independence for all Mandatory Palestine and establishing an All-Palestine Government, which was destined to fade away, as we have seen. The irony of these two events is obvious. The 1948 congress and the 1996 council convened in the same city, Gaza. The first established the All-Palestine Government (negating the existence of Israel), and the second confirmed Palestinian recognition of the State of Israel, which now has the first say in molding the Palestinian entity in a small part of Mandatory Palestine.

What is no less ironic was the timing of the Palestine National Council resolution. The Syrian military presence in Lebanon and the military engagement of the Lebanese Hizballah with Israel, in the final analysis, are but two remnants of the forty-eight-year broader Arab engagement with Israel for the sake of the Palestinians. It is against this background that one should view the resolution of April 24, 1996. In historical terms, it was a turning point not only in the Palestinian-Israeli conflict but also in the Arab-Israeli one. In the Palestinian-Israeli context, the Palestine National Council resolution, in my opinion, was tantamount to a final unequivocal departure by Israel and the PLO from their mutual denial of Jewish and Palestinian nationalisms and an arrival at mutual recognition. In the Arab-Israeli context, as the irony of the timing reveals, the resolution was concrete evidence that the Arab-Israeli conflict has now broken down into subconflicts, and each party has to cope with its own conflict independently. Indeed, this was the logical outcome, though it came thirty-two years later, of establishing the PLO in 1964 to represent the Palestinian entity.

THE ASSERTION OF PALESTINIAN INDEPENDENCE

The ultimate objective of the Palestinian struggle as it crystallized in the late 1920s was to establish an independent Arab state of Palestine, like Syria, Lebanon, Transjordan, Iraq, and Egypt, though some of the Palestinian political leaders called either for unity with Transjordan under Emir (later King) Abdullah or for a broader Arab unity. As has been described, the nation-state system was introduced to the former Ottoman territories in the eastern Mediterranean region after World War I. The foundation of the Arab League in 1945 as a loose confederation of individual Arab states institutionalized the status quo and accentuated the already strong tone of independence among the Palestinians. In fact, the foundation documents of the Arab League referred to the independence of Palestine explicitly. The October 7, 1944, Alexandria protocol devoted a special resolution to

Palestine. In one of its paragraphs, the resolution states, "The committee holds that the binding British pledges to stop the Jewish immigration, to protect the Arab land and to bring Palestine to independence are inalienable Arab rights." The Arab Charter (or Arab League Covenant), which was signed by the seven Arab states on March 22, 1945, included a "Special Appendix on Palestine." Among other things, this appendix maintains that

> since the end of the last World War, the Arab countries that were part of the Ottoman Empire seceded from it, and each of them, including Palestine, became a country in its own right; and under the Lausanne Treaty each of these countries is entitled to run its own affairs. Though Palestine was not able to exercise this right, the League of Nations' Charter of 1919 would not have decided the regime under which it was placed [in other words, the mandate] had it not been recognized as an independent entity. . . . The signatories on the Arab League Charter hold that due to the special situation of Palestine and until this country is able to practice its actual independence, the League's Council will assume the job of choosing an Arab Palestinian representative to participate in its proceedings.

On December 4, 1945, the Arab League council adopted the following resolution:

> The Council decides that Palestine be represented by one delegate or more, not exceeding three, and that the delegation participates in all the proceedings of the Council in accordance with what the Charter of the Arab League provided for. It is to be understood that the participation of the Palestinian delegation means that it has the right to vote on the Palestinian issue and on other issues that Palestine can commit itself to implement. The Palestinian delegates are to be nominated by the Higher Arab Committee (HAC) and appointed by the League Council. If the nomination is not possible, the whole task [that is, nomination and appointment] becomes the Council's responsibility.[2]

The council gave itself the prerogative to appoint the Palestinian representative because of the differences that had raged among the Palestinian political parties over who was to represent Palestine when they were asked to participate in the proceedings of the league's preparatory committee, which held its meetings in Alexandria in September and October of 1944. More important, there was no elected Palestinian national body that could delegate representatives to the Arab League. Finally, a neutral Palestinian personality, Mousa al-Alami, was chosen to represent Palestine on the committee. On June 12, 1946, the council of the Arab League decided to set up a Palestinian committee under the name of al-Ha'ia al-Arabiya al-Ulia, as distinct from al-Lajna al-Arabiya al-Ulia, which was set up in 1936 to supervise and guide the Palestinian general strike. After June 1946, this new HAC represented Palestine in the Arab League. On June 29, 1963, Ahmad Hilmi Pasha, the prime minister of the defunct All-Palestine Government and the representative of Palestine in the Arab League, died. Egypt lobbied for appointing Ahmad al-Shuqairi, a Palestinian lawyer originally from Acre, as his successor. Al-Shuqairi was anti-Hashemite and was known to have cherished some ideas incompatible with the unity of the West Bank and the East Bank of Jordan. Perhaps because of these political leanings, he was chosen by Egypt as a candidate to succeed Ahmad Hilmi Pasha; Nasser at that time was very enthusiastic about developing and activating the concept of the Palestinian entity. On September 19, 1963, the council of the Arab League appointed al-Shuqairi as representative of Palestine in accordance with the Arab League Charter. Their resolution entrusted al-Shuqairi with the task of forming and heading a Palestinian delegation to attend the eighteenth session of the General Assembly of the United Nations to present the case of Palestine. The council recommended that the member states instruct their permanent representatives at the United Nations to subscribe to this delegation and help it to accomplish its mission. The council also decided that at the end of the UN session (that is, the General Assembly's), al-Shuqairi was to tour the Arab states to discuss the Palestinian cause in all its aspects and the means to rejuvenate it.[3]

Al-Shuqairi, a veteran politician, was also experienced in UN affairs because he had been the Saudi representative to the United Nations before his appointment as Palestinian representative to the Arab League. His academic background and his training as a lawyer, as well as his work at the United Nations and the Arab League, gave him impressive expertise in multilateral diplomacy. In his political discourse, he was fond of rhetoric and had demagogic tendencies.

Not surprisingly, Jordan, aware of al-Shuqairi's enthusiasm for establishing a Palestinian entity, opposed his appointment. In June 1961, the Palestine Experts Committee had met to discuss the Palestinian entity. Al-Shuqairi participated in the meeting as an expert and proposed two plans. The first envisaged a Palestinian National Congress with 150 representatives that would convene once a year in Jerusalem, and the second was to reestablish a genuine Palestinian government that would operate within the Arab League framework. Jordan opposed both plans. When the "Palestinian entity" was a hot issue among the Palestinian intellectuals in the early 1960s, al-Shuqairi was one of the prominent figures in the debate. He was known to have embraced a position hostile to the Hashemites. His thesis was "the road to Palestine should go through

Amman." Jordan viewed the decision to appoint al-Shuqairi as the representative of Palestine as a preliminary step by Egypt toward establishing the Palestinian entity. Jordan's position was that the Palestinians would decide on their political future only after the liberation of Palestinian land, which could be achieved through the cooperation of the Arab states. However, Egypt, even before Nasser came to power, had always held that the Palestinians should have their own entity in order to protect the Palestinian cause from drifting into oblivion. The death of Ahmad Hilmi, the prime minister of the defunct All-Palestine Government, provided Egypt with the opportunity "to abolish this institution [the All-Palestine Government] once and for all and to move the issue of Palestinian representative institutions from the realm of words to deeds."[4]

In May 1964, the first Palestinian National Congress convened in Jerusalem. At the end of the convention the establishment of the PLO was announced. The second Arab summit, held in Alexandria in September 1964, "welcomed the establishment of the PLO as the basis of the Palestinian entity and as a pioneer in the collective Arab struggle for the liberation of Palestine."

POLITICAL ADJUSTMENT, DEMOGRAPHIC FRAGMENTATION

After the armistice agreements were signed in 1949 between Israel on the one hand and Egypt, Jordan, Lebanon, and Syria on the other, the 1,300,000 Palestinians woke up to a horrible fact. They were fragmented and scattered all over the region, and their country was dismembered. Some of them became Jordanian citizens, some Israeli citizens. Others, like the local inhabitants of the Gaza Strip, remained Palestinians but were stateless, and 750,000 became refugees. The dream of an independent Arab Palestine was destroyed, the All-Palestine Government was a myth, and they had to adjust to the tragic new situation as best they could. Regardless of the economic troubles they had to face in the first decade after 1948, the Palestinians who became Jordanian citizens after the unity of the West Bank with Transjordan were in better shape than their fellow Palestinians in the Gaza Strip, Lebanon, and Syria. Those who remained in Israel also had to suffer from being an unwelcome minority in a state that was meant to be Jewish. UNRWA stepped in to help the refugees. Omar Massalha, in *Towards the Long-Promised Peace*, writes:

> After the failure of the Conciliation Commission, the international community effectively shelved the political file of Palestine, reducing the question merely to

a humanitarian refugee problem. This attitude, which overlooks the existence and political rights of the Palestinian people, was mirrored in the omission of the Palestinian question from the agenda of the U.N. General Assembly (October 14–December 21, 1952). From 1952 until December 10, 1969, Palestine was only mentioned in the UNRWA Commissioner-General's Annual Report.[5]

The growing awareness among the Palestinians of their political situation horrified them. How to maintain their cause as a national one—as a fight for a land and a people rather than as a humanitarian issue involving refugees—became the major concern of Palestinian activists. Their dismay was exacerbated by their fragmentation. Egypt, which assumed the role of big Arab brother—or rather, leader—had the same worry about the Palestinian question becoming simply a refugee issue. Such concerns would lead to instability and confrontation with Israel. In a military confrontation, Egypt would shoulder the largest share of the burden. That is why Egypt in March 1959 raised the issue of the Palestinian entity in the ordinary session of the Arab League council. As mentioned earlier, Kassem in Iraq responded to Egypt's initiative by supporting the establishment of a Palestinian republic and later by establishing the nucleus of a Palestinian army, providing military training to young members of the small Palestinian community in Iraq.

The dispersing of Palestinians in different territories under different governments transformed them over the years into several societies; each community developed within the framework of the host country and took on some of its characteristics. The only bond that united them as one people, until the 1967 war, was their common plight and their hope for return. They maintained their customs and folklore as a means of staying connected with their homeland across the armistice lines. They found in transnational political parties convenient institutions through which, they believed, they could promote their cause and achieve their national objectives. In Israel, for example, the Palestinians until the early 1980s identified politically with the Israeli Communist Party (ICP), less for ideological reasons than for their quest for acceptability. The ICP was a binational party; its members were both Jews and Arabs. It was also the representative of the interests of Israeli Arabs in the 1950s and 1960s. It raised issues related to Arab demands in the Knesset and in the party's papers. In the Arab world, the Palestinians joined or supported, according to individual leanings, pan-Arab parties like the Ba'athists or the Arab Nationalists and pan-Islamic parties like the Muslim Brotherhood and communist parties. Nasserism, for the vast majority of Palestinians, was the most appealing of all, and it was viewed as being more credible than the programs of the political parties. Nasser's credentials as an anticolonialist were solid, especially after he had allied Egypt with the Soviet Union and nationalized the Suez Canal. In addition, he was the revolutionary leader of Egypt, the largest Arab state. And supporting Nasserism was less perilous because it was not a political party. The average Palestinian preferred to support Nasser over joining a banned political party whose members were exposed to the threat of arrest, harassment, or even persecution by Arab governments, depending on who was in power. In brief, the Palestinians did not form political parties based on Palestinian nationalism after 1948.

THE DRIVE TO REGAIN CONTROL OVER PALESTINIAN DESTINY

Thanks to the Israeli occupation of the Gaza Strip in 1956–57, activists inspired by the Algerian, Vietnamese, and Cuban revolutions felt the need to resort to armed struggle against Israel. They felt that such an armed struggle should be independent of Arab control, though it should seek Arab cooperation. They did not want to repeat the experience of the Palestinian fedayeen, the Egyptian-trained Palestinian guerrillas whose operations against Israel were halted by Egypt after the Suez War. Operating under Egyptian command would mar their national objectives. Massalha, who was the "permanent observer" for Palestine at UNESCO from 1980 until 1993, writes:

> The political means was spawned with the creation in Gaza, in 1957, of the Palestinian national movement, Fatah, and, since 1959, with its publication entitled "Our Palestine." Fatah's political program comprised the following main objectives: achieving the renaissance of the Palestinian entity as the resistance's point of departure; relying on its own means, with the support of friends throughout the Arab world and other countries; a call for armed resistance, for a long-term popular war; and the creation of a secular, democratic state, in which Jews, Christians, and Muslims would live together, to be inspired by the pluralist and tolerant history of the Palestinians. Fatah's slogan could be summed up in the words: no to tutelage, no to dependence, no to being politically hijacked by other states.[6]

GAZA: HOTBED OF PALESTINIAN NATIONALISM

It was only natural that Palestinian nationalism should be more vibrant in the Gaza Strip than anywhere else. First, this was a Palestinian territory whose population was wholly Palestinian, either local or refugee. Though it had come under Egyptian administration in the wake of the 1948 war, it was not annexed to Egypt, the only adjacent Arab country. Unlike the West Bankers and the Arab Israelis, who also continued to live on Palestinian territory, the Palestinians in Gaza were stateless. They soon found themselves in a sort of limbo. The Gaza Strip is a desertlike enclave with very limited natural resources. Its population before 1948 lived on agriculture, trade, and fishing. As a result of the 1948 war, the Gaza Strip became stranded and was host to a large concentration of Palestinian refugees. The United Nations estimated that by September 1949 there were 726,000 refugees located behind the armistice lines; 200,000 of them were in the Gaza Strip, and the rest were scattered over Transjordan, the West Bank, Syria, and Lebanon. The boycott that the Arab states imposed on Israel in the wake of the war left the strip with just one exit, or rather one neighbor to deal with—Egypt. The scarcity of natural resources, the density of the population, and the boycott contributed to the plight of its people. UNRWA projects and relief services barely allowed the refugees to survive. Jobs became scarce and the standard of living deteriorated.

Egypt, the neighbor and the administrator, was not a land of opportunity for the Gazans simply because Palestinians, except for university students, were not allowed to reside there. The grand mufti, right after the 1948 war, asked the Egyptian authorities not to allow Palestinians from Gaza to live in Egypt. For him it was imperative that the Gaza Strip continue to be the symbol of the Palestinian entity. And to be an entity, it must not be evacuated by its own people. Thus, the Egyptians, who have consistently supported the notion of a Palestinian entity, would not permit Palestinians to live in Egypt. In fact, for a Palestinian from Gaza to visit Egypt, he or she had to get a permit from the Egyptian governor general's office in Gaza. And if a Gazan had to stay in Egypt beyond the permitted time, he or she had to report to the governor general's office in Cairo to get an extension. Libya and the oil-producing Arab countries in the Gulf constituted the only job opportunities for the Gazans. The governments and peoples of those Arab countries showed genuine sympathy for the Palestinians in general and for those from the Gaza Strip in particular. Nevertheless, it was not easy for the Gaza Palestinians to get work contracts or entry visas to any of these countries, not only because they had to compete with other Arab job seekers, including fellow Palestinians from other host countries, but also because they were stateless. A Palestinian from Gaza had to go to Cairo to file an application at the consulate or the recruitment office of one of those countries. And in order to go to Cairo, one had first to visit the governor general's office. While I was a schoolteacher in Kuwait in the late 1950s and early 1960s, my colleagues from the Gaza Strip told me that it was very common in those days for the family to celebrate when a refugee was contracted to work in one of the oil-producing Arab countries; friends and relatives would rush to his home to extend their congratulations. To a destitute refugee, such a contract was not only a salvation from immediate needs but also a promise of a much better life. It was not unfamiliar for the father of a single woman with a job in one of these countries to stipulate that the salary of his daughter, or a percentage of it, should continue to go to him even if his daughter were to get married.

It is useful to contrast the situation of the Gazans with that of their fellow Palestinians on the West Bank of Jordan. The West Bankers had two major choices in terms of employment: the oil-producing Arab countries and the East Bank of Jordan, which was booming after the unification and whose intelligentsia and skilled labor were limited in number, while the unskilled preferred to join the army. So the West Bankers who had become Jordanian citizens could move to the other part of their country not only freely but also without worrying about competition from East Bank fellow citizens.

Another difference between the Gaza Palestinians and the West Bankers was that the former were under the administration of an Arab country, Egypt, which maintained its belief in a Palestinian entity, even before the inception of Israel; this fact could only have enhanced their nationalism. Nationalism without a state is a recipe for restlessness that can lead to national struggle. The West Bankers, in contrast, had become citizens of a state. Their nationalism would lead less to national struggle and more to political activism in order to influence their government's foreign policy. The highest degree of intensity they might reach would be to stage demonstrations in an effort to raise the priority of their national issue on the government's political agenda; otherwise, they were absorbed in the process of developing the identity of the state. As for the Palestinian refugees in Lebanon and Syria, they were mostly preoccupied with the daily issues they had with the UNRWA and with cherishing their dreams of a solution to their national problem. Such a solution, as they envisioned it, could be attained either militarily, through an all-out Arab-Israeli war that would result in the dismantling of Israel, or politically, through the international community. This accounts for the two attitudes that characterized the Palestinian refugee mentality regarding the solution for their national problem. One attitude was litigious and the other bellicose. The more they realized that litigation was useless, the more they tended to be belligerent. The Palestinian activists in Gaza had a third area to explore. The refugees in Gaza shared the concerns of their fellow refugees in the host countries, but being on Palestinian territory, the Gazans had a special urge to be proactive. This urge undoubtedly sprang from two roots: the harsh socioeconomic situation in Gaza and the sense of moral responsibility among the activists toward the Palestinian cause. Their situation was different not only from that of their fellow Palestinians in Jordan, who were in the process of being integrated into their new state, but also from that of Palestinians in the refugee camps in Syria and Lebanon, who were helplessly located on non-Palestinian territory, and from that of Palestinians in Israel, who formally had become citizens of a state but were really second-class citizens, or rather helpless prisoners from a national perspective. Hence the activists in Gaza were inspired by the Algerian, Vietnamese, and Cuban revolutions, since each of these revolutions had been mounted and sustained by people who lived on their national turf or in an adjacent foreign territory (a sanctuary). The issue theoretically was how to start their liberation struggle against Israel while they were under the administration of Egypt. For Egypt, after the Suez War in 1956, had agreed to station on its territory the United Nations Emergency Forces (UNEF) and had embraced a strict policy of managing conflict with Israel rather than confronting it.

Nasser's call for an Arab summit to discuss the Israeli plans to divert the waters of the River Jordan late in 1963 and the 1964 Arab summit resolution to implement counterplans were the most concrete manifestations of this policy. Nasser intended to avoid military confrontation with Israel, and he succeeded. This policy became an open secret, known not only to other Arab governments but also to the Palestinian activists. This situation was bound to create a latent tension between Nasser, who called for the liberation of Palestinian land and nurtured the concept of the Palestinian entity on the one hand, and the young Palestinian activists in Gaza on the other. This fact accounts to a large degree for Fatah's slogan: "No to tutelage, no to dependence, no to being politically hijacked by other states." For all these reasons, it was natural that the national Palestinian leadership was to emerge from Gaza.

WHY NOT THE WEST BANK?

But what about the Palestinian territory on the West Bank? Why didn't this region produce national Palestinian leadership? The West Bankers were citizens in a state whose political system is a ruling monarchy. Under such a system, there is always only one national leader, the king, who does not alternate power with others as long as he lives. Of course, there are community leaders and political leaders, but none of them becomes a national leader unless one is ready to run the risk of rebelling against the whole regime. In such a case, one would pay the price of being a dissident, and this is what happened in 1970 when the PLO, growing in power, challenged the regime and disputed King Hussein's authority, forcing the king to defend his regime and expel the PLO from Jordan.

In the case of the West Bankers before 1967, one might assume that a Palestinian national leadership would not challenge the authority of the king throughout the country but only on the West Bank. In other words, a national revolution could have been mounted to separate the West Bank from the East Bank and create an independent state. Yet even that did not happen. And as mentioned earlier, no Palestinian political protests against the central government reached the point of demanding secession, and not a single political leader of the opposition challenged the authority of the king over the West Bank on a Palestinian national basis. In other words, the West Bank leaders of the political opposition did not rise to the rank of Palestinian national leaders because they neither represented nor claimed to represent Palestinians elsewhere and because they never pressed for the secession of the West Bank from the kingdom. I believe that there were three reasons for this. The first was the awareness among the public and the political leaders alike of the built-in limitations of an independent West Bank, especially at that time when independence on the part of a Palestinian territory did not also imply making peace with Israel. If secession were achieved, the independent West Bank would not have been able to defend itself against Israeli occupation. Even assuming that Israel did not make such a move, a landlocked West Bank—squeezed between Jordan, from which it had seceded, and Israel, with which it hadn't made peace—would be doomed; it would not be able to survive economically, even if an air supply line like the one provided to a besieged Berlin in 1948 was maintained.

The second reason was related to the prevalent notion before 1967 that the Palestinian question could be solved either politically through the United Nations or through an all-out Arab-Israeli war. If these were the only two options, there would not be any meaningful role for a Palestinian national leadership in Jordan, since each of the two options implied a state's role rather than that of an unofficial national leadership. Besides, as mentioned earlier, Jordan is a ruling monarchy, where there is no room for national leadership except for the monarch, who is the head of state. Under such circumstances a Palestinian national leadership would have been both meaningless and risky. It would be meaningful only after a solution was reached either politically or militarily. Furthermore the sentimental majority in the West Bank until the 1967 war viewed their situation as temporary. This perception was psychologically comfortable to the West Bankers—it allowed them to sustain their national dreams, since it implied a potential change—and it was equally comfortable to the government because it helped control what otherwise might have been a rebellious community. This fact perhaps accounts for the official political discourse before 1967, which focused on the theme of restoring Palestinian rights, and for the tendency of the political leaders of the West Bank to reconcile themselves to the prevailing situation.

The third reason had to do with the accumulated historical experience of the Palestinians. Throughout the Ottoman rule and the British mandate, the Palestinians had grown accustomed to viewing the community leadership as the highest authority, always going through a middleman when they had to deal with any official authority. Even in the 1930s and 1940s, when the grand mufti emerged as a national leader, he was not the undisputed one. He had rivals who commanded loyalty and support from their followers, mostly within their own communities. The majority supported the grand mufti, and many did so in conformity with the political leanings of their community leaders, who were usually the major landowners or the scions of big influential families in the cities. In those days, nongovernmental organizations (NGOs) were almost nonexistent. Therefore, community leaders who derived their leadership from managing and organizing specific collective services in the community did not exist. Even most of the political parties in the 1930s and 1940s were formed and maintained on a family-relationship basis. King Abdullah relied on just such community leaders—who were viewed as national leaders by the desperate Palestinians at that time (from May 1948 to December 1948)—in organizing the Jericho Conference, which led to the unification of the two banks in 1950. After the unification, these community leaders neither claimed nor retained the common perception of them as national leaders, since the West Bank became part of a kingdom whose ruling monarch was ipso facto their new national leader. Thus, they continued to be community, rather than national, leaders whose legitimate role "was based mostly on the social structure of local communities and not on more integrative nationalist values or structures."[7]

Even the young leaders from the West Bank intelligentsia who emerged during periods of political unrest did not develop into national leaders; they remained Jordanian politicians who "tended to enhance popular identification with the pan-Arab political leadership rather than lead to the development of a national leadership in its own right. . . . The weakness of a leadership comprised of educated men lay in its inability to draw power either from its institutional or its socioeconomic status. Nor, given the lack of meaningful party activity, could it find effective channels for participation in the existing Jordanian political system."[8]

Furthermore, the West Bankers were reconciled to the status quo. To them it was a temporary arrangement. Their community leaders were as effective as ever; they continued to play the role of middlemen between the local community and the central government in Amman, whether on issues of security or of the distribution of the government's material resources. The West Bankers' attachment to their locality—whether a village, a town, a neighborhood, a clan, or a family—was so strong that the community leader was quite satisfactory. They didn't feel a compelling need to have a Palestinian leader, because there was Nasser, the pan-Arab leader, who was stronger, more inspiring, and more influential than any Palestinian leadership in coping with their national concerns. The less you believe in your own power, the more you wish to believe in that of the rest of the nation. The Jordanian government indirectly fed this feeling through its policies. On this issue Shaul Mishall argues:

> The regime in Amman maintained its control over the loci of power in the context of co-existence by justifying its policy towards the Palestinians in broad terms of Arab unity. . . . It controlled the Palestinians not only through its use of material resources but also through its ability to manipulate the meaning of Palestinian desires, thus limiting the political options open to the Palestinians. This ability became its secret weapon.[9]

Therefore, when King Hussein faced the establishment of the PLO in 1964, he could not counter the Arab League's initiative as King Abdullah had in 1948, mobilizing the Palestinian leaders in Transjordan against the All-Palestine Government in Gaza and succeeding in aborting the rise of a Palestinian entity. In 1964 the Palestinian leadership in Jordan fell into two categories. One category consisted of the local community leaders who had already become part of the system and were perceived by the West Bankers more as middlemen than as political leaders. So they did not qualify, especially as the issue under discussion was one that would influence the unity of the two banks, to which these community leaders were committed and in which they had developed their own vested interests. The other consisted of the younger, educated, pan-Arab–oriented political leaders who either were political fugitives, had been tamed or scared into inactivity, or were practicing their political activities underground. Thus, neither their political convictions nor their self-image or status as opposition leaders would make them accept the task of countering the establishment of the PLO, which was Nasser's baby. Moreover, it was too late for the king to restructure the kingdom within a federal framework in which the West Bank would carry the name of Palestine and which would allow him to preempt the Arab League's position to maintain the Palestinian identity of the West Bank. Realizing that he was in a difficult situation, the king decided to cooperate with the Arab League rather than confront it, and he inaugurated the first Palestinian National Congress, which convened in Jerusalem in May 1964, and declared the establishment of the PLO. But before the king reached this crucial point, he made sure that the composition of the congress would guarantee Jordanian control over it by securing a pro-Jordanian majority. Jordan intervened in the appointment of its own delegates. Furthermore, the king arranged to have the West Bank members of the upper House of Deputies be appointed members of the Palestinian National Congress. The king's arrangements and diplomacy had favorable results as far as Jordan was concerned. The Palestinian charter and the PLO constitution emphasized that the PLO would not intervene in the internal affairs of the Arab states. They stated that "the PLO will not assert any territorial sovereignty over the West Bank, nor over the Gaza Strip, nor over al-Hama area" (the latter was a small Palestinian enclave under Syrian control). It also emphasized that "the Palestinian people will achieve self-determination after completing the liberation of its homeland." To the leaders of the underground Palestinian organization Fatah, these principles were evidence that the PLO was to sustain the Arab guardianship of the Palestinians.

In retrospect we can note two significant phenomena. The first is that Gaza after 1948 was the hotbed of Palestinian nationalism, and the second is that Egypt was the incubator of the seeds of "the Palestinian entity." Jordan, although it accommodated the largest Palestinian community and comprised the largest Palestinian territory (the West Bank), was neither the hotbed nor the incubator, basically because the Palestinians in Jordan, relatively speaking, were in a more comfortable situation. They were citizens of a state. Thus, the influential leaders of Fatah were not

Palestinian-Jordanians; they came mainly from the Gaza Strip. To a certain extent this contributed to their suspicious attitude toward Jordan when, three years later, they had to deal directly with the king in moving their headquarters to Jordan after the 1967 war. This attitude was based not only on lifelong suspicions of the Hashemites' ambitions in Palestine, which the Palestinian nationalists resented, but also on their perception of the king, developed outside Jordan during the media warfare between Jordan and the revolutionary pan-Arabists from the mid-1950s until the 1967 war. The Palestinian suspicion of the king, in turn, generated Jordanian suspicions of the Palestinian leaders of the fedayeen movement.

As for the other phenomenon, Egypt, out of strategic convictions, volunteered to germinate the seeds of the "Palestinian entity" after the defeat of the Arab armies by Israel in the 1948 war. The seeds became seedlings, the first of which was planted in Gaza in 1948, but it was destined to die. The second seedling was the establishment of the PLO, which was nurtured by Egypt in the Arab League with the support of the majority of Palestinians. Some Palestinians, however, did not support the PLO simply because it was under Arab patronage. One such group was the Fatah organization. From its inception in the late 1950s and 1960s, Fatah called for the emancipation of the Palestinian national movement from Arab patronage. Fatah did not view the PLO initially as an independent Palestinian institution. Al-Shuqairi, to them, was an Egyptian protégé and an Arab appointee. That is why Fatah operated after 1967 under an independent umbrella called the Military Organizations of the Palestinian Resistance. The PLO, to Fatah, was a weak seedling of the Palestinian entity because it was sown in an Arab soil that allowed Arab weeds to grow around it. One of Fatah's main objectives after 1967 was to weed out the Arab influence on the PLO and make it truly independent. Chairman Arafat took the first major step toward this objective in February 1969, at the fifth session of the Palestinian National Congress, which convened in Cairo. At that session the leaders of the political and military organizations of the Palestinian resistance joined "independent" members. At the end of the session, Arafat, then the spokesman for Fatah, was elected chairman of the PLO executive committee, replacing Yahia Hammuda, who had been the second chairman.

About that session, Massalha writes, "It is important to emphasize three important provisions among the amendments made to the Charter, which filled a void in the first text and reflect Fatah's views. These were: the rejection of any form of intervention, patronage, or dependence vis-à-vis the Arab countries; the assertion of the Palestinian people's sovereignty over the land and its right to self-determination; and armed struggle as a strategy to liberate Palestine."[10]

The second step that Arafat took to finalize the independence of the Palestinian national movement came five years later, when the Arab summit at Rabat (Morocco) adopted a resolution recognizing the PLO as the sole legitimate representative of the Palestinian people. It was then that Arab guardianship was completely removed. It is noteworthy that after the foundations of its independence were laid in 1969, the PLO fell out with the four Arab states bordering Israel. Ironically, its first confrontation was with Nasser's Egypt over U.S. secretary of state William Roger's peace plan in 1970. The second was with Jordan in the same year; the third with Lebanon from the mid-1970s until 1984; and the fourth was with Syria in 1983, when the Syrian army in Lebanon destroyed Fatah's base in the Tripoli area.

THE IMPACT OF THE ESTABLISHMENT OF THE PLO ON JORDANIAN-PALESTINIAN INTEGRATION

The establishment of the PLO in 1964 came fourteen years after the unification of the two banks of Jordan. Though the journey of the Palestinians in Jordan during this period was not always smooth, the situation of the West Bankers was much more comfortable than that of their fellow Palestinians elsewhere. Indeed, their situation was coveted by the Palestinians in other Arab countries.

In spite of the tumultuous years of the 1950s and the many political dislocations that Jordan witnessed through the fourteen years that preceded the establishment of the PLO, the process of merging the two banks and of integrating the Palestinians into Jordan never ceased.

In that time, Jordan underwent two mutually reinforcing parallel processes. One was the process of Palestinian adjustment to the state, and the other was the state's assimilation of the new Palestinian community. Though the Palestinians outnumbered the Jordanians two to one, it was the Palestinians who had to adjust. We should note that when the unification took place, the East Bank (Transjordan) was a full-fledged state. It had all the institutions of the modern state: a government, a parliament, courts, press, police, and an army. The West Bank was a district resulting from the dismemberment of a country, and its people, besides the refugees, lived in small disconnected communities as a result of the fragmentation of the

Palestinian people. When the two banks were welded into one country, it was obvious that the Palestinians had to adjust to a state that had already been shaped economically, politically, and culturally, while the state had to incorporate and assimilate the newcomers to achieve an organic unity of the land and people. Indeed, at this point Jordan entered a new phase of nation building, which "is a matter of building group cohesion and group loyalty for international representation and domestic planning."[11]

The pronounced similarity in cultures made it easy for the Jordanians and Palestinians to communicate and act as one people. Almost in no time, the Jordanian and Palestinian intelligentsia shared membership in the same political parties. Intermarriages, which had occurred before the unification, now continued on a larger scale. Close social relationships of all kinds were established. The younger generation of Palestinian male students who resided on the East Bank and went to its schools picked up a Transjordanian accent, while the younger generation of Transjordanian women picked up a Palestinian accent from their fellow students. Each community selected from the other some of its customs and practiced and internalized them. Many Palestinian artisans and skilled laborers moved to the East Bank, especially Amman, which was experiencing rapid growth in population and new construction. Amman became the magnet for West Bankers' savings and a center for their investments, especially in real estate. Civil servants from the West Bank were appointed on the East Bank and vice versa. The Transjordanian families of some of the military and police moved to the West Bank, where their units were deployed.

This socioeconomic integration process was preceded by institutional political integration. Later, under King Hussein, the unsupervised compliance of the West Bankers was secured. In the mid-1950s, the Jordanian army was too small and insufficiently equipped to defend every single village. The Palestinian villages along the armistice lines provided the army with a low-paid National Guard to watch the first line and help the army defend their villages against Israeli retributive attacks. In 1956, when the king dismissed General Glubb, the West Bankers supported the king; without their support, this revolutionary step might have spawned political disruption and threatened security. And when Egypt was attacked by Anglo-French-Israeli forces, King Hussein publicly and vehemently took a very risky position in supporting Nasser and calling for general mobilization. The West Bankers responded quickly to his call and went to the training centers with great enthusiasm. All these examples, interestingly, are related to the need for security. We noticed earlier (see chapter 3) that the inhabitants of Kalkiliya cheered King Abdullah on his visit to their town as *"hameena,"* our defender. The Palestinian attachment to the state as the entity that met their needs, especially the security need, was entrenched by 1964. This is what Herbert Kelman calls "instrumental attachment." Kelman argues that "instrumental attachment refers to people's attachment to a group [in this case, the Jordanian state] based on perception of that group as meeting their personal needs and interests and those of the other members of the social category encompassed by the group. Insofar as the group is seen as instrumental to the achievement of their goals, they extend loyalty to it."[12]

Kelman also identifies another source of attachment, which he calls sentimental attachment. This type, according to Kelman, "refers to people's attachment to a group [the state] based on the perception of that group as representative of their personal identity—as somehow reflecting, extending, or confirming their identity. Insofar as it represents them, as persons and as parts of a collectivity, they extend loyalty to it."[13]

Kelman further argues that "the two sources are analytically distinct . . . , but they do tend to generate and reinforce one another. That is, instrumental attachment to a group also tends to strengthen the perception of that group as representative of one's identity, and sentimental attachment also encourages members to look to that group for the fulfillment of their needs and interests."[14]

The PLO came into existence at a crucial point in the all-encompassing process of integration between the West Bank and the East Bank. Palestinian instrumental attachment to the Jordanian state was already established. This attachment was manifested in Palestinian acceptance of the laws and regulations of the state, their "entanglement in social roles," and commitment to the state's "institutional arrangements and operating values," as Kelman defines them. Furthermore, this instrumental attachment was developing into sentimental attachment within large Palestinian sectors. Already large segments had identified themselves as Jordanians both technically and emotionally. The establishment of the PLO in 1964, just as sentimental attachment was approaching its peak, confused some of the sentimentally attached, strengthened the sentimental attachment of others, and preempted the potential attachment of still others. Instrumental attachment was not affected and persisted as strongly as it had before, even for the two decades following the occupation of the West Bank by Israel in 1967; but the foundation of the Transjordanian-Palestinian relationship in Jordan was cracked, and grave problems were bound to arise.

6

The Interaction between Jordan (the State) and the Palestinian Entity (the Organizations)

THE SAFEGUARDS

While the establishment of the PLO in 1964 marked a new era in the Arab-Israeli conflict, in Jordan it activated the Transjordanian-Palestinian dynamic. From the beginning Jordan was concerned that the rise of a Palestinian entity, whether in the form of a real state or of an organization representing the Palestinian people, would eventually have an adverse impact on the Hashemite Kingdom of Jordan, which encompassed the largest Palestinian community. With the establishment of the PLO, King Hussein found himself in a situation similar to King Abdullah's in September 1948, when the Arab League announced the establishment of the All-Palestine Government. But King Hussein's problem was even graver than his grandfather's, since King Abdullah's major concern had been his competition with the mufti over the West Bank; for King Hussein, the survival of the regime and of the country as a whole was now at stake. Nevertheless, the king approved of the establishment of the PLO for several reasons.

Foremost among those reasons, was that, on the eve of the first Arab summit in Cairo in January 1964, Jordan was on bad terms with Egypt because of the Yemeni civil war. King Hussein thought that appeasing Nasser, who stood behind the establishment of the PLO, might improve Jordanian-Egyptian relations. On December 23, 1963, Nasser had called for an Arab summit to counter Israel's plan to divert the River Jordan. Nasser asserted that he could not wage war against Israel to abort her plans, and he would not jeopardize the destiny of his country in a game of rhetoric. He called on the Arab governments to put an end to political overbidding. Jordan, suffering from Arab propaganda and subversive activities, heartily supported this first Arab summit, which marked the beginning of Arab political reconciliation. The PLO was a product of this summit. According to Kamal Salibi, "having effected a successful political reconciliation with Nasser, the Jordanian king was not going to take chances with it."[1]

Besides, the Arab summit discussed two issues that would benefit Jordan: the first was building a dam on the Yarmouk River (a tributary of the River Jordan), from which Jordan gets the majority of its irrigation water; and the second was the modernization of the armies of some Arab countries, including Jordan. In both plans the major costs were to be paid by other Arab countries.

Based on what occurred after the establishment of the PLO, I believe Jordan cherished the notion that it would be able either to confine the PLO within the "limits of ineffectiveness" or to prove that the PLO was a detriment to national Arab security and solidarity rather than an asset. The Jordanian historian Suleiman Mousa reports that

> the Jordanian government based its consent to the establishment of the PLO on two major foundations:
>   1. that the PLO should not carry out any activity that would lead to a cleavage between Jordanians and Palestinians in Jordan, because both communities had been living together and amalgamating in the social, economic, political, and day-to-day life since the unification of the two banks in 1950.
>   2. The PLO should not stimulate Israeli retributive actions.[2]

Asher Susser, the former director of the Moshe Dayan Center for Middle Eastern and African Studies in Tel Aviv and an Israeli scholar specializing in Jordan's political affairs, argues that ever since the unification of the two banks in 1950,

> one of the guiding principles of Jordanian policy had been to prevent the creation of an independent power base among the Palestinian population of the kingdom. The danger of such a power base was inherent in its potential to erode the regime's staying power by competing for influence and control with the mainstay of the regime—the army and other security forces. Such an erosion could have undermined the stability of the regime and finally even have

toppled it. It was clear to Hussein that there could be difficulties in the relationship with the PLO, and it is quite possible that he understood from the very beginning that, sooner or later, Jordan and the PLO would find themselves on a collision course.[3]

Jordan took an obviously cautious approach. King Hussein contributed to the wording of the resolutions of the first and second Arab summits, and he adhered to the letter and spirit of the resolution relating to the PLO when the time for implementation came. How conservative the wording should be was not difficult to resolve because Nasser favored a controlled PLO rather than an unsupervised one, and this suited Jordan well. After all, Nasser had called for the first Arab summit to dissipate the belligerency of the Syrians, Iraqis, and Palestinians over Israel's diversion of the River Jordan's water. An unsupervised PLO would have defeated his purpose; Nasser wanted to avoid war with Israel while Egypt was engulfed in the Yemeni civil war.

When in late 1962 Jordan had come up with a white paper presenting its plan to establish the "United Kingdom of Palestine and Jordan," Nasser had considered the plan a Jordanian ploy to outbid Egypt on the Palestinian question. He had not only rejected it but also launched a propaganda campaign against it and had then announced in one of his speeches that "he who claims that he has a plan to liberate Palestine must be dishonest and unfaithful."[4] Nasser now hoped to establish a PLO that would be under his control, since this not only would allow him to avoid war with Israel but also would place in his hands the Palestine card, one of the most important political cards in inter-Arab politics. To support this strategy, the fifth resolution of the first Arab summit was made to read, "Mr. Ahmad Shuqairi, the representative of Palestine to the League of Arab States, should continue his consultations with the member states and the Palestinian people on the purpose of laying the sound foundations to organize the Palestinian people and enable them to carry out their role in liberating their homeland and attaining their self-determination." In other words, Shuqairi was not to mobilize the Palestinian people into organizations without first consulting the Arab states. Under the circumstances, this was reassurance enough for Jordan.

The first Arab summit also adopted other significant resolutions. The second resolution provided in article 1 for "the prompt establishment of a United Arab Command (UAC) for the Arab armies." Article 2 provided for "the appointment of a general commander for this command from the United Arab Republic. The government of the UAR will appoint this commander." With this resolution Nasser secured for himself the decision of war, if it ever were to happen.

By the time the second Arab summit was held in Alexandria (September 1964), the PLO had already been established. The fourth resolution of the second summit supported the establishment of the Palestine Liberation Army (PLA). Article 2 of this resolution read, "The formation, the armament, and the training of these forces are to be implemented in accordance with a plan to be set by the UAC in participation with the PLO." Article 3 read, "The location of these forces is to be selected by the PLO upon approval of the concerned state." Again, this was acceptable to Jordan, which would have the final say regarding the deployment of the PLA.

King Hussein went beyond the favorable wording of the summit resolutions by attempting to contain the PLO. This goal became obvious during the preparations for the first meeting of the Palestinian National Congress (PNC) in May 1964. If Nasser controlled Shuqairi to keep the Palestinian card in his hands, King Hussein wanted to control the PLO to keep his country intact. Moshe Shemesh, a senior lecturer on Middle Eastern studies at the Ben-Gurion University in Israel, writes:

> Hussein left nothing to chance. In his talks with Shuqairi he made sure that the PNC's decisions would reflect Jordan's inclinations. In this he succeeded; Shuqairi accepted his demand [that the PLO should not compromise Jordan's sovereignty over the two banks]. . . . Hussein made sure that only a few days before Congress convened [May 28, 1964], the West Bank members of the Senate and House of Deputies joined the PNC. To sustain his control over the PNC, Hussein ensured that the Jerusalem Congress was turned into a permanent National Congress and that Shuqairi was elected chairman of the executive committee, with the authority to appoint members to it. Hussein believed it would be easier to deal with one person rather than a group of leaders.[5]

The outcome of this convention, which was held in Jerusalem and opened by King Hussein, was quite satisfactory to Jordan. In the first place, the majority of the members of the congress were Jordanians and had been appointed with Jordan's approval. Shuqairi's report to the second Arab summit had included a special section classifying the PNC members according to their geographical distribution, including representatives from the East Bank of Jordan. According to this classification, Jordan was allocated 216 seats out of 396. Besides, the National Palestinian Charter reassured Jordan; as Mousa reports, it "emphasized the Palestinian territorial unity and Israel's illegal existence. Although the charter asserted that the goal of the PLO was the liberation of Palestine, it stressed that the

PLO would not exercise any sovereignty over the West Bank or Gaza Strip, and it would cooperate with all Arab states and would not intervene in the domestic affairs of any of them."[6]

It is important to note here Fatah's position regarding the Jerusalem Convention. At the time, Fatah's leaders were busy recruiting members for their clandestine organization. They were invited to attend the convention, and after some initial hesitation, they decided to participate. Abu Iyad (Salah Khalaf), who by the time of his assassination in 1991 had become second in command to Arafat, records:

> The issue to us was whether to boycott the conference. The sponsorship, structure, goals, and other factors pulled us toward boycotting it. Yet there were other reasons that pushed us to participate. Among those reasons were our anxiety not to be isolated from the Palestinian political life and the urgent need to benefit from the resources that will be available to such a rich and strong organization [the PLO]. It was possible to employ it in a useful manner as a front for our clandestine activities. Eventually some of our comrades participated and through their participation they promoted Fatah's primary theses, especially the thesis of the armed struggle.[7]

JORDAN'S ATTEMPTS AT CONTAINMENT

Having established the PLO and secured approval from the second Arab summit to form the PLA, Shuqairi set out to translate the summit and PNC resolutions into realities. He had his own agenda. To him, Jordan was the major arena precisely because of the number of Palestinians in the country. He set up a PLO office in Jerusalem and presented Jordan with a number of demands that Jordan viewed as dangerous, threatening to mar Jordan's sovereignty and its national unity. Shuqairi began to work among the West Bankers to set up the Palestinian Popular Organization (PPO), which was assumed to be the organizational framework for the PLO. Its charter, which had been approved by the second PNC, defined its goal as highlighting the Palestinian entity by building up the popular Palestinian base. To put pressure on the king, Shuqairi activated the dormant opposition inside Jordan and started to solicit the support of the Jordanian opposition who had fled the country in 1957–58 and been given political asylum in Egypt and Syria. Shuqairi's conduct revealed his ill will toward Jordan's regime. It became quite reasonable to assume that Shuqairi's policy might lead to securing a sort of personal autonomy for the West Bankers, an autonomy that might be followed by the separation of the West Bank from the Hashemite Kingdom of Jordan. The king had to move to thwart Shuqairi's plans and perceived intentions, making use of the summit spirit to which Nasser still adhered. On February 13, 1965, King Hussein again appointed Wasfi al-Tal prime minister. According to Suleiman Mousa, the king chose al-Tal to form a new cabinet because the prevailing domestic stability and Arab reconciliation seemed to offer the right climate for dynamism, creativity, and rejuvenation.[8]

I believe the king's appointment of al-Tal was based on three different reasons: the first was al-Tal's experience in dealing with Palestinian organizations through his involvement with the Arab Rescue Army in 1948. The second had to do with al-Tal's white paper of 1962 (described in chapter 4); Hussein believed that al-Tal had a substantive vision for dealing with the PLO in case Shuqairi started to make problems—and by the end of 1964, it looked like he might. The third reason was related to the assumption that since Shuqairi was in Nasser's grip, Jordan would fall out with Nasser if relations between Jordan and the PLO developed into a conflict; al-Tal, unlike his predecessor Bahjat al-Talhouni, was ready to confront Nasser. According to Susser,

> there was a fundamental incompatibility between the PLO's ambition to exercise authority and patronage over the Palestinian population and the demand of the regime for complete sovereign authority over the territory of the kingdom and its citizens. It is reasonable to assume that the appointment of Wasfi al-Tal as prime minister in February 1965 was intended, inter alia, to place a resolute and uncompromising personality at the head of the team which was to handle most of the contacts with the PLO.[9]

Al-Tal's choice of Hazem Nusseibeh as his foreign minister foretold his strategy. Nusseibeh had been a co-author of the 1962 white paper. When friction between Jordan and the PLO flared in 1965 and developed into a public conflict in 1966, it was Nusseibeh, a West Banker, who had to explain to Arab diplomats Jordan's position. A West Banker myself, I was in a similar situation in 1970–71, when, as minister of information and the government's spokesperson, I had to explain and defend Jordan's position regarding the armed confrontation that had erupted between the government and the Palestinian organizations. In both cases we can deduce that the king was eager to sustain national unity through various means, including the visibility of a senior Palestinian official defending the state's position on a Palestinian issue. This made the conflict appear to be between the government and dissidents rather than between the government and Palestinians.

THE SEEDS OF CONFLICT

In 1965, Shuqairi gradually fell under two pressures. The first came from militant Palestinians, especially the PLA command, who were pressuring Shuqairi to steer the PLO more toward the military direction than toward the diplomatic one. The second came from the growing embarrassment caused by the popularity among the Palestinian public of Fatah, which was launching ever more operations against Israel. To relieve these pressures, Shuqairi sought to establish a foothold in Jordan, the majority of whose inhabitants were, in Shuqairi's eyes, first and foremost not Jordanian but Palestinian. The West Bank, after all, was a Palestinian territory populated by Palestinians. Besides, the West Bank was intermittently subjected to Israeli military attacks. Therefore, if he pushed for a Palestinian military presence in the West Bank to help the Jordanian army defend Palestinian villages, his demands would be welcomed by the West Bankers. If Jordan rejected this, he would mobilize the Jordanian opposition to his side. With this sort of logic, Shuqairi pressed his demands.

Less than two weeks after al-Tal assumed office, Shuqairi arrived in Amman with two suggestions: (1) the formation of a military force to be linked to the PLO, and (2) the deduction of 5 percent of the wages of Palestinian civil servants, with the money to be transferred to the Palestinian National Fund. The Jordanian government rejected both demands on the grounds that they encroached on Jordan's sovereignty and that it was impossible to have two separate military forces under two separate commands in one country. Al-Tal, who was aware of the implications of Shuqairi's demands and had never trusted him, set out to preempt Shuqairi's quest to win over those Jordanian army officers and members of the opposition who had fled the country in 1957–58. Al-Tal felt that these people, who resented their plight, might well side with Shuqairi in his conflict with Jordan. Since many of them, especially the army officers, were of Transjordanian origin, al-Tal thought that it was imperative to abort any attempt by Shuqairi to win them over. On April 6, 1965, al-Tal's government enacted a law of general amnesty that allowed all these people to return to Jordan free of any charge or sentence. To further forestall Shuqairi, the government took a number of measures to integrate the National Guard (the paramilitary body manned mainly by Palestinians along the armistice line on the West Bank) with the regular army. At the parliamentary session that convened on May 9, 1965, Prime Minister al-Tal announced the government's rejection of the PLO's demand to set up its own military units. He stressed that the Jordanian army was the army of Jordan and Palestine. On May 15, the king reaffirmed al-Tal's statement: "Since the integration of the two banks and the amalgamation of the two peoples," said the king, "Palestine has become Jordan and Jordan has become Palestine."[10] King Hussein was not the only one to refer to Jordan as Palestine and Palestine as Jordan. Shuqairi used the same theme in the debates at the third Arab summit (Casablanca, September 13–17, 1965) when he referred to Jordan as a Palestinian territory. King Hussein obviously intended by this argument to help preserve the unity of the two banks by excluding Shuqairi's PLA, while Shuqairi was using it to emphasize his right to deploy the PLA on the West Bank.

To undermine once and for all Shuqairi's argument that the PLA should be established in Jordan in order to defend the West Bank, the Jordanian government passed the Law on Defense of Front-Line Towns and Villages and followed it, beginning on June 16, 1965, with the distribution of arms to the villages and the training of their inhabitants. On June 20, "the PLO and Jordan approved in principle a draft agreement prepared and presented by Amir Khammash, the Jordanian chief of staff, involving fortifications of the front lines and the formation of guard units of 15,000 to 20,000. These forces, which would be armed with light weapons only, would be financed by the PLO."[11] However, this agreement was not put into effect. It was fiercely opposed by the PLA military command.

THE SHOWDOWN

In addition to his proposal for deploying the PLA within Jordan, Shuqairi urged that Jordan grant diplomatic immunity to the PLO center in Jerusalem, to members of the Executive Committee, and to PLO officials. He also demanded that Jordan allocate time on Jordanian radio for the Palestinian nationalist programs.

Jordan viewed Shuqairi's demands as laying the foundation for creating a state within a state, a nightmare that Jordan dispelled by rejecting most of the demands. Shuqairi kept pressing until he finally carried his conflict with Jordan to the third Arab summit in Casablanca. Due to the king's resistance, Shuqairi failed to put through his agenda at the summit. "On the demands of the PLO for providing full freedom for the PLO and for conducting direct general elections to the PNC, the summit recommended that the PLO maintain contact with the concerned member states to achieve understanding on the necessary measures," Mousa reports.[12]

In spite of the summit resolutions, Shuqairi continued his propaganda campaign against Jordan. He personally attacked the king in a speech transmitted on Palestine radio from Cairo. The king, who chose not to retaliate promptly and directly, sent Nasser a letter on October 8 in which he accused Shuqairi of making seditious attempts aimed at dividing the Jordanian Palestinians of the West Bank from their brethren on the East Bank. In particular, the king referred to "Shuqairi's subversive calls and slogans as well as his clique's." Hussein's letter concluded with an appeal to Nasser to redress the situation in conformity with the principles of the Arab Solidarity Covenant, and he stressed that an insult to his dignity constituted an insult to the dignity of Nasser and the Arab nation. Such insults should not be tolerated.[13]

The king obviously considered Nasser the ultimate arbiter, one who would side with Arab solidarity, which, according to Hussein, Shuqairi was trying to undermine. We can also rightly deduce that the king was preparing for the inevitable showdown with Shuqairi. To triumph at the least political cost, he had to win Nasser to his side or at least neutralize him through presenting Jordan's just case. By referring in his letter to the fact that Palestine radio transmitted from Cairo, the king implied that Nasser tolerated Shuqairi's campaign. This suggestion was intended to preclude or at least to mitigate Nasser's potentially hostile reaction. Indeed, the fact that Palestine radio transmitted from Cairo was a nuisance not only to Nasser but to Shuqairi himself. It allowed Fatah to accuse Shuqairi of being a tool in Nasser's hands. To prove otherwise, Shuqairi refused the Egyptian offer to give the PLO free transmission time. Instead he insisted on paying.[14]

Without waiting for a reply from Nasser to the king's letter, al-Tal held a press conference in Amman three days later. He warned of what he called the "hostile campaign" that emphasized that "Jordan is Palestine." Jordan, he said, would not accept duality either in efforts or in institutions, and he concluded by pointing out that the Jordanian army's scheme to defend the front line had been conceived in cooperation with the UAC.[15]

On December 18, 1965, the Executive Committee approved the final version of the PNC's election law. According to the new law, Jordan's share of representatives in the PNC was to be reduced from 53 percent, where it had been for the first PNC, to 40 percent. Jordan would no longer hold an absolute majority. Obviously Jordan was alarmed, and the mutual propaganda attacks intensified.

Out of fear that the Jordanian-Palestinian relationship might deteriorate further, the secretary general of the Arab League brokered a temporary agreement between Jordan and the PLO on January 10, 1966, according to which the two sides would cease the mutual propaganda attacks and resume negotiations. These negotiations led to another agreement, reached on March 1, 1966. This agreement was especially interesting. Except for the item dealing with the people's campaign to raise funds for the PLO, the other items did not refer to the PLO, Palestine, the West Bankers, or any other term that would indicate that the agreement was meant to serve the PLO's purposes. The PLO was to receive funds, but all other functions were to be carried out by Jordan.

The exclusion of the PLO from mobilizing Palestinian-Jordanians was obviously meant to preserve Jordan's national unity by keeping the Palestinians away from the PLO leadership. At that time, the members of the banned parties in Jordan, who were aware of Nasser's support for the PLO, saw in the PLO a means by which they could continue their political opposition to the Jordanian regime. Moshe Shemesh writes that "al-Tal, in a secret memorandum to his ministers and the directors of the general [public] security and general intelligence, gave clear directions about exactly what PLO activity would actually be allowed in Jordan." All avenues for penetration into the PLO by "opportunists, destroyers, saboteurs who serve party and opportunists' interests" must be closed. "All contact between the PLO and citizens, for whatever purpose, without permission of the state and its special officers and not in accordance with its laws, must be prevented. The War Laws regarding communism and parties must be carried out immediately and literally. Any printed or photographed material must be prohibited."[16]

By the end of 1965, King Faisal of Saudi Arabia and the shah of Iran had issued a joint communiqué in which they called for a pan-Islamic conference. Both monarchs were allies of the United States. This call, coming at the peak of the Cold War, provoked the Soviet Union's ally Nasser. When King Faisal paid a state visit to Jordan in January 1966 to promote the proposed Islamic conference, the Egyptian media launched a campaign against Jordan and Saudi Arabia, accusing them of trying to establish an Islamic pact. Nasser compared the proposed conference to the Baghdad Pact, stressing that the Islamic pact was an American ploy. It was during this period that Nasser's position shifted from that of arbiter in the Jordan-PLO conflict to that of staunch supporter of the PLO. During the early months of 1966, then, the Arab summit spirit of conciliation and cooperation began to wane. Contributing to the deterioration of this spirit was the Syrian military coup in February 1966, which placed a more militant

Ba'athist regime in power. The new regime adopted the slogan of the "Popular Liberation War" for Palestine.

Syria now gave practical support to Fatah, which was in dire need of a base from which to operate against Israel. Yet the new regime was keen on avoiding Israeli retributive military acts, so it forbade Fatah to send its fedayeen into Israel directly from Syria. According to Salibi, "instead, these fedayeen were directed to infiltrate into Israel either by way of Lebanon or preferably by way of Jordan, where the long armistice line could be easily infiltrated at many points. . . . For Syria, the repeated Fatah infiltrations through Jordan yielded the added bonus of embarrassing the Jordanian regime and scoring a point over Nasser, who had no wish to provoke Israel into war."[17]

According to Suleiman Mousa, the Arab states, in light of these recent developments "aligned once again into two camps: (1) the camp of the revolutionary states, which comprised Egypt, Syria, Iraq, Yemen, Algeria, and the PLO; (2) the camp of the moderate conservative states, which comprised Saudi Arabia, Jordan, Tunisia, and Morocco. Other states like Kuwait, Lebanon, Libya, and the Sudan did not take sides."[18] Obviously, the PLO aligned itself with the revolutionary camp. With Shuqairi's escalation of his hostile policies, especially his alliances with activists among the Jordanian political opposition, the PLO became a real threat to Jordan's national security. So was the leftist regime in Syria, which provided the Fatah fedayeen with support and a safe haven.

The third Palestinian National Congress was scheduled to convene in Gaza on May 20, 1966. The Jordanian government, aware of the implications of its reduced representation in the PNC, attempted to dissuade all Palestinian-Jordanian representatives from attending, but it failed. Some of the representatives felt that their attendance was necessary precisely so that they could change the proportion of representatives in Jordan's favor, but they too failed.

The third PNC did not augur well from a Jordanian point of view, since, among other things, one of its resolutions repeated Shuqairi's demand for Jordan to release political activists, many of whom were of Transjordanian origin. King Hussein's earlier hope of controlling the PLO by controlling the PNC with a majority of Palestinian-Jordanian representatives was dashed, and the split with the PLO looked imminent.

In April 1966, the government cracked down on those activists who were communists, Ba'athists, PLO supporters, and members of the Arab Nationalist Movement. Scores of them were arrested. Though technically this was purely a domestic Jordanian issue, Shuqairi launched a media campaign in which he demanded that the government release the arrested activists. Jordan considered Shuqairi's demand to be tantamount to intervention in its domestic affairs and further evidence of his hostile agenda.

Yet, sources of Jordan's worry during this period were not confined to Syria, Nasser, Shuqairi, and Fatah. Israel was a major concern because it posed a highly likely military threat. Israel's disproportionate retributive acts against the West Bank villages always triggered some sort of chain reaction: public demonstrations protesting the government's failure to defend the villages, government suppression of the demonstrations, arrests of activists and suspects, more government alienation from the local and vocal Arab mainstream, and perpetuation of the government's worries about national security. To Israel, Jordan was both a neighbor who had to be reckoned with for geographic and demographic reasons and an easy target. Israel's disproportionate retaliations were intended not only to penalize the villagers who sympathized with the fedayeen but also to trigger the usual political chain reaction, forcing Jordan to further intensify security measures against the fedayeen. On April 30, 1966, Israeli troops attacked two West Bank villages near the armistice line and blew up fourteen houses. On May 14, 1966, Israeli forces opened fire on Jordanian soldiers, and the tension along the armistice line flared to unprecedented highs.

Meanwhile, Jordan continued to come under attack from Syria and Shuqairi. Nasser failed to check Shuqairi's campaign against Jordan and continued his own campaign against the proponents of the "Islamic alliance," including Jordan.

The situation in Jordan in May 1966 was so precarious that the king decided to put an end to it. According to Shemesh, "the Jordanian leadership began by assessing the situation confronting them. Their conclusions were to break off contact with the PLO, to eliminate completely PLO activities in Jordan while eliminating its representativeness of the Palestinians, and to cast aspersions on Shuqairi's leadership."[19]

THE SPLIT

King Hussein was distressed to see the Arab consensus collapse after two years of conciliation and cooperation. This time the absence of Arab consensus was even more threatening to Jordan, because the new hostile actor, the PLO, had transformed the Palestinian factor in Jordan into an organized body acknowledged by the member-states of the Arab League.

To the mainstream Palestinian, the PLO was not only a spokesperson but also a focal point that had not existed before. What made the situation worse from Jordan's point of view was the fact that the PLO allied with the revolutionary Arab camp, whose prominent members, Egypt and Syria, were currently on bad terms with Jordan. After all, both Egypt and Syria had supported the Jordanian antiregime activists in 1957–61. The Arab consensus had temporarily pacified the Jordanian activists.

Now, with Syria, Egypt, and the PLO in one camp, the Jordanian activists (especially in the West Bank) were more willing to confront the government. The Jordanian government could not live with this situation for long, especially as the war cry for "the liberation of Palestine" fueled Arab, and particularly Palestinian, emotions. The king, once he had exhausted all means of getting Nasser and Shuqairi to understand his position, could not wait.

On June 14, 1966, King Hussein addressed the nation through his commencement speech at the Teacher's Training College for Women at Ajlun (a small town in northern Jordan). In his speech, he spelled out Jordan's views about the conflict with the country's Arab adversaries. He addressed the issues of Arab nationalism, Arab unity, the Arab summit, the Palestinian question, the PLO, the fedayeen, and the national security of Jordan. Most important, he referred to the Syrian and PLO leaders as communists. He also suggested that the Arab revolutionary camp was itself in the hands of international communism. Without mentioning his name, the king described Shuqairi as a clown and an agent.

As for the Palestinian question, the king stressed that it was the most important and gravest issue because "to Jordan, it is an issue of life or death, survival or extinction." He also asserted that it was an Arab, not a Palestinian cause: "Palestine the cause had lost its absolute Palestinian tinge at the moment when the Arab armies trod on its turf in 1948. Nevertheless, many in the Arab world, as it seems, have chosen in the face of the challenge to consider the Palestinian cause as one that concerns only the Palestinians, in spite of the quiescence and myopia this attitude implies." Here the king was criticizing not only Nasser and Shuqairi but also other Arab governments that supported the Palestinian entity.

The king also addressed his major concern, the territorial unity of Jordan:

> The unity of the two banks was blessed by God and supported by the people. It is the nucleus of the broader Arab unity. It is this pioneering sacred unity that succeeded in preserving the rest [the West Bank] of the usurped motherland [Palestine] to become eventually the center for mobilization and to make of

our vigilant army the army of liberation and the army of Palestine. . . . Any call for duality or for the dismemberment of this unity is seditious. Any whim that might provoke aggression on this front before we complete our preparations in accordance with the UAC plan is detrimental. Any effort exerted for liberation should be integrated into our efforts. . . . Any hand to be stretched to undermine this unity or this one united country will be severed. Any eye that looks at us with contempt will be pierced. As of now, we are not going to condone or tolerate any trespassing.[20]

The gist of the king's speech was that Jordan now refused to acknowledge the PLO's leadership, structure, and strategy as representative of the Palestinian people or as the epitome of the Palestinian cause. If the Arab states were sincere about liberating Palestine, they should give their support and funnel their assistance to Jordan, the representative of the Palestinians, since the Hashemites had addressed the Palestinian problem from its inception and since the majority of the Palestinians were Jordanian citizens.

As a demonstration of the Jordanian people's support of the king's determined position, "delegations representing Palestinians in the East Bank and the Nablus, Hebron, and Jerusalem districts went to the royal court on June 20–22 to express their condemnation of Shuqairi's campaign [against Jordan] and their support for the position of the Jordanian government."[21] This demonstration was followed by a special session of the Jordanian Parliament, which unanimously adopted a resolution expressing the Parliament's support for the government's policy and condemning the PLO for having "diverted from its charter." By the end of June, representatives of the Arab heads of states convened in Cairo. At this meeting, Shuqairi presented a report in which he demanded that King Hussein abdicate. On July 4, 1966, in retaliation for Shuqairi's ongoing campaign against the king, al-Tal announced that Jordan could not cooperate any more with the PLO.

Deeply disturbed by an Israeli air strike on a water-diversion construction site in Syrian territory on July 14, 1966, King Hussein sent Nasser a lengthy letter in which he addressed all the issues that had caused the crack in Arab relations:

I am sorry to tell your excellency that my worries have turned out to be true despite all the attempts that were made to straighten up the diversion. . . . It has become clear from Shuqairi's conduct since the eve of the third PNC that the objective of the PLO after it has been dominated by partisans, saboteurs, and subversive elements . . . lies east of the armistice line, not west of it. Their aim is to undermine serious meaningful Arab efforts and to replace the UAC, which

is our last resort in the war of liberation, with emotional, extremist, irresponsible, and futile whims that will push all of us to fight a war before we complete
our preparations on which we agreed in our behind-closed-door discussions in
Casablanca.[22]

SPIRALING DOWN INTO THE ABYSS

Jordan's decision to throw down the gauntlet to Egypt, Syria, and the
PLO was intended to protect Jordan's national security. Shuqairi's consistent demands implied the emergence of a two-headed state, which could
only result in conflict and national disintegration. Such a situation could
have occurred if the elections to the PNC had been held in Jordan before
August 1, 1966, as scheduled. According to the PLO election procedures,
Palestinians had to vote in their countries of residence for their representatives to the PNC. In the case of Jordan, where Palestinians were Jordanian
citizens represented in the Jordanian Parliament, such an arrangement
would have created and institutionalized a dual loyalty—a recipe for national disintegration. This fact contributed to the timing of the Ajlun speech.
Despite its efforts, Jordan failed to generate any effective Arab pressure on
Shuqairi to change his attitude. In the Saudi-Iranian call for an Islamic
conference by the end of 1966, Jordan found a loophole through which it
could bring Saudi Arabia, a neighboring influential Arab country, to its
side. Jordan's goal in supporting the Islamic conference was mainly to
seek Saudi support as Jordan wrestled with the PLO and Nasser. Nasser,
whose main problem was his involvement in the Yemeni civil war, where
he had fifty thousand troops, now viewed Jordan as an ally of Saudi Arabia,
his major enemy in the Yemeni war, rather than as a major partner in the
Arab-Israeli conflict. This new Egyptian perception of Jordan made it even
more difficult for Nasser to appreciate Jordan's genuine worries.

When King Hussein made his Ajlun speech, the situation in the eastern
Mediterranean region had already been tense. It was both volatile and
uncontrollable. The then prevailing political scene could be roughly drawn
up as follows:

- The major actors were Syria, Egypt, Jordan, the Palestinians (the PLO
  and Fatah), and Israel.
- Syria's major concerns as a state were Israel's diversion of the water of
  the River Jordan and the implementation of the Arab's counter water
  projects. The ruling party in Syria had a different agenda. It wanted to
  be the ideological leader of the Arab world, and its strategy was to

motivate the Arab public and outbid Nasser on the Palestinian question, raising the slogan of the "liberation of Palestine" through "the
popular liberation war." The Israeli strike on the Syrian construction
site on one of the River Jordan's tributaries in July 1966 gave popular
support to this Syrian war cry throughout Syria and among the Palestinians and the general Arab public. The Israeli policy of aborting the
Arab's counter water projects not only nullified Nasser's strategy to
avoid military confrontation with Israel over the water resources but
also made it possible for the new Syrian leftist regime to transform the
conflict from one over water resources into one of liberation. As a result, Fatah, with its basic tenets of armed struggle with Israel, now
became Syria's natural ally, instead of the PLO, which had to abide by
Nasser's strategy. Implicitly, the Syrian leftist regime was defying Nasser's
strategy and competing with him over the leadership of the "Arab
masses."

- Egypt had two major concerns: (1) to get out of the Yemeni quagmire
  in an honorable way, and (2) to avoid an early confrontation with Israel. These concerns were obviously interrelated. To the Egyptians, Fatah
  was a dangerous actor because its strategy might accelerate the
  Arab-Israeli conflict and undermine Nasser's avoidance of early confrontation. Hence the Egyptian and pro-Egyptian Arab media were
  critical of the first operation carried out by Fatah against Israel on December 31, 1964. Abu Iyad wrote, "We [Fatah], to the Egyptians,
  were fanatic Muslim Brotherhood and agents of imperialism. The
  Beirut-based daily al-Anwar, which was pro-Nasser, ran a front-page
  story [on the event]. Its headline asserted that we were CIA agents."[23]
  Egypt was not publicly critical of the Syrian policy of verbal escalation,
  though in private Nasser was very critical. The PLO continued to be
  Egypt's Palestinian card.

- Jordan also had two major concerns: (1) keeping its territorial integrity
  and national unity intact, and (2) fending off Israel's disproportionate
  military retributive acts. Again, these two concerns were interrelated.
  From a Jordanian viewpoint, the question of water resources could be
  solved through fair sharing among the concerned Arab states and Israel. Unlike Egypt and Syria, Jordan viewed both the PLO and Fatah as
  threats. The former jeopardized Jordan's national unity, and the latter
  activated the infiltration-retribution cycle with all its adverse ripples. In
  other words, Jordan's essential concerns were internal—namely, the
  Palestinian land and people.

- Israel at the time had three major concerns: (1) aborting the rejuvenation of the Palestinian entity epitomized by the PLO, (2) nipping Fatah in the bud as a Palestinian organization believing in and practicing armed struggle, and (3) aborting the Arab plan to counter its diversion of the River Jordan's water. To Israel, all three concerns had to do with its national security. Israel viewed all Arab actors as enemies, though it differentiated among them in the degree of danger each represented. For each of the three Arab states (Egypt, Syria, and Jordan), Israel had drawn a red line. The red line for Jordan was the arrival of Iraqi tanks and mechanized troops at H3, the farthest Iraqi point on its western borders with Jordan. If such troops reached that point, then Israel would consider Jordan to have crossed the line and would respond.

- The Palestinians in general were high-spirited in 1966 because the Palestinian question was no longer merely a refugee issue. To them, the Arab commitment to the Palestinians differed from that of 1948 because now the skipper was Nasser, and the Soviet Union was on the Arab side. A minority of cynical Palestinians, living mainly on the West Bank, were worried about the Egyptian and Syrian approaches to the Palestinian question. They were against any policies that would lead to a war with Israel. Their argument was that not only would the Arab states lose such a war but also that the West Bankers would lose their homeland. The Palestinian refugees would lose nothing, as they had already lost their homeland. In the heat of emotions, this minority was unable to make its views heard.

- Fatah's strategy was predicated on a number of convictions. One was that Jordan should be its safe base because of its long borders with Israel and because of the Palestinian majority in the country. During 1966, Fatah continued to carry out its strategy of violent engagement with Israel. Its operations increased in number; most of them were staged from Jordan, fewer from Lebanon, and very few from Syria. In response to this increase in Fatah's operations, Israel stepped up its disproportionate reprisals.

- The situation was delicately poised, with the different actors arranged like dominoes in a row. Fatah, for example, though the smallest of the actors, could have effected the collapse of the entire setup.

The Arab scene in the year between June 1966 and the June war of 1967 witnessed further tensions in inter-Arab relations. The Arab leaders seemed to lose focus. King Hussein's speech at Ajlun on June 14, 1966, could be read not only as a shift in Jordanian strategy from conciliation to confrontation but also as the first Arab voice of protest against the prevailing Arab political mess. The June war of 1967 was the culmination of a yearlong process of deterioration between Israel on the one hand and Egypt, Jordan, Syria, and the Palestinian fedayeen on the other. The same period witnessed another process of deterioration between Jordan and each of the other Arab actors—Egypt, Syria, and the PLO. These two processes were intertwined.

Three major events set off or enhanced the first process. Two of them were initiated by Israel and the third by Syria. We have already mentioned the first Israeli action—its air attack on July 14, 1966, on a water-diversion project on one of the Jordan River's tributaries in Syrian territory. The Israeli attack conformed to a strategy spelled out by the Israeli prime minister ten months later. On May 13, 1967, Prime Minister Levy Eshkol said, "We are going to stop any terrorist attack on our territory. We shall continue to block any scheme to divert the resources of the Jordan River and we shall defend free navigation in the Red Sea."[24] The Israeli attack brought Nasser closer to Syria, the Arab actor with whom Nasser had been least comfortable because of Syria's outbidding policies and potentially provocative acts toward Israel. But this time Israel had provoked the confrontation. What made the event even more disturbing, from Nasser's point of view, was that it was over the diversion of water from the Jordan River. The Israeli attack implied that Nasser's judgment in calling for the first Arab summit had not been sound, since the attack proved that the Arab counterproject was as provocative to Israel as destroying the Israeli project itself through outright war would have been. The question of whether Israel was aware beforehand that the air attack would bring Egypt closer to Syria, increasing the chances of war, still persists. At the time, the most salient manifestation of the Egyptian-Syrian rapprochement was the joint-defense pact reached by the two countries on November 4, 1966.

The second event, initiated by Israel, was the November 13, 1966, attack on al-Samu^c, a Jordanian village near the armistice line in the Hebron province of the West Bank. Though the attack, as Israel announced, was in retaliation for a fedayeen operation in Israeli territory nearby, its effects and size exceeded the bounds of simple retaliation. Fifteen Jordanian soldiers, a fighter pilot, and six villagers were killed. In the village, Israeli soldiers destroyed 125 houses, a mosque, a police station, a health clinic, and a flour mill. This attack ignited Jordan's anger. West Bankers took to the streets of all West Bank cities, condemning the attack and criticizing the government for its "failure to arm the villagers." They demanded military training, distribution of weapons among the people, and the deployment of PLA units on the West Bank. Shuqairi seized this opportunity to launch a scathing propaganda attack, calling for replacement of the monarchy with a republican regime. He called on the West Bank members of the Jordanian cabinet to resign. No one responded to this request. A curfew was imposed on the cities of the West Bank, yet the agitation continued throughout the rest of November and part of December. The most interesting reaction was the attempt of West Bank political activists of all stripes to hold a popular conference in Jerusalem in early December, "to discuss the developments which had taken place in Jordan since the al-Samuᶜ operation. At first [the king] authorized the conference but when he realized that it was intended to serve as a platform for the pro-PLO opposition to assail al-Tal government, [he] withdrew his consent and ordered its cancellation."[25] Jordan arrested the political activists of the West Bank, while Shuqairi intensified his propaganda campaign against Jordan. This process culminated in Jordan's closing the PLO's offices in Jerusalem on January 4, 1967, and withdrawing its recognition of Shuqairi as the representative of the Palestinian entity.

To absorb the anger of the West Bankers and defuse their demand for weapons and military training, the government introduced a conscription system through which men over eighteen would receive basic military training for three months, after which they would be enlisted as reserves. The impact of the al-Samuᶜ episode on Jordan was enormous. It reactivated the triangular negative interaction among the Palestinians, Israel, and Jordan. The major outcomes were that more West Bankers drew closer to the PLO and Shuquairi's demand to deploy PLA units in Jordan gained popularity. In other words, the two Israeli attacks on Syria and Jordan tipped the balance in favor of the belligerent Arab actors, Syria and the PLO.

The third event was the Syrian shelling of an Israeli tractor operating in the no-man's-land between Syria and Israel on April 7, 1967. The attack provoked an Israeli air attack on Syrian fortifications in the Golan Heights. Syrian fighter planes intercepted Israeli planes, which shot down a number of Syrian jets. This event accelerated the deterioration process leading toward war. On May 18, 1967, Nasser terminated the mission of UNEF that had operated on the Egyptian side of the cease-fire lines since 1957. Four days later, Nasser closed the Tiran Straits to Israeli navigation, and on June 1, Israel formed a national unity government.

Meanwhile, Jordanian-Egyptian relations reached their nadir on February 23, 1967, when Jordan recalled its ambassador from Cairo after withdrawing its recognition of Egypt's ally, the Republic of Yemen, five days earlier—a step that Jordan took to cement its alliance with Saudi Arabia. Jordan's relations with Syria seriously deteriorated after Syrian agents exploded a car bomb at the customs checkpoint at Ramtha, a Jordanian town bordering Syria. The explosion killed twenty-one Jordanians. Until May 30, 1967, when the king made an abrupt visit to Cairo, Jordan was at odds with all three of the Arab actors, who, like Jordan, were directly involved in the Arab-Israeli conflict.

The action-reaction process occurred so quickly in the last days before the war that two joint-defense Arab pacts were signed in five days: one between Jordan and Egypt on May 30 and the other between Iraq and Egypt on June 4. The Arab defense arrangements represented an attempt at a quick fix for the deep political differences that had characterized Arab interrelations for more than a year. Against this background, Israel launched its attack on Egyptian air bases on the morning of June 5, starting the shortest war in modern history—a war that was destined to change not only the course of the Arab-Israeli conflict but also the history of the Middle East in the twentieth century.

7

The 1967 War
Structural Changes in Geography, Demographics, and Attitudes

THE TRAUMA OF THE SIX DAY WAR

Only twenty-seven hours passed between Jordan's announcement at 11:30 A.M. on June 5, 1967, of its military engagement with Israeli troops on the Jerusalem front and King Hussein's receipt at 2:30 P.M. on June 6 of a classified cable from the Egyptian deputy president Abdul-Hakim Amer, notifying him that Egypt would exert every effort to reach a cease-fire. At 11:15 P.M., the king received a cable from Nasser himself supporting the withdrawal of the Jordanian troops from the West Bank that same night, based on General Abdul-Mun'im Riyadh's recommendations. (Riyadh was the Egyptian staff officer entrusted with the job of commanding the Jordanian armed forces in accordance with the Jordanian-Egyptian joint-defense pact, signed a few days before the war.) Nasser's cable also applauded the king: "When history is written, your courage and bravery will be acknowledged, and so will be the courage of the Jordanian people who joined this battle without reluctance as soon as it was imposed." Nasser added, "Give-and-take is part of the history of nations and so is progress and retreat."[1]

The Arab military defeat in the June 1967 war was extremely abrupt. The Israeli blitzkrieg did not even offer the historian the opportunity to monitor advances and retreats. The defeat consisted of a knockout at the very beginning of the first round. It was shattering and sweeping. It was followed immediately by a trancelike state, interrupted on June 9 by Nasser's resignation in Egypt and the sight of refugees crossing the bridges over the River Jordan from the West to the East Bank, traveling on foot or in all kinds of vehicles—buses, trucks, cars, tractors. They climbed the hills heading for Amman or nowhere. They were lost in a wilderness of uncertainty and despair. Most of them, arriving from West Bank refugee camps, were now refugees for the second time. Some of them came from the Gaza Strip. Some had a faint hope of being hosted by relatives in East Bank towns or refugee camps. The others were looking for government relief.

A few hours after the Israeli military engagement with the Jordanian army, King Hussein addressed the people: "As we have expected, the enemy launched an attack, an aggression on our Arab land, sky, cities. All of us are soldiers in this drastic battle that has already started. We hope that it will soon end up in the victory that we have always cherished and lived for."[2]

Forty-eight hours later, the whole picture was quite the opposite. "At one stroke, the war had stripped Hussein of two of the most important justifications for his claim that Jordan represented the Palestinians: the West Bank as part of Filastin, and the largest concentration of Palestinian population."[3] Those forty-eight hours sowed the seeds of a great change in attitude toward Israel. Israel gradually came to be viewed as a reality to live with rather than as an alien body to be rejected. Those hours also brought about a new kind of Transjordanian-Palestinian interaction on the East Bank. The West Bank, which King Hussein had done his best to retain as part and parcel of the Hashemite Kingdom of Jordan, now came under Israeli occupation. East Jerusalem, which had been the "jewel in the crown" for nineteen years, was occupied and became a continual source of pain and a reminder of loss and defeat. The number of Palestinians on the East Bank increased by tens of thousands in a matter of days. The Jordanian army—always a source of pride for the king and the backbone of the nation's independence and security—was largely destroyed. The sight of embattled, aimless soldiers crossing the River Jordan was traumatic. A mood of despondency and uncertainty reigned. The people needed hope, and the hard-pressed country needed rebuilding. The government now came under the direct leadership of the king, and martial law, announced on June 5 when the war broke out, continued. In many people's eyes, Jordan was on the verge of collapse. The fact that it managed to survive was largely due to the king's statesmanship.

ABSORBING THE SHOCK

The king's first step was to raise the morale of the army and to find excuses for its defeat in order to preempt any anger that might translate into agitation against the regime. As early as June 7, the king addressed the army, saying, "Jordan, with its soldiers and citizens, men and women, has proved that it deserves the honor we are defending."[4]

On June 8, after the cease-fire, the king's address to the nation elaborated on the same theme:

> As for you, our soldiers, who missed martyrdom not because of cowardice or quiescence but because of God's will, I feel proud of your manhood and valor, brotherhood and friendship. I appreciate your performance, which made you worthy of being the children of Khalid ibn al-Walid [commander of the Yarmouk battle in 640 A.D., which opened the way for the conquest of Damascus] and of Saladin. My feelings toward you are the product of your heroism and sacrifice. My happiness lies in the fact that you are my family and clan, besides being my friends and comrades.[5]

In a telephone call early on the morning of June 6, Nasser communicated to King Hussein that there were hints of American and British airplanes participating on Israel's side, and the king supported Nasser's statement. The Israelis, who intercepted and recorded the call, broadcast it on Israeli radio. This telephone call proved to be of great help for Nasser and Arab dignity, at least for the first few weeks after the war. The Arab masses believed that the Arab defeat was due to the Americans and British offering military assistance to Israel. Thus they vented their anger on these two countries in particular. When Nasser stepped down on June 9, the Egyptian masses took to the streets of Cairo in huge demonstrations; many were crying, begging Nasser to cancel his decision and return to office. Interestingly enough, the Arab public, including the West Bankers now under Israeli occupation, shared the Egyptian people's feelings; they wanted Nasser to remain in office. To them, Nasser had been defeated not by Israel but by the Western superpowers. But most important, Nasser, to the Arab masses, remained the epitome of Arab dignity; his resignation would symbolize acceptance of the defeat of all Arabs—a fact they did not want to acknowledge. Nasser changed his mind and remained in office as the Egyptian president and the leader of Arab nationalism.

Nasser's reneging on his resignation in response to the Egyptian people's appeal was tantamount to his exoneration of the defeat. King Hussein was vicariously exonerated. After all, it was Nasser who had led the Arab camp before and during the war. Besides, the Jordanian army had been commanded by an Egyptian general during the war, and Nasser himself had already commended the king's courage in his cable of June 6.

Another factor that helped Jordan survive the fallout of the defeat and helped shield the king from dangerous accusations was the fact that the king's political position had been proved right. Before the war, the king had perpetually warned against demagoguery and emotional reactions to Israel, lest the Arabs be pushed into a catastrophe. The military defeat boosted the king's credibility.

Furthermore, the Jordanians were more concerned with the fate of their relatives, whether they were soldiers (as true of most Transjordanians) or civilians (as true of most Palestinians). In general, all were interested in listening to personal stories from those who had just arrived from the West Bank. Obviously, these stories were depressing, and together with the shattering defeat, they started to weave in the people's psyche two paradoxical inclinations: to accept Israel as a reality and to take revenge on Israel. During those months, officials and nonofficials began to realize that the loss of lives in the war was considerably less than that reported by the official Jordanian media. The actual loss amounted to 696 officers, soldiers, and conscripts, while the media had given the impression that tens of thousands had been killed or injured. On July 5, the prime minister had reported that 6,094 had been killed or were missing in action and that 762 had been injured.[6] The emphasis of the media and the official statements on the fact that the army was destroyed enhanced the exaggerated figures about the loss of life. During the war, there was no way to ascertain accurate numbers or even to offer estimates about the loss of lives because the war was so short. After the war, the failure to give accurate figures was for a different reason. When the order for withdrawal from the West Bank was given at 10:00 P.M. on June 6, many soldiers withdrew on their own in an undisciplined, unprofessional manner. Once they crossed the river and reached a safe area, most of them headed for their families in towns, villages, and bedouin encampments. Others headed for the military bases. The armed forces command was initially unable to identify how many had been killed or lost. By the end of July, most soldiers, with the exception of the prisoners of war and the injured still in Israeli hospitals, had once again reported to their military commands.

Before more accurate figures of the losses started to leak to the public, Israel had already announced its decision to subject East Jerusalem to Israeli law, a step that the Arabs took to be a symbol of annexation and a provocative manifestation of Israeli victory. The loss of Jerusalem and the West Bank, in the eyes of both Transjordanians and Palestinians, constituted an even greater loss than the now accurate figures on the loss of lives. Transjordanians, who highly valued gallantry and had contributed most of the soldiers in the combat units as well as all of their commanders, started to develop a timid sense of guilt, while the Palestinians felt that this new figure of 696 lives lost suggested that the army had not fought hard and that Jordan had conspired to help Israel defeat Nasser. In August, rumors began to circulate that the Jordanian military commanders had issued orders to the combat units contradicting General Riyadh's. Such misperceptions and rumors were enhanced by the professional political opposition, who within a month of the defeat began to aim for local targets. Nevertheless, the Transjordanian sense of guilt and the Palestinian sense of betrayal were destined to influence Transjordanian-Palestinian relations for many years to come.

JORDAN'S NEW AGENDA

The occupation of the West Bank meant that Jordan now had to draw up a new national agenda for domestic, regional, and international affairs. Domestically, Jordan's first major concern was to keep the country quiet and under control. After absorbing the shock of defeat, Jordan had to resume its normal life, especially in the economic sphere. It had to take into account the loss of the West Bank, which until the June war had contributed 38 percent of Jordan's gross domestic product. Now Jordan had lost all its revenues from tourism, which relied almost entirely on Jerusalem and Bethlehem, and this loss amounted to ten million dinars ($30 million in 1967) in hard currency. In his statement at the American National Press Club on November 7, 1967, King Hussein described the adverse impact of the loss of Jerusalem on the Jordanian economy: "Jordan without Jerusalem is like England without London, France without Paris, or Italy without Rome."[7] In addition, the foreign and private investments ceased. The closure of the Suez Canal paralyzed the Aqaba port. Rebuilding the armed forces both in terms of organization and of weapons and equipment was another major concern (the air force had lost all its planes, and the army 80 percent of its tanks and armor). Stimulating the economy and rebuilding the armed forces required finances that hard-pressed Jordan did not have.[8]

King Hussein wasted no time in attempting to secure as many resources as possible from the Arab states. On June 7, just the second day of the war, in light of the desperate military situation, Hussein addressed the armed forces, still withdrawing in a chaotic manner from the West Bank. Although this speech was directed to the army, the king appealed to the Arab nation:

> As for you, our Arab brethren in every place, I am telling you that your dear Jordan holds steadfast in confrontation of our enemy, in defense of our nation's heritage, the glory of our faith, and the dignity of our homeland. Our troops are sacrificing their blood and youth to achieve only one goal—martyrdom for the sake of God. That is their obligation to you, but as to your part, I leave it to your discretion and gallantry. Any material or moral assistance with which you might provide your sons, your brethren, the youth of your nation in their trenches, will be highly appreciated by God, people, and history.[9]

In response, Saudi Arabia, Abu Dhabi, Qatar, Bahrain, and Dubai donated twenty-two million dinars ($60 million), earmarked for rebuilding Jordan's armed forces. This donation was of great significance because as a result of Jordan's participation in the June war, the United States suspended the annual financial assistance it had given Jordan since 1957. On June 8, the king followed up on his speech with a letter to all Arab kings and heads of state in which he called for an Arab summit "to discuss the question in all its aspects and to encounter the situation with all its material, political, and military requirements."[10]

Another item on the domestic agenda was coping with the problem of the new refugees, or "the displaced," as the United Nations called them. The number of the displaced continued to increase over the years; by June 19, 1967, for example, their number amounted to one hundred thousand people, while on June 15, 1968, a year after the war, the official number was 354,248. The Jordanian government provided makeshift camps that have become the permanent dwelling place of the displaced. These refugees also needed minimal supplies, since they had lost their jobs on the West Bank; to look after these needs, a special governmental committee was established. Those who were refugees for the second time continued to received their monthly rations from UNRWA. Later, poor Transjordanians came to resent the government's regular assistance to the displaced, viewing it as evidence of the government's bias toward "the Palestinians" at the expense of the Transjordanian poor. It is noteworthy that the Palestinians of the Gaza Strip, who had been cut off from the West Bank since 1948, were now allowed by Israel to travel not only to the West Bank but also from there on to the East Bank. In other words, Israel allowed thousands of these Palestinians to seek refuge in Jordan. This Israeli policy during the very early stages of occupation betrayed Israel's demographic strategy, which was to reduce to as few as possible the number of Palestinians in Mandatory Palestine. In some towns, such as Bethlehem, the Israeli occupying authority went so far as to use loudspeakers and call on inhabitants "to leave their town and to go to the East Bank, otherwise their lives will be endangered."[11]

To the West Bankers who fled their towns, villages, and refugee camps for Jordan, their movement to the East Bank was a movement from the war-stricken areas to safer ones within their own country. But to the Palestinians of Gaza, taking refuge in Jordan constituted a move to a foreign country. In the immediate aftermath of the war, the Jordanian authorities, for humanitarian and administrative reasons, did not distinguish among all the refugees who were flowing into the East Bank from the West Bank.

Right after the war, Jordan's strategy was based on the restoration of the West Bank. For the first time since 1948, the Israeli occupation provided West Bankers with a new option regarding their political allegiance— the option of secession from the Hashemite Kingdom. According to Shemesh, "the West Bank's relationship with Jordan became a subject for negotiation in the Arab, Palestinian, and international arenas, while its future was becoming inextricably bound up with the solution of the Palestinian issue."[12]

Jordan's strategy required above all the maintenance of strong bonds with West Bankers, while it continued to represent Palestinians in both the Arab and the international arenas. In this respect, Jordan adopted a number of policies. The most important of these was the open-bridge policy, allowing the movement of persons and goods over the bridges connecting the West and East Banks (though trade was allowed to move only in the East Bank direction). This became a de facto, rather than a negotiated, arrangement between Jordan and Israel, and it was convenient for Israel as long as the movement of people and goods occurred under its control on the other side of the bridges. After all, such movement would relieve the congestion of the Palestinian population on the West Bank, an objective cherished by Israel for security and demographic reasons. Most important for Israel from a political standpoint was that the open-bridge policy would normalize relations with Jordan.

The Jordanian government made use of the open-bridge policy to sustain official and nonofficial institutions. In other words, the Jordanian government maintained what Kelman terms an "instrumental attachment" with West Bankers. Nevertheless, a few West Bankers claimed that it was time for the Palestinians to have their own state. Those who spelled out this attitude were blacklisted by the Jordanian government. On June 21, Prime Minister Sa'ad Juma' made a statement emphasizing the unity of the two banks and Jordan's determination to restore the West Bank as soon as possible. He warned West Bankers of the enemy's plots and propaganda and added, "The government emphasizes that every single one is, and will continue to be, a Jordanian citizen. Therefore the government considers the cooperation of any one of them with the enemy as a treason that will inflict on him everlasting disgrace and make of him a criminal who will be severely punished in the very near future."[13]

Israel did not spell out its position on the future of the West Bank, and this ambiguity left room for speculation by the Jordanian government and West Bankers alike. When Israel annexed East Jerusalem on June 28, the Jordanian government and the West Bankers read the event as a prelude for drastic changes in the status of the West Bank. One of the first steps taken by senior officials of the Israeli military administration was to approach community leaders and notables to ascertain their attitudes about the future and to float some general ideas about the Israelis and Palestinians cooperating and living together. The substance of these meetings was reported to the government in Amman, which took the matter seriously. On July 5, Prime Minister Juma' held a meeting in the Parliament building in Amman that was attended by politicians, senior officials, businessmen, and civil society representatives. At that meeting, the prime minister spelled out the government's policy:

> Jordan's policy was, is still, and will continue to be predicated on the following:
> The Palestinian cause is an all-Arab cause. No Arab State has the right to solve that question.
> The Jordanian entity of the two banks is sacred. We believe in it as much as we believe in God and in our religion. We will never at any time relinquish this sacred unity.
> The West Bankers should realize that their lives, souls, and future are all tightly and sacredly bound to this bank. That bond will never be broken under the leadership of King Hussein.[14]

Jordan continued to stress the unity of the two banks. The king's letter of commission to the new prime minister in October 1967 stated, "The

Palestinian question is the cornerstone in Jordan's internal, Arab, and external policies. If this cause is sacred to our Arab nation, to Jordan it is a question of life or death."[15]

The West Bank community leaders and senior officials complied with the king's position. On July 20, the Israeli assistant administrative governor sent a letter to the mayor of East Jerusalem, Ruhi al-Khatib, asking him and the members of the East Jerusalem Council to meet with him on July 23. In this meeting, the Israeli senior official planned to explore whether the mayor and his colleagues on the council were ready to join the Israeli Jerusalem Council after Israel's annexation of East Jerusalem. The plan was to amalgamate the East and West Jerusalem councils into one council.

On July 22, the Israeli official received a memorandum from the East Jerusalem Council members rejecting his invitation on the grounds that joining the Israeli Jerusalem Council would be tantamount to accepting Israel's decision to annex their city. The annexation was illegal and in violation of the UN Charter.

Though this memorandum was connected solely with East Jerusalem's status, it triggered a wave of protest by official representative bodies and others all over the West Bank against the Israeli annexation decision. In published statements to the Israeli military governor of the West Bank, the protesters proclaimed their loyalty to the unity of the two banks. Religious leaders, chambers of commerce, labor unions, professional federations, party leaders, notables, and community leaders participated in this protest. A new unwritten social contract began to govern the relationship of the West Bank and the East Bank, whose gist was "We, the West Bankers, will stick to unity, and you, the government in Amman, will support our efforts to stick to the land while you work to end the occupation." But the position of the West Bankers was not congruent with that of the PLO leadership.

Yahia Hammuda, who had just succeeded Shuqairi in December 1967 as the chairman of the Executive Committee of the PLO, said in answer to a question about the future of the West Bank after the Israeli withdrawal, "The destiny of this part [of Palestine] should be determined by the Palestinian people. There is no state that has the right to determine the West Bank's destiny. Certainly this attitude hurts the feelings of those committed to the standing unity of the two banks. As for us, our ambition is to liberate all Palestine. After liberation, we shall let our people decide, even if we feel that the people tend to expand the limits of unity with Jordan [meaning that all liberated Palestine would unite with Jordan instead of only the West Bank uniting with the East Bank]."[16] In other words, while Jordan considered the West Bank to be part and parcel of the Hashemite kingdom, the PLO leaders asserted that the unity between the West Bank and the East Bank was open to referendum.

Hammuda's statement betrayed not only his optimism about an early Israeli withdrawal from the West Bank but also his sense that a Jordanian-Palestinian dispute over the future status of the West Bank was highly probable. It is interesting to compare Hammuda's statement with King Hussein's answer in Amman on June 19 to a journalist's question about whether Jordan would be able to survive without the West Bank: "The West Bank is an essential part of the Jordanian territory. Jordan is a part of the Arab homeland. The issue [to Jordan] is not one of survival. It is a question of right."[17]

Exploring the positions of the influential Western countries regarding the future of the West Bank was of special significance to King Hussein. He wanted to make sure that the new realities would not entice the United States in particular to adopt or support a conflict-resolution policy at the expense of Jordan or Jordan's territorial integrity. On June 19, one week before the king's address to the UN General Assembly, President Johnson announced five principles for peace in the Middle East. His statement included the following:

> Our country is committed—and we reiterate that commitment today—to a peace that is based on five principles:
> • First, the recognized right of national life;
> • Second, justice for the refugees;
> • Third, innocent maritime passage;
> • Fourth, limits on the wasteful and destructive arms race; and
> • Fifth, political independence and territorial integrity for all.
>
> We are not the ones to say where other nations should draw lines between them that will assure each the greatest security. It is clear, however, that a return to the situation of June 4, 1967, will not bring peace. There must be secure and there must be recognized borders. Some such lines must be agreed to by the neighbors involved as part of the transition from armistice to peace. At the same time, it should be equally clear that boundaries cannot and should not reflect the weight of conquest.[18]

King Hussein was not wholly satisfied with Johnson's statement. Though it emphasized the principle of territorial integrity, its indication "that a return to the situation of June 4, 1967, will not bring peace" was especially worrying.

Assuming that the occupation would have to be temporary, and in the hopes of securing a UN resolution that would force Israel to withdraw from the West Bank, the king addressed the General Assembly on June 26. There he declared that he spoke on behalf of the Arab nation. "What Jordan and the Arab nations are requesting is peace and justice," he said. "The lines that Israel crossed were not natural borders but the armistice line drawn nineteen years ago. They were the same lines that hundreds of thousands of Palestinian refugees crossed in panic in 1948. The fact that there are 1,300,000 refugees is by itself a reprimand to this international organization. The current war is not a new one. It is a part of an old war that might continue for many years to come if the moral and material wrongs afflicted on the Arabs are not redressed." The king emphasized that the war was the result of Israeli aggression: "It was Israel who started the war at the time and place that she chose, quite as she had bragged before the aggression. She also ended the war in the same manner, violating the Security Council cease-fire resolution." And he referred to Jordan's losses and the social and economic dislocations resulting from the war: "In addition to the thousands of refugees who fled their camps in which they had lived for nineteen years, a new category of refugees came into existence. . . . The largest part of our most productive land is now under occupation. Jerusalem has fallen into foreign hands for the second time in 1,300 years, and so has Bethlehem, Hebron, Jericho, and a large part of the fertile Jordan Valley." The king went on, "There is nothing to do but to promptly condemn the aggressor and to force the Israeli troops to withdraw to the June 4 lines." Urging the United Nations to take a firm position and warning of establishing a precedent in terms of condoning aggression, the king concluded, "If the aggressor is allowed to gain one square foot of the land, the UN should not expect compliance with its cease-fire resolutions anywhere in the world or under any circumstances as of today."[19]

Though Hussein's address to the General Assembly suggested the need for a final peaceful settlement, it did not address specific components of the conflict except for the complete withdrawal and the issue of refugees. In fact, before the Arab summit had convened, it was difficult for the king to be more specific.

After his speech to the United Nations, Hussein met with President Johnson in Washington. According to Mousa, the king expressed "Jordan's readiness to offer Israel peace if she withdraws from the West Bank, which Jordan accepts to have demilitarized. Johnson's reaction was that Jordan should negotiate directly with Israel in order to reach a general settlement conducive to a final peace that will resolve the Middle East problem in its entirety. Johnson's reaction was disappointing to the king because it revealed the American bias toward the aggressor."[20]

During his tour in the Western countries, the king also met British prime minister Harold Wilson; his foreign secretary, Harold Brown; and President Charles de Gaulle of France. About these discussions in Europe, the king said, "In London, we reached mutual understanding in spite of the hostility of the public opinion to me personally, to my country, and to the Arabs in general. In Paris, General de Gaulle was so perceptive. I found him deeply knowledgeable of the problem and its various aspects. I was extremely touched by his concern regarding us and by his friendly attitude. Still I remember his words, 'If Israel has the right to live in peace and security, Jordan, by the same token, deserves that same right.'"[21]

KING HUSSEIN'S NEW APPROACH ON THE ARAB POLITICAL SCENE

Jordan's Arab policy in the wake of the June war was anchored in four interconnected goals: restoration of the Arab consensus through the resumption of the Arab summit, rationalizing the Arab attitude and approach regarding the Arab-Israeli conflict, reinstating Jordan's undisputed representation of the Palestinians, and working with Nasser. Jordan had always suffered from Arab divisiveness, but this time Arab consensus was needed for other reasons. The king needed it as a safety net in his quest for the restoration of the West Bank by peaceful means. Jordan was also in dire need of Arab material support to cope with the new domestic challenges resulting from the military defeat. As early as June 8, the king began calling for an Arab summit to secure Arab financial support and to rationalize the Arab attitude and approach to the problem at hand before sentimentalism took over and dominated the Arab scene. To him, Israel was now a reality, and the Arabs should reconcile themselves to it; yet peace and justice should go hand in hand, for otherwise there would be no lasting peace. The king espoused the formula of trading land for peace, but how to complete this transaction was a knotty question. On the one hand, he had to persuade the Arabs to transform their attitudes toward Israel and reverse their thinking, from belligerency to pursuing peaceful means to resolve the Arab-Israeli conflict. He also needed to reinstate his representation of the Palestinians to support his restoration of the West

Bank as the second half of the Hashemite Kingdom. On the other hand, he had to facilitate dialogue with Israel, his strongest adversary, which was now in control of the occupied territories and whose intentions about the future of the West Bank were still unclear. In this complicated situation Nasser was an indispensable partner; his appeal to the Arab public and influence on Arab governments were still effective. The king's credentials in terms of his partnership with Nasser had never been stronger. He had gone along with Nasser more than the Syrians had. He had accepted an Egyptian general to command the Arab army. Unlike the Syrians, he had gone to war by Nasser's side just a few hours after the conflict flared up. And Nasser not only had praised the king and the Jordanians for their courage and fortitude in his June 6 cable but also had made the following pledge to King Hussein on June 22: "The United Arab Republic is fully prepared to link its destiny with the cause of the brave Jordanian people under your patriotic leadership, which proved its dedication to the people under the toughest and most dangerous circumstances."[22]

The king correctly interpreted these messages to mean that Nasser was open to cooperation with him and was prepared to support the king's representation of the Palestinians. Nasser's reference to the king's "commitment to the people" referred specifically to his dedication to the interests of the West Bankers. Nasser's recognition of the king's courage and dedication was both reassuring and encouraging to King Hussein. Yet the situation was not simple.

To implement the king's land-for-peace formula, Hussein had to make his way through a minefield of Arab rejectionists and Israeli expansionists. Again, for the king, the Arab military defeat was not a mere *naksa* (setback) but a question of Jordan's life or death.

Egypt had termed the military defeat a *naksa*, and the term had been quickly picked up by the official Arab media, becoming a keyword in Arab political discourse at that time. The term was first used to dilute the devastating effect of the military defeat on the Arab public and to immunize Arab leaders and governments against potential popular scathing criticism that might develop into violence or military coups, as had happened after the 1948 war. Yet *naksa* implied the hope of resuming the war in order to achieve victory, and thus it was not a helpful term for those like King Hussein who believed in settling the Arab-Israeli conflict by peaceful means. Jordan could not afford to fight another war. Salibi argues that "the Sinai desert lost by Egypt in the war was important mainly for its strategic value. The same was true of the Golan Heights lost by Syria. But this was not the case for the Jordanian West Bank. Effectively, this area comprised about half the inhabited Jordanian kingdom, and its fall to Israel could in no way be dismissed as a mere *naksa*. Little wonder that among the Arab losers in the war, Jordan came out particularly crestfallen."[23]

Jordan's participation in the war, its loss of half the inhabited kingdom, Nasser's testimony in favor of Jordan and his pledge to link Egypt's destiny with Jordan's new cause (the restoration of the West Bank), the familiarity of the Arab governments and the public with King Hussein's prewar warnings against emotional policies—all these factors helped the king shape his postwar moderate approach. It was an approach characterized by dynamism and aggressiveness that reflected the king's concern—that time was not on his side. Nasser too felt that time was not on his side, and this shared feeling brought the two leaders closer still.

The king, I believe, was aware that such aggressive diplomacy, especially for a small, resource-poor country like Jordan, had an expiration date. As the biggest loser in the war, Jordan was like a bereaved person whose anger, emanating from anguish, would be tolerated for a while but not forever. King Hussein's policy was to strike while the iron was hot. He hoped to lay the foundations for a new type of political thinking on the Arab scene, as well as new norms for inter-Arab relations.

A short, extemporaneous speech made in Beirut on August 24, just five days before the summit meeting, best exemplifies the king's new aggressiveness in the service of his goals. In response to the welcome given by the Lebanese president, the king said,

> In the past we went along a path that was proved to be wrong because it did not take us to our goal. There were also mistakes and reasons that led us to what has happened. . . . The war was imposed on our nation, and in Jordan we fought this war with all our resources, resolve, and determination. The will of the exalted God might have chosen to test our endurance and faith in our cause. He provided us with the opportunity to reexamine all the previous, superficial positions on the basis of which we had tried to address issues with emotions instead of planning. . . . We have to give up demagoguery and turn instead to building and preparing for the battles that our nation has to fight."[24]

(By using the word *battles,* instead of *war,* he clearly was referring to political, diplomatic, and public relations efforts.)

Next, in his speech at the Arab summit in Khartoum, the king reiterated his criticism of the Arab attitudes before the war and his call for reassessing prewar positions and concepts. "It seems to me," he said, "that the most important thing is to reexamine our positions and calculations before and during the war and until this moment. We have to face realities and mistakes with honesty and courage. To sing of glory does not make glory. . . . We insist that as of today a new brighter era should dawn in the Arab world, an era devoid of the fragmentation, quiescence, and weakness that characterized the prewar era." The king spoke with noticeable self-confidence, taking the tone of knowledgeable instructor. To justify addressing his fellow Arab leaders in this way, the king said, "Jordan, which has always been entrenched in the front line of defense of the Arab nation, was destined to come out of the aggression with the deepest wound in its heart. . . . Jordan has lost, as you well know, its Western Bank, and half of its people have fallen under occupation and in hideous captivity." Emphasizing his representation of the Palestinians, he said, "Our pride in the steadfastness of *our family on the West Bank of Jordan* and in their sincere nationalism and patriotism should not mask the danger implied in the continuation of their present situation."[25]

The Arab summit in Khartoum was desired not only by the king and Nasser as a new point of departure but also by the West Bankers, who believed that their salvation could come only through a united Arab effort.

The Khartoum summit resolutions, announced on September 1, 1967, did not fully meet the king's expectations. The third resolution was particularly obstructive from the king's point of view. It read, "The Arab heads of state have agreed to unite their political efforts at the international and diplomatic level to *eliminate the effects of the aggression* and to ensure the withdrawal of the aggressive Israeli forces from the Arab lands which have been occupied since the aggression of June 5. This will be done within the framework of the main principles by which the Arab states abide: no peace with Israel, no recognition of Israel, no negotiations with Israel, and insistence on the rights of the Palestinian people in their own country."[26]

The three principles of no peace with Israel, no recognition of it, and no negotiations with it placed relatively tight restrictions on the king's future diplomatic activity. Since these principles were militant and inconsistent with logical expectations after the Arab military defeat, they became synonymous with the Khartoum summit worldwide. Nevertheless, the commitment of Saudi Arabia, Kuwait, and Libya to make annual regular payments totaling $325 million to Egypt and Jordan ($228 million to Egypt and $97 million to Jordan) was partly gratifying to Jordan, sorely in need of financial support. The first resolution, which emphasized the conference's commitment to the "unity of Arab ranks, the unity of joint

action, the need for coordination and for the elimination of all differences," was satisfactory to the king. The West Bankers were particularly
satisfied with the second resolution, which read, "The Conference has
agreed on the need to consolidate all efforts to eliminate the effects of
aggression on the basis that occupied lands are Arab lands and that the
burden of regaining these lands falls on all the Arab states."[27] This resolution enhanced their hope that the occupation would not last long.

The Khartoum summit was held almost three months after the war,
and during this period the Arab governments and public developed a number of common perceptions that contributed to the wording of the summit resolutions. Two of these perceptions were destined to govern the
Arab attitude toward regaining the occupied territories for quite a while.
The first stemmed from the 1956 Arab experience, when the United States
put pressure on Israel to withdraw from the Egyptian Sinai. In the first few
months after the June war, both Arab officials and public recalled that
1956 episode and thought that Israel might once again be forced to withdraw in 1967. In their opinion, the Soviet Union was in a better position
than it had been in 1956, so it could put pressure on the United States to
force the Israeli withdrawal. The second perception was that the United
Nations would not tolerate the acquisition of territory by war. After 1956,
the United Nations' approach to ending international conflict—by man-
dating a third party who would broker a deal—had gained currency in the
Arab mind.

Over the three months since the end of the war, King Hussein's repeated emphasis on the unity of the two banks had revived the worries of
the PLO, especially Shuqairi. In this context, the Khartoum summit was
not only an embodiment of Arab consensus but also an arena for the first
Jordanian-Palestinian political encounter since the war. Shuqairi, who like
the majority of Arab leaders and public believed that the Israeli occupation was only temporary, wanted to make sure that the West Bank would
not return to Jordan. At the conference, he tried to convince the Arab
leaders to adopt a resolution to this effect, but he failed. However, he was
able to introduce the three famous "no's" in the resolution. Shemesh
writes that Shuqairi "walked out of the Khartoum summit on the final day
after the rejection of his demand that 'no stand will be taken regarding the
future of Palestine and the outcome of aggression [the June war] without
the participation of the PLO' and that 'no Arab state will sign a separate
agreement resolving the problem of Palestine.' Shuqairi continued to defend the PLO as the sole representative of the Palestinian people, and

called for the Palestinians' right to self-determination."[28] Thus, we might say that at Khartoum the king won the first round in the encounter with the PLO after the June war.

Though the Khartoum summit's political resolutions sounded belligerent, reading between the lines reveals that it was a relatively advanced platform when compared with the prewar Arab position. For example, the third resolution stressed the "political" and "diplomatic" efforts for the first time in the history of the Arab-Israeli conflict. In addition, the phrase "to eliminate the effects of the aggression," found in four out of the eight summit resolutions, was a positive development. For many years to come, this would be the key phrase in Arab political discourse. Stressing the "elimination of the effects of the aggression" was quite different from going after the "liquidation of Israel," which had been the prewar catch phrase for the majority of Arab governments and people. Perhaps unbeknownst to the Arab leaders, these three principles hinted at a fundamental change in the Arab position, from the intention to destroy Israel to that of regaining the occupied territories. Ironically, this change was not acknowledged by the Western media, though it caused Syria and Algeria not to attend the conference. (Through diplomatic channels, both countries had been aware that the change was going to happen.) The failure of Syria and Algeria to attend the conference implied that the summit had not secured Arab unanimity about adopting peaceful means "to eliminate the effects of the aggression." The germ of renewed inter-Arab conflict lay dormant, waiting for the right moment to reawaken.

At the Khartoum summit, the king achieved more or less all his objectives in the Arab domain, at least temporarily. The Arab consensus was reestablished. His partnership with Nasser was confirmed when Nasser declared at the conference that the "only open avenue before them was the political one, and that it was imperative that King Hussein should approach the Americans in order to regain the West Bank, since the United States alone could put pressure on Israel to relinquish it. Nasser also voiced his full support for the king."[29] The political approach to eliminate the effect of the aggression was ensured.

After these achievements at the summit, the king resumed developing his international contacts with more self-confidence. The king's political activity in the international arena was aimed mainly at regaining the West Bank by securing an early Israeli withdrawal.

On October 2, the king made his first official visit to Moscow, where he held talks with President Podgorny and Prime Minister Kosygin. This visit rounded out the king's efforts to convince the Big Four to adopt a strong resolution in the Security Council that would force Israel to withdraw from the occupied territories.

King Hussein summed up these visits and discussions with world leaders in this way: "One point became very clear to me. In spite of all that has happened since the Palestinian question developed into a catastrophe, the world public opinion is convinced that Israel was established in our region in order to exist. It was necessary to accept the fait accompli. Besides, I also felt that the public opinion was anxious first to help us define our position regarding the recognition of Israel and, at the same time, to make sure that peace deprives Israel of the right to expand; and second, to achieve a just and lasting peace and the elimination of the effects of the aggression."[30]

Thus, Hussein's diplomatic activity, intended to influence the attitudes of other states, came to influence the king's own attitudes as well. This fact widened the gap between his stance and that of the rejectionists, including the PLO. The gap widened further on November 22, when Jordan and Egypt accepted Security Council Resolution 242, which addressed the refugee problem by discarding Palestinian national rights. Most resentful was Fatah, the staunchest advocate of Palestinian nationalism.

Only Jordan and Egypt accepted Resolution 242. Syria rejected it, while the Palestinians themselves at that time were a subject to be discussed by others rather than a recognized partner in the discussions. Resolution 242 superseded the Khartoum principles and has become, in the years since, the gospel of Middle Eastern peacemaking and the rubric of Middle Eastern political discourse. In spite of strong Arab reservations early on, it has proved its viability and has since gained Syrian and Palestinian approval. The third article in Resolution 242 requests "the secretary general to designate a special representative to proceed to the Middle East to establish and maintain contact with the States concerned in order to promote agreement and assist efforts to achieve a peaceful and accepted settlement in accordance with the provisions and principles in this resolution." The secretary-general appointed Gunnar Jarring, a senior Swedish diplomat, as the special representative to the Middle East. With his appointment, Jordanian and Egyptian diplomacy began to revolve around his mission. But parallel to this diplomacy, an opposite activity was quickly building steam: the Palestinian fedayeen movement was destined to play a huge role not only in influencing the course of events in the Middle East, including the peace process, but also in reshaping the Transjordanian-Palestinian relationship.

8

From Consensus to Contention

In 1981, Abu Iyad, the PLO's second in command after Arafat at the time, wrote in his book, *Filastini bila Huwiya* (A Palestinian without Identity):

> The Six Day War opened before us a new horizon for development. The Jordanian regime became too weak to challenge our program. King Hussein released hundreds of Palestinian nationalists who had been imprisoned in the years preceding the conflict. He also closed his eyes to us when we embarked on establishing bases along the River Jordan [on the eastern side] to be used as staging points for our commandos. Neither did we lack the support and sympathy of the local inhabitants nor the support and sympathy of the Jordanian army with whom we had established excellent relations. Officers of Transjordanian origin who were to "massacre" the Palestinians two years later used to greatly facilitate the execution of our mission.[1]

Abu Iyad's remarks are absolutely correct. The Palestinian fedayeen, who had been joined by a number of Arab volunteers, did not seek Jordan's permission either in organizing themselves, in bringing weapons into Jordan, or in establishing bases for their combatants who were to launch guerrilla attacks against Israel after the Arab military defeat in the June 1967 war. After that devastating war, Jordanian authorities were in no position to prevent the landless Palestinians from organizing and carrying

151

weapons in order to resist the Israeli occupation. However, Abu Iyad's last sentence in the quotation here provides us with the key notion for this chapter.

On September 26, 1970, while Arab leaders were convening in Cairo for an Arab summit to resolve the ongoing fighting between the Jordanian army and the fedayeen organizations, King Hussein said in Amman, "They [the fedayeen] always talked about resistance to Israel. As things turned out, it was not Israel that the fedayeen were after, it was Jordan. I have always been puzzled by their term the 'Palestinian revolution.' I could comprehend very well the 'Palestinian resistance' but not the 'Palestinian revolution.'[2]

King Hussein's statement could be an answer in advance to Abu Iyad about the change that took place. What really did happen between 1967 and 1970? According to Herbert Kelman, chair of the Middle East Seminar at the Harvard Center for International Affairs, the Six Day War triggered three processes. First, it initiated among the Arab states a reassessment of their conflict with Israel. Israel's occupation of territories belonging to Egypt, Syria, and Jordan created bilateral issues between Israel and these countries, a fact that led the Arabs to exchange their goal of dismantling Israel altogether to that of negotiating "land for peace." They gradually accepted Israel and began to search for ways of disengaging from the conflict. Second, it accelerated the development among the Palestinians of an "independent Palestinian nationalism." The Palestinian grievances resulting from Israel's occupation of the West Bank and Gaza became the focus of their national mobilization. Third, it reactivated in Israel the question of the country's borders, which had lain dormant since the 1949 armistice agreements. Some Israelis saw in the occupied territories an opportunity for peace (through trading with them), while others saw in them an opportunity to establish greater Israel in all Mandatory Palestine.[3]

JORDAN'S CENTRALITY AFTER THE JUNE WAR

Jordan was deeply involved in the first process (the Arab reassessment of the conflict with Israel), overwhelmingly entangled with the second (the development of an independent Palestinian nationalism), and structurally affected by the third (the rejuvenation of Israeli expansionism). In the first process, which technically took almost five months, Jordan played a pivotal role, both in securing Arab consensus in Khartoum and in making Security Council Resolution 242 possible.

Without the Arab consensus in Khartoum subscribing to peaceful means to "eliminate the effects of the aggression," it would have been almost impossible for Jordan and Egypt to accept Resolution 242, whose more detailed text would have made the shift in Egypt's and Jordan's positions too abrupt to be acceptable. Yet the comprehensiveness of Resolution 242 allowed it gradually to supersede the Khartoum resolutions as a basis for a peaceful settlement for the Arab-Israeli conflict. (Syria accepted Resolution 242 on October 22, 1973, when it accepted Security Council Resolution 338 in the wake of the October war. The second clause in Resolution 338 called on "the parties concerned to start the implementation of 242 in all its parts immediately after the cease-fire." The PLO accepted 242 in 1988.)

THE CONSENSUS TO BREED CONTENTION

The outcome of these two events, the Khartoum summit and Resolution 242, favored Jordan's strategy to regain its sovereignty over the West Bank by peaceful means. Jordan's satisfaction with the outcome contrasted sharply with the PLO's and Fatah's objectives, a fact that made of Jordan an arena for political rivalry and military confrontation for the four years following the war.

Indeed, the conflict between Jordan and the PLO transformed Jordan's satisfaction with its diplomatic accomplishments into a deep concern over its survival. By mid 1968, Jordan had become a point of attraction and interest to the world and a center of Arab political rivalries and contradictions. Thus, two of Kelman's three processes were active in Jordan—so much so that King Hussein became the central figure in Middle Eastern politics between the 1967 June war and the 1973 October war.

While King Hussein was deeply preoccupied in the weeks and months that followed the June war with pursuing his peace diplomacy in Arab and foreign capitals, Arafat was equally preoccupied with preparing the ground for guerrilla war. In June 1967, just a few days after the war, Arafat undertook a daring mission by infiltrating the occupied West Bank in disguise with a number of his lieutenants. His mission was to establish resistance cells and to evaluate the readiness of the Palestinians under the Israeli occupation for his strategy. At the same time, a number of Fatah leaders visited Cairo, Damascus, Baghdad, and Algiers, the capitals of the Arab revolutionary countries, to explore the "feasibility of resuming the Palestinian fedayeen activities."[4] They also met with the leaders of the oil-producing Arab countries to secure financial support. These countries showed sympathy and pledged financial support for Fatah.

One of the most interesting responses the Fatah leaders received was from the then Syrian president, Nur ed-Din al-Attassi, who "warned us strongly against launching fedayeen activities against Israel because 'you will lose and you will drag us into the catastrophe.' He kept begging Fatah's delegation, saying, 'Give us time to catch our breath.'"[5]

While Fatah leaders were soliciting Arab governments' support, Fatah activists were collecting weapons. Arafat, in turn, dispatched reports from the occupied territories indicating that the people there supported the continuation of the Palestinian struggle by all means; as Abu Iyad later recorded, "the Arab defeat did not weaken the resolve of the people of the West Bank and Gaza."[6]

In August 1967 and after Arafat's return from the West Bank, Fatah leaders made a firm decision that their fedayeen would launch attacks on Israel beginning August 31, 1967. Fatah's choice of this date was not arbitrary, since it was the scheduled date for the Arab summit in Khartoum. By choosing August 31 as its D-day, Fatah wanted to affirm to the Arab leaders that its path differed from that of the Arab states. From that day on, Fatah became the de facto Palestinian protagonist, representing Palestinian aspirations and forging Palestinian policies. Helena Cobban, an American correspondent in Beirut from 1976 to 1981 and an authority on the PLO's political history, writes that

> by the end of 1965 . . . Fateh had already laid down the basis of its activities for the years to come. It had proved itself able to sustain a constant level of guerrilla operations against Israel; and while these certainly did not threaten to bring the Jewish state to its knees overnight, they were a constant irritant to it, whilst acting as a powerful rallying-point for Fateh in the Palestinian communities of the diaspora as well as a potential, and uncontrollable, source of instability for several Arab regimes.[7]

Fatah worked hard and fast to establish its bases in Jordan. Although Fatah was closely monitored by the Jordanian security apparatus, it continued to grow and flourish, mainly because the government chose not to block its way. The fedayeen movement then enjoyed high popularity among both Transjordanians and Palestinians. Mousa accurately characterizes the mood of the people right after the war:

> There was a strong feeling that the enemy [Israel] should not rest, losses should be inflicted on it, and its arrogance should be checked. All over the Arab world sympathy with the fedayeen intensified, as well as the hope that they [the

fedayeen] would attain what the professional, regular armies had failed to accomplish. The Arabs, in the wake of the defeat, were in need of those who would restore Arab self-confidence in confronting the enemy and retaliating against its blows. It became widely acknowledged that those *Mujahideen* [the fedayeen] were eligible to stand up to the hegemony of the occupying forces like the Vietnamese were in Vietnam.[8]

To the Arabs in general, the fedayeen in those days constituted the heroes who would heal injured Arab dignity. Besides, King Hussein hoped he could merge his political path with the fedayeen's in order to bring real pressure on Israel to respond positively to Security Council Resolution 242. The king expressed this hope in many different ways and contexts. For example, on February 16, 1968, King Hussein addressed the "armed Jordanian forces and all the members of the one Jordanian family," saying,

> No one on this territory can outbid us in our quest to attain our goals or realize our hopes. . . . Any sincere [combatants] should move through us on the land and in compliance with our planning and preparations. We call on every party that is eager to fulfill its duty with sincerity and honesty to join us on our path, the path of organized work that is conducive to restoring our rights and regaining our land as well as our Jerusalem, the Arab and Muslim Jerusalem.[9]

But the king's hopes never materialized. The undercurrents of tension continued to build in an atmosphere of confused inter-Arab relations. Cobban writes, "But it was in the collapse of the previously existing system of inter-state relations in the Arab World, its checks, balances and interrelated ideologies, that Fateh's most explosively dynamic chance for growth arose, the chance that was to catapult Fateh into the leadership of the PLO."[10]

TRIANGULAR INTERACTION

One of the salient features of the period following the June war was the continuation of the prewar triangular interaction among Jordan, Israel, and the Palestinian nationalist movement (the fedayeen)—but with two differences: now the three actors interacted mainly on the East Bank instead of the West Bank, and their postwar interaction was larger in magnitude, deeper in implication, and more devastating in manner. Indeed, one could argue that the June war both made Israel an unsolicited partner in shaping the future of the Hashemite Kingdom of Jordan and made the Palestinian fedayeen a de facto partner in running the state. For more than three years, the East Bank became an arena where three, not just two, contenders wrestled ferociously with each other. The entanglement of these three actors invariably brought about fear, violence, and suffering for all of them. In addition to weapons, the tactics of intimidation, manipulation, and diplomacy were also lavishly employed. This fierce contest on the East Bank revealed important realities that have not yet been sufficiently analyzed in the quest for peace in the Middle East. These realities include the fact that three nationalisms exist on both sides of the River Jordan, no one of which can be eliminated by the other two. If peace is ever to reign, all three must find a way to coexist on equal footing.

Within the context of this bloody interplay (1967–71), each party developed short-term concerns and intermediate goals that determined its agenda and policies. Israel's main objective was to keep the West Bank under control. In the summer of 1969, Hisham Sharabi, an Arab-American and professor of history at Georgetown University, wrote in his paper "Palestinian Guerrillas: Their Credibility and Effectiveness":

> Following the 1967 war, one of the first things the Israeli occupation authorities did was to facilitate investigation by various social scientists of the conditions and psychological attitudes of the Arab inhabitants of the West Bank of the Jordan River and the Gaza Strip. . . . Motivated primarily by instrumental considerations, the analysts seem to have been influenced in their conclusions more by the need to control than to understand.[11]

To attain its goal, Israel on the one hand adopted a repressive security policy while on the other it developed a lenient economic approach toward the Palestinians. The policies worked in tandem to keep the West Bank and Gaza pacified. Israel's security policy, hoping to nip in the bud Palestinian resistance in the occupied territories, included arrests and deportations of Palestinian activists and potential resistance leaders. Israel went even further, invoking a British law that allowed the demolition of houses of those convicted of security offenses. (The law was introduced by the British authority during its mandate in Palestine, before the establishment of the State of Israel in 1948.) This repressive security policy occasionally took the form of curfews imposed on cities, villages, and camps as well as other types of collective punishment.

Israel's economic policy in the West Bank and Gaza was quite the opposite of its security policy: it was intended to make life more bearable for the Palestinians. Hence, the open-bridge policy, which allowed West Bankers to keep their East Bank markets open and helped young, unemployed people find jobs on the East Bank and elsewhere, notably in the Gulf Arab states. It also facilitated the flow of money into and out of the West Bank, especially after Israel replaced all Jordanian banks on the West Bank with Israeli banks, which Palestinians in the first years of occupation almost entirely boycotted. In addition, Israel gradually employed a Palestinian labor force in Israel proper.

A psychological factor also helped to pacify the Palestinians under occupation. I call it "the savior will come from outside" syndrome. Since 1948, the Palestinians had developed a comfortable myth that others from outside their borders would come to their rescue. This myth had its roots in the Arab League's 1948 pledge to liberate Palestine. Even the Arab states' failure to deliver in the 1948 war did not kill the myth, since Nasser, a few years later, took power in Egypt and became the undisputed leader of pan-Arabism; his credibility as a savior was established by nationalizing the Suez Canal Company in 1956 and by standing up to the tripartite British-French-Israeli attack on Egypt. After Nasser's military defeat in the 1967 war, the Palestinian fedayeen, who operated out of neighboring territories, revived the myth by becoming the potential saviors. Besides, the Arabs continued to place their hopes in the international community, especially the Soviet Union, an ally to the Arab cause. With the adoption of Resolution 242, the United Nations itself became another outside savior. Jordan's political discourse toward the West Bankers emphasized the theme of *al-sumud*, steadfastness, which was interpreted by the West Bankers as their share in the struggle against occupation. All of this influenced their lack of rebellious behavior for two decades. Many Western journalists were so puzzled by this passive behavior, which tolerated the building of Israeli settlements, that some of them mistakenly described the West Bankers as "docile." That myth was punctured only in 1987 with the *intifada* (the Palestinian uprising), which became a glorified milestone in the history of the Palestinian national struggle and a turning point in the Israeli-Palestinian conflict.

Israel, which did not want to recognize the existence of a Palestinian people, did not engage in serious political dialogue with the West Bankers during the four years following the June war.

The West Bankers, for their part, likewise refrained from serious political dialogue. They continued to emphasize during this period that they were part of Jordan. This policy was comfortable for the West Bankers because it protected them from punishment from the big rivals, Jordan, Israel, and the PLO. If they reached a unilateral deal with Israel—which, after all, was not offering them a specific formula—Jordan would punish them by terminating unilaterally the open-bridge policy, while the PLO would launch a terrorist war against their leaders.

Meanwhile, Fatah had become the dominant organization in the PLO, especially after Arafat was elected chairman of the Executive Committee in February 1969. In fact, Arafat's election was the culmination of Fatah's efforts to be recognized by both the Palestinian people and the Arab governments as the leader of the Palestinian struggle. Cobban writes:

> Hand in hand with Fateh's military efforts after the June defeat went its efforts to gain political recognition in the Palestinian and inter-Arab arenas for the role of the guerrilla action in general, and the role of Fateh in particular. On 9 December 1967, Fateh presented a memorandum to a conference of Arab Foreign Ministries in Cairo expressing concern at the "misleading statements" made by Shuqairi and demanding the closure of Arab information media to him.[12]

Fatah resumed its guerrilla war against Israel less than two months after the Arab defeat. Such a war required financing, weapons, training, a staging ground, and a safe haven for planning and preparation. The East Bank, where Fatah received support and sympathy from almost all the people (Transjordanians and Palestinians), represented the ideal staging ground for the fedayeen.

In the immediate postwar period, East Bankers were left with just one worry—Israeli retributive acts—but they were willing to suffer these as the price of regaining their lost dignity. A year later, however, this support had quietly begun to crumble. The East Bank was not entirely a "safe" haven. Though the inhabitants were sympathetic and supportive of Fatah, the government was cautious, reserved, and reluctant for good reasons. Thus, Fatah had to maintain a delicate balance between the people's support and the qualms of government leadership. Fatah leaders in the beginning were equally cautious in considering the East Bank a safe haven. They knew that their strategy conflicted with that of the host country, and this made them distrust the government. The seeds of this distrust had been sown before the war. In addition, the fedayeen certainly knew that their activity against Israel would provoke increasingly ruthless reprisals, which Jordan could not long endure. Nonetheless, when Fatah started to establish its bases along the cease-fire line, they were friendly with the Jordanian officers and soldiers with whom they cohabited in the Jordan Valley and the surrounding hills. The Jordanian army reciprocated with sympathy and assistance. Encouraged by the army's attitude and the people's genuine support, the fedayeen gradually abandoned their caution, if not their distrust. One of the safeguards Fatah sought was to establish rapport with Transjordanian community leaders, yet without incorporating Transjordanians into its cadres. This tactic was compatible with Fatah's basic principle of conducting an independent Palestinian struggle.

> To avoid appearing as a regional [purely Palestinian] organization, Fatah established rapport and alliances with Transjordanian figures. Part of its activity was centered on inviting sympathetic figures to attend the PNC meetings as observers . . . Hawatmeh [the secretary general of the Popular Democratic Front for the Liberation of Palestine] was the only Transjordanian who was accepted as a member of the PNC on the grounds that he was the leader of a Palestinian organization. . . . In the midst of this tide [the rising strength of the fedayeen] some of those Transjordanians volunteered to put on the fedayeen uniform, and a number of them who were high-ranking officials even came to their offices in this uniform.[13]

Fatah won the public to its side temporarily, but its relations with Arab governments remained complex. Nasser, like King Hussein, was fully aware of the inherent contradiction between his goal and Fatah's goal. Fatah needed Nasser because he remained the prominent Arab leader, setting the tone for Arab policy toward Israel. Fatah's attempts to gain his support bore fruit after al-Karama (a military confrontation on March 21, 1968, between Israel on the one hand and Jordan and the fedayeen on the other.) According to Shemesh:

> Nasser regarded [fedayeen] activities as an integral part of the military struggle against Israel. He classified Egyptian military activity on the canal front into different stages of escalation. In April 1968, a first official meeting took place between Nasser and the Fatah leadership, agreement being reached on aid and coordination; on April 10, 1968, he emphatically declared for the first time his support for and intention of aiding the Palestinian resistance. Nasser saw [fedayeen] activities in the occupied territories as an important way of harassing Israel.[14]

The Fatah alliance with Nasser withered by the end of July 1970. The Palestinian fedayeen staged demonstrations in Amman in protest at Nasser's acceptance on July 23, 1970, of the Rogers Plan, a U.S. peace initiative. (William P. Rogers was U.S. secretary of state during the first Nixon administration.) One particular demonstration "humiliated Nasser and caused him, in his anger, to send Hussein a message which the king wrongly interpreted as backing from Cairo to move against the fedayeen at a time of his choosing."[15] Arafat discussed the demonstrations with Alan Hart in 1988 and said that "it [the demonstration] was very rude, very offensive, very stupid. It was also our fatal mistake. Nasser was our protector. . . . Nasser was dealing with us as a godfather."[16]

When by the end of 1967 the fedayeen had become synonymous with Arab resolve, nationalism, courage, and dignity, Syria decided to establish its own fedayeen organization consisting mainly of the Palestinian Ba'athists. In Jordan, this organization (al-Sa'iqa) became the military wing of the Ba'athist party, which was banned in that country. In December 1968, the Jordanian Ba'athists loyal to the Iraqi Ba'ath formed their own organization, called the Arab Liberation Front (ALF), which was to be trained, armed, and financed by Iraq. But the most important organization was the Popular Front for the Liberation of Palestine (PFLP), which arrived on the scene in December 1967. It constituted the major rival to Fatah within the Palestinian resistance. Its leader, George Habash, was a Palestinian refugee physician, a militant Arab nationalist, and later a Marxist-Leninist. Nayef Hawatmeh, a Transjordanian and a prominent figure in the PFLP, broke off with a group of his supporters to establish their own fedayeen group late in 1968, the Popular Democratic Front for the Liberation of Palestine (PDFLP), and it became more Marxist-Leninist than the PFLP.

Ironically, then, Fatah found itself both competing and cooperating with Palestinian organizations controlled by other Arab governments. Even the PFLP relied on South Yemen as its Arab government sponsor. All of them were offshoots or extensions of revolutionary pan-Arabist parties. They espoused socialism and believed in overthrowing the "reactionary" Arab regimes, which included Jordan's. Cobban writes:

> The core ideology of Fateh . . . included a stress on Palestinian non-intervention in the internal affairs of existing Arab states, but this concept was not shared by many of the other Palestinian guerrilla groups gaining influence in Jordan in the late 60s. The PFLP still clung to the pan-Arabist ideological approach of its Arab Nationalists' Movement origins; the DFLP, despite Fateh's midwifery to its birth, was soon thereafter calling for the establishment of soviets . . . in some areas of northern Jordan; Saiqa and the Arab Liberation Front were the Palestinian guerrilla sections of respectively the pro-Syrian and the pro-Iraqi wings of the (pan-Arabist) Ba'ath Party respectively, and so on. For all these groups, a confrontation with Hussein . . . was considered not only desirable, but also ideologically necessary. Thus, in direct contradiction to Fateh's long-held ideology, throughout late 1969 and the first half of 1970, the Palestinian guerrillas' challenges to Hussein's authority multiplied as rapidly as their traffic-control roadblocks spread throughout more and more of his capital.[17]

Why didn't Fatah crack down on these groups, especially the PFLP, or unify them by force? Sharabi touched on this issue as early as 1969:

From the standpoint of Fatah, the PFLP represented an ideological, doctrinally committed party. Insisting on the futility of ideological commitment at this stage of development, Fatah stood for a broad national front. Its leaders did not wish to alienate important portions of the population whose backing and financial support were essential to the development of the movement at least in its initial phases. . . . Despite its pragmatism, Fatah has tended, partly as a result of pressure from its own leftist elements and partly because of criticism by the PFLP, to give increasing attention to political organization and to develop more focused political positions. The transformation of the guerrilla nucleus into a political organization was under way much earlier than anticipated.[18]

Sharabi was right. If he had written his report six months later, he would have said that the transformation of the guerrilla nucleus into a political organization had already transpired. The confrontation with Jordan was accelerated because of this early transformation. By early 1970, the leftist ideologies reigned. The fedayeen discourse in Jordan had become considerably political, revolving around the fedayeen's political dispute with King Hussein. The more ruthlessly Israel hit the fedayeen bases, the more the fedayeen moved into Amman and other cities, the more political they became, and the more ideology displaced resistance. Hart wrote in 1988:

> The majority view among Fatah's top leaders was and still is that Fatah should have used as much force as necessary to isolate and control the leftists and radical groups to prevent them provoking a confrontation with Hussein. Very candidly, Hani [Hani al-Hassan, one of Fatah's leaders] said: "I think we lost Jordan because Arafat refused to discipline the leftists. I think we were right to debate with the leftists and radicals without putting any pressure on them, but when we decided our line, which was to cooperate with Hussein, we should have disciplined and punished those who did not follow it and who broke the many cease-fire agreements we made with the king."[19]

The third actor on the East Bank scene was the major one: Jordan itself. Politically, King Hussein had to deal with four interrelated fronts simultaneously: the foreign, the Arab, the West Bank, and the local fronts. Any action on one of the four fronts would immediately provoke a reaction on one or more of the other three.

The king felt he had no choice but to go along with the political solution backed by the Khartoum Arab consensus. The implementation of Security Council Resolution 242 was his objective. Nasser's partnership was essential, because it guaranteed the maintenance of the Khartoum consensus. In turn, King Hussein was an essential partner to Nasser because Jordan was the only Arab state besides Egypt that had accepted Resolution 242 and because Hussein was more acceptable to the Western countries as the Arab interlocutor than Nasser.

The relations between Jordan and Syria continued to be characterized by tension and distrust. In the first place, Syria had not participated in the Khartoum Arab consensus, calling instead for the "popular liberation war" and becoming the major support base for the fedayeen, though they were not allowed to use Syrian territory as a staging ground in their operations against Israel. Jordan tried to improve relations with Syria and to coordinate the two governments' policies concerning fedayeen activities. For this purpose, in the summer of 1968, I accompanied a senior Jordanian intelligence officer on a visit to Colonel Abdul-Karim al-Jundi, the Syrian director of intelligence in Damascus.

The main theme on which the senior Jordanian officer focused was that it was in the best strategic interests of Syria not to lose Jordan—yet if the fedayeen groups continued their increasingly undisciplined behavior, there might come a day when there would be neither Palestinian resistance nor the State of Jordan. The fedayeen lack of discipline made it possible for Israel's agents to penetrate these groups and for these groups to cause chaos in Jordan. Jordan's intelligence had already uncovered a number of such agents. Jordan's suggestion was that the two governments should coordinate their policies in order to discipline the fedayeen and secure genuine and effective resistance. Though Colonel al-Jundi expressed his understanding of the Jordanian position, this coordination did not materialize.

The Iraqis, who had sent troops to Jordan on the eve of the June war, now kept one division on the East Bank at Jordan's request. When Iraq formed its own fedayeen group, these forces supplied this new group with weapons and remained their immediate sponsor. As for the other Arab states, the king kept up the best possible relations with them in order to maintain Arab consensus.

In the international arena, the king's peace diplomacy followed two parallel lines. First, he focused on maintaining direct contact with the Big Four to generate their pressure on Israel to implement Resolution 242. Then he had to deal with the UN secretary-general's special representative.

The United States was obviously the most important and influential of the Big Four. Between 1967 and 1970, the United States was making the transition between the Johnson and Nixon administrations. Under Johnson, nothing tangible happened along the path of peacemaking in the Middle East except the adoption of Security Council Resolution 242. William Quandt, professor of political science and director for Middle Eastern affairs on the National Security Council staff under the Carter administration, writes:

Johnson and his advisers were mindful of how Eisenhower had dealt with the Israelis after the Suez War. They were determined not to adopt the same strategy of forcing Israel to withdraw from conquered territories in return for little in the way of Arab concessions. The need, as American officials saw it, was to establish a diplomatic framework for a peace settlement, and then to allow time to pass until the Arabs were prepared to negotiate to recover their territories. Johnson apparently did not believe that the U.S. should launch a high-level, intensive peacemaking effort immediately.[20]

The Johnson administration's diplomatic framework was based on the five points Johnson spelled out on June 19, 1967, which were incorporated into Security Council Resolution 242. But time passed without any tangible result. Quandt writes:

> The key areas of disagreement between Israel and Arabs, as well as between the U.S. and the Soviet Union, rapidly emerged. The Arabs insisted upon full Israeli withdrawal from newly occupied territory prior to the end of belligerency. Israel, on the other hand, held out for direct negotiations and a "package settlement" in which withdrawal would occur only after the conclusion of a peace agreement. The Soviet Union generally backed the Arab position, whereas the U.S. agreed with Israel on the "package" approach, but was less insistent on direct negotiations.[21]

What complicated the execution was the fact that the text of Resolution 242 was ambiguous, citing "withdrawal of armed forces from occupied territories." According to Quandt, "the ambiguity was intentional and represented the maximum that Israel was prepared to accept. The resolution fell just short of calling on Israel to withdraw from all territories and on the Arabs to make full peace with Israel. Much of the diplomacy of the subsequent years revolved around efforts to make more precise and binding the deliberately vague language of Resolution 242."[22]

Satisfied though King Hussein seemed after Security Council Resolution 242 had been adopted, the path was not as smooth as he had hoped. He had hoped that an Israeli withdrawal from the West Bank would preclude the growth of Palestinian resistance in Jordan and the eventual domination of its extremist line of thinking and action. But Israel was in no hurry. It did not want to see the Eisenhower precedent repeated. Time was on its side, because the armies of the three Arab countries who wanted Israel to withdraw lay in ruins. Israel wanted the Arabs to negotiate directly, and it aimed at full peace.

The king invested much time trying to urge the Johnson administration either to put pressure on Israel to implement 242 or to come up with a workable initiative. According to Quandt:

Johnson was clearly preoccupied with Vietnam . . . and in late March he announced his intention not to seek the presidency for another term, a decision which set off an intense political campaign within his own party and, after Hubert Humphrey's nomination, between the two parties. In this atmosphere, major initiatives for peace in the Middle East could not be expected. Instead, Johnson acted to ensure that the post 1967 status quo would not be disrupted by Soviet arms shipments to Syria and Egypt.[23]

THE FAILURE OF JARRING'S MISSION

With the U.S. administration preoccupied with presidential elections domestically and Vietnam externally, Ambassador Jarring, the UN's representative, filled the diplomatic vacuum. Jarring's efforts during 1968 brought to the surface two inherent handicaps: one related to Resolution 242 and the other to the Khartoum resolutions, on which the king was leaning in his peace diplomacy. The ambiguity of 242 made it possible for Israel to adopt a maximalist position, while the Khartoum's three "no's" made it difficult for Egypt and Jordan to meet the two Israeli conditions of direct negotiations and full peace. Although Jordan's and Egypt's acceptance of 242 implied their acceptance of the Israeli state, Israel tended to consider this major concession the fruit of its military victory rather than a positive and fundamental shift in the Arab position. The Arab concession was a fruit of Israel's victory, but given the nature, origins, and cultural implications of the Arab-Israeli conflict, it would have been wiser and much more constructive for Israel to appreciate and build on the Arab concession rather than to bask in the ecstasy of victory. This acceptance marked the vital turn in the course of the Arab-Israeli conflict without which the peace process would not have been possible. Unfortunately, Israel still fails to appreciate this Arab concession, which strikes deep in the Arab psyche. Israeli appreciation of the Arabs' concession is the key to lasting peace and full normal relations between Israel and the Arabs. This appreciation would not consist merely of a verbal compliment accorded the Arabs. Rather, it would involve a change in attitude and, consequently, in the Israeli political position, especially vis-à-vis the Palestinians, so that Israel would no longer focus on securing the maximum booty and would instead concentrate on attaining coexistence and a lasting peace. What Israel, the Arab governments, the United States, and the world at large call "snags" in the peace process and normalization are in my opinion rooted in this issue.

In brief, the Arab interpretation of 242 fell short of what Israel called for, while Israel's interpretation went far beyond what Jordan and Egypt could accept. Jarring's contacts with the concerned parties revealed this early in 1968. The more he explored their positions, the more issues were raised. In March 1969, Jarring sent written questions to the parties. The answers of the three parties reflected the wide gap between the Israeli position and that of Jordan.

Having received the discouraging answers, Ambassador Jarring went back to his post in Moscow as the Swedish ambassador in April 1969.

JORDAN'S QUANDARY

In late 1967 the East Bank stage was properly set for the PLO, Israel, and Jordan to perform their bloody drama.

The policies of Fatah emanated from the following five convictions: (1) the Palestinian resistance (led by Fatah) was the representative of the Palestinian people; (2) the West Bank was a Palestinian, not a Jordanian, territory; (3) Israel was the enemy that should be fought; (4) King Hussein was a rival, but it was possible to force him to serve the PLO's goals; and (5) the unity of the Palestinian factions was necessary to protect the Palestinian armed struggle.

Israel's policies within the triangular interplay also emanated from five convictions: (1) there was no such entity as the "Palestinian people"; (2) the partner with which Israel should continue to engage in diplomatic activity toward a peaceful settlement of the conflict was Jordan; (3) Israel should sustain its ambiguous position toward the future of the West Bank; (4) fedayeen resistance should be nipped in the bud; and (5) Jordan should be forced to forbid fedayeen activities.

King Hussein's policies likewise emanated from five convictions: (1) the West Bank was the second half of the Hashemite Kingdom; (2) he was the representative of the West Bank in the regional and international arenas; (3) the Palestinian resistance groups were not representative but could be a helpful instrument in ending Israeli occupation of the West Bank; (4) any Israeli-PLO dialogue or agreement should be precluded because it would be at the expense of Jordan's very existence; and (5) Israel was an adversary yet also a peace partner.

Examining these convictions, we can see that there was no point of convergence between Israel and Fatah, while there were two points of convergence between Jordan and Israel—namely, that the PLO was not representative of the West Bank and that a peaceful settlement should be arranged. These two points of convergence obviously strengthened the

PLO's distrust of Jordan—so much so that all of King Hussein's efforts to use the fedayeen to forward the peace process were destined to fail.

In this context of conflicting convictions, the fedayeen had to take the initiative in activating the violent interaction among the three actors, if for no other reason than to assert its very raison d'être. That the fedayeen movement, which operated out of Jordan, was in Jordan's view a political adversary yet also a potential ally in putting pressure on Israel and that Israel was an adversary yet also the ultimate peace partner placed Jordan in a messy and confused position. Jordan's quandary grew increasingly tangible with the waning of hope for an imminent Israeli withdrawal and with the growth of the fedayeen movement in Jordan, especially the PFLP, PDFLP, ALF, and al-Sa'iqa, which I will henceforth call the "synthetic groups." (I call them *synthetic* because they were offshoots of ideological political parties, and they neither maintained the essential qualities of political parties nor did they become purely freedom fighters. They were a blend of the two with distinctly new objectives and means.)

Jordan's quandary was best expressed by King Hussein in an interview conducted by a BBC correspondent in May 1968:

> Correspondent: It seems that your Majesty's position on the fedayeen is a hard one. A while ago you criticized their actions, now you look as if you have turned to support them. What is your real position?
>
> The King: I believe that the issue is one of a people who have lost everything. They practice their right of resistance because the peace efforts have failed to make any progress. By resistance they [the fedayeen] want to demonstrate to the world that the problem is still there. . . . Nevertheless, I am against lack of discipline and disorder. . . .
>
> Correspondent: It seems that you support the fedayeen and you only wish to see them better organized?
>
> The King: I am not necessarily supportive. But at the same time, I cannot be responsible for the safety of occupying forces in the West Bank. If those forces are not there or if they withdraw in implementation of S.C. Resolution 242, there will be no problem.[24]

Throughout the three years that followed the June war, Israel and the fedayeen initiated violence. Through their guerrilla war against Israel, the fedayeen asserted their reason for existence. Israel's reprisals set the pace for the fedayeen's movement into the Jordanian cities and inadvertently stimulated the transformation of their goals and concerns. In this interplay, Jordan was reactive and sustained the biggest losses. As a result, Jordan's major goal of regaining the West Bank was supplemented by a mounting desire to reduce hostilities on its territory and sustain the rule of law, which was eroding as the fedayeen developed into a parallel authority. Indeed, changing the defiant behavior of the fedayeen became the king's obsession.

Israel's contribution to the transformation of the bloody drama in Jordan occurred in three stages. The first involved blocking off the cease-fire line in an attempt to prevent fedayeen infiltration into the occupied West Bank or Israel. The second included the escalation of air strikes against and shelling of fedayeen bases wherever they existed. And the third consisted of striking the Jordanian infrastructure and hurting Jordanian citizens— Transjordanians in their villages and Palestinians in the refugee camps. Throughout the three stages, the Jordanian army's positions and fortifications along the cease-fire line and behind it were targets of Israeli attacks; the Jordanian army engaged almost daily with Israeli forces across the River Jordan or with Israeli airplanes during their attacks on army positions and fedayeen bases. This engagement helped forge an intimate cooperative relationship between the army and the fedayeen, contrary to what Israel had expected. Aware of this situation, the Israeli prime minister on February 12, 1968, warned Jordan against shelling Israeli positions. He said, "Israel's patience has its limits, for the blood of its soldiers and citizens cannot go without revenge."[25] Later, when the Israeli attacks increased in intensity, the army started to resent the fedayeen operations, which were viewed as nothing more than provocation to Israel to strike the army and East Bank villages from which a sizable portion of the military came. In other words, as of late 1968, the army began to view the fedayeen as accomplices with Israel rather than as the army's allies. The fiercer the Israeli strikes, the more the king's call for coordination with the fedayeen made sense and the more the fedayeen activity looked ineffectual.

The fedayeen activity fell into three stages in conformity with Israel's escalation of its reprisals. The first stage was mainly marked by the fedayeen crossing the cease-fire line to operate against Israeli targets in the occupied West Bank and Israel proper. The second was mostly marked by the fedayeen shelling Israeli settlements, positions, and patrols across the cease-fire line. And the third stage was the massive movement of the fedayeen into Jordanian cities and refugee camps. During this stage the fedayeen activity became mostly political, and the extremist discourse of the synthetic groups began to prevail.

In this military and political context, the Jordanian government's activity was three-pronged. It had to keep the West Bankers under remote control lest they become pro-PLO or reach a separate deal with Israel.

Thus the open-bridge policy was maintained, and relations with the West Bank community leaders and functionaries were sustained. The king never ceased to stress in his speeches and statements the unity of the two banks and to promise the West Bankers salvation.

The government also had to cope with the mounting Israeli military attacks and their damaging effects, morally and physically.

Finally, Jordan had to deal with the fedayeen organizations. This activity, which was almost entirely in the king's sphere, also went through three stages. In the first, the king attempted to win the hearts and minds of the fedayeen by persuasion, appeal, and appeasement. In the second, the king tried to subordinate the fedayeen to the law of the land, and in the third the king decided to eliminate the synthetic groups and control the fedayeen activity.

With a new American administration under President Nixon, with Jarring back at his post in Moscow, and without the basic conditions or resources necessary to execute a war with Israel, King Hussein was left alone to deal with the rapidly deteriorating internal situation in Jordan. Nasser, his ally, had started to lose hope of a peaceful effort to regain the Sinai and now raised the slogan "What was taken by force cannot be regained but by force." By mid-July 1969 Nasser charted his own course to regain the occupied Sinai.

The king, who had also begun to lose hope of securing a total Israeli withdrawal from the West Bank, could not raise this slogan, not only because Jordan could not afford a war but also because it was so dangerous, since it would nurture the already volatile mood built by the fedayeen activity and the media.

9

The Battle for Jordan

The army-fedayeen honeymoon was short-lived. The Jordanian army and Palestinian fedayeen embraced each other as comrades in arms in September 1967, then parted in mutual resentment seven months later, competing over who deserved the glory for a battle that they had fought jointly against Israel. But the state-fedayeen relationship had been ruptured even earlier. The three-year process of conflict between the two, marked by tension, changes in attitudes and priorities, agreements, clashes, and an all-out confrontation, would shape the future Palestinian-Jordanian relationship. Israel, meanwhile, continued to be an actor in this process through the inevitable triangular interaction. After the short honeymoon, the symbiotic relationship between Jordan and the fedayeen went through three stages: the rift, the polarization, and the showdown.

THE RIFT

As noted in chapter 8, the fabric of the Jordanian-fedayeen relationship had two weaknesses—the conflicting goals and the conflicting means of the two entities. The fedayeen armed struggle invited Israeli reprisals, which most of the time did not distinguish between fedayeen and nonfedayeen or between Transjordanians and Palestinians. The two major concerns for nonfedayeen civilians were their security, especially of course as it related to life or death, and their means of earning a living. Israel's reprisals, which frequently disrupted the ability of the state to satisfy these needs, aroused both the people's and the government's indignation, first against Israel and later against the fedayeen.

Among the hundreds of Israeli attacks on the East Bank, I will select two for analysis here because of their impact on the rift between Jordan and the fedayeen.

The first one occurred in February 1968, when Israeli long-range artillery and airplanes attacked thirteen villages in Irbid Governorate and one refugee camp in the Jordan Valley. The death toll reached fifty-six, including ten soldiers. Eighty-two others were injured, and dozens of houses were demolished. The implicit message of the attack was that civilians (both indigenous and refugees) would be as much a target as the fedayeen as long as the civilians gave support and shelter to the fedayeen. The attack was so devastating that the king had to address the nation and warn that "anyone who chooses to operate from our territory should do that through us and according to our planning."[1]

The next day, the minister of the interior stated: "We shall not allow any group to act on its own in such an extemporaneous manner. The government is determined to protect the security of Jordan and to establish the rule of law."[2] The statement provoked a wave of protest against the government among the fedayeen and their supporters. Two days later, Prime Minister Talhuni announced that he disagreed with the minister's statement. The government backed off, and the fedayeen concluded that opposing governmental attempts to subordinate them to the law of the land would pay off. Still, it was obvious that both the king and the minister blamed the fedayeen, not Israel, for the attack.

The major effect of the February 15 Israeli attack was the government's evacuation of refugees and local inhabitants, in response to their demand, from the fertile valley to the safer highland. The government established a new camp for them and started to dispense relief rations. As a result, agricultural production fell immediately, and Transjordanians became refugees for the first time.

The second and most significant Israeli attack was on al-Karama on March 21, 1968. Al-Karama was a refugee camp established in the Jordan Valley in 1949 that had developed into a flourishing agricultural village.

Two days before the attack, the Jordanian chief of military intelligence warned Fatah leaders of an imminent Israeli attack on the fedayeen bases in the valley. He recommended that they evacuate their bases, because their light weapons were no match for the Israeli tanks, artillery, and air force. Fatah leaders refused to evacuate the village and decided to fight. In its attack, Israel used armored force, heavy artillery, and airborne troops. The Jordanian army engaged the attackers in an attempt to stop the advance. The front of engagement extended thirty miles along the River Jordan. Israeli paratroopers engaged the fedayeen in the village where they were entrenched. The fedayeen fought bravely, sustaining more than a hundred casualties. The Jordanian army, which used tanks, artillery, infantry, and special forces, had not fought an army-to-army battle since the June war. They too fought selflessly and obstinately to hold their ground and repel the Israelis, as though they wanted to avenge their military defeat on the West Bank nine months earlier. The Israelis occupied the village and destroyed the fedayeen bases in a fierce battle, during which Israel asked for a cease-fire from Jordan. Jordan refused to accept the cease-fire until the Israeli force withdrew. Under Jordanian heavy fire the Israelis withdrew, leaving behind nineteen destroyed vehicles, including tanks. Two days later those vehicles, as well as some Israeli weapons, were placed on display in one of Amman's squares, where citizens streamed to see them.

The battle at al-Karama was the most significant military episode in the triangular interaction after the 1967 war. At al-Karama, the three parties engaged in a fifteen-hour battle with Jordan and the fedayeen fighting against Israel. After the battle, the two allies continued to fight among themselves; they were embroiled in psychological warfare over who had fought the battle and who had won it.

Al-Karama allowed the Jordanian army to regain its self-confidence. From the king's point of view, the battle rehabilitated the army. It provided him with solid credentials to ask for more Arab financial assistance to sustain Jordan's "steadfastness" and to provide the army with more modern weapons. To the Transjordanians, who had not been able to fight for their independence, al-Karama was a central event in the Transjordanian national narrative.

It is not surprising, therefore, that in Jordan nowadays only three national monuments take human form. The first is a horseman in the traditional figure of Saladin wearing a helmet and brandishing a sword (it is in a square in Kerlak, a town known for its Crusaders' castle, which Saladin destroyed in the twelfth century); the second is a horseman in a traditional Arab outfit placed at the main entrance to Parliament; and the third is a soldier with a helmet on his head and a rifle in his hand, placed at an intersection south of al-Karama village. The first symbolizes Jordan's broader identity, namely, Islam; the second symbolizes the Arab Revolt led by the

Hashemites; and the third commemorates the army's heroic accomplishment. March 21 has become a Jordanian national occasion commemorated annually by the army in a ceremony held at the monument. To the Israelis, al-Karama was a military setback on the road to destroying Palestinian resistance. Israelis in Jerusalem and Tel Aviv demonstrated to express their anger with the government because of the losses sustained by Israel's attacking force. Ten days later, Prime Minister Eshkol warned Jordan against supporting the fedayeen. Most important, perhaps, is that al-Karama helped effect a structural change in the hierarchy of the PLO. In the fourth PNC, which convened in Cairo four months later (July 1968), for the first time seats were apportioned to the fedayeen organizations in the PNC. As a result, the real power in the PNC shifted to the fedayeen organizations away from the independents. The fifth PNC (February 1969) elected Yasser Arafat for the first time as chairman of the executive committee of the PLO. At the same time, representatives of fedayeen organizations were allocated a number of portfolios in the PLO Executive Committee. With this change, decision making became the mandate of the fedayeen organizations.

To Fatah, al-Karama was a vindication of its strategy, a source of Palestinian pride, and a solid credential for soliciting Palestinian and Arab support. Indeed, it opened wide the door for thousands of Palestinians to join Fatah. It is interesting to compare two records of al-Karama: one Palestinian, written by Abu Iyad, and the other Transjordanian, written by Suleiman Mousa. Abu Iyad's description reads:

> The whole Arab world celebrated al-Karama battle, considering it a glorious victory. Myths were woven around our feat. Tens of thousands as well as prominent Jordanian figures, military and civilian, came to the town of [al-Karama] to bow before our martyrs who exceeded one hundred in number and who were lined in a big tent. The Palestinian masses were overwhelmed with fervor and pride by al-Karama victory. After decades of submission and humiliation they viewed this victory as the threshold of their liberty. Tens of thousands of old and young people rushed to join Fatah. . . . King Hussein, who had viewed us as rivals and a revolutionary replacement of his regime, had to announce in public two days after al-Karama battle, "All of us are fedayeen."[3]

Suleiman Mousa, on the other hand, writes:

> The Jordanian artillery forced the enemy to retreat, leaving in the battlefield its vehicles, tanks, and killed soldiers, something that never happened before or after in any battle between the Arabs and Israel. . . . With all due respect to the fortitude of the fedayeen, the battle in its reality was the Jordanian army's battle

with its heavy weapons, namely artillery and tanks, from the very beginning to the end.[4]

The two descriptions reflect how al-Karama became an issue of contention between the army and the fedayeen. The distinguished performance of the army at al-Karama placed the Jordanian soldier for the first time on an equal footing with the fedayeen in the realm of sacrifice. And that was the harbinger of the army-fedayeen polarization.

To prevent the rift between Transjordanians and Palestinians from widening, the king made a two-pronged effort: continuing to call for coordination with the fedayeen while hammering home with the people the oneness of the Transjordanian-Palestinian plight.

In his unceasing attempts to persuade the fedayeen of the need for coordination, the king went so far as to call for an Arab summit to discuss the Arab-Israeli situation in view of the new developments. He hoped that a new Arab summit would update the Khartoum resolutions and offer an Arab consensus that would give Jordan and Egypt greater leeway in their joint quest for a political settlement as well as increase Arab financial assistance and set a reasonable parameter for fedayeen activity. The summit that convened in Rabat, Morocco, twenty-one months after al-Karama failed to reach any resolutions.

As for his efforts with the people, the king picked *al-sumud* (steadfastness) as a rallying theme. Now he equated the East Bank with the West Bank in *al-sumud*, an equation that was underscored by Israel's escalated attacks on the East Bank. "The bereaved of Irbid, Salt, and Kerak as well as the orphans of Shuna, al-Karama, and Kufur Assad [all East Bank towns] are like their peers in Jerusalem, Nablus, Ramallah, Hebron, and Jenin [all West Bank towns],"[5] the king said. Since the Transjordanians and Palestinians were suffering the same plight, it only made sense to coordinate their efforts.

Another theme the king employed at this stage was self-determination. This theme appealed not only to the Palestinian nationalists represented by the fedayeen movement but also to Transjordanians and Palestinians at large, who might have been having second thoughts by then regarding the unity of the two banks. The first time the king used this theme was in Amman in December 1968, during an interview with Gavin Young, correspondent for Britain's *Observer* newspaper. When Young asked the king if he was ready to renounce sovereignty over the West Bank and if this would help achieve a settlement, the king quietly answered, "Yes, if that is what the people want."[6]

One month later, the king was interviewed in London by Frank Giles, deputy editor of the *Sunday Times*. When asked about his comment to the *Observer*, the king said, "I can never renounce the West Bank or the Palestinians. This idea of a so-called entity has no reality in fact. The Arabs do not want it, the Palestinians do not want it; it is simply an Israeli diversion. What I am ready to do once the West Bank is restored is to ensure that a greater measure of decentralization is granted to the Palestinians there."[7]

Nevertheless, the king came back to the self-determination carrot in a more official manner seven months later. In his letter of commission to the new prime minister, the king said, "We have to intensify our efforts and potential in the service of one goal, namely the elimination of the effects of aggression, the realization of peace on the basis of right and justice, and the restoration of all our rights, holy shrines, and the usurped land of our nation. Our brethren, who shoulder with us the burden of struggle and sacrifice, shall exercise their right to self-determination once the hideous occupation comes to its end."[8]

THE POLARIZATION

All the king's attempts to prevent the rift from widening failed. The Israeli attacks and reprisals against the fedayeen activity drove the latter back into the cities, where the synthetic groups flourished and violations of law and order increased. Such violations ranged from breaking traffic laws to kidnapping, detaining, and torturing citizens suspected of collaborating with the government and, in some cases, even executing those suspected of collaborating with Israel. Fatah also encouraged its Palestinian-Jordanian supporters to set up organizations that duplicated elements of Jordanian civil society. For instance, a Palestinian Red Crescent society was established side by side with the Jordanian Red Crescent. A fedayeen authority parallel to that of the state was growing. The king's priority changed from bridging the rift to precluding polarization. By the end of 1969, he had given up on changing the fedayeen behavior through appeals, dialogue, and agreements that were never implemented; in early 1970, he decided to try enforcing law and order.

On February 10, 1970, the government made a new attempt to subordinate the fedayeen to the law of the land, just one day after the king had returned from a conference of Arab confrontation states (Jordan, Egypt, Syria, and Iraq) in Cairo (February 7–9). The timing suggested that the king had been given the green light by the leaders with whom he had conferred to put an end to the growing disorder in his country. The cabinet issued a list of twelve items by which the organizations had to abide to restore order. In a show of force, the organizations mounted a huge demonstration in which thousands of their members and supporters took to the streets of Amman, many firing their automatic weapons in the air. The army, in turn, placed checkpoints on the roads leading to the capital. The next day, the king, eager to avoid bloody confrontation, instructed the government to freeze its decision. The majority of the people, who viewed the government's decision to discipline the fedayeen as a saving step, were frustrated by the king's backing off. Disenchantment with the fedayeen was growing among middle-class Palestinians, low-level government employees, small merchants, and those with considerable business success. In light of this growing popular disenchantment, the palace set out to mobilize its supporters, beginning with the Transjordanian tribes. A series of gatherings were held in which tribal chiefs declared their support of the government's decision to restore the rule of law. This move implied that the king had now accepted polarization as a fact. The question was how and when he should use the polarization to subordinate or perhaps even eliminate the synthetic groups. At this point, a new break between Transjordanians and Palestinians emerged.

Scared by the implications of this popular movement among Transjordanians, the synthetic organizations began to mobilize their own supporters among the people. At the fedayeen's behest, three hundred activists (community leaders, former ministers, party members, trade union leaders, and leaders of professional organizations) formed a political national command, which in turn formed a follow-up committee whose task was to prepare for a comprehensive national conference.[9] The idea was to counter the tribal mobilization with a similar popular mobilization and to take the initiative on questions related to Palestinian resistance on both the domestic and foreign levels.

By the end of March 1970, there were two camps: the king, supported by the army and the Transjordanian tribes, versus the fedayeen, supported by the Palestinian refugees in the camps and the cross-communal National Front, consisting of professional associations and political activists of all stripes. The majority of Palestinians and Transjordanians who were disenchanted with the fedayeen's public behavior chose to remain on the fence.

The first test of who had a hold on Palestinian affairs came in April 1970. At that time, Joseph Sisco, the American assistant secretary of state for the Near East and South Asia, visited the Middle East to discuss with Nasser and King Hussein new American peace proposals. While he was holding his scheduled talks with Nasser in Cairo, demonstrations were mounted in Amman against Sisco's upcoming visit to Amman. Sisco canceled his visit at the recommendation of the American ambassador to Jordan. The king, who resented the decision, requested the withdrawal of the American ambassador. Hussein took Washington's response to the ambassador's recommendation as an ominous sign indicating that Washington had doubts about the king's ability to maintain law and order in his country. (Before this episode, the king had already anticipated such an unfavorable international impression. In 1969 one of his themes had been that "the fedayeen activity against occupation is being practiced because we wanted it.")[10] This episode increased the pressure on the king to demonstrate who ruled the country. The fedayeen's success in blocking Sisco's visit made them more difficult to control and fueled the synthetic groups' ambitions. Their political discourse against the regime became more militant. To Syria and Iraq, the episode was of special interest. Both thought the Hashemite regime was on the verge of collapse; thus, they increased their moral and material support to the fedayeen. Iraq went so far as to conceive of a plot against the monarchy in Jordan. According to Abu Iyad, "During an official visit by an Iraqi delegation to Amman in May 1970, three senior Iraqi delegates—Abdul-Khaleq al-Samirra'i, Zeid Haidar [members of the Ba'ath command], and Mahdi Ammash, the Iraqi minister of the interior—met with Arafat and myself. They said to us, 'If you stage a coup to overthrow the royal regime and replace it with a people's government, we shall support you through the Iraqi troops stationed in Jordan.' They had conceived of a plot according to which the Iraqi troops would occupy Zarqa and Irbid [two Jordanian towns] while the fedayeen organizations would win control over Amman."[11] Unlike the Iraqis and Syrians, Nasser looked on the developments in Jordan with great concern. He was disenchanted with the fedayeen behavior, and he hoped that King Hussein would be able to straighten up the situation. He was morally committed to the king, who was also his only partner in the peace process. For him, a stronger Jordan was better than a weaker one.

THE COUNTDOWN

From June 1970 on, the situation in Jordan deteriorated without respite. There was no break between one confrontational event and the next until September 17, when the showdown occurred. This period witnessed intense violations of the law and all kinds of provocations, including the slogan that the PDFLP raised: "No authority above the authority of resistance." The people were expecting the decisive battle at any moment. Some of them started to leave the country. Others moved their families from Amman to their hometowns and villages. A member of the royal family was murdered in her house, an American diplomat was killed, hotels were stormed and placed under the control of synthetic groups, courts were almost paralyzed, and the streets as well as residential neighborhoods in Amman came under control of the fedayeen. Most important, more assaults and acts of humiliation were directed at the soldiers as they moved from one place to another. People almost forgot about the relationship between the fedayeen and resistance; they started to see the organizations as another arbitrary, disorganized authority to be feared but not respected. In brief, the situation resembled a big explosive waiting to be detonated.

The most potentially incendiary event was the attempt on the king's life on June 9, 1970, when his motorcade was ambushed and attacked by machine-gun fire while he was on his way to visit the Intelligence Department. One of his bodyguards was killed, and four others were injured. When the event was announced, some bedouin crack units shelled two refugee camps in Amman. The army reaction was both revealing and alarming. The choice of two refugee camps as the target for the army's anger implied that the army looked on all Palestinians as an extension of the fedayeen and vice versa. This fact was especially alarming to the king, who rightly judged that if he gave leeway to the army and Jordanian tribes, a civil war would break out. To defuse such an explosion, the king addressed the nation, warning the people of sedition. This approach was helpful because it implied condemnation of the attempt on his life without having to point to the actor. In Islamic tradition, "the sedition is dormant, cursed be he who awakens it." The introduction of the theme of sedition made it possible for the king and the fedayeen to blame the crisis on an illusory third party without having to exchange accusations and inflame the situation any further. Two days after the assassination attempt, the organizations, including Fatah, called for the ouster of the commanders of the Jordanian army and the armored corps, arguing that they were the ones who had stirred up the troubles in the country. Since both were members of the royal family, this fedayeen demand confirmed the king's conviction that the Hashemite regime, rather than Israel, had become the target of the organizations.

The king complied with their request, but at the same time he sent a circular to all army and security units, stating, "Until now we have chosen to keep the army out of Amman. . . . In Amman there are some armed bands that are committing robbery, looting, and killing. . . . Amman is under the worst of circumstances. . . . I accepted to relieve them [the two commanders] of their posts after they had appealed to me to do so. . . . Now I personally assume the direct command of the armed forces. It is the last opportunity. There will be no other opportunity."[12]

The circular not only issued an ultimatum to the fedayeen but also alerted the army to be ready to rescue the capital. But the fedayeen misread the king's response to their demand, taking it as another victory. Fatah, for example, published its unlicensed daily newspaper four days later.

From June 20 until June 22, the king was in Libya to participate in the ceremony marking the American evacuation of the Wheelus Air Base. There the king had the opportunity to explain the situation in Jordan to thirteen fellow Arab leaders. In his briefing, the king distinguished between Palestinian organizations (those who were committed to resistance) and non-Palestinian organizations (the synthetic groups). He also said that he could accept fedayeen along the cease-fire lines but not in the cities. The Arab leaders responded by deciding to form a four-member Arab Reconciliation Committee consisting of Algerian, Egyptian, Sudanese, and Libyan representatives. Notably, neither Iraq nor Syria, which had other agendas, were represented on the committee. The king's resorting to and accepting an Arab committee whose goal was to broker an agreement between Jordan and the fedayeen was less motivated by his belief in its potential effectiveness than by his need to neutralize Arab governments or gain their support in case he had to take action against the organizations. Seeing the situation for themselves, Arab officials would understand the king's case better. In other words, the Arab involvement in solving the Jordanian-fedayeen conflict indicated that the king was nearing the point of decision to destroy the synthetic groups. The fedayeen were no match for the Jordanian army. The problem, to the king, was the potential intervention of Syrian and Iraqi troops in Jordan on the side of the fedayeen. The Arab Reconciliation Committee, after meeting with Jordanian officials, fedayeen leaders, and activists, brokered an agreement on July 10. By the terms of the agreement, the government undertook to consider the Palestinian Central Committee as the body in charge of the fedayeen movement, to permit the fedayeen free activity, and to cancel all emergency measures, in return for the fedayeen undertaking to disband their bases and arms depots in the cities, to respect the law of the land, and to cease carrying weapons in public places. This agreement was supposed to relax the situation, but tension reached another peak on July 26, when Jordan accepted the Rogers Plan.

The gist of the Rogers Plan was for Egypt and Israel to reach a cease-fire for three months, during which the two of them and Jordan would resume peace talks through Ambassador Jarring on the basis of Resolution 242. Once Egypt and Jordan accepted the plan, the fedayeen and their supporters burst into demonstrations in the streets of Amman. The Central Committee issued a statement expressing its disapproval, and Iraq and Syria took a similar position. Radio Baghdad announced on July 29 that all Iraqi troops in Jordan were placed at the disposal of the Palestinian resistance. The reaction to the Rogers Plan accelerated the drift toward the September showdown. To the fedayeen, it was tantamount to a danger signal. According to Quandt, "their position was endangered as President Nasser, their most prestigious backer, was apparently joining Hussein in a political settlement that could only be at their expense."[13] Therefore, the Central Committee decided to undermine the peace initiative by all possible means. Protest demonstrations alone would not do the job. They needed a broader, more cohesive antipeace base, in Jordan and among all Arabs. Obviously, Syria and Iraq sympathized with this orientation. On August 27–28, the PNC convened in an emergency session in Amman to discuss the peace initiative. On August 29, the PNC and the revolutionary Arab forces (the pan-Arab and leftist factions) held a joint session in which they characterized the Rogers Plan as a conspiracy and called for killing it. On September 1, another attempt on the king's life occurred when his motorcade was attacked on his way to the airport to receive one of his children. The next day, the World Symposium on Palestine was held in defiance of the government. These events were covered by the media and attended by a show of force in the streets. The best description of the situation was contained in the king's address to the nation on September 3:

> The citizens are scared and worried of what might happen at any moment as a result of shooting, which exposes innocent people to danger, the public life to damage. People's business and trade have been stalled. The public potential and the state's resources are sustaining big losses. The government's departments, institutions, and schools have ceased to function.[14]

King Hussein was not the only one in a quandary, for Arafat's position was no less difficult. Arafat was aware of the implications of mounting fedayeen defiance to the king's authority. He urged the synthetic groups to stay out of Jordanian politics. He was especially alarmed when the leaders of the PFLP and PDFLP formally advanced proposals at the emergency session of the PNC calling for the overthrow of the royal regime. But Arafat refrained from taking drastic measures to deter these organizations out of his desire to maintain the unity of Palestinian resistance. The reasoning of the fedayeen during this period is best portrayed by Abu Iyad. In an emergency meeting held by the Central Committee of Resistance in Amman in July 1970, Abu Iyad asked two questions: "Do you want to take over the authority in Amman? If you do, does your assessment of the balance of power indicate that we shall win?" The majority answered the two questions in the negative. In view of their answers, Abu Iyad suggested that they should relax tension with the king before it was too late. When he called on them to go with him to the royal palace to negotiate an accord with the king, "the majority did not move." Abu Iyad concludes from this encounter that "the majority of the Central Committee gave priority to tactics over strategy" and that his colleagues held a false assumption that the king would not "risk a massacre in his capital" and that "the royal army or at least part of it, would disobey the orders to fire arbitrarily at the people. As for me, my conviction was quite the opposite."[15] No sooner did the fedayeen complete their propaganda-oriented conferences than the PFLP members on September 6 and 9 hijacked a number of airplanes, three of which (American, Swiss, and British) were flown to Dawson Field in the desert east of Amman. More than four hundred passengers and crew became hostages. The PFLP demanded the release of Palestinian prisoners from Swiss, British, and Israeli prisons. The PFLP, releasing most of the passengers but keeping fifty-four in custody, then blew up the airplanes. The king was furious. Dozens of journalists arrived in Amman to cover the event. President Nixon urged a strong response. The Eighty-Second Airborne Division was placed on semi-alert. The fedayeen controlled the streets, hotels, and public places in Amman. British journalists, in a joint dispatch, described Amman as a battlefield.[16] One day before the first hijacking operation (on September 5), a scheduled meeting of the Arab League council took place in Cairo. Among its decisions was the reactivation of the Arab Reconciliation Committee, with a fifth member from the Arab League secretariat added to it.

PREPARATIONS FOR THE SHOWDOWN

One afternoon in the summer of 1988, King Hussein, in a reflective mood, was chatting about the difficult days he had faced in the past. I asked him which was the toughest decision he had ever taken. Without hesitation he answered, "Our decision to regain Amman in September 1970."

By mid-September 1970, with the world expecting him to do something to obtain the release of the fifty-four hostages held by the PFLP in his capital, the king was weighing one option against another. While reason was wrestling with emotion, a significant development tipped the balance toward taking drastic action to end the chaos once and for all.

On September 14, the High Council of the Jordanian Trade Union Federation, which was dominated by pro-fedayeen members, decided to stage a strike by all officials and employees of the public and private sectors starting September 19. The strike was to continue until the government responded to their demands and their "national authority" was established in the country. According to the plan, the strike would develop into civil disobedience to paralyze the state, which was already nearly frozen. The fedayeen were in control of most of Amman's streets, so much so that the newly appointed American ambassador to Jordan, Dean Brown, had to be driven in an armored troop carrier from his office to the royal court to present his credentials to the king. The king reacted promptly to the High Council's decision, forming a military cabinet on September 15. By then, he must have conceived of a plan and alerted the army and security forces of this development.

The cabinet consisted of twelve members—three West Bankers and nine East Bankers—representing the various security bodies, such as the army, the Public Security Office, and the General Intelligence Department. The prime minister, Brigadier Mohammad Dawoud, was a West Banker. Retired Field Marshal Habes al-Majali, from an influential tribe from Kerak, was appointed military governor general. Tribal and provincial representation was also taken into consideration. Five district military governors were appointed, making the East Bank tribal representation more comprehensive. The structure of the military cabinet, consisting of East and West Bankers, and the appointments of district military governors were meant to suggest a national consensus on the king's new move.

In contrast with the established tradition in Jordan, where the prime minister designate chooses the cabinet members, the king himself chose the members of the military cabinet. I was the first to be appointed directly by the king, and the second was Brigadier Dawoud—both of us West Bankers. This approach was not arbitrary. In my opinion, the king, known for his caution, intended to conduct a last-minute litmus test of the Palestinian reaction to his move. Wasfi al-Tal was in the king's residence during the formation of the military cabinet, an indication that he coengineered the move.

Right after my appointment as minister of information, I asked al-Tal about the reason for forming a military cabinet. His answer was "*Bidna nu' mur ᶜalayhum* [We are going to bully them (the fedayeen)]." He added that the mere formation of the cabinet would bring them to the negotiating table, where we would have the stronger position. The PFLP and similar groups should be disbanded. They were the cause of the prevailing chaos. Fatah and the PLA were the only sincere fedayeen groups. If Fatah disassociated itself from the insincere ones, Jordan would cooperate.

Thus, the complete liquidation of fedayeen activity was a Jordanian fallback position in case Fatah proved to be recalcitrant and took sides with the synthetic groups. Nevertheless, liquidating all fedayeen activity was the goal of many senior army officers who would be in control right after September.

The king's mandate to the military cabinet was spelled out in his letter of commission to Brigadier Dawoud and his statement on September 16. The king emphasized cooperation between the honest fedayeen activity and the army, as well as the restoration of law and order. A contingency plan had been established in case the synthetic organizations did not comply with the government's requests.

Dawoud, whose office was in the building of the armed forces headquarters, started work on September 16 by contacting Chairman Arafat directly as well as through the chairman of the multilateral Arab Reconciliation Committee, which had brokered an agreement between the outgoing government and the PLO the day before. The gist of this agreement was similar to that of July 10. Dawoud asked Arafat to sit down with him to implement the new agreement. Arafat's answer, which came through a member of the Central Committee at 10:00 P.M., was that the Central Committee of the Palestinian Resistance refused to discuss anything with the military government.

The formation of the military cabinet was interpreted by the Central Committee as a signal that the king was going to liquidate fedayeen activity. Instead of trying to defuse the king's plan, the fedayeen chose confrontation, indicating that they believed either that they would win or that the king would back off. They had a contingency plan too, as one of many documents seized by the army during the hostilities showed. At dawn on September 17, the fedayeen in Amman simultaneously attacked all the enclaves of the security forces in the capital, including the royal palace, the army headquarters, and the offices of Public Security and General Intelligence. The army, already poised for action, embarked on its offensive. On the first day of hostilities, the army used artillery and tank fire to scare the fedayeen into surrender, especially in the refugee camps in Amman. When this was not successful on a large scale, the hostilities turned into street fighting.

THE SHOWDOWN

The battle for Jordan went through two stages. The first took ten days (September 17–27), lasting until King Hussein and Chairman Arafat signed an agreement under the auspices of an Arab summit convened in Cairo. The second (July 12–17, 1971) ended when the army evicted the fedayeen from their last stronghold in the wooded area of Jerash, north of Amman. In reality, the two stages overlapped, because the ten-month period between them witnessed continual clashes. Except for a few hundred Palestinians in the army who defected to the fedayeen camp, the others fought the battle against the fedayeen until the end. Transjordanian fedayeen likewise fought against the army until the end. Large sectors of Palestinians remained aloof from the hostilities. The battle lines between the two communities were not clearly drawn. The notion of the "civil war" crystallized after the showdown of September when

> the differences and divisions between Palestinians and Jordanians were reinforced by myths and countermyths. The Palestinians spoke of huge casualty figures, massacre, and rape, particularly on the part of bedouin units in the Jordanian army. The purging of the security forces and civil service and the army's searches in September's wake increased Palestinians' fears. . . . Jordanians had their own atrocity stories and myths, and these tended to dwell on the dishonesty and ingratitude of the Palestinians. There were stories that soldiers' heads had been chopped off and used as footballs and of soldiers' families being wiped out by guerrillas.[17]

Ironically, a civil war was not fought in September, but the confrontation was conveniently characterized as such by the foreign media as well as by Jordanian and Palestinian nationalists afterward.

During the first stage, the army won control over the whole country except two cities: Irbid and Amman. Arafat declared Irbid Governorate on the Syrian border a liberated area on September 16, one day before the hostilities began. The king, who had decided to evict the fedayeen from the capital first, did not challenge Arafat's declaration because it would have taken him away from his primary target. Arafat appointed an East Banker, also a member of Parliament, as governor general of the "liberated area." This move reflected Arafat's keenness to suggest to the Jordanians that Palestinians were not intent on ruling Jordan. Amman was the hard knot, because it was there that the fedayeen had concentrated their force. They had fortified themselves in public and private houses as well as in the refugee camps in Amman. When the army advanced into the city, it faced strong resistance. Although the army quickly controlled some neighborhoods, the fedayeen were still fighting in most of the city. The casualties were heavy, especially among civilians, whose situation started to grow desperate when the power and running water were shut down and telephones ceased to work. This situation pressured the king to reach a cease-fire with Arafat, who went into hiding to escape arrest by units of the army that were searching for him. A number of other PLO leaders were arrested, including Abu Iyad. From his hideout, Arafat addressed the Arab summit in Cairo on September 22: "There is a sea of blood. Some twenty thousand of our people are killed or wounded. . . . From amidst the dead, the debris and our patient people . . . I appeal to you to move your conference to Amman immediately so that you can see for yourselves the magnitude of the crime and the ugliness of the massacres."[18] Arafat's appeal was widely covered in the press and on radio.

On the same day, the king and Abu Iyad, who was still in custody, reached an agreement for a cease-fire. By the terms of the agreement, the fedayeen had to respect the law of the land, dismantle their bases in the cities, and establish new ones along the borders of the occupied territory. In return, Jordan had to deal with the PLO as the legitimate representative of the Palestinian people and to withdraw the army from the capital and its suburbs. It is obvious that the face-saving item for Fatah was Jordan's recognition of the PLO as the Palestinians' legitimate representative. Jordan announced the agreement on September 23.

The showdown raised deep concern among the Arabs and invited different reactions. Algeria, Syria, and Iraq supported the fedayeen with official statements and media campaigns. Libya and Kuwait suspended their financial assistance to Jordan. Nasser's position was neutral and his approach constructive. His main concern was for the parties to reach a cease-fire as quickly as possible. He appealed to both the king and Arafat to stop fighting, sending his chief of staff to Amman on the first day of hostilities with this message. Neither his emissary nor his appeals bore fruit. When his personal effort failed, he called for an Arab summit, which convened in Cairo on September 22. On September 24, the summit sent a delegation, headed by Numeiri, then president of Sudan, to Amman, where they met with the king and Arafat separately. The delegation supported the agreement reached by King Hussein and Abu Iyad and returned to Cairo accompanied by Arafat in disguise. On the same day, Dawoud, who was representing the king at the summit, resigned as prime minister, and a civilian cabinet was formed on September 26. Ahmad Toukan, a prominent Palestinian figure, was appointed prime minister. His appointment was a renewed signal that the fighting was not between Palestinians and Jordanians but between the state and the fedayeen.

On September 27, the king joined the summit in Cairo, and by the end of the day he and Arafat had signed an agreement. This agreement called for the two parties to terminate all hostilities and media campaigns. The army had to withdraw from Amman to their previous positions. The fedayeen had to evacuate Amman to new bases reflecting the appropriate fedayeen activity outside the cities. A trilateral follow-up committee was established, headed by the Tunisian prime minister Al-Bahi Al-Adgham and comprising a Jordanian representative and a Palestinian representative. Interestingly enough, Arafat chose the lawyer Ibrahim Bakir, a Palestinian-Jordanian and a member of the PLO Executive Committee, for the job. Though this appointment might have been prompted by Arafat's desire to benefit from Bakir's negotiating capabilities, it turned out to be a symbolic event used by Transjordanian nationalists in their argument that "there is nothing called a Jordanian-Palestinian. One is either a Jordanian or a Palestinian. Otherwise, how should we interpret Bakir's negotiations with the Jordanians in 1970 except that he was a Palestinian?"

It was this trilateral committee that ultimately evacuated the fedayeen from Amman and Irbid. One of the measures on which the committee agreed was the regrouping of the fedayeen in the wooded area of Jerash before they moved to their allocated bases.

Nasser's relentless effort between September 17 and 27 to broker a cease-fire agreement between the king and Arafat was interrupted by a Syrian move that put the whole Middle East on the brink of an East-West confrontation. Around midnight on September 18–19, PLA units that were stationed in Syria crossed the borders into Jordan. On the morning of September 20, a Syrian armored brigade with three PLA battalions took positions in the southern plain of Irbid around a vital crossroads. The small Jordanian force in the area engaged them, but by the end of the day the Jordanians had begun to retreat. Early in the evening the military cabinet members were driven in armored troop carriers to the king's residence west of Amman, where he told them that in view of the grave situation in the north, he had given orders to concentrate whatever forces available around Amman to defend the capital. Although the force that was fighting bravely against the Syrians would be reinforced, Jordan might need the help of foreign friends, and the king asked the cabinet to authorize him to call in such a friendly foreign force. After some reluctance, the cabinet authorized the king "to take whatever measure he deems necessary to defend the kingdom, its sovereignty, and independence against any setbacks and threats to its national existence, pan-Arab interest, and the decisive cause [the Palestinian question]."[19]

The United States for some time had been concerned about King Hussein's weakened position vis-à-vis the fedayeen. In September, the United States was especially worried that other actors, such as Israel, Iraq, and Syria, might be drawn into the fighting in Amman. If Egypt were drawn in, a U.S.-Soviet confrontation would become more likely. According to Quandt, "Nixon clearly wanted Hussein to crush the fedayeen, but he also wanted the conflict contained within Jordan. His role, as he saw it, was to encourage Hussein to act, while restraining the Israelis from precipitating military moves. At the same time, an American and Israeli show of force might help to deter the Syrians, Iraqis, and Soviets."[20]

Nixon's first move was to warn against outside intervention. His second move came after the Syrian troops arrived in Jordan on September 19. He ordered the Eighty-Second Airborne and units in West Germany to be placed on high alert, and the Sixth Fleet was ordered further east. American diplomatic contacts with the Soviets were made, stressing that both Israel and the United States might be forced to intervene unless the Syrians pulled back.[21]

The third American move, according to Quandt, was Nixon's authorization on September 21 of National Security Adviser Henry Kissinger to work out a plan for intervention with Rabin, then the Israeli ambassador to the United States. The United States "agreed in principle to an Israeli air and land strike [against the Syrian troops], subject to review at the last moment. The U.S. would not be just an onlooker."[22]

However, the king did not call in friendly forces, nor did the Israeli strike materialize. While the reinforced Jordanian units in the north were engaged again in heavy fighting with the Syrians on September 22, the Jordanian air force effectively attacked the Syrian tanks. On the same day the Syrians began to withdraw. The Jordanian resistance, the ostentatious movement of the Israeli forces toward the cease-fire lines, the American show of force, and the Soviet pressure on the Syrians had all worked together to bring about Syrian withdrawal.

The first stage of the battle for Jordan ended technically on September 27. Nasser died one day later, and a new era dawned in the Middle East.

THE IMPLEMENTATION OF THE CAIRO AGREEMENT

On September 28, the follow-up committee began its work, and on October 28 the king formed a new government whose prime minister was Wasfi al-Tal. This appointment implied that al-Tal would continue the September move by other means—namely, by implementing the Cairo agreement through the follow-up committee. No matter how good had been the intentions of King Hussein and Arafat when they signed the Cairo agreement, the disaffected would mostly set the tone and pace for its implementation. This group included the officers and soldiers who had never forgiven the fedayeen for the latter's humiliating behavior before the showdown and who resented the fact that they had failed to evict them from Amman by force. Obviously, they resented the synthetic groups as well as ordinary fedayeen who had come out of the September battles with a hostile view toward the army. Since both groups existed in the same streets, neighborhoods, roads, and hills, friction was highly likely. Four agreements were reached between the government and the PLO between September 1970 and January 1971. Between September 28, 1970, the end of the first stage, and July 13, 1971, the beginning of the second stage, tension subsided a little, but clashes continued intermittently. Nevertheless, the fedayeen finally abandoned their bases in Amman on April 9, 1971. Then on April 13, the head of the follow-up committee resigned his post, not because the hardest part of the job was done but because he suspected that the government, whose sole concern was to maintain the sovereignty of the state, intended to liquidate the fedayeen in stages.[23]

On July 13, 1971, some army units attacked the fedayeen regrouped in the Jerash area. The commander accused the fedayeen of assaulting farmers in the area and destroying some farms. On July 17, the fedayeen were completely evicted from their last stronghold in Jordan. Some 2,300 fedayeen surrendered, seventy sought and were granted refuge in Israel, and the rest were killed or injured. Those who surrendered were given the choice of retiring to civilian life or being evacuated to Syria. The majority went to Syria, from where they moved on to Lebanon. From the Jordanian point of view, July 17 marked the end of the battle for Jordan. From a fedayeen point of view, the date marked the end of an era in Palestinian history. Abu Iyad writes, "On July 18, the Jordanian minister of information, Adnan Abu-Odeh . . . announced to journalists with rude fluency that the October 13 [1970] agreement between the king and the resistance was null and void. With that, a leaf of our history was turned for good."[24]

THE ASSASSINATION OF WASFI AL-TAL

After their eviction from Jerash, the fedayeen developed a vengeful attitude toward the ruling elite in Jordan. Abu Iyad admits that Fatah created a secret apparatus in Jordan to work toward overthrowing the regime and that he was chosen to run this apparatus. He adds that "since it was impossible to conduct a traditional guerrilla war across the Israeli lines, [the fedayeen] were anxious to practice another type of revolutionary violence, the type that is called 'terrorism' in other contexts."[25]

On November 28, 1971, al-Tal, in Cairo to participate in a regular meeting of the Arab Defense Council, was assassinated by four terrorists. The fedayeen held al-Tal responsible for their cruel eviction from Jerash, since he was the one who had suggested that location for their regrouping. Once they were evicted, they interpreted al-Tal's suggestion as a trap to have them "massacred en masse."

While it is true that al-Tal coengineered the first stage of the September 1970 hostilities with the king, it is not true that he engineered the second stage in July 1971. To the best of my knowledge, al-Tal neither knew nor was consulted about the Jerash operation. Even he was fooled by the army. His pride as prime minister and minister of defense impelled him to claim he had been privy to the army's plan. Al-Tal considered the September move an act aimed at purifying, not liquidating, the fedayeen. He believed that it was in the best interest of Palestinian resistance to be purified of alien bodies such as the synthetic groups. Early in August 1968, al-Tal had sent the king a memo with his suggestions on how to counter Israel's hostile strategy toward Jordan. He had proposed a national plan that would transform Jordanians into productive, fighting people like the people of Carthage in the third century B.C. In his plan he addressed the fedayeen role: "The fedayeen activity should be a part and parcel of this plan. To achieve this objective, the fedayeen should be united under a high command. Besides, they should be provided with training, planning, financing, as well as with men and weapons."[26]

Al-Tal's insistence on going to Cairo was, in my opinion, motivated by a strong urge to acquit himself of the accusation that he was responsible for liquidating all fedayeen activity in Jordan. His credentials for acquittal, as he viewed them, were his participation in the 1948 war as an officer in the Palestine Salvation Army and his "Carthage plan." The military plan he carried with him to the Arab Defense Council was predicated more or less on these ideas and on building a pan-Arab force in which the fedayeen would play an integral part. As Susser notes, "Wasfi al-Tal's position toward Israel was complex and pragmatic. On the one hand, he struggled for the Palestinian cause and described Zionism as 'an aggressive, racist, expansionist, fascist movement, a base for imperialism and a bridge for war against liberation.' On the other hand, al-Tal respected Israel's power and even admired its prowess."[27]

Al-Tal's assassination triggered a wave of anger among Transjordanians. At the time, he was already revered as a Transjordanian national hero. Mousa writes, "There was a general feeling that Wasfi [al-Tal] was killed for the sake of Jordan and the Transjordanians."[28] The current Jordanian nationalists glorify him as the epitome of Jordanian nationalism. He has become a salient part of the Jordanian nationalist narrative.

Al-Tal's assassination also produced a designation that became known all over the world: "Black September." To justify their terrorist act, his assassins used this name to remind the world of the wounds that had been inflicted on the fedayeen in Jordan in 1970–71.

THE OUTCOME

The September showdown had its fallout in Jordan. It was to have far-reaching implications for Jordan's domestic politics over the next two decades. Two of the three Arab states, Libya and Kuwait, that had been committed by the Khartoum resolutions to provide Jordan with a fixed annual financial support now suspended their assistance. Syria closed down its borders with Jordan on July 25, 1971, during the second stage of the conflict, and the closure continued until October 30, 1972. The West Bankers, as the vital Palestinian constituency that the king had been so eager to keep on his side, were adversely affected. They had followed the news reports about the "fierce fighting" with great concern, and these reports were favorable toward Jordan. After the cease-fire, exaggerated stories about the "savage fighting" snowballed, traveling rapidly among the West Bankers and the Palestinians in the diaspora, whose attitudes toward Jordan grew hostile as a result. Nevertheless, West Bank traditional community leaders, businessmen, big farmers, and civil servants who still received their salaries from Jordan continued to maintain normal relations with Amman, since it was instrumental in their lives. Because the working class and the younger generation did not feel that Jordan had this same instrumentality in their lives, they became vocal critics of Jordan and supporters of the PLO. Indeed, these two segments would form the backbone of the *intifada*—the Palestinian uprising against the Israeli occupation in the West Bank and the Gaza Strip—in 1987–91.

As for the East Bank Palestinians, the September showdown had two salient effects. The first was a stronger, though hushed, sense of Palestinian nationalism. The second was a blend of a sense of guilt and of hatred toward the state. Due to their firsthand experience of the conflict, the East Bank Palestinians, unlike the West Bankers, recognized the role of the fedayeen in bringing about the military collision. They felt that they were themselves partly responsible for what had happened because they had not checked the fedayeen excesses. The Transjordanians' sense of guilt toward the Palestinians, which had developed after the June 1967 defeat, was eradicated and replaced by a Palestinian sense of guilt toward Jordan, the state.

It was this sense of guilt that helped the Jordanian government carry out what might be called the mopping-up process. After the September showdown, the government embarked on a purge of the public sector and security services of the fedayeen's supporters (Transjordanians and Palestinians alike). When this process later developed into a de-Palestinianization process, there was no serious collective Palestinian protest. Of course, there were other factors besides the sense of guilt that contributed to this lack of protest—notably, the availability of job opportunities in the Jordanian private sector and the Gulf states.

One important effect of the September 1970 collision was the erosion of the historical alliance of the Transjordanian-Palestinian opposition or the unofficial amalgamation of the intelligentsia. Fatah was almost exclusively a Palestinian organization. The Transjordanians who joined in fedayeen activity found room in the synthetic groups. Fatah, in the eyes of the Transjordanian public, was the main organization that provoked Israel's disproportionate military retaliation from which they suffered (through loss of life or property). The synthetic groups were the main actor that disrupted law and order and humiliated East Bankers' siblings in the army or public security. After the eviction of the fedayeen, it became quite unpopular among Transjordanians to identify with these groups or their goals. The struggle for Palestine declined as the motivating force behind the historical alliance of the Transjordanian-Palestinian opposition. One of the positive effects of this phenomenon, from the Jordanian government's perspective, was the absence of any serious opposition to the Jordanian-Israeli peace treaty when it was concluded in October 1994. The alliance was trying to put itself together once more, not over the "liberation of Palestine" but over "Jordan's normalization with Israel."

Some of the Transjordanian nationalists who believed that the Palestinian-Jordanians constituted a basic threat to the Transjordanians' very identity rather than just to its regime were heartened by the army's accomplishment in 1970–71. They considered this accomplishment to be phase one; phase two would consist of excluding the Palestinians at large, and not just the fedayeen, from Jordan's public sector and political life. Only then would the job be complete. When the mopping-up operation was entrusted to the Mukhabarat (the intelligence service), these Transjordanians established a rapport with the Mukhabarat command and officers. To them, the Mukhabarat was like the army, an embodiment of Transjordanian nationalism. For the first time in the Middle East, the Mukhabarat was looked on favorably by political activists outside the political ruling elite. Those nationalists included professionals, university professors, and former political activists in the opposition. One of them, in a gathering of Transjordanian elite, said that if the Palestinians were to stay in Jordan, they shouldn't be more than unskilled labor employed by Transjordanians. Some of these nationalists went even further by volunteering to give information about their Palestinian colleagues' fedayeen inclinations in hopes that the mopping-up process would target these colleagues. I don't exclude the possibility that such behavior was motivated by selfish urges as well, since these people were aware that the Mukhabarat could recommend them to coveted administrative or political posts. The mopping-up policy, which developed into a process of Transjordanizing the government, gradually phased the Palestinian-Jordanians out of the national consensus.

Although King Hussein came out of September's fighting as the epitome of Transjordanian nationalism, Transjordanians for the first time since the inception of the state in 1921 started to deal with the Hashemite monarch as a first among equals, rather than as the supracommunal Hashemite ruler, whenever an issue dealt with Palestine or the Palestinians. This represented a profound change in attitude. The king continued to be viewed, though, as the supratribal Hashemite monarch if the issue in question was a purely Jordanian one. After the September showdown and especially after the assassination of Wasfi al-Tal, Transjordanians began to believe that the king should stop clinging to his policy of being the official representative of Palestinians on the West Bank. Instead, they felt that they should have a real say in such matters because all issues pertinent to Palestine necessarily had a bearing on Transjordan and its people. Jordan was not only King Hussein's kingdom but also their homeland. After all, Transjordanian combatants had put an end to the threat the fedayeen had posed. This type of Transjordanian national thinking ushered in a new era in Jordan's nation-building process. The integration of Palestinians and Transjordanians started to give way to separation of the two peoples. For the first time Fatah (the PLO), as an advocate of independent Palestinian nationalism, found a Transjordanian party that agreed with its basic ideology. Fatah, which had lost the East Bank as a staging ground for its guerrilla war against Israel, had now won a strong core of Transjordanian activists who believed in an independent Palestinian nationalism, since this implied, in turn, an independent Transjordanian nationalism. Now it was the Jordanian-Palestinians on the East Bank who were torn between the two nationalisms. Concomitant to this ideological split, the gulf between Transjordanians and Palestinian-Jordanians grew wider in the wake of the September showdown.

Though the fedayeen had been evicted from Jordan, they had not been evicted from the minds of Jordanian decision makers. The PLO continued to be a strong influence on all diplomatic activities that the king and the Jordanian government conducted. According to Moshe Shemesh, "the immediate result of the September 1970 crisis was that the issue of Palestinian representation became central to the struggle between the regime and PR [Palestinian resistance]."[29] Israel was only partly relieved. Soon Israel had to engage the bulk of the fedayeen on the Lebanese front. The triangular interplay continued.

10

The Dynamics of Retrogression
The Status of Palestinian-Jordanians

In November 1995, a heated debate over Jordanian-Palestinian relations exploded in the Jordanian press, involving columnists, lawyers, politicians, members of Parliament, and university professors. This debate was brought on by the Oslo Declaration of Principles (DOP), signed by Israel and the PLO in September 1993, and the Jordanian-Israeli peace treaty, signed in October 1994. The two accords dispelled the ambiguity in which the status and destiny of Palestinian-Jordanians had been shrouded by the Rabat Resolution of October 1974, which recognized the PLO as "the legitimate and sole representative of the Palestinian people." The DOP has come to represent a reconciliation between Israelis and Palestinians, in which Israel accepted the establishment of a Palestinian entity on the West Bank and in Gaza, destined to be the Palestinian homeland. In July 1988, King Hussein announced Jordan's disengagement with the West Bank, and the Israel-Jordan Treaty of Peace indirectly confirmed this disengagement. Taken together, the two accords implied that "Jordan is Jordan and Palestine is Palestine," a concept long cherished by

Transjordanian nationalists. The lines having been established, these nationalists could now treat the Palestinian-Jordanians as an alien community whose legal status had to be reconsidered so that the Jordanian identity would not be compromised.

The debate was sparked by two coinciding events. The first was the publication in the Jordanian press in October 1995 of the results of an opinion poll about the type of relationship that should exist between Jordan and the would-be Palestinian entity. The poll, which was conducted jointly by a Jordanian and a Palestinian institute, showed that 74 percent of those questioned were in favor of some kind of union, 22 percent were against, and 4 percent expressed no opinion.

The second event was the king's instruction to the government to resume issuing five-year passports to West Bankers, a procedure that had been halted on July 31, 1988, when the king decided to disengage Jordan legally and administratively from the West Bank. Until the disengagement decision, five-year passports were issued to Jordanian citizens whether they were Transjordanians or Palestinian-Jordanians. In order to distinguish East Bankers (both Transjordanians and Palestinian-Jordanians) from West Bankers, the government issued two-year passports to the latter. The king's 1995 instruction followed the accusations that the then minister of the interior (a Transjordanian) had been depriving many Palestinian-Jordanians who were living in the East Bank of their right to five-year passports. This category of Palestinian-Jordanians were considered Jordanians entitled to five-year passports in accordance with the disengagement decision. After the Oslo agreement, the Ministry of the Interior, which is commissioned to issue passports, did not abide fully by the new arrangement. In some cases, the ministry refrained from issuing five-year passports to Palestinian-Jordanians who were entitled to them. The motivation, it seems, was to reduce the number of Palestinian-Jordanians.

These two events obviously relate to the essence of Transjordanian nationalism, with its proposition that Jordan is for Transjordanians. Though the government stressed that the five-year passports for West Bankers and other displaced persons were for travel only and did not connote nationality, the king's instruction fueled the ongoing debate, which was characterized by four attitudes. The first, professed by Transjordanian nationalists, called for the exclusion of all Palestinians from Jordanian citizenship and for separate Jordanian and Palestinian entities. The second, reflecting the attitude of Palestinian-Jordanians, emphasized their right to full citizenship and equal rights and called for the termination of all forms of discrimination against them. The third attitude was articulated by some pan-Arabists, who argued that the unity of the two peoples was an undisputed principle. The fourth was voiced by the "deferrers," who called for the suspension of the discussion until the Palestinian question was settled.

Of the many articles addressing this debate that were published in the Jordanian press from September to December 1995, I will quote two writers because of their candor in articulating the grievances and concerns of the two communities. The first is Marwan al-Saket, a Transjordanian nationalist who wrote in December 1995 that Palestinians had come to Jordan to seek refuge; now, Jordanians asserted that "Jordan is not a substitute homeland for all Palestinians including their offspring." Al-Saket went on to propose a solution for the issue of "naturalized Jordanians of Palestinian origin." He suggested that these people should respond soon to the PLO's call for every Palestinian to carry a Palestinian passport and should lose their Jordanian citizenship to become Palestinian residents in Jordan, where they could work as they did in the Gulf states.[1]

Oraib Rantawi, a Palestinian-Jordanian columnist, addressed the issue from a different angle. In October 1995, he argued that the rancorous government-PLO interaction had led more or less "to the division of labor in Jordan along bicommunal lines. One community [Palestinian-Jordanian] pays taxes while the other [Transjordanian] consumes them." He called on the political and economic Palestinian-Jordanian elite to abandon indifference and become deeply involved in public life in order to protect their civil and political rights as secured by the constitution and law.[2]

Rantawi, in touching on the issue of discrimination, was obviously blaming it partly on the Palestinian community leadership. A U.S. Department of State report issued in April 1996 confirmed Rantawi's account of discrimination: "Palestinians suffer disproportionate scrutiny in taxation and discrimination in the award of university scholarships and appointments to senior position in the government and the military."[3]

Kamal Salibi tackles the issue of discrimination and makes his own interpretation. He writes that the quarrel of the Jordanian regime, in principle, was with the fedayeen as an armed movement and not with the Palestinians as a people. According to Salibi,

> The fact that such discrimination did exist derived from the peculiar structure of Jordanian society rather than from state policy. As far as the Hashemite monarchy was concerned, all Jordanians were equal, regardless of origin. But to most Transjordanians as to most Palestinians, the question of origin remained

politically important. With the Transjordanians dominating the army and holding the key posts in the administration, the status of the Palestinians as Jordanian citizens of full rank and standing was compromised in various ways, especially in cases where their political loyalty was suspect.[4]

Though not entirely wrong, Salibi's interpretation has two flaws: (1) the
Transjordanian domination of the army *was* a policy, and (2) the key posts
in the administration until 1971 were occupied by both Transjordanians
and Palestinian-Jordanians.

The status of the Palestinians, as fairly characterized by Rantawi, did
not decline overnight. It involved a long process that started more or less
with the government-fedayeen showdown (1970–71) and has been sustained by a consistent state policy. Nevertheless, many actors, including
the king, the Jordanian ruling elite, the PLO, the Arab states, Israel, and
the Palestinian-Jordanians and Transjordanians themselves, contributed
to this process either deliberately or inadvertently. The overwhelming
majority of people holding middle-management positions in the public
sector today are Transjordanians. The exact percentage of Palestinians in
the army, public security, and Mukhabarat is unknown, but few observers
would describe it as other than insignificant. One can easily feel that the
state is specifically Transjordanian rather than just Jordanian.

As for the private sector, in 1996 Jordan University's Center for Strategic Studies conducted a study on Palestinians' and Transjordanians' capital participation in the country's economy. This study showed that Palestinian participation amounted to 82.6 percent of the capital, while
Transjordanian participation amounted to 11 percent. The rest reflected
the participation of other minorities—Circassians, Armenians, Kurds, Syrians, and Lebanese. In Amman, the economy is dominated by Palestinian-
Jordanians.

According to the most recent census (1994), the population of Jordan
is 3,823,000. Though the government chose not to publish the breakdown of Palestinians and Transjordanians, interested people are usually
satisfied with the assumption that Palestinians represent 50 percent of the
population.

Thus, Palestinian-Jordanians are obviously underrepresented in the
public sector, while Transjordanian participation in investment capital is
remarkably low. This communal division—or rather national deformation—
along the private and public sector lines has not been accidental. It is due
in part to the prevailing system of social values and in part to domestic
politics. Whatever the reason, this situation, as the opinion poll reveals, is

a source of dissatisfaction for both communities. On the one hand, Transjordanian complaints of Palestinian-Jordanian dominance in the private sector are understandable—since the limited wages of public-sector employees cannot in general match the income of those who work in the private sector—but they are not justified—since the private sector is not off limits to Transjordanians. In contrast, Palestinian-Jordanian complaints of Transjordanian dominance in the public sector are not only understandable—accurately reflecting the discrimination they experience—but also justified. Stories of civil servants who obstruct Palestinian official transactions abound in Jordan today. As a result, Palestinian businesspeople have resorted to employing Transjordanians whose job it is to ensure that their company's official transactions get through the obstructive bureaucracy. Some Palestinian-Jordanian businesspeople who returned to Jordan in the wake of the Iraqi invasion of Kuwait and the Gulf War (1990–91) have adopted the Gulf states' model, in which one cannot start a business without an indigenous partner. When such businesspeople do not find a willing Transjordanian with whom to start a business, they resort to seducing one with free shares. The higher the Transjordanian's official connections, the better. Ironically, then, the discriminatory attitude of the Transjordanian bureaucracy has generated new jobs and perhaps a different means of redistributing income.

Transjordanian control of the security apparatus has had a more adverse impact on national unity than Transjordanian dominance of the civil administration. The state—any state—holds the monopoly on violence. But when the security apparatus is controlled by one group in a society where tribal kinship supersedes the rule of law, then neutrality of repression, an essential factor for intercommunal harmony, disappears. The dominated group members feel that they are in either a xenophobic country or one that is occupied by a foreign power. As a result, a sense of victimization has grown among Palestinian-Jordanians over the last two decades.

The biased attitude and behavior of the police have adversely affected the business of Palestinian-Jordanian lawyers. One of them told me about a new phenomenon in which Palestinian-Jordanians tend to hire Transjordanian lawyers in criminal cases, not because of the latter's professional capabilities but because of the former's belief that the police are more responsive to their requests than to the requests of Palestinian-Jordanian lawyers.

If this is true, this interaction between Transjordanian security officers and Palestinian-Jordanian lawyers does not result from the direct implementation of actual policy but rather reflects an orientation or is a response to signals. De-Palestinianization is an orientation that might have produced an attitude, now reflected in some officers' behavior. In a patriarchal society, children (dependent citizens) are skilled in and intent on reading signals from the father (the official authority) in order to adjust their behavior so as to avoid the father's anger or to gain his affection. If the security apparatus is staffed almost exclusively by one group, the message is obvious: this group is loyal and the other is not. The de-Palestinianization of the security apparatus has triggered a self-perpetuating divisiveness. Transjordanians look on Palestinian-Jordanians as disloyal or, perhaps, as permanent suspects, and thus see no reason why they should be part of officialdom. (The conspiracy theme is, after all, a common justification for ethnic or religious discrimination.) For Transjordanians, excluding Palestinians from the public sector is not a moral issue. What Palestinian-Jordanians call discrimination, Transjordanian nationalists view as fair. Palestinian-Jordanians, meanwhile, have reacted passively to these Transjordanian nationalist attitudes and discriminatory behavior. Since the authority of the state in Jordan is felt most strongly through the Transjordanian-dominated security apparatus, the Palestinian grassroots feel that the state is not theirs. In the 1970s and (to a much lesser degree) in the 1980s, they identified with PLO goals, which often conflicted with Jordan's goals. This identification, in turn, heightened suspicion of their loyalty, given that the PLO sabotaged Jordanian targets in the years immediately following the September showdown and that Transjordanian diplomats were targets of terrorist attacks conducted by the Abu Nidal group in the 1980s. Such activities prompted the government to tighten security measures against Palestinians in general.

The exclusion of Palestinian-Jordanians from the public sector means not only reducing their employment opportunities but also depriving them and their families of the fringe benefits that go with government jobs, such as health insurance and subsidized goods (food, clothes, and appliances) to which the army, security personnel, and civil servants are entitled. This fact arouses the resentment of Palestinian-Jordanian lower-middle-class families, just as the ration given by UNRWA to Palestinian refugees arouses the resentment of Transjordanian lower-middle-class families.

THE REVERSAL OF THE 1967–70 PALESTINIAN TIDE

Distinct as the division between Transjordanians and Palestinian-Jordanians is, it has not developed into polarization—that is, the two communities

are not on the brink of conflict. After the 1970–71 showdown that resulted in the eviction of the fedayeen from Jordan, the king had three
major domestic priorities: (1) to prevent the fedayeen from reentering
Jordan, (2) to restore normalcy to the country, and (3) to consolidate his
power base. On the whole, both Palestinian-Jordanians and Transjordanians,
except for the revolutionary party members, were relieved by the outcome
of the 1970–71 showdown. Both groups wanted the restoration of law
and order and a return to normalcy after the years of chaos. Yet other
sentiments were developing and taking hold at the grassroots level.

The Transjordanian grassroots were proud of the army's accomplishment in September 1970, viewing it as a victory over the Palestinians. It
was *their* victory, not only because the army was the state's symbol of sovereignty but also because its soldiers and officers were their siblings. Since
the inception of Jordan, the army had been part and parcel of Transjordanian
society. It has always been the largest employer. Almost every Transjordanian
family has had one of its members in the army. Furthermore, many
Transjordanians had felt humiliated, either directly or vicariously through
their siblings in the army, by the derogatory attitude and behavior of the
fedayeen. Abu Iyad admits, "Though we strove to secure the support of
the whole people irrespective of their origins, we tended to favor Palestinians over [Trans]jordanians. Besides, the fedayeen, who were boastful of
their strength and deeds, frequently displayed their sense of superiority,
sometimes even arrogance, without taking into consideration the sensitivi-
ties and interests of [Trans]jordanians. What was even more grave was the
fedayeen attitude toward the Jordanian army, which they treated more as
an enemy than a potential ally."[5] As victors, many Transjordanians felt they
were entitled to their share of the prize. In their view, the king, in preserving his throne, already had his share; at stake was *their* share. On the individual level, the reward to which they aspired was simple: a prompt and
personal favor from the king or his government, such as a job, a promotion, free medical treatment abroad, or bounty of any sort. They also wanted
to be favored over the Palestinians permanently. They expected the king to
be responsive to their requests because he had to be grateful for their support. In a society where kinship and personal connections outweigh the
dictates of law, one often appeals to gratitude to achieve one's objectives.
The king was aware of these feelings. He was responsive to general and
individual requests not only because the prize was available, especially in
government jobs, but because he wanted to consolidate his power base.
The government's responsiveness to Transjordanian requests and the

replacement of purged Palestinian-Jordanians by Transjordanians in the security apparatus was tantamount to an official declaration that Transjordanians were the favored, trusted community. The more this self-image was enhanced, the more Transjordanians asked for government jobs, and the more domineering Transjordanian officials became. As Transjordanian influence in day-to-day affairs increased, Palestinian-Jordanian middlemen, except for the very few who had direct access to the prime minister or the palace, almost vanished and were replaced by Transjordanian middlemen. In fact, a new phenomenon emerged: that of Palestinian-Jordanian sub-middlemen who forwarded the demands of their constituents to Transjordanian middlemen with access to state resources. These changes further alienated the Palestinian-Jordanians and enhanced both the sense that Transjordanians dominated Jordanian society and the Transjordanian tendency to patronize the Palestinian-Jordanian grassroots. Patronizing, in turn, both confirmed Transjordanian domination and provided Transjordanians with votes outside their clans in municipal and in general elections—from the Palestinian-Jordanians who were expected to show their gratitude to the new Transjordanian community leaders.

For their part, Palestinian-Jordanians, knowing that they were perceived as suspects, did not protest their unfair sacking by the government, since protesting might lead to investigation and investigation to arrest. Why should they bring evil on themselves? Thus, they behaved exactly as suspects would, avoiding places frequented by security agents.

The government's policies, partly proactive and partly reactive, triggered a mutually perpetuating process: the Palestinian-Jordanian was gradually alienated from the state, and the Transjordanian gradually came to feel that the state was his. Under such conditions, the Transjordanians felt relaxed and satisfied, while the Palestinian-Jordanians were watchful and alert, and this "us-versus-them" mentality nurtured the dichotomy.

The king was extremely anxious about this dichotomy, since it could lead to polarization and conflict. Before his assassination, al-Tal suggested an institutionalized reconciliation. The idea was to set up a political organization along the lines of the one-party system in socialist countries. The king would preside over the "Jordanian National Union," which was to be run by a secretary general and would mobilize the nation behind the king's policies. The real objective was to preempt potential communal polarization and achieve national reconciliation by bringing Palestinian-Jordanian and Transjordanian political activists together under the king's helmsmanship.

The objective of national reconciliation was spelled out in the king's opening address at the first conference of the union: "Last year's events [the September showdown] with all its distress and suffering, followed by the loss of a sense of direction, which carried us further away from our usurped rights in Palestine and our nation from regaining its lost dignity, enhanced my conviction and belief in setting up a national union that brings together the people of the two dear banks and unites their efforts on the path of victory and liberation."[6]

From November 1971 to February 1976, when the National Union was terminated, it was run by three consecutive secretary generals. All of them were Palestinian-Jordanians (I was one). The implicit message was obvious: Palestinian-Jordanians and Transjordanians are one people. Other attempts at reconciliation were made, notably the commutation of death sentences of a number of convicted conspirators against the regime and the issuance of amnesties for all those convicted and serving their sentences as well as for those convicted in absentia. Though the Palestinian-Transjordanian rupture persisted, the king's efforts succeeded in preventing its deterioration into a clear-cut polarization. Neither Transjordanians nor Palestinian-Jordanians wished to revisit the recent chaotic past.

However, other factors worked to maintain the rupture. The assassination of Wasfi al-Tal was only the beginning of a series of such attacks. On December 15, 1971, an attempt was made on the life of Jordan's ambassador in London, Zeid al-Rifa'i. By the end of 1972, letter bombs had been mailed to three Palestinian ministers (including myself), but they had all been intercepted at the post office before they reached their destination. In February 1973, seventeen Fatah members were arrested after they had infiltrated the country with weapons. Their mission was to storm the offices of the prime minister during the weekly cabinet meeting and hold him and other ministers hostage until their demands were met. Such events made it clear that the rupture had not been healed.

THE JORDANIAN ELITE BREAKS UP

One of the major casualties of the September showdown was the Jordanian-Palestinian alliance. When the two banks were officially united in 1950, the process of integrating them traveled three parallel yet interconnected paths: institutional (government and Parliament), socioeconomic, and political (the parties). In the 1950s and 1960s, West Bankers criticized the official integration process, while the unofficial routes toward integration—namely, the socioeconomic and political paths—went unscathed. Palestinian-Jordanian and Transjordanian political activists worked voluntarily together within the political parties both before and after they were banned in 1957. The bonds that pulled them together were the ideologies they had embraced and were struggling to promote. Because they were in the opposition, they came to be known as the Jordanian National Movement. Their ideology and programs were cross-communal, helping to unite the two peoples. But this unofficial alliance or bond was badly injured by the fedayeen activities that resulted in the September showdown, and the bond finally broke down.

Fahad al-Fanek, a columnist, former Ba'athist, and articulate Transjordanian nationalist, accurately describes these developments:

> The fedayeen activity concentrated all political activity in Jordan on the Palestinian issue. In so doing, it obscured almost completely the Jordanian National Movement, which before 1967 had been intermittently crippled by the government's arrest of its activists [Transjordanian and Palestinian-Jordanian]. The fedayeen activity had a worse effect on the movement than the government since it not only paralyzed the movement but transformed it into a tail of the fedayeen. As a result, Transjordanian activists became too timid to identify with Jordan. The Transjordanian National Movement rose from the ashes of the Jordanian National Movement and as its substitute. The regime [the king and the army] became the Transjordanian *fedayeen* group.[7]

In the wake of the 1970 September showdown, King Hussein drew new battle lines with the PLO, refusing to readmit the fedayeen in Jordan, maintaining his representation of the West Bank, and insisting on a peaceful solution to the Arab-Israeli conflict. Simultaneously, a new low-profile Transjordanian political force that did not see eye to eye with the king began to emerge. This force consisted of middle-class Transjordanians, including senior officials, former members of the Jordanian National Movement, professionals, relatives and friends of Wasfi al-Tal, and some members of the royal family, who believed that the king's Palestinian policy should be changed. They believed that it would be in Jordan's best interests if the king gave up trying to represent the West Bank, leaving it to the PLO. The West Bank, they argued, had been a source of trouble for Jordan even before its occupation by Israel in 1967. After the occupation, the troubles caused by the Palestinians had increased; Palestinians had not only killed Wasfi al-Tal but also threatened the very existence of Jordan. These attitudes made them the undeclared allies of the PLO. For understandable reasons, they did not confront the king in public; they made their beliefs felt through the senior officials and intelligence officers among them who had access to the palace. In public, they mainly chose to support the right of Palestinians to self-determination, which implied Jordan's eventual separation from the West Bank. The fact that the king had relied mainly on Transjordanian support in repelling the fedayeen during the September showdown gave this group the courage to express an attitude that ran counter to the king's.

This unpublished challenge to the Hashemite patriarchal monarchy differed from that in 1957 in two ways. During the Nabulsi episode in 1957, the challenge had been to the monarchical system itself and had come from political parties that comprised Palestinian-Jordanians and Transjordanians, motivated mainly by ideological considerations. This challenge was to the monarch's Palestinian policy and came from Transjordanians motivated mainly by their concern about their identity. The policy of the monarch, not the monarchy, had to be changed.

These people represented the nucleus of the resurgent Transjordanian nationalism that was to take shape in the next two decades. What was especially interesting about this nucleus was the fact that many of its members belonged to pan-Arab parties, namely, the Ba'ath and the Arab National Movement, and ideologically they were supposed to cling to the unity of the two banks, rather than supporting their separation. They did not perceive the contradiction in this position for good reasons. First, the rubric of Arab nationalism during this period was the support for the Palestinian struggle for liberation and statehood, and they supported it; second, Fatah, the leading faction in the PLO, had pan-Arabists among its leading members, and they were doing the same; and third, every Arab subgroup was sticking to its independent state in practical terms, so why should Jordanians be any different? Comparing them to Fatah is especially intriguing. Fatah was a national front struggling for liberation. Usually liberation movements accommodate all political stripes. But what were the Transjordanian elite struggling for that would justify forming a kind of national front? Since they were not struggling for liberation, the implicit objective was to exclude Palestinian-Jordanians from Jordan. This sowed the seeds of the current exclusivist nationalism.

The nationalist overtone in this argument was nevertheless obvious. The term *intima'* (membership), a euphemism for "loyalty to Jordan" or "Transjordanianism," later became the litany of their political discourse, soon permeated the media, and became a salient term in the Jordanian political lexicon.

THE PALESTINIAN-JORDANIAN ELITE: DIVIDED AND CONFUSED

Unlike most of the Transjordanian elite, who could identify their goals and path after the September showdown, the Palestinian-Jordanian elite were divided into two major categories: those who linked themselves with the king and what he stood for—the unity of the two banks and the king's representation of the Palestinians in Jordan—and those who linked themselves with the PLO and what it stood for—its exclusive representation of the Palestinian people and their right to self-determination and statehood. Both categories belonged mainly to the middle class. They were professionals, businesspeople, and journalists. A remarkable number of them were seasoned party members. Among the PLO-linked category, however, were prominent activists who also supported the unity of the two banks. To them, the Palestinian struggle was for liberation rather than separation. Many of them had a great stake in the status quo since they came from the middle class.

The future status of the Palestinians in Jordan was never an issue for public debate among Transjordanian and Palestinian-Jordanian elites during the 1970s and 1980s, as this would have put them on a collision course that they chose to avoid. Those Palestinian-Jordanians who linked themselves to the king accepted the notion that they would continue to be full citizens and a party to the Jordanian national consensus. Those in the PLO-linked category never cared about the future status of Palestinian-Jordanians because their focus was on the establishment of an independent Palestinian state. As for the Transjordanian elite, they viewed their problem with the Palestinians as twofold: one related to the land (the unity of the two banks), the other related to the people (the large number of Palestinians on the East Bank). For the first, the solution was separation, which they supported indirectly by supporting the PLO as the sole representative of the Palestinians. The second issue was publicly raised by the Transjordanian elite only after the Oslo DOP. Before that, they had found an answer for their concerns in the king's federal plan of March 1972, announced eight months after the eviction of the fedayeen from Jordan (the federal plan is described in the next section). In other words, the Transjordanian elite were provided with an answer to their concerns at a very early stage, even before they started to be conscious of their existence as a new political force.

Throughout the two decades after the September showdown, the only public forum in which politics was practiced legally was the Federation of

Professional Associations. (Political parties were legally licensed only in 1992, after they had been delegitimized for thirty-five years.) Since professionals comprised both Transjordanians and Palestinian-Jordanians, their associations created an ideal forum for dialogue and interaction between the political activists among them. Many Palestinian-Jordanians and Transjordanians belonged to the same pan-Arab party or supported the same fedayeen group as an offshoot of a certain party—not as combatants but as promoters of its tenets and positions. But the king-linked Palestinian-Jordanian elite were almost completely excluded from this political discourse. Neither the Transjordanian elite nor the PLO-linked Palestinian-Jordanian elite viewed them as eligible Palestinian interlocutors, since they did not have a stand of their own. They looked like minors excluded from a game of adults. After the Rabat Resolution of 1974, the king-linked group gradually fell into a kind of limbo. Most of them, while in office, viewed themselves and were viewed by the Transjordanians as mere technocrats or token appointments, not really a part of the decision-making process.

The retrogression of the Palestinian-Jordanians' status in Jordan since the September showdown has been proportionate to the divisiveness process that has been nurtured by internal and external pressures alike. Arthur Day, an American diplomat who specialized in Middle East affairs, has commented: "The most suspect seam in Jordanian society is that which binds Palestinian-Jordanians to East Bank Jordanians—a seam especially vulnerable to the kind of external pressure that appears most likely to threaten the cohesion of the state."[8]

THE UNITED ARAB KINGDOM

One internal factor that contributed enormously to the divisiveness process was the king's federal plan. According to the plan, a federal United Arab Kingdom, consisting of two autonomous provinces—a Jordan province (East Bank) and a Palestine province (West Bank)—would replace the Hashemite Kingdom of Jordan. Each province would have its own parliament and government, whose members would be wholly Jordanians in the Jordan province and wholly Palestinians in the Palestine province. Amman would be both the federal capital and the capital of the province of Jordan. Jerusalem would be the capital of the Palestine province. The king would be the head of state and would assume executive power, which he would practice through a central government. He would also assume legislative power along with the federal Parliament, which would consist of equal numbers of representatives from each of the two provinces. The central government would be responsible for foreign affairs and defense, and the United Kingdom would have one army, whose supreme commander would be the king.

The United Kingdom plan, which the king announced on March 15, 1972, was drafted by a joint Palestinian-Jordanian and Transjordanian royal committee, of which I was a member. The king's motivation, as he spelled it out to the committee, was that it was time to recognize the Palestinian identity. It was unrealistic to return to the formula that had preceded the 1967 war. Though the plan was meant "to make some concessions to their [Palestinians'] regional particularism," it also emphasized Jordanian particularism.[9] In other words, though the plan was put forward to allay Palestinian concerns, it also allayed Transjordanian concerns. For the Palestinian nationalists, dropping "Hashemite" and "Jordan" from the proposed name of the state implied the recognition of their identity and had a visceral appeal. Although Transjordanians resented changing the name, the plan allayed their growing concern over the increasing members of Palestinians on the East Bank. According to the plan, the Palestinians on the East Bank would vote for their representatives in the "Palestine province"; this would make them mere residents of the East Bank. Thus, they would not be able to dominate Jordan through democratic means. Besides, the federal plan was designed to upstage the PLO, whose major appeal to the Palestinians was the reinstatement of Palestine on the Middle Eastern map. Announcing the plan just eleven days before municipal elections were scheduled to be held on the West Bank attested to the goal of reducing the PLO's appeal. The king's address to the nation that introduced the federal plan summed up his goals: "In the new stage to which we aspire, we shall put the Jordanian-Palestinian house in order so that intrinsic strength and ability to attain our ambitions and goals will be enhanced. This formula [the federal plan] will tighten the bonds of the two banks."[10]

Israel, I believe, was another audience to which the plan was addressed. In those days, despite Israel's ambiguous policy toward the future of the West Bank, conventional wisdom in Amman held that Israel was looking for Palestinian interlocutors from the occupied West Bank and Gaza with whom to reach a settlement in order to preempt the PLO. The federal plan was also meant to attract support for the king from the Western democracies, especially the United States. In fact, the king announced the plan just before he made a scheduled visit to Washington. In his address, he stressed the principle of self-determination: "This is our pledge to our people to exercise their right of self-determination. It is our reply to everyone who has shed doubts on our pledge, which is heard today by every citizen in this country, every individual in our nation, and everyone in the world."[11]

In spite of the fact that the federal plan took Palestinian and Jordanian concerns into consideration, it received a mixed response from the Palestinians of both banks. The PLO denounced the plan "as a devious plot aimed at robbing the Palestinian people of their right to self-determination and independence."[12] Conservative Arab states did not give their expected support. Revolutionary Arab states viewed it as a flagrant intervention in Palestinian affairs. Egypt, in particular, demonstrated strong opposition to the plan by severing its diplomatic relations with Jordan. Israel, too, rejected the plan "on the grounds that the king was putting the cart before the horse. . . . If he wanted to have this [Israeli-occupied] territory returned, he had first to talk to them."[13]

Ironically, the implications of the plan survived the plan itself. The first implication was that the unity of the two banks was no longer a given, since the Hashemite king himself had initiated a plan that would rescind the 1950 unity. The second was that the status of Palestinians in Jordan could be demoted from citizens to residents if a separate Palestinian entity emerged on the West Bank. This notion is the pivot around which dialogue between Palestinian-Jordanians and Transjordanians revolves today. Among other things, the federal plan revived the question of who represented the Palestinians in the occupied territories, the king or the PLO. The Palestinian Popular Congress (PPC)—which consisted of PNC members and other Palestinian activists representing various political groupings, trade unions, and so forth—convened in Cairo on April 6, 1972, to discuss the king's plan. The PPC condemned the plan and called for the overthrow of the king. To achieve this goal, a Palestinian-Jordanian National Liberation Front (PJNLF) was to be set up. In March 1972, the PLO Planning Center had already prepared a working paper in which it defined the objective of the PJNLF as follows:

> The removal of the regime in Jordan, liberation of Palestine from the Zionist occupation, and the establishment of a federal state on the land of Palestine and Jordan which will ensure the preservation of sovereignty of the two peoples and strengthen the relationship of brotherhood and equality [between them] by means of equal rights in the constitutional, legal, cultural, and economic aspects.[14]

After the September showdown, the PLO began to emphasize Transjordanian nationalism as the equal of Palestinian nationalism. The themes of the two peoples, their joint struggle, and the bonds of brotherhood and equality that linked them were reaffirmed in the tenth and eleventh PNCs (April 1972 and January 1973, respectively). Ironically, just as the king's federal plan had a counterproductive effect, so did the PLO's emphasis on a separate Jordanian nationalism. To Transjordanians, the federal plan implied that unity was not sacrosanct. The PLO's association of the overthrow of the monarchy with Transjordanian nationalism missed a significant point—that the rising Transjordanian nationalism viewed the Hashemite monarchy as part and parcel of the Transjordanian identity. In the final analysis, the PLO's emphasis on Transjordanian nationalism strengthened Transjordanian exclusivist nationalism rather than bringing the two peoples closer. Eventually, both the king's federal plan and the PLO's reaction nurtured the divisiveness.

THE SADAT FACTOR: RADICAL CHANGES

The decade of the 1970s in the Middle East could be rightly called Sadat's decade, for it was Sadat of Egypt who made war (1973) and opened the road for peace (his visit to Jerusalem in 1977), generating profound changes in the war-torn region. Sadat came to power after the death of Nasser with a new approach to the Arab-Israeli conflict based on his convictions that it was unrealistic to obliterate Israel, that the state of no-war–no-peace was unacceptable, that the stalemate could be broken by intermediate steps, that it was possible to reach a peace agreement with Israel, and that the United States held 90 percent of the cards for a peaceful settlement. He believed that the Palestinian issue should be solved through self-determination for the Palestinians and that the PLO was the sole legitimate representative of the Palestinian people. Egypt's task, as far as the Palestinian issue was concerned, was to help restore the occupied West Bank and Gaza to the Palestinians. He believed that Arab solidarity was essential and that to maintain it, he had to support the Palestinians and help them establish their entity or state on the West Bank and Gaza. President Carter arranged and chaired direct discussions between President Sadat and Prime Minister Begin of Israel at Camp David on September 5–17, 1978, and Sadat adhered to his position during and after these talks. Quandt writes that "Sadat sent a message to Carter on November 8 saying there must be unequivocal agreement on what was to take place on the West Bank and

Gaza. Otherwise he would be accused of making a separate deal with the Israelis and abandoning the Palestinians."[15]

Having failed to reactivate the peace process in his first two years in office, Sadat engineered the October war with President Assad of Syria. On October 6, 1973, Egyptian and Syrian forces launched a simultaneous surprise attack on Israeli occupying forces across the cease-fire lines in the Golan Heights and the Suez Canal. On October 22, 1973, the Security Council adopted Resolution 338, calling on the belligerents to cease fire, to begin implementing Resolution 242, and concurrently and immediately to start negotiations under appropriate auspices aimed at establishing a just and lasting peace in the Middle East.

On October 16, 1973, before the guns fell silent, Sadat announced a peace plan in which he called for, among other things, an international peace conference that would include Egypt, Syria, Jordan, the PLO, and Israel. Resolution 338 produced two issues for the Arab side: direct negotiation and representation of the West Bank and Gaza. These required an Arab summit to give a new mandate to the Arab parties who would participate in the upcoming peace conference in Geneva. That summit convened in Algeria on November 26–28, 1973. The summit's resolutions defined the Arab interim aim. As for the Palestinian question, the resolution provided for "adherence to restoring the national rights of the Palestinian people in accordance with the resolution of the PLO, which is the sole representative of the Palestinian people." Jordan, as was expected, objected to this article. The Geneva conference convened on December 21, 1973, under the chairmanship of the UN secretary-general and was attended by Egypt; Syria; Israel; and the cosponsors, the United States and the Soviet Union.

Between November 1973 and October 1974, when the Rabat summit convened, a fierce diplomatic battle raged between Jordan and the PLO over the issue of representation. Jordan suggested a number of alternatives to the PLO's status as "sole" representative. The king's thesis was that a large number of Palestinians in Jordan were Jordanians. They were organically integrated into the state. How could he not represent them? He suggested "legitimate" instead of "sole." He even suggested restoring the West Bank and letting its people decide whether to unite with Jordan or separate from it after the Israeli withdrawal. He suggested that the PLO could be part of the Jordanian delegation to the peace conference. All the king's suggestions were rejected by the PLO, which fought its diplomatic battle equally fiercely.

The new political realities resulting from the October war prompted the PLO to shift its position—except on the issue of representation. The most significant shift was its adoption of the "ten-point plan" or the "phased program" proposed by the twelfth PNC session (June 1–8, 1974). Under the rubric of the "interim aim," the PNC decided that the PLO would struggle with all possible means at its disposal—the foremost of which was armed struggle (political activity was implied)—to liberate Palestinian territory and establish the people's independent national authority over that territory. This new position was particularly hailed by Sadat, who had tried to persuade Fatah of the strategy of stages.

When King Hussein went to Rabat for the Arab summit, he was aware of the difficulty he faced. He relied, nevertheless, on three factors: a vague promise by Sadat to side with him, the rationality of his argument, and Israel's rejection of the PLO as the Palestinian interlocutor. However, after lengthy debates and discussions, the king joined the Arab consensus on the famous resolution that emphasized "the right of the Palestinian people to establish an independent national authority under the command of the PLO, the sole legitimate representative of Palestinian people in any Palestinian territory that is liberated." In another resolution, the summit decided to support Egypt, Syria, Jordan, and the PLO financially. Jordan's share was $300 million. Most important, Arab leaders implored the king to continue Jordan's assistance to and maintain linkage with the West Bank to prevent the emergence of a vacuum that Israel might exploit. The Rabat Resolution ushered in a new era for the PLO and the Arab-Israeli conflict, and at the same time it accelerated the divisiveness among Palestinians and Jordanians.

According to Adam Garfinkle, the PLO was "enthroned" at Rabat.[16] According to Shemesh, "Egypt under Sadat continued to be the leader in advancing the notion of a Palestinian entity. While Nasser laid the conceptual foundation for its establishment, Sadat laid the practical foundations for an independent entity."[17]

THE RIPPLES OF THE RABAT RESOLUTION IN JORDAN

The repercussions of the Rabat Resolution in Jordan were prompt and strong. The Transjordanian elite were as happy with the resolution as was the PLO. Usually when the king returned to Jordan from an official visit abroad, he was received by senior officials. On his return from Rabat, his reception was exceptional. Community leaders and senior officials welcomed him at the airport. Students lined the road outside the airport, waving Jordanian flags and welcoming placards.

On November 23, 1974, twenty-five days after the Rabat summit, a new cabinet was formed by Zeid al-Rifa'i, the prime minister from the outgoing cabinet. On the same day Parliament was suspended. The percentage of Palestinians in the new cabinet dropped from 46 percent to 20 percent. According to Salibi, "the king wanted to make it perfectly clear that he intended to abide by the Rabat Resolution to the letter."[18] The drop in the Palestinian percentage in this post-Rabat cabinet sent an obvious signal to both Jordanians and Palestinians. But these developments required an explanation from the king. On November 30, 1974, one week after the formation of the cabinet, King Hussein addressed the nation:

> If some matters had to be readjusted in order to give substance to the Rabat summit resolution, Jordan will not cease to be the homeland of every Arab Palestinian who chooses to be one of its citizens, with all the rights and obligations of citizenship without prejudicing his or her natural rights in Palestine. Those who choose the Palestinian identity will be dear Arab brethren enjoying whatever rights Arab citizens enjoy [residency] in this genuine Arab country.

The king called on the people to receive the Rabat Resolution "with pride and satisfaction," because it represented "the collective Arab will to sustain strong Arab solidarity in order to uphold the Arab position." He urged the people to accept this development only in this context and "not to distort it or get worried and puzzled." Aware of the Jordanian-Palestinian rupture and of the arguments of Transjordanian nationalists, and eager to prevent the rupture from developing into polarization, the king addressed the people as *muhajirin* (emigrants)—the Palestinians—and *ansar* (supporters)—the Transjordanians.

> You are one family and one clan that will not be divided as a result of this development. Being one of the most magnanimous and noblest peoples, no one of you is going to be biased in his sentiments, intentions, or treatment of the other. If anything of this sort happens, God forbid, I will consider it an insult to me and to every other citizen through me. The new development came to strengthen the Arab position, not to weaken it.[19]

The king's reference to Palestinians and Jordanians as *muhajirin* and *ansar* was a first after the confrontation with the fedayeen in September 1970. Obviously, the king intended to invoke traditional Islamic terms to ensure national unity. But Transjordanians and Palestinian-Jordanians understood these terms as drawing a distinctive line between the two

communities.[20] To present-day Transjordanians, these terms have conno-
tations of "guests and hosts" more than emigrants and supporters. The
guest-host dichotomy suggests a more temporary relationship than that
implied by *muhajirin/ansar* in the Islamic tradition. The king's speech,
then, included three themes that inadvertently nurtured divisiveness, albeit
short of polarization: the distinction between Palestinian-Jordanians and
Transjordanians, the temporariness of the guest-host connotation of
muhajirin and *ansar*, and the implicit notion that Jordan was doing the
Palestinians a favor (Jordan would be the homeland of any Palestinian
who so chose).

The Rabat Resolution was received with relief and joy by Transjordanian
nationalists, Palestinian refugees in general, and supporters of Fatah in
particular. Encouraged by the distinction between Palestinian-Jordanians
and Transjordanians that was made by word (the king's speech) and deed
(the low Palestinian-Jordanian percentage in the cabinet and the suspension of Parliament in which West Bankers occupied 50 percent of the
seats), Transjordanian nationalists shifted to phase two of their arguments.
Phase one had been concerned with the issue of representation, which
implied the unity, or disunity, of the two banks. Phase two was about the
status of Palestinian-Jordanians. With the encouragement or at the behest
of senior officials, Transjordanian rallies were held in districts throughout
the country. In one rally, a Transjordanian betrayed one of the major concerns of Transjordanian nationalism when he said jokingly, "Now my son
has a chance to become a minister."

Palestinian refugees, in contrast, celebrated the Rabat Resolution by
passing out candies. The resolution boosted their morale, which had ebbed
tremendously after the September showdown. In November 1974, Arafat
addressed the UN General Assembly in New York. The PLO was allowed
to have an observer delegation at the United Nations, and the General
Assembly endorsed the Rabat Resolution. All these developments gave
hope to the Palestinians that a Palestinian state was imminent. In the midst
of this radical change, the king-associated Palestinian-Jordanian elite became confused and felt that they had entered a gray zone. Pan-Arabist
Transjordanians and Palestinian-Jordanians alike were unhappy about the
new development, and so were some of the older-generation
Transjordanians who had helped create the union of the two banks since
the time of King Abdullah.

On July 13, 1976, Mudhar Badran formed a new cabinet. The cabinet
included four Palestinian-Jordanians (of whom I was one) out of eighteen

ministers. Four of the fourteen Transjordanian ministers were known to be Transjordanian nationalists – an indication that the de-Palestinianization process was to take a steadier course.

THE LIKUD FACTOR

Likud's assumption of power in Israel was a new factor that fed the divisiveness, exacerbating Transjordanian fears about the existence of Palestinians in Jordan. According to Likud political ideology, Jordan, or the East Bank, was originally part of Palestine and had been arbitrarily carved out by the British to become Transjordan. Thus, the Palestinians already had their state, and that was Jordan. When Likud came to power in May 1977, Prime Minister Begin chose Ariel Sharon as his minister of defense. In that capacity, Sharon, the most outspoken about the Likud's notion of "Jordan is Palestine," became responsible for the occupied territories. According to Garfinkle, the Likud policy as it evolved "was to feed a graduated de facto annexation that had earlier grown not out of design but the habit of power." Sharon's "ultimate motive was to depopulate them [the occupied territories] of Arabs, and by so doing, topple Hashemite Jordan."[21]

Even before the Likud came into power in Israel, Transjordanian concerns had been fed by three other alarms. The first alarm was Arab, triggered by a statement made on July 6, 1973, by Tunisia's President Bourgiba. He proposed a Palestine state to replace the Hashemite regime in Jordan. The second alarm was Palestinian, triggered by an article authored by Isam Sakhnini, a PLO activist at the Palestinian Research Center. The Sakhnini article called for the establishment of a "Palestinian East Jordan" as a "substitute entity that embodies the present and historical characteristics of the Palestinians and the East Jordanians."[22] The third alarm was triggered by Farouk Kaddumi, head of the PLO's political department. Around the time when Sakhnini's article was published, Zeid al-Rifa'i and Kaddumi discussed how to coordinate their efforts in view of the Rabat Resolution. During these discussions, Kaddumi wanted to know about the number of Palestinian-Jordanians and their geographical distribution in the refugee camps and outside. The request irritated al-Rifa'i, who said that the PLO had nothing to do with the Palestinians in Jordan simply because they were Jordanians under Jordanian jurisdiction. Kaddumi withdrew his request when al-Rifa'i threatened that if the PLO insisted on Jordan dealing with Palestinian-Jordanians as Palestinians, Jordan was ready the next day to sort out Palestinians from Jordanians.

The Likud factor was important not only because it triggered the fourth alarm among Transjordanians but also because it fed the illusion of a potential Israeli-Palestinian conspiracy to make Jordan a Palestinian state. What persuaded the Transjordanians of PLO-Israel complicity was their perception of the twelfth PNC (1974) adoption of the policy of stages, reflected in the decision to establish a Palestinian national authority by the PLO. They believed that the new PLO position was the first step in a process of PLO backtracking. Due to Israel's position—which rejected talking to the PLO and relinquishing control of the West Bank and instead promoted the building of settlements in the West Bank to pave the way for thousands of Israelis to move into the occupied territories—such a process might ultimately lead to the PLO's acceptance of establishing a Palestinian state in Jordan. In this case, Israel's strategy and the PLO's weakness might weave themselves into a conspiracy against Jordan.

While we are on the subject of a perceived conspiracy, a recent official expression of a conspiracy came in December 1994, after the conclusion of the Jordanian-Israeli peace treaty in October of that year. In a lecture at the War College, Jordan's highest military institute, Khaled al-Karaki, a Transjordanian nationalist who was the chief of the royal court, the second highest senior post after the prime minister's, said:

> The 1970 sedition perpetrated by regionalist organizations [Fatah] aimed at breaking the unity between *muhajirin* and *ansar*. The 1974 Rabat summit and the disengagement decision in 1988 aimed at the same objective. Then came the Gaza-Jericho agreement [the PLO-Israeli agreement to establish a Palestinian self-governing authority in the two cities as a preliminary step] and the self-government as a climax in this process; or perhaps, all these effects are a prelude to what is even more dangerous if the Palestinian national scheme chooses to fall into the embrace of the Zionist scheme, in which case both of them will turn to the east in search of *al-Watan al-Badil* [substitute Palestinian homeland] given the fact that the issue of demography is the most threatening in the region, and Jordan is the most susceptible to it.[23]

As the number of settlements built by the Likud government in the West Bank grew, so did the credibility of the conspiracy notion. As a result, the government turned on Palestinian-Jordanians, precluding an increase in their numbers in Jordan and reducing their visibility. The Palestinian-Jordanians were visible in four areas: the private sector, the public sector, the press, and unofficial political forums such as professional associations and universities. The private sector remained untouched because the government could not afford to damage the economy. The government even naturalized Palestinian individuals from Gaza (who had never been

Jordanians) in return for their investment in Jordan. However, the government continued to reduce Palestinian visibility in the public sector, especially in the foreign ministry, through the de-Palestinianization process. The government could do little about Palestinian visibility in the press because the Palestinian question was the major item on Jordan's Arab and foreign policy agenda. As for the universities, the government subjected faculty and students at state universities to the Transjordanization process, favoring the appointment of Transjordanian faculty over Palestinian-Jordanians; screening lecturers and professors for security (a candidate would not be contracted if he or she was a member or sympathizer of a banned party or Palestinian organization); and admitting students through district quotas, which allowed more Transjordanian students to join the cheaper and more prestigious state universities than Palestinian-Jordanian students.

In the late 1980s and early 1990s, Transjordanian student associations or clubs were founded by Transjordanian nationalists and politicians and backed by the government. One of their prominent activities was to celebrate Jordan's national events, like the king's birthday, Independence Day, the Arab Revolt day, and so on. Until then student national activities had been mostly confined to national occasions linked with the Palestinian cause and to other major political events in the Arab world. Later, organized Transjordanian students began mounting demonstrations on university grounds on Palestinian occasions to drown out the cheers of Palestinian-Jordanian demonstrators. This development was strongly supported by the government, especially during the period when the *intifada* on the West Bank was at its peak. It became common to see two distinct groups of students in university squares shouting Transjordanian and Palestinian slogans at the same time. Such activities nurtured the divisiveness among the younger generation.

As for Palestinian visibility in professional associations, nothing much could be done. But one incident betrayed how eager the government was to reduce Palestinian visibility even before the Likud assumed office in Israel. Late in 1976, Ibrahim Bakir, a prominent Palestinian-Jordanian lawyer, ran for the presidency of the Lawyers' Association. He was approached several times by the minister of the interior, who tried to dissuade him from running. When Bakir asked the minister why the government did not want him to run, the minister's answer was "Because you are a Palestinian!" When Bakir retorted that there were several Palestinian-Jordanians occupying senior posts in the government, the minister said, "But you are too much of a Palestinian. You negotiated for the PLO in

1970."[24] The minister was referring to the trilateral follow-up committee that had been set up by the Arab summit in Cairo during the September showdown and at which Bakir had represented the PLO.

The implementation of government measures to reduce Palestinian visibility in Jordan deepened divisions, yet there were several reasons for which communal polarization did not occur. First, the economic boom that the country experienced during this period (per capita income rose from $291.83 in 1973 to $1,089.20 in 1979)[25] diluted Palestinian-Jordanian resentment. Second, Palestinian-Jordanians were not associated with a specific territory like the Tamils in Sri Lanka, the Turks in Cyprus, the Maronites in Lebanon, or the Kurds in Turkey. In addition, the growing sense that their situation was temporary made Palestinian-Jordanians behave like guests, rather than citizens. Indeed, in comparing their condition with that of their refugee brethren in Syria and Lebanon, Palestinian-Jordanians were thankful. As a result, rather than protesting against the discrimination of which they were the targets and demanding that their civil rights be upheld, Palestinian-Jordanian discourse became filled with expressions of gratitude to Jordan. By disregarding the basic reality that they were Jordanian citizens, Palestinian-Jordanians inadvertently further impaired their status.

THE AMERICAN FACTOR

U.S. Middle East policy has contributed remarkably to shaping many developments in the region, including the Palestinian-Jordanian dynamic. After the first meeting of the Geneva Peace Conference on December 21, 1973, the Arab parties to the Arab-Israeli conflict viewed the conference as the most convenient mechanism for implementing Security Council Resolution 242. Their diplomatic efforts concentrated on reconvening the conference, and Sadat was eager for the PLO to participate in the conference when it reconvened. The Rabat Resolution and the ten-point program adopted by the twelfth PNC made it possible for Sadat and other Arab states to promote the PLO as the eligible Palestinian interlocutor.

To forestall this possibility, Israel was able to reach with the United States a "Memorandum of Agreement on the Geneva Peace Conference." Signed by U.S. secretary of state Henry Kissinger and by Israel's foreign minister Yigal Allon on September 1, 1975, this agreement in its second paragraph reads, "The U.S. will continue to adhere to its present policy with respect to the PLO whereby it will not recognize or negotiate with the PLO so long as the PLO does not recognize Israel's right to exist and does not accept Security Council Resolutions 242 and 338."[26]

This American-Israeli position sustained Jordan as the representative of the Palestinians, at least until the PLO fulfilled the conditions of the memorandum, and this in turn fueled the rivalry between King Hussein and the PLO, despite Jordan's endorsement of the Rabat Resolution. By the same token, it enhanced the Transjordanian nationalists' concern that Jordan might be directly involved in conspiracy regarding the Palestinian question that would work to the detriment of the Transjordanians.

The American factor could also be traced back to 1974 and 1975, when the United States brokered three military disengagement agreements between Israel on the one hand and Egypt and Syria on the other, excluding Jordan. This exclusion produced two conflicting attitudes. The king was extremely unhappy with Jordan's exclusion; it seemed to imply that Jordan's regional role was receding and that the Palestinian issue was being put on the back burner. These turns made Jordan's future path seem more ambiguous and perilous. Transjordanian nationalists, in contrast, were ambivalent about Jordan's exclusion from the disengagement agreements. In part, they were satisfied because the exclusion implied Jordan's aloofness from Palestinian issues. But they were also worried because the exclusion might mean that Israel would not give up the West Bank, causing its people to move into Jordan and exacerbate the already scary issue of how many Palestinians resided in Jordan.

The American factor resurged once again in the Camp David accords, signed by President Carter, President Sadat, and Prime Minister Begin on September 17, 1978. The accords consisted of two documents. One was a framework for the conclusion of peace between Egypt and Israel, the other a framework for peace in the Middle East, focusing on the establishment of a self-governing authority in the West Bank and Gaza. In this accord, Jordan was given an essential role in negotiating with Israel and Egypt the modalities for establishing the elected self-governing authority and for determining the final status of the West Bank and Gaza.

Lukacs reports that "Jordan is mentioned fifteen times in the document even though it was not a signatory to the agreement."[27] Jordan viewed the accords negatively and refused to participate in the process they instigated. The official reason for this refusal was that Jordan had no legal or moral obligations to matters that Jordan had not participated in discussing or formulating. The PLO, which was excluded as an actor, condemned the Camp David accords strongly and warned Palestinians in the occupied territories against participating in any function related to them. The Arab states held a summit in Baghdad (November 1978) that Egypt failed to attend, and the summit ostracized Egypt.

The rejection by Jordan and the PLO of the Camp David accords placed them in the same camp. As a result, their public political rivalry receded in favor of cooperation. The Jordanian-Palestinian relationship entered a new phase. Arafat visited Jordan in March 1979 to discuss "the upcoming Egyptian-Israeli peace treaty and the necessary steps to be taken. The joint communiqué that was issued after the discussions emphasized the development of Jordanian-Palestinian relations and abiding by the Baghdad summit resolutions. As a result of this visit, the PLO office in Amman was reopened and became like a PLO diplomatic mission in Jordan. To prove its good intentions, the government released a number of detained fedayeen."[28]

The best manifestation of the cooperation between Jordan and the PLO was the setting up of the High Jordanian-Palestinian Committee on the Affairs of the Occupied Territories. Its task was to fulfill the needs of the Palestinians under occupation, a job made possible by the annual $150 million that the Baghdad summit had allocated in support of the Palestinians' steadfastness. The Baghdad summit had also allocated $1.25 billion for Jordan and $150 million for the PLO annually. Syria's share was $1.8 billion.

The Jordanian-Palestinian cooperation continued, though at a slow pace, within the parameters set by each party—namely, Jordan's unwillingness to lift the ban on fedayeen operations against Israel from Jordan's territory and the PLO's adherence to the Rabat Resolution. According to Lukacs, "not until Israel's invasion of Lebanon in June 1982 and the subsequent September 1, 1982, peace plan proposed by President Reagan did Jordan come back to the limelight."[29] On June 6, 1982, the Israeli army invaded Lebanon, destroyed the PLO's infrastructure, and besieged Beirut. Ambassador Phillip Habib, President Reagan's special envoy, brokered an agreement between the PLO and Israel by which the fedayeen evacuated Beirut. The American factor once again triggered the Jordanian-Palestinian dynamic. On September 1, 1982, as the PLO was poised to leave Beirut, Reagan announced his peace plan. This plan, based on yet more specific principles than the second of the Camp David accords, emphasized the land-for-peace principle and called for a self-governing authority in the West Bank and Gaza Strip in association with Jordan and the freezing of Jewish settlements in the occupied Arab territories. Reagan expressed his opposition both to the establishment of an independent Palestinian state and to permanent control of the occupied territories by Israel. Obviously the plan placed King Hussein in a quandary not unlike the one he faced in 1967: to act or not to act. According to Salibi, "the Reagan plan, in essence, was similar to the United Arab Kingdom project advanced by the king in 1972. Accordingly, the king proceeded to reactivate the project on September 20, in preparation for the expected peace talks."[30]

JORDAN'S QUEST FOR A PEACEFUL SETTLEMENT WITH A PROPER COVER

By the time Reagan launched his plan, the Israeli policy of building settlements in the West Bank was in effect and continuing at a steady pace. Jordan viewed this policy as the Likud's strategy for depopulating the West Bank. This was Jordan's nightmare, and had forced it in early 1979 to file a complaint with the Security Council against Israel's settlement policy. In addition, two other events had taken place of special significance to Jordan. The first was Israel's large-scale operation in March 1978, when Israeli troops, in retaliation for a fedayeen raid on the Israeli coast that had killed thirty-seven people, attacked the fedayeen bases in Lebanon and occupied a six-mile-wide strip in southern Lebanon. As a result, twenty-five thousand Lebanese villagers fled north, and the United Nations Interim Force in Lebanon (UNIFIL) was deployed along the Lebanese-Israeli cease-fire lines, according to Security Council Resolution 425 of March 19, 1978. The special significance of this event to the king was the fact that while Israel carried out its operation, there had been no Arab military reaction to defend Lebanon. The king concluded that the same could happen to Jordan, but with more dangerous results.

The second event was the 1981 elections in Israel, which provided the Likud with another term in office. To the king, the continuation of Likud rule implied the continuation of its settlement policy and the possibility of thrusting hundreds of thousands of West Bankers into the East Bank through a military operation similar to the 1978 invasion of Lebanon.

At the core of the king's quandary was Israel's position not to relinquish the occupied territories, including Jerusalem, in a political settlement. If Israel had been ready to withdraw from all the territories with minor rectification of the borders on a reciprocal basis, the king would have taken action without worrying about the PLO's reaction. But the Israeli position made it impossible for Jordan to take the plunge, and it became imperative for the king to look for a cover under which he could reach a political settlement and eventually save Jordan and the regime. To find such a cover, the king tried three approaches: searching for PLO partnership, calling for an international conference, and soliciting Palestinian partnership in the occupied territories.

All these attempts, which occurred over six years (1982–88), failed. The first attempt started three days after Reagan launched his plan. On September 3, 1982, the king delegated the chief of the royal court and the foreign minister to meet Arafat in Athens after he had evacuated Beirut on September 1. The delegation expressed to Arafat the king's interest in the integrity of the PLO. At this time, the PLO was at its nadir, and the king saw this weakness as a loophole through which he might convince Arafat to fulfill the American conditions. Jordan viewed Reagan's plan as a formula for Jordanian-Palestinian confederation, and it solicited Arafat's approval on this basis. Arafat found Jordan's fervor for the confederal relationship a positive sign, since it implied a shift away from the federal relationship suggested by the king's 1972 plan. Though the PLO did not accept Reagan's plan, the sixteenth PNC, convened in Algiers (February 14–24, 1983), underscored the "special relationship" between Jordanians and Palestinians and expressed the PLO's hope of building future relations on the basis of a confederation between two independent states. The PLO's new attitude came after several months (October 1982–February 1983) of intensive discussions between Jordan and the PLO. The goal of these discussions was to reach a Jordanian-Palestinian position that would enable them to work together for the implementation of Reagan's plan. A draft agreement was reached on April 5, 1983, but Arafat suspended his final approval until he had sought the counsel of other PLO members. On April 10, the Jordanian government issued a statement announcing that the PLO had not approved the agreement. It went on:

> We in Jordan, having refused from the beginning to negotiate on behalf of the Palestinians, will neither act separately nor in lieu of anybody in any Middle East peace negotiations. . . . We shall continue nevertheless to provide support for our brethren in the occupied territories. . . . As for us in Jordan, we are directly affected by the results of the continued occupation of the West Bank and the Gaza Strip through the accelerating colonization program and the economic pressures systematically brought on the Palestinian people to force them out of their land. . . . In light of these facts, and in the no-war–no-peace situation that prevails, we find ourselves more concerned than anybody else to confront the de facto annexation of the West Bank and Gaza Strip, which forces us to take all steps necessary to safeguard our national security in all its dimensions.[31]

Nevertheless, the king did not give up on the notion of a partnership with the PLO. A window of opportunity was reopened in late December 1983, when Arafat and his fedayeen supporters were evicted from Tripoli (Lebanon) by his opponents, who had split from Fatah, with the help of the Syrians. By the end of 1983, Arafat was even weaker than in September 1982, when he had evacuated Beirut, and this represented another opening for the king. To further pressure Arafat, the king decreed the resumption, as of January 16, 1984, of Parliament, suspended since November 1974 (after Rabat). The activation of Parliament with half its members from the West Bank sent an implicit message that Jordan had another choice for Palestinian partnership—the West Bankers. I myself, a West Banker, was appointed as minister of the royal court. Anticipating the worries of Transjordanian nationalists that this message would spark, he chose Ahmad Obeidat, a Transjordanian, to form a new cabinet on January 10, 1984. As a former minister of the interior and former director general of the Mukhabarat, Obeidat was a soothing factor.

Arafat, at his low point as a result of losing ground in all the countries bordering Israel and because of the split that had occurred within his own faction (Fatah), started to see Jordan as a way out of his predicament. After all, political coordination with Jordan would enable him to maintain the PLO's bonds with the Palestinians in the occupied territories.

Early in 1984, the contacts between the PLO and Jordan intensified. Arafat asked to convene the seventeenth PNC in Jordan, and the king gave his consent. When the king opened the PNC session on November 22, 1984, he underscored the significance of Jordanian-Palestinian joint action to get out of the no-peace–no-war situation and save the West Bank. He proposed an initiative based on Resolution 242, the land-for-peace principle, as well as peace negotiations held within an international conference in which the PLO would participate with the other parties on an equal footing.

It is to be noticed that Reagan's plan did not mention an international peace conference. King Hussein brought it up as a new element, believing that it would strengthen Arafat against his opponents within the PLO and that it would placate Syria and the Soviet Union (both of whom opposed Reagan's plan). An international conference would allow the Soviet Union to be a partner, and Syria would not be excluded from the peace process. Both had cultivated Palestinian opposition to Arafat's initial response to the king's call for cooperation.

The second round produced the February 11, 1985, Amman accord, in which Jordan and the PLO called for total Israeli withdrawal from the occupied territories, the resolution of the refugee problem, Palestinian self-determination within a Jordanian-Palestinian confederation, and an international conference to be attended by the parties to the conflict as well as by the five permanent members of the Security Council. The PLO, according to the accord, would be part of a single Jordanian-Palestinian delegation.

The Amman accord was overwhelmingly supported by the Palestinians in the occupied territories, but within the PLO a disagreement emerged. The PFLP and PDFLP opposed it, as did Syria. An Arab summit in Casablanca (Morocco) blessed it. The United States was intensely involved in diplomatic discussions with Jordan over the international conference and the qualification of the PLO. The United States was hesitant about calling for an international conference because it hoped to exclude the Soviet Union. George Shultz, the U.S. secretary of state in the Reagan administration, writes, "Explanatory messages came in saying that such a conference would come only at the end of the negotiations, to ratify and guarantee whatever outcome would be reached by means of direct Arab-Israeli negotiations, and so we shouldn't worry about the conference. I was not reassured."[32]

To put flesh on the Amman accord, King Hussein and Arafat planned to send a joint Palestinian-Jordanian delegation to the capitals of the five permanent Security Council members. Neither the Soviet Union nor the United States received them. Unlike the Soviet Union, which refused to support the accord, the United States did not reject it, yet it also did not accept all its items.

The PLO was very reluctant to accept Resolution 242 unequivocally. Arafat insisted on American endorsement of Palestinian self-determination and a direct dialogue with the PLO. A year of intensive diplomatic efforts failed to change Arafat's decision. On February 19, 1986, the king announced in an address to the nation "our inability to continue political coordination with the PLO." The irony in this painstaking diplomatic exercise was that while the king thought the weakness of the PLO would make it flexible, Arafat realized that no progress would ever be made on the Palestinian issue without the PLO. Hence, Arafat's well-known term for the PLO: *al-raqam al-sa'b* (the hard figure). George Shultz, who more than any other secretary of state was embroiled in the Jordanian-Palestinian issue, grasped the king's problem: "For all my frustration with King Hussein, I know that the problem of Palestinian representation was a legitimate one for him, and a big one. He had not been able to solve the problem himself, and we had not been able to solve it for him."[33]

LOOKING TO THE PALESTINIANS IN THE OCCUPIED TERRITORIES

The official termination of Jordan-PLO coordination did not terminate the king's concerns about *al-Watan al-Badil*. His February 19 address to the nation included this reference: "In addition to our national, religious, and moral commitment to Jerusalem, the holy shrines, the Palestinian people, and their homeland, there are our obligations toward our national security." He pointed out three Israeli schools of thought on the Palestinian question. "The third school," he said, "calls for expelling the inhabitants (Palestinians) eastward by using military force. . . . The advocates of this school occupy a number of seats in the Knesset [Israel's Parliament]."

The king had considered partnership with the Palestinians in the occupied territories as a fallback position in case he failed to secure the PLO partnership. He had already told the United States about his strategy. According to Shultz, "again King Hussein told us that if Arafat would not cooperate with him in dealing with Israel about the territories, he would move without the PLO to build a pro-Jordanian constituency among West Bank Palestinians and try to form a delegation from them."[34]

After the king's February 19 speech, PLO relations with Jordan deteriorated. In July 1986 the government ordered the closure of all PLO and Fatah offices, which had been reopened in 1978. This measure was intended to cut the PLO's umbilical chord to the Palestinians in the occupied territories. Next, the government approached the Palestinians with a $1.292 billion five-year development plan for economic, social, and educational projects on the West Bank and in Gaza. The plan was inaugurated in Amman with a conference attended by representatives of Arab and foreign aid agencies—in other words, the prospective donors and lenders. It was also attended by some West Bankers, especially from the public sector.

The rationale behind the development plan was to improve the Palestinians' quality of life, create jobs, and eventually stop or at least slow down Palestinian emigration to Jordan. The plan was also designed to create a local Palestinian leadership free of PLO influence. Such a leadership would, at the right time, become Jordan's Palestinian partner in negotiating a peaceful settlement with Israel within an international conference.

To give this strategy a greater chance of success, Jordan moved on two fronts: the functional front in cooperation with Israel (known as the "condominium strategy") and the political one in cooperation with Arafat's adversaries. The sub rosa Jordanian-Israeli interaction intensified. The outcome was the Hussein-Peres agreement, concluded in London in April 1987. Peres at the time was Israel's foreign minister in the national unity government. The agreement provided for convening an international conference within which direct negotiations would be concluded, and the Palestinians would participate as members of a Jordanian-Palestinian delegation. As to its prerogatives, the conference would not intervene and veto any agreement reached between the parties unless the parties themselves agreed. At the functional level, much was achieved. Lukacs sums it up: "Israel and Jordan agreed to reopen the Cairo-Amman Bank, facilitated the Jordanian development plan, and agreed on the appointment of West Bank mayors, notably Zafir al-Masri, the mayor of Nablus."[35]

On the political front, the Jordanian government cultivated a prominent Fatah member who had broken away from Arafat and settled in Jordan. Jordan wanted to give its strategy a PLO flavor and thought that if such an ex-Fatah member were involved in the West Bank political activity, he might be the answer. In the early stages, Jordan's strategy required a low-key approach, but the chosen figure, an outspoken show-off, did not cooperate. He soon became known in Amman as the protégé intended to replace Arafat, and his image generated broad-based Palestinian-Jordanian opposition before anything serious could be accomplished.

While Jordan was busy carrying out its strategy, a new actor was looming on the horizon. This new actor appeared in the Palestinian uprising that began in December 1987; the *intifada,* its Arabic name, was destined to change almost all the rules of the game in the Palestinian political sphere.

JORDAN'S DISENGAGEMENT WITH THE WEST BANK

In December 1987, while the PLO was still at its ebb, a Palestinian popular uprising against the Israeli occupation broke out in Gaza and spread to the West Bank. It came quite unexpectedly after twenty years of occupation, during which many reporters had grown used to describing the Palestinians under occupation as docile. Soon the *intifada* produced leadership that issued occasional communiqués about its confrontations with the Israeli occupying forces as well as giving instructions and guidance to the people. The Jordanian government and people came out in support of the *intifada.* Government and popular committees were set up to raise funds for the Palestinian victims of Israel's repressive response. On March 11, 1988, the United Command of the Uprising issued its tenth communiqué, calling on the people to intensify the mass pressure against the occupation army and the settlers and against collaborators and personnel of the Jordanian regime. We are proud of our people for punishing them and pressing them to desist from their ways by publishing this resolution in mosques, churches, and before the popular committees. We also call upon the [Palestinian] deputies in the Jordanian Parliament who were appointed by the king to represent our people, to promptly resign their seats and align with their people. Otherwise, there will be no room for them on our land.[36]

The king described the communiqué as a "horrible sign of ingratitude" and soon came to realize that his strategy of substituting a partnership with the Palestinians in the occupied territories for one with the PLO had fallen apart. He had spent six years trying to solicit a Palestinian partnership in order to reach a peaceful settlement with Israel and safeguard Jordan from becoming the substitute Palestinian homeland. He had reinstated the suspended Parliament with 50 percent West Bank seats and launched an ambitious five-year development plan in the West Bank and Gaza—all in vain. Only one thing persisted: the substitute-homeland nightmare. During the six-year crusade, Transjordanian nationalists had been unhappy with the king's attempts. In their view, Jordan would be safer without the West Bank and without the Palestinians. They were happy with every failure the king faced in his quest to secure a Palestinian partnership. The government, however, never stopped the de-Palestinianization process. The one-time increase in the number of Palestinians in the cabinet to the pre-Rabat level occurred in April 1985 to symbolize the equal partnership that the February 11 confederal agreement between Jordan and the PLO had envisaged.

In March 1988, the king began to consider disengaging from the West Bank. He had to act under five constraints—four rational and one emotional. The four rational constraints were the following. (1) Internationally, especially in the West, Jordan's disengagement from the West Bank must not jeopardize Jordan's regional role, which functions as the guarantor of Jordan's national security. Up to this point, Jordan's attempts to reach peace with Israel had been appreciated by the West in general and by the United States in particular. (2) In the Arab arena, the disengagement decision must not provide the oil-producing Arab countries with a pretext to stop their financial assistance. (By 1988 all the Arab countries except Saudi Arabia had stopped living up to their Baghdad summit financial commitments.) (3) Israel must not take the disengagement decision as a warrant to annex the West Bank. (4) The disengagement decision must not reflect on the Jordanian-Palestinian relationship in Jordan; national unity should be maintained.

The emotional constraint related to Jerusalem. As a Hashemite, the king was eager that his forthcoming decision would not further jeopardize the status of that city.

In June 1988 an Arab emergency summit convened in Algiers to discuss the ways and means of supporting the *intifada*. Here was the proper forum in which the king could pave the way for his upcoming historical decision. Indeed, the Algiers summit, in its resolution to support the *intifada* financially through the Jordanian-Palestinian Committee rather than through Jordan, spurred the king to take the decision.

On July 28, the government canceled its five-year development plan for the occupied territories, and on July 30, the king dissolved Parliament. On July 31, the king announced his decision to commence "administrative and legal disengagement from the West Bank," though he emphasized that Jordan was to continue its administration of the Muslim holy shrines in Jerusalem and al-Awqaf (the Islamic endowment). He described Jordan's relationship with the Palestinians since the occupation of the West Bank until this decision as a "suspending situation under which neither Jordan nor the Palestinian cause were best served." Elaborating on the reasons supporting his decision, the king went on:

Of late, it has become clear that there is a general Palestinian and Arab orientation toward highlighting the Palestinian identity in full in all efforts and activities that are related to the Palestine question and its developments. It has also become obvious that there is a general conviction that maintaining the legal and administrative relationship with the West Bank . . . goes against this orientation. It would be an obstacle to the Palestinian struggle, which seeks to win international support for the Palestine question, considering that it is a just national issue of a people struggling against foreign occupation. Since this is the orientation that emanates from a genuine Palestinian wish and a strong Arab willingness to promote the Palestinian cause, it is our duty to be part of this orientation and to meet its requirements.

One of the major issues the king addressed was national unity:

However, it is to be understood in all clarity, and without any ambiguity or equivocations, that our measures regarding the West Bank concern only the occupied Palestinian territory and its people. They naturally do not relate in any way to the Jordanian citizens of Palestinian origin in the Hashemite Kingdom of Jordan. They all have the full rights of citizenship and all its obligations, the same as any other citizen irrespective of his origin. They are an integral part of the Jordanian state. They belong to it, they live on its territory, and they participate in its life and all its activities. Jordan is not Palestine; and the independent Palestinian state will be established on the occupied Palestinian land after its liberation, God willing. There, the Palestinian identity will be embodied, and there the Palestinian struggle shall come to fruition, as confirmed by the glorious uprising of the Palestinian people under occupation. National unity is precious in any country; but in Jordan it is more than that. It is the basis of our stability and the springboard of our development and prosperity. It is the foundation of our national security and the source of our faith in the future. It is the epitome of the principles of the Great Arab Revolt, which we inherited, and whose banner we proudly raise. It is a living example of constructive pluralism and a sound nucleus for broader Arab unity.[37]

The emphasis on national unity was noticeably strong, and not without good reason. When the king asked me to write the disengagement speech and gave me his directives, including the themes to be addressed, the national unity theme was one of them. I suggested that the speech should be very clear and specific on this theme, as I was concerned that many Transjordanian nationalists, especially in the public sector, might go beyond the limits that the king wanted to set and take the upcoming decision to mean that Palestinian-Jordanians in Jordan would no longer be Jordanian citizens. The king's response was "A^{c}udhu bi-llah" (Impossible!). But I was aware that the de-Palestinianization process had not ceased even during the six-year period when the king had sought Palestinian partnerships and despite the fact that the 1985–89 cabinet included ten Palestinian-Jordanian ministers out of the total of twenty-three and also despite the resumption since January 1984 of the suspended Parliament with 50 percent of the seats for West Bankers. Indeed, I had drawn the king's attention to the discriminatory practices of the bureaucracy against Palestinian-Jordanians twice in the mid and late 1980s, once during a meeting of the inner cabinet always chaired by the king. My remark was not taken favorably by the other members.

The first reaction of the PLO to the king's disengagement decision reflected the former's suspicions that the king had an ulterior motive. Soon, however, the PLO welcomed the decision and moved quickly to capitalize on it. On November 15, 1988, the PNC held an emergency session in Algiers in which it approved the text of the Declaration of the State of Palestine, with Jerusalem as its capital. Jordan and other Arab states recognized the State of Palestine. The PNC also decided to accept Security Council Resolution 242, a step toward meeting the American conditions for negotiations with the PLO. On April 2, 1989, Arafat was elected president of the State of Palestine by the Palestinian Central Committee in

Tunis. On December 13, 1988, Arafat addressed the General Assembly of the United Nations in Geneva, calling for a peaceful settlement and the establishment of a Palestinian state that would renounce terrorism in all its aspects. On December 15, President Reagan announced the U.S. government's decision to start a direct dialogue with the PLO. The separation between Jordan and Palestine was formalized on January 7, 1989, when Jordan considered the PLO office in Amman as the Palestinian embassy and a Palestinian ambassador presented his credentials to the king.

Contrary to what the king had stressed in his disengagement speech on July 31, 1988, Transjordanian nationalists within the bureaucracy and outside took the speech as an endorsement of the ongoing discriminatory practices against Palestinian-Jordanians and a signal to start lobbying for the institutionalization of Transjordanian domination over Palestinian-Jordanians in Jordan. The Palestinian-Jordanians, in contrast, took the disengagement decision as the king had spelled it out in his speech: Jordan is Jordan for all its inhabitants irrespective of their origin, and the West Bank is Palestine for its Palestinian inhabitants and any other Palestinians who wish to settle there or affiliate with it once the Palestinian state is established.

The declaration of the State of Palestine and the U.S. decision to start a dialogue with the PLO gave Palestinian-Jordanians hope that the end of uncertainty regarding their status was imminent. They expected that the nightmare of *al-Watan al-Badil* would fade away, to be replaced by a reamalgamation process putting an end to the September showdown rupture and to the implications of the Rabbat Resolution. Soon they realized that their expectations were wrong, and frustration began to replace relief: the nightmare of *al-Watan al-Badil* persisted. They could do nothing but wait for salvation. The idea that these conditions were only temporary was their haven. Indeed, temporariness was the psychological haven for both Transjordanians and Palestinian-Jordanians. For Transjordanians, it justified the de facto demotion of Palestinian-Jordanians, since to them, Palestinian-Jordanians were guests until their problem was solved and their state established. Temporariness helped Palestinian-Jordanians tolerate discrimination because they felt it was bound to come to an end. It was during this period that I became familiar with the Arabic expression *ana ibn al-balad* (I am a genuine Jordanian), used when a Transjordanian would call to ask for my help in getting a job, a scholarship, or medical treatment abroad. *Ana ibn al-balad* was supposed to strengthen the person's credentials. Of course such people sought my assistance because

I was a senior official at the royal court, a middleman with access to the resources of the state.

To Transjordanian nationalists, the disengagement decision was tantamount to dismantling a company or splitting a legacy among heirs. Each partner or heir was to receive his or her fair share. The East Bank was the Transjordanians' share as much as the West Bank was the share of the Palestinians, including those who had settled on the East Bank since 1948. After all, it was the Palestinian partner who chose to liquidate the company. According to this reasoning, any Palestinian-Jordanian complaint of discriminating practices was shrugged off as unwarranted after the split of the legacy. Transjordanian nationalists saw no moral problem in the de facto demotion of Palestinian-Jordanians who were supposed to be fellow citizens.

Still, the notion of temporariness was an essential psychological factor in precluding polarization, and it was sustained by the king's consistent reference to Palestinian-Jordanians and Transjordanians as *muhajirin* and *ansar.*

FROM REACTION TO PROACTION

The July 1988 disengagement decision brought Jordan back to its pre-1950 geographical map but not to its previous demographic structure. Now at least half the population were of Palestinian origin, a fact that the government and Transjordanian nationalists had to reckon with when the state began to put its house in order.

Restructuring political life addressed three interconnected areas, and each one reflected the Palestinian factor. The first one was the legislation of a new election law for the House of Deputies (the lower house of Parliament). Naturally, the new legislation excluded the West Bank. Over the course of ten years, the government increased the number of governorates three times. The first time was in 1985, before the disengagement decision, when Jordan added three governorates by redividing the existing ones. This decision was appreciated because it matched the demographic and economic changes that had occurred over the preceding thirty years. The two other times were in 1989, when the government added three more governorates, and in 1995, when it added another one. Increasing the number of governorates also increased the number of districts and subdistricts (*alwiya* and *aqdiya*). According to current administrative divisions, Jordan consists of twelve governorates, thirty-nine districts, and thirty-four subdistricts. Except for one governorate (Zarqa) where

Palestinian-Jordanians are concentrated, the other six new governorates are overwhelmingly populated by Transjordanians. The increase in the number of governorates implied an increase in the number of seats for deputies, from thirty for the East Bank before the disengagement decision to eighty for Jordan after the decision. Out of the eighty, three seats are allotted for Circassian and Chechen minorities, six are allotted for bedouins, and seven are allotted for Christians (six of these are allotted to constituencies in which most Christians are Transjordanians). With these allocations for ethnic, religious, and social minorities, only the Christian seat in the Amman constituency could be competed for by both Palestinian-Jordanians and Transjordanians. In the worst-case scenario for Transjordanians or the best-case scenario for Palestinian-Jordanians, fifteen out of sixteen seats for minorities will be occupied by Transjordanians in any election. (The Amman Christian seat in the 1993 elections was occupied by a Transjordanian Christian.) The remaining seventy-four seats are to be competed for by Transjordanian and Palestinian-Jordanian Muslims. Since the number of seats in the House of Deputies for each constituency is not determined by the size of the population, the administrative divisions of the kingdom have predetermined the highest number of Palestinian-Jordanian deputies in Parliament, even if Palestinian-Jordanians were to cast their ballots purely on a communal basis, banding together to elect only Palestinian-Jordanian candidates. In such a case, and without regard for the number of inhabitants in each constituency, the Palestinian-Jordanians could secure nineteen seats at most for Muslims and probably one seat for Christians out of eighty—25 percent. So it is not surprising that Palestinian-Jordanians occupied only thirteen seats in the House of Deputies between 1993 and 1997. Theoretically the number of Palestinian-Jordanian seats would exceed twenty only if Palestinian-Jordanian candidates ran for elections in Transjordanian districts and were able to win Transjordanian votes. Thus, Jordanian geography was used to emasculate Palestinian demography as a safeguard against the Palestinian-Jordanians achieving political domination through democratic means.

Abdul-Salam al-Majali, a prominent figure among the Transjordanian political elite and the prime minister of the government that signed Jordan's peace treaty with Israel, has said about the disproportionate representativeness of Palestinian-Jordanians in Parliament, "I do not agree that the number of seats for every constituency should reflect the size of the population. Geographical groups should be represented. Otherwise the population of Amman, which has increased tremendously in recent years, would rule the whole country." He supports the view that if Palestinian-Jordanians occupied half the number of seats in Parliament, the illusion of *al-Watan al-Badil* would be nurtured afresh, and he stresses the need to use the two criteria—the numbers of inhabitants and geographical representativeness—in deciding the number of seats for each constituency. As to Palestinian-Jordanians being underrepresented in the government, al-Majali says, "New formulas related to the structure of society, its districts, and the sentiments of the people should be taken into consideration. Competence is not the only criterion. Such a situation should be gradually redressed through increased awareness, as well as through social, cultural, and intellectual development." He adds that "the problem of Palestinian-Jordanians is that they do not exist in a specific governorate."[38]

Concrete evidence of this policy, standing since 1974, is the structure of the upper house in Parliament (see table 3). The members of the chamber are appointed, not elected. The members of the seventeenth upper house were appointed on November 23, 1993, when al-Majali was prime minister. Palestinian-Jordanians, who constitute 50 percent of the population, accounted for only seven members out of forty (17.5 percent). Table 3 shows the percentages of Palestinian-Jordanians in the government, Parliament, and high administrative posts as of August 1997.

The second area that witnessed political restructuring after the disengagement from the West Bank lay in the formation of political parties. For the first time since the unity of the two banks in 1950, some political parties were founded on "Jordan for Jordanians" principles, excluding or at least reducing Palestinian-Jordanian participation in the national consensus. One of these parties, al-Ahd, was able to secure more than ten seats in the House of Deputies in the 1993 elections. This party set out to

Table 3. Palestinians-Jordanians in Positions of Power, August 1997

	Transjordanians	Palestinian-Jordanians	% of Palestinian-Jordanians
Cabinet ministers	18	6	25.0
Ambassadors	39	6	13.3
Key and senior posts	80	20	20.0
Members of Parliament			
(a) Lower house (elected)	67	13	16.25
(b) Upper house (appointed)	33	7	17.5

enlist Transjordanian members right after the disengagement decision. Many of its prominent members are retired Transjordanian army officers. The third area was the establishment of safe parameters within which the political parties would operate. One of the most dangerous political experiences that Jordan had undergone occurred in 1956–57, when the political parties had banded together against the monarchical regime. When the king decided on political liberalization, he was determined not to see 1957 revisited. The Jordanian National Charter, described in chapter 4, solved the problem by setting the principles for pluralism. Among other things, the charter addressed the Jordanian-Palestinian relationship. The "substitute homeland" was a central theme in defining their relationship. The second and third articles of chapter 7 read:

> Second: Political variables at the Arab and international levels, together with developments in the Jordanian-Palestinian arena, resulted in the severing of administrative and legal ties with the West Bank, with which the PLO agreed. They also led to the declaration of an independent Palestinian state under the leadership of the PLO and to recognition by Jordan of the Palestinian state. This has given rise to a new reality that emphasizes the special and distinctive nature of the Jordanian-Palestinian relationship and establishes the conditions for placing it on a right footing and basing it on a clear set of principles.
>
> Third: On this basis, the Jordanian-Palestinian relationship must not be understood or exploited under any conditions whatsoever to imply any curtailment of the rights of citizenship or to lead to a weakening of the Jordanian state from the inside or to create conditions leading to the realization of Zionist designs to make Jordan the substitute Palestinian homeland. From this perspective, a commitment to Jordan's national security becomes the responsibility of all citizens and serves to emphasize their continued struggle and sacrifice for the liberation of Palestine and the preservation of Jordan and its ideology.[39]

If anything, the concerted efforts of the king, the government, and Transjordanian elite to put the Jordanian house in order by establishing safeguards to preempt any potential political domination by Palestinian-Jordanians that might lead to *al-Watan al-Badil* reasserted the Jordanian state-centered nationalism.

THE SURFACING OF THE DEMOGRAPHIC FACTOR

On August 2, 1990, Iraq invaded and annexed Kuwait. An American-led international alliance evicted the Iraqi troops on February 28, 1991. Many Arab states, including Egypt and Syria, joined the alliance. Jordan did not. During the Iraqi occupation, hundreds of thousands of expatriates who had jobs in Kuwait either fled the country or were expelled by the Iraqi occupation authority. Scores of thousands of them were Jordanians of Palestinian origin. After the restoration of Kuwaiti rule over the country, Kuwaiti authorities expelled the remaining Palestinian-Jordanians (except for a few thousand) as an expression of Kuwait's disaffection with King Hussein's and Arafat's positions. Other countries of the Gulf Cooperation Council (GCC) terminated the residence permits of many Jordanians. The total number of Palestinian-Jordanians who returned to Jordan amounted to more than two hundred thousand. This large number struck a sensitive chord for Transjordanians, who had barely begun to rejoice at the disengagement decision, when they were shocked once more by an intensification of the Palestinian demographic factor. About this particular episode, Laurie Brand, a U.S. scholar, has written:

> The influx of 200,000 Jordanians (most of them Palestinian) mainly from Kuwait exacerbated what was already a serious unemployment problem, strained state services, and drove up food and housing prices. These developments strengthened the perception among many Transjordanians that they were gradually losing control of their country to successive waves of "outsiders" seen as possessing the kingdom's wealth and therefore poised to acquire more and more power. The result has been the gradual development of a much broader sense of Transjordanianness reminiscent of the "'East Banker First" surge in the wake of Black September. This emerging sentiment, expressed outside the state, most often takes the form of opposition to the role of Palestinians and Palestinian institutions in Jordanian affairs.[40]

RELAXATION OF THE LAST CONSTRAINT

For Jordan, making peace with Israel had never been an issue of principle but one of timing. Indeed, Jordan had always considered peace with Israel a national security imperative and a panacea to all its problems, especially its economic malaise. For more than four decades, conventional wisdom in Jordan held that all the problems Jordan faced stemmed from the state of war with Israel, which was employed by other Arab states in the Arab power struggle.

As far as peace with Israel was concerned, Jordan was under constraints from two sources: Arab and Palestinian. The Arab constraint faded away when Iraq invaded Kuwait and when Syria, one of the most vocal Arab countries against Israel and the United States, joined the American-led coalition against Iraq. The Palestinian constraint disappeared on September 13, 1993, when Israel's prime minister Rabin and Chairman Arafat signed the DOP in Washington. Nevertheless, when a PLO spokesperson announced on August 26, 1993, that an agreement was about to be reached between Israel and the PLO, Jordan's government and the Transjordanian nationalists grew deeply worried because the government had not been notified about the secret talks between Israel and the PLO. This secrecy revived among Jordanian officials the fear of potential Israeli-Palestinian complicity against Jordan. At the time, Jordan was busy preparing for its scheduled general elections in November. Some editorials in the local press reflected this fear of a conspiracy. They questioned whether Palestinian-Jordanians were eligible to participate in the elections, since a Palestinian Authority was to be established in the West Bank and Gaza. The Jordanian authorities reduced enormously the number of Palestinians who crossed the bridges into Jordan. The American embassy used its good offices to persuade the government to stop these measures. As Mousa writes, "the agreement [DOP] was the 'biggest surprise' to Jordan. No one had known about it before it was announced, though Jordan is the closest to Palestine and has the strongest bonds with it."[41]

However, just one day after Israel and the PLO signed the DOP, Jordan and Israel signed the "Jordanian-Israeli agenda" in Washington, and this included the principles and goals of the Jordanian-Israeli peace negotiations. The agenda had been formulated between the two countries several weeks before the DOP was signed. But the Palestinian constraint had prevented Jordan from signing it. Lukacs sums it up, "Without the breakthrough agreement between Israel and the PLO, Jordan would not have been able to sign the treaty with Israel. The PLO legitimized the idea that a separate agreement with Israel was no longer treason as was also true when Egypt made peace with Israel."[42]

On July 25, 1994, Jordan and Israel signed the Washington Declaration signaling the end of the formal state of war between the two countries. On October 26, the peace treaty was signed.

The DOP and the peace treaty did not meet strong—or rather, visible—opposition. Transjordanians were happy because the treaty, as Prime Minister Majali said, "had buried *al-Watan al-Badil*" and because it was portrayed by the king and the government as a panacea to Jordan's problems. Two factors in particular forestalled any visible opposition. The first was the absence of a Jordanian political alliance between Palestinian-Jordanians and Transjordanians, and the second was the king's ongoing reference to Palestinian-Jordanians and Transjordanians as *muhajirin* and *ansar*. This phrase implied that "if any Palestinian wants to protest against the peace treaty, he had better protest against the DOP in his homeland, since the peace treaty does not relate to him."

The DOP and the peace treaty improved relations between Jordan and the PLO, but they did not salvage the status of Palestinian-Jordanians in Jordan. As far as the PLO is concerned, the Palestinian-Jordanians' status is not an issue, at least for the time being. The PLO's focus has become its political negotiations with Israel to move toward defining the borders of the Palestinian state.

Unlike the PLO, Jordan views Palestinian-Jordanians as an issue to be discussed, examined, and resolved. The peace treaty, which reassured Jordan about its territorial integrity and ensured that its borders are acknowledged by Israel, paved the way for thinking about the other pillar of the state—the people.

The DOP not only removed the Palestinian constraint on Jordan but also triggered a chain reaction among Palestinian-Jordanians. It shattered the hope of return for Palestinian refugees (the largest group of Palestinian-Jordanians), which in turn eliminated the sense of temporariness that had been such a soothing factor. Never had the divisiveness between Palestinian-Jordanians and Transjordanians been felt so strongly as it was after the signing of the DOP. Now it was not only Palestinian-Jordanians who wanted to redefine their status. Transjordanians also felt that it was time to decide on the final status of Palestinian-Jordanians. The irony is that while Palestinian-Jordanians, especially the refugees, have given up the notion of temporariness, Transjordanians still consider the refugees' existence in Jordan temporary and their loyalty to the state to be watched until their case is settled. In other words, while the PLO pushed Palestinian-Jordanians into limbo, Jordan placed them in purgatory. After the DOP, Palestinian-Jordanians realized that their case was no longer on the PLO agenda; they would have to present and defend it themselves.

In 1995, I met with a group of refugee leaders in al-Baqah Camp near Amman. The group consisted of traditional community leaders, professionals, and one member of Parliament. I discussed with them their general affairs, activities, and concerns. Their first major concern was their status in Jordan ("We want to know our rights and obligations"), and the second was the compensation issue—when and how the refugees would be compensated in terms of the UN resolution concerning them, which is based on the principle of return or compensation. The DOP has indeed effected a profound change in Palestinian-Jordanian priorities, encouraging Palestinian-Jordanians to discuss their issues in the local press (as mentioned at the beginning of this chapter) and to challenge the Transjordanian nationalist arguments that have long dominated the media. The concerns and grievances of the two communities were identified through a poll, conducted by the Jordanian Center for Strategic Studies in late 1994 and published in September 1995. Transjordanian concerns, according to the poll, included the following: the private sector is mostly in the hands of Palestinian-Jordanians; the mounting number of Palestinians in Jordan is alarming; Palestinian-Jordanians have a dual loyalty (to Jordan and to the PLO); Palestinian-Jordanians do not appreciate the benefits they have reaped as a result of their Jordanian citizenship. In turn, Palestinian-Jordanians complained about the following: the public sector is mostly manned by Transjordanians; Palestinian-Jordanians are not proportionately represented in the executive and legislative branches; sensitive government posts are exclusively staffed by Transjordanians; the government departments favor Transjordanians over Palestinian-Jordanians in various official transactions.[43]

To conclude, the retrogression of Palestinian-Jordanians' status was the outcome of internal and external pressures, at the heart of which were the fedayeen episode (1968–71), with its divisive effects, and the perceived nightmare of *al-Watan al-Badil,* a product of the triangular interaction in which Israel, through its policies, has played a central role. These pressures forced Jordan to adopt defensive policies, some of which were reactive while others were and are proactive. Together these pressures and policies contributed to crystallizing a sense of a distinct Palestinian community in Jordan, a community that shares the same aspirations and concerns as other Palestinian communities in the diaspora and in the occupied territories but that also has its own concerns, interests, and grievances—the special agenda of the Palestinian-Jordanians.

The same pressures and policies crystallized a sense of a Transjordanian community as distinct from the Palestinian community. Since the Transjordanian community has become almost exclusively the one in power and since it derives its name from the state, its distinctness has nurtured Transjordanian nationalism. Thus communal distinctness has become a source of tension and potential polarization.

11

Transjordanian Nationalism

A National Defense Mechanism

I n the early 1980s, author and leading Syrian intellectual George Tarabishi wrote,

> It is the age of statism, this era in which we live. Every regional [Arab] state claims to be a nation [on its own merits] and a substitute for the hoped-for pan-Arab state. For most regional states [*al-duwal al-qutriya*] there is a national assembly, a national economy, a national security council, a national airline, a national tourist bureau, a national costume, a national dish, besides the national anthem and the national flag.[1]

Despite the sarcasm behind Tarabishi's lament, his characterization of Arab nation-states is highly accurate. Jordanian nationhood is no exception to the rule of every other Arab nation-state developing its own national identity. Following the British drawing of the map, the country, under Emir and then King Abdullah, went through the usual steps of nation building: Transjordan was recognized as an autonomous entity as of 1923; a new state apparatus was solidly implanted and extended; supratribal structures were formed; the loyalty of the people to a stable government was, after 1925, assured; the formerly tribally differentiated inhabitants became Transjordanians, superseding their subnational identities. Thus, like many contemporary states, Jordan was made before

Jordanians. The Jordanian national identity was its effect, not its cause. As Eric Hobsbawm argues, "nations do not make states and nationalism, but the other way around."[2] All Jordanian national achievements under Emir-King Abdullah—namely, Jordan's independence (1946) and the unification of the East and West Banks (1950)—were initiated and realized by the emir-king. Herein lie the seeds of Jordan's state-centered nationalism. This is not to say that popular Transjordanian nationalism did not exist. It did. It manifested itself in the late 1920s and early 1930s through national conferences, especially the 1928 conference that criticized the organic law. But because of economic, cultural, social, and political factors (see chapter 1), Transjordanian nationalism lay dormant until 1964. Sown in the 1920s, its seeds bloomed in the 1970s. If anything is unique about Transjordanian nationalism, it is that, compared to other Arab regional nationalisms, it has been a late bloomer.

WHY A LATE BLOOMER?

The seeds of popular Transjordanian nationalism sown by the colonial map were submerged by the pan-Arabism that King Abdullah stood for. The patriarchal political system, coupled with the social patriarchal value system, made it possible for state-led nationalism to prevail. There was no room in this system for national leaders. Through co-optation, they withered away as soon as they emerged. After all, in a ruling monarchy the only national leader is the monarch himself. The 1950 unity of the Jordanian East Bank and the Palestinian West Bank vindicated King Abdullah's pan-Arabism and submerged further the seeds of Transjordanian nationalism.

It is worth noting here that one reason Transjordanians looked favorably on unity in the early 1950s, despite their concern that the much larger number of Palestinians would blur their identity, was the need to protect their Palestinian brethren from the Israeli threat. This need was promoted by pro–King Abdullah Palestinian notables to convince West Bankers to unite with East Bankers. Simultaneously, this need appealed to Transjordanians, whose tribal value system highly esteemed the allocation of protection to those who sought it. The 1967 defeat in the June war shattered this jointly cherished notion. In fact, the loss of the West Bank was later perceived by Transjordanians as the Palestinian-Jordanians' loss of their share of the company (the East Bank–West Bank unity) rather than the loss of part of the kingdom. This perception was strengthened by the PLO's insistence on representing the West Bank. However, it was this perception that laid the foundations for the host-guest theme that emerged in the 1970s.

In contrast, King Hussein's strategy regarding nationalism emanated from his defensive considerations, though it adopted aggressive methods most of the time. In the early 1950s, following Hussein's accession to the throne, precursors of popular Jordanian (not Transjordanian) nationalism began to sprout, based on what Laurie Brand calls "the hybrid (pan-Jordanian) identity."[3] It made itself felt from 1955–57 on two national occasions: the blockage of Jordan's quest to join the Baghdad Pact in 1955 and the termination of Jordan's treaty with Britain in 1957 after the king ousted General John Bagot Glubb from the army. Yet this version of Jordanian nationalism was more a convergence of politically like-minded people leaning on a broad popular base than a wholly national movement. It crystallized under the political liberalization of 1956. It was cross-communal and appealed to a sizable portion of the Jordanian (Transjordanian and Palestinian) grassroots. It grew outside the boundaries of the state-centered nationalism and became its rival. It was affected more by Nasser's pan-Arabism than by Hashemite pan-Arabism, and eventually this fact would polarize rather than unite the people. The king's 1957 crackdown on political parties opened a window of opportunity for him to fill in the resulting vacuum with an all-encompassing Jordanian nationalism (Transjordanians and Palestinian-Jordanians together) in which the king would be at the center, rather than at the other pole as he was during the upsurge of opposition-centered nationalism (1955–57). The king and the ruling elite had been inspired by that cross-communal opposition alliance; it offered a prototype of a nationalism that stemmed from a hybrid identity. They thought they could mobilize both Palestinian-Jordanians and Transjordanians, just as the opposition had, but along different lines. In addition to Hashemitism, the new king-led popular nationalism put emphasis on three pride-inspiring themes as rallying forces. The first was that Jordan was the custodian of the holy shrines in East Jerusalem, which the Jordanian army defended alongside Palestinian combatants against Israel's military attempts to occupy it during the 1948 war. The second was that the Jordan of the two banks represented a successful example of the yearned-for Arab unity. And the third was that Jordan was holding the longest lines of confrontation with Israel. This last theme inspired fear too, because it referred to an external enemy that was a permanent threat to Jordan. The pride-inspiring component in the three themes was more appealing to Transjordanians because they were more or less linked with the army, which was and still is an essential ingredient of Transjordanian identity. The fear-inspiring component was more appealing to Palestinian-Jordanians, especially West Bankers, because they had to take the brunt of any potential Israeli attack. Though this fear-inspiring theme made the West Bankers more pliant than defiant, it confirmed their conviction that Jordan alone could not defend the West Bank. Jordan should ally with other Arab states, especially Egypt, Syria, and Iraq, to be able to defend them. The king took this conviction into consideration when he decided to strike an alliance with Egypt just a few days before the outbreak of war in June 1967.

Promoting these themes was sufficient to lay the foundation for a Jordanian nationalism that encompassed Transjordanians and Palestinians. To a certain extent, it provided all Jordanians with the unifying and liberating ingredients that until 1948 Transjordanian nationalism had lacked. The defense of Jerusalem symbolized liberation, and so did the pledge to restore Palestinian rights. The unity of the two banks was the unifying ingredient. The fear-inspiring notion of the external enemy supported the other two.

It is easy to understand that the refugees would be less impressed by Jordanian nationalism. They had lost their homeland, and they wanted liberation, not symbols. Under these circumstances, even unity was meaningless unless it was tied to liberation. Simply put, it was difficult for them to appreciate unity while they resided in refugee camps. In this context, it was even difficult for them to identify with the West Bankers (fellow Palestinians). Nonetheless, the nascent Jordanian nationalism was effective enough to give a boost to the growing sentimental attachment of Palestinians to the state of Jordan.

TRANSJORDANIAN NATIONALISM REVIVED

In preceding chapters, I have examined the Transjordanian-Palestinian dynamic within Jordan during the late 1960s and 1970s. One effect of this dynamic—the retrogression of the status of Palestinian-Jordanians—was addressed in chapter 10. Another effect was the rejuvenation of Transjordanian nationalism that had lain dormant for almost four decades. This rejuvenation, which had an adverse impact on Palestinian-Jordanians, was due to internal and external pressures we have already identified and analyzed.

Due to these pressures and attendant perceptions, the once dormant Transjordanian nationalism resurged in 1970 as a product of the adverse triangular interaction among Jordan, Israel, and the PLO. In its new mold as a national defense rather than liberation mechanism, it has continued to grow. At first, it was a reaction to the perceived Palestinian threat to Transjordanian identity and to Israel's seemingly permanent occupation of the West Bank with its implications of more Palestinian emigration to the East Bank, more pressure on Jordan's meager resources, more demographic imbalance, and eventually the establishment in Jordan of a substitute Palestinian homeland. To the ruling elite, nationalism was an easy way to make common cause with the people. Since Palestinian-Jordanians were viewed by the Transjordanian elite as one aspect of the perceived enemy, they were to be excluded from the process of mobilizing Transjordanian nationalism. But because of Palestinian-Jordanians' large numbers in Jordan, it was dangerous to antagonize them into confrontation. They had to be controlled and appeased. This constraint was best manifested by catchphrases such as *muhajirin* and *ansar* that permeated the domestic political discourse.

Not all Transjordanians joined the march of Transjordanian nationalism. A good portion of them remained Jordanian nationalists—advocates of the pan-Jordanian identity and Palestinian-Jordanian integration. Others are staunch pan-Arabists and Islamists. Their voice has been drowned out by the louder voice of Transjordanian nationalism, which the state, especially after signing the peace treaty with Israel, tends to amplify for domestic political reasons. Today these enclaves of Jordanian nationalism, combined with Palestinian-Jordanians in general, constitute the reserve for the revival of pan-Jordanian nationalism, should the state deem it necessary to reverse the tide of Transjordanian nationalism.

In its drive since 1970, Transjordanian nationalism has produced three groups: the pragmatic group, the clan/tribe-based group, and the radical group. The first group grew within the boundaries of the state, and its leaders and proponents come from the Transjordanian ruling elite. Most of them are former senior government officials or retired army officers. They belong to the middle and upper-middle class, and some are prominent businesspeople. A number of political parties belong to this group, the most prominent of which is al-Ahd. Its leader, Abdul-Hadi al-Majali, is a member of Parliament and former minister, chief of staff of the army, ambassador, and director general of public security. He also comes from an influential tribe from Kerak. His party could rightly be considered an extension of the state, or its unofficial mouthpiece and the promoter of its policies. In a lecture he gave on January 19, 1997, entitled "National

Identity and Dual Political Loyalty," al-Majali said, "The issue of identity is crucial. If it is not clearly defined, division and rupture will inflict the people and society. Conflicts, which might pose danger to the country, might break out." Attempting to define the Jordanian identity, he said, "I believe that the national identity is the formula composed of the components of the homeland (the state), the people, the territory, and the framework that was accepted by the people to live within."[4]

In an interview a year earlier, he defined national identity in the same terms. When asked to elaborate further on the "framework," he added, "The throne and the constitution."[5] So, according to this group, the Hashemite monarchy is an indispensable component of the Jordanian identity. As to the destiny of Palestinian-Jordanians and the future relationship with the Palestinian identity, al-Majali said in his January 1997 lecture,

> I present to you my party's view. Since we believe, and so does our leadership [the king], in the establishment of a Palestinian state on Palestinian territory, we are to ask, "Who are the people of the prospective Palestinian state?" Although there might not be a clear-cut answer to this question, we should define a scenario that answers the ongoing legitimate questions as to the destiny of those [Palestinians] who exist in Jordan. Some of them are part of the people of the Palestinian state in the making. Those Palestinians who originally came from the West Bank and Gaza are the closest to the Palestinian state, while the 1948 refugees are the remotest from the West Bank. Therefore, our party believes that our people [Transjordanians] should accept those 1948 refugees as full Jordanian citizens, because of the difficulty of having them return to Israel. . . . As for the West Bankers, wherever they are in the diaspora, they should practice their political rights on Palestinian territory. . . . He who chooses to remain Jordanian, though it is preferable that he practices his political rights in his country, Palestine, we shall find a solution for his case. He has to apply to become Jordanian. In this way, the [Jordanian] identity and loyalty will be reaffirmed.[6]

Al-Majali is consistent; in my interview with him, he emphasized the same ideas. When I asked him why he would not reverse his proposition that West Bankers in Jordan must apply to become Jordanians and make it, instead, "those Palestinian-Jordanians who choose to become Palestinians have to apply for that since they are Jordanians by law," he replied, "We reject the premise that a Palestinian-Jordanian is Jordanian. We come from the premise that a Palestinian-Jordanian is Palestinian." Then he asked me, "What difference does it make?" I said, "Your proposition will give you the right to be selective, and it will make the Palestinian who is accepted as a Jordanian citizen for the second time feel that his status is shaky and that he is a Jordanian because you did him a favor. This is a kind of patronizing." But he held fast to his position.[7]

As to the future relationship with the Palestinian entity, al-Majali in his lecture expressed his belief in a federal relationship that would maintain the Palestinian particularism that was disregarded in the Jericho conference of 1948.

It is interesting to notice that while this group is prepared to "accept" the 1948 refugees as full citizens—even though they came to Jordan (as their name suggests) involuntarily and have felt most of the time that their existence here was temporary—yet al-Majali's group insists on disenfranchising the West Bankers who settled in the East Bank during 1950–67 voluntarily, thus confirming their loyalty to the state. This paradox is related to the Transjordanian ruling elite's concept of the Jordanian regional role—a subject discussed in the concluding chapter.

One last thing to be said about this group is that it is not ideologically inflexible. I think it is accurate to call it the pragmatic school because it is resilient enough to develop its positions; after all, it is associated with the Transjordanian ruling elite and is state sponsored.

The second school grew within the boundaries of the tribal system, much like the army. Both the clans and the army are central to Transjordanian identity. No specific political party represents this school, but there are active individuals who articulate its attitudes in the local press and others who are members of certain political parties. Prominent among them is Ahmad Owaidi al-Abbadi, a tribal historian. Al-Abbadi also is a former police officer, who in November 1997 was elected for a second time as a member of Parliament.

The first Transjordanian group to be worried by the growing challenge to Jordan posed in the late 1960s by the Palestinians in general and by the fedayeen in particular consisted of al-asha^{c}ir (the clans), not only because their siblings were in the army but because the potential ruler was the urban Palestinian. Palestinian rule implied a threat to the tribal character of Jordan. The September showdown triggered a lively tribal discourse in reaction to the idea that all citizens (Transjordanians and Palestinian-Jordanians) might be equal and anonymous members of a Jordanian community. Such a situation would erode the tribal power structure. The tribal rebound from their perceived loss of political standing was made possible first by the state, which sought their support in order to strengthen its power base, and second, by the effects of Jordanian mass education and communications. According to Dale F. Eickelman, a renowned American anthropologist who made pioneering field studies on Arab tribes, the effects of mass education and communications

> since the mid-twentieth century are especially salient in the Arab world. Mass education, especially mass higher education, has rendered more explicit the intricate, yet shifting, relationship between the "imagined" communities encouraged by the print and broadcast media and other, alternative shared senses of collective and personal identities.[8]

After the September showdown, bedouin stories, folklore, and poetry started to be viewed, listened to, and read almost daily, and the tribal component of Transjordanian identity was boosted. Transjordanian tribal historians began to adapt their oral traditions to print. Andrew Shryock, assistant professor of anthropology at the State University of New York, who recently conducted a field study on Jordanian Balga tribes, writes, "The urge to render oral histories textual and (somehow) national is part of an ongoing reaction to Jordan as a political idea. It is an attempt to embrace and, at a deeper level, to resist 'Jordanianness' as an official identity designed to co-opt, supersede, and sometimes even replace popular attachments based on allegiance to family and kin."[9]

Al-Abbadi, perhaps the most articulate proponent of this tribe-embedded version of Transjordanian nationalism, sums up his views in this way: "Jordan is our father and the tribes are our mothers."[10]

As to the Hashemite monarchy, this group concurs with the first group that the Hashemite rule is an essential ingredient of the Transjordanian identity, but unlike the first group, its proponents do not accept the king's authority unconditionally. They hold that there is an unwritten compact (*al-bai^c a*) between the monarchy and the tribes, which give loyalty in exchange for economic security.

In one of his articles, al-Abbadi protested the government's decision to issue five-year passports to Palestinian-Jordanians (whom al-Abbadi terms "Palestinians") like those issued to Transjordanians (whom he calls "Jordanians"): "This is a rejected measure, because it is in conflict with *al-bai^c a*. The government and others [the king] have forgotten that it is we, the Jordanians, who give legitimacy to all; and no one gives us legitimacy or bestows upon us his blessings that are derived from Peres or Rabin [Israel's foreign minister and prime minister, respectively]."[11]

As to the issue of Palestinian-Jordanians, this school believes that the Transjordanians have given Palestinian-Jordanians land, economy, identity, and security, while the Palestinian-Jordanians have given nothing in return. Al-Abbadi believes that the policy of the state did not favor

Transjordanians because it "placed the economy in the hands of Palestinians and the stick in the hands of Jordanians. If the Palestinian became a threat, the state would use the Jordanian stick to repress him; and if the Jordanian became a threat, the government would deprive him of his source of living. Thus, this state has been able to prosper and survive on the Jordanian-Palestinian division, which she herself created. Hence the Jordanians' view that they are threatened by both the Palestinians and this policy of the state." Al-Abbadi adds:

> The sensitive government posts that Jordanians assume are to protect Palestinian wealth: I really wonder why the Palestinians covet these jobs that make of us mere guards to protect their property. I believe, however, that government jobs should be confined to Jordanians and the priority in everything should be given to them, such as a director, a minister, a scholarship, etc. The crumbs should be given to the Palestinians. Besides, Jordanians are entitled to a share of the Palestinian wealth, which they couldn't have gained without the Jordanian passport. This share should amount to 51 percent. Palestinians should not have any political rights whether in the executive or legislative branch. A brave decision should be taken that the Jordanian [i.e., Transjordanian] is Jordanian and the Palestinian [i.e., Palestinian-Jordanian] is Palestinian. . . . Therefore I believe in withdrawing Jordanian passports from the Palestinians and giving them instead travel documents.[12]

Especially interesting is al-Abbadi's statement that he considers it a Transjordanian right to seize 51 percent of the wealth of Palestinian-Jordanians. The key to understanding this attitude lies in what he said earlier about Jordan giving land to the Palestinians. Until the late ninth century, when "the maritime trade of the Red Sea and the Mediterranean was already beginning to revive, to an increasing extent at the expense of the overland trade passing through Transjordan," the present Jordanian territory was the crossroads of what is called today the Middle East.[13] And Transjordan continued to constitute the approaches to Mecca and Jerusalem for both Muslim and Christian pilgrims traveling overland. Transjordanian tribes in those days derived a source of income from the protection of pilgrims traveling through the tribal territories. In this practice lie the roots of the business of selling territorial facilities to the foreigner. This notion was rejuvenated, sustained, and developed after the establishment of modern Jordan. It was reflected in the tribal conviction that the British bases in Jordan were not a manifestation of colonial occupation but rather a transaction whereby Jordan provided land facilities to the British in return for an annual rent. This notion was further developed by the royalties Jordan earned from the oil pipelines that crossed its territory—the Iraq Petroleum Company (IPC) pipeline from Iraq to the Mediterranean (it ceased to operate as a result of Israel's establishment in 1948) and the Tapline from Saudi Arabia to the Mediterranean. In my opinion, al-Abbadi's demand to seize 51 percent of Palestinian wealth derives from this concept. The basic premise behind it is that the Palestinian-Jordanians are as much foreigners as the Muslim and Christian pilgrims, the British, and the IPC and Tapline pipelines.

In his writings about Transjordanian tribes, al-Abbadi is motivated to compose a national story that he feels is lacking. According to Shryock, who worked with al-Abbadi during his field study in Jordan and was privy to Abbadi's ideas,

> Dr. Ahmad [al-Abbadi] is writing against the clock. . . . What would constitute moral victory for him—apart from tribal dominance over outsiders—is unclear, and much of this uncertainty springs from the ambiguity and ambivalence that accompany attachment to a Jordanian state that, even after seven decades in place, is not yet the source of any moral community Dr. Ahmad is willing to imagine.[14]

Third is the radical school, whose proponents came from the banned revolutionary political parties—specifically, the communist and Ba'ath parties and the pan-Arab movement. Its core consists of frustrated leftists who deserted their parties. Though they are not organized in a political party, since 1982 the members of this school have called themselves the "Jordanian National Youth Federation." They consider themselves to be the nucleus of the modern Jordanian National Movement. The Jordanian weekly paper *al-Mithaq* is their mouthpiece. This group's most prominent and articulate proponent is Nahedh Hattar, editor in chief of *al-Mithaq* and a former communist. The majority of its members are young Transjordanian civil servants with tribal connections. Another sizable portion of them are professionals and retired officers. Perhaps because they come originally from ideological parties, they have been eager to formulate their own new ideology, and this has distinguished them from the two other schools. Their ideology is a unique blend of radical leftist principles grafted onto a rightist orientation. In an interview, Hattar spelled out the following convictions, principles, and goals of the movement:

> The [Trans]jordanian particularism emanates from the conviction that there was a cohesive [Trans]jordanian society, culturally, socially, and economically in the mid-nineteenth century. Recognizing this fact is imperative because it implies that Jordan was ripe enough to become a state before the arrival of the Hashemites in 1920. [The movement clearly wants to undermine the alleged

notion about the artificiality of Jordan as a state, which draws on the conventional wisdom that had it not been for Emir Abdullah there would have been no Jordan.]

— The [Trans]jordanian national entity is in opposition to the Zionist entity, since the former is an extension of the surrounding Arab entity that is in opposition to Israel.

— The continuing existence of the Zionist entity necessitates the negation of the [Trans]jordanian entity, because Israel is willing to expel the Palestinians who will find in Jordan *al-Watan al-Badil* (the substitute Palestinian homeland).

— Therefore, the movement supports strongly the establishment of a Palestinian state with East Jerusalem as its capital. And by the same token it is against the DOP, which would turn the West Bank into cantons.

— East Jerusalem as a capital for the Palestinian state is crucial not only emotionally but also because it reassures the Transjordanians that the Palestinian state is permanent, not temporary.

— The Transjordanian national thought is in need of an Arab ideological cover. So the movement stands for unity with Syria and Iraq but not with Palestine unless it becomes a sovereign, independent state. [In my opinion, the movement feels the need for a legitimizing cover in order to dilute the negative impression created by the movement's nationalistic exclusivist views.]

— By the same token, the movement is against a confederal or federal relationship with Palestine before the establishment of the sovereign, independent Palestinian state.

— The movement is against the establishment of an economic pact with Israel on the Benelux model, because it implies Jordanian subservience to Israel and the creation of a cantonized Palestine.

— The movement is against privatization because it is conducive to the transfer of public services and property to the private sector, which is dominated by Palestinian and foreign capital. Privatization is one of the mechanisms that could realize *al-Watan al-Badil.*

— The movement is against normalization with Israel, because normalization provides Israel with influence over Jordan, an influence that Israel might employ to implement its strategy of dominating the Middle East.[15]

The members of this movement are prolific and defiant writers. They criticize the first school as subservient to the monarchy and the second school as overly tribal and lacking substantive thought. Like the tribe-based school, they believe that the king plays Palestinian-Jordanians off Transjordanians and vice versa. According to Tareq al-Tal, a nephew of Wasfi al-Tal as well as a Transjordanian nationalist and young scholar who is close to this school, the movement on its own account "will face a formidable list of enemies as well as King Hussein: the Center for Strategic Studies in Jordan University [which publishes opinion polls suggesting a kind of Jordanian-Palestinian relations contrary to Palestinian exclusion], the centers of Palestinian bourgeois power in Jordan, the mercantile comprador wing of Jordanian bourgeoisie, the pseudo-intellectuals in the pay of the 'Jordanian' and 'Palestinian' authorities, and regrettably that part of the Palestinian masses in Jordan moved by narrow self-interest or regional chauvinism to support its enemies and torturers."[16]

As for this school's attitude toward the Hashemite monarchy, Tareq al-Tal compares them to the pragmatic school: "Where the radicals are often Transjordanian nationalists or protonationalists who place loyalty to Jordan before allegiance to King Hussein, the pragmatists are fervent monarchists."[17]

About the Palestinian issue, this group holds to the principle of "Jordan first." Its literature so far has focused on negating all arguments that the Palestinian factor is essential for Jordan's survival and well-being. The issues of the size of the Palestinian population, the history of Transjordan, and the Palestinian contribution to the country's economic and political development are their focus. Their aim is to prove that Jordan would be better off without the Palestinians, hence their ultranationalism and exclusivist views.

Al-Tal makes his own prediction on the future of this school: "No doubt they will console themselves, as perhaps Arafat and his comrades did in launching Fatah as a militant Palestinian movement in 1965, that despite the enormity of their task and the condescension of all the world, they occupy the moral high ground of all who seek self-determination on their own soil."[18]

THE PREDICAMENT OF TRANSJORDANIAN NATIONALISM

No matter how many versions of Transjordanian nationalism there are or what similarities and dissimilarities they have, all of them stem from one root—official nationalism, which according to Benedict Anderson is "an anticipatory strategy developed by dominant groups which are threatened with marginalization or exclusion from an emerging nationally imagined community."[19] Even the third Jordanian group, the ideological ultranationalist that grew outside the boundaries of the state, would not have crystallized as it stands today had it not been for the fertile ground that the ruling elite created for the revival of Transjordanian nationalism. The government's deeds, symbols, and signs, discussed in chapters 9 and 10, attest to the applicability of Anderson's definition of official nationalism to the rising Transjordanian nationalism.

At its rebirth, Transjordanian nationalism identified one adversary: the intensive Palestinian presence in Jordan. A few years later it identified another one in the "Jordan is Palestine" notion. Each of these adversaries had two aspects, practical and perceptual, that Transjordanian nationalism had to address. The practical aspect of the Palestinian demographic factor was coped with by the de-Palestinianization of the public sector and the election law. The practical aspect of the second adversary was addressed through intensifying the state's peacemaking efforts with Israel. This element of Jordan's peacemaking is reflected in Prime Minister Majali's oft-quoted remark after the peace treaty was signed with Israel: "We have buried *al-Watan al-Badil.*"

The fight on the perceptual front was not easy because of the complexity of the issues. Transjordanian nationalism had to defuse the rationale behind *al-Watan al-Badil* and undermine the general impression of the "overwhelming Palestinian majority" in Jordan. The two issues are, of course, perceptually intertwined.

The overriding predicament that Transjordanian nationalism has faced emanates mainly from its lack of a national master narrative that could serve as a glue for national cohesiveness, certifying that Transjordanians were a nation before the state was established. Hence al-Abbadi's work "against the clock" to write Jordan's narrative and Hattar's assertion that "Jordan was an integrated society as of the mid-nineteenth century."

THE ARTIFICIALITY ISSUE

Why should the artificiality issue be so central to Transjordanian nationalists, given the fact that scores of other modern states are the product of colonial mapping? What makes it so, I believe, is the perception by Transjordanian nationalists that "artificiality" implies that Jordan is a state without solid foundations, a fragile, perhaps nonviable state that lures stronger neighbors to tamper with it, annex it, or substitute it for something else. Most important, artificiality could make *al-Watan al-Badil* plausible if it proved to be the only way to resolve the complicated Palestinian question. Therefore, Transjordanian nationalists find it imperative to prove the opposite. Perhaps a master narrative assembled from disconnected subnarratives that have occurred on Transjordan's soil could be a reassuring answer. "History," according to Shryock, "is being posed as the answer to diverse array of challenges nationalism proposes. Those challenges are moral and political."[20]

Paradoxically, the issue of artificiality has turned out to be a constructive one because it has triggered a number of scholarly studies about Transjordan, its cities, its rulers, its historical sites, and the civilizations that have flourished on its soil. The goal of this intellectual activity has been to prove Jordan's territorial contiguity and its people's unbroken historical continuity. To realize this goal, two types of scholarly work are required. One has to concentrate on place—cities and historical sites— and the other has to concentrate on time—historical milestones creating an imaginary line that, by connecting the highlighted places, would make of Jordan, the land, a conceptually integrated unit. Another imaginary line connecting the landmarks of history would make Jordan, the people, part of an uninterrupted line of Jordanians who have settled in the land, cultivated it, and built civilizations since ancient times.

If such lines can be established, Jordan cannot be called an "artificial" state. But without highlighting certain dots of place and time, the lines cannot be drawn to produce the desired image. According to Kelman, "Insofar as a group of people have come to see themselves as constituting a unique, identifiable entity, with a claim to continuity over time, to unity across geographical distance, and to the right to various forms of collective self-expression, we can say that they have acquired a sense of national identity."[21] On February 4, 1997, Bilal al-Tal, a Transjordanian columnist and nationalist, criticized the "self-appointed" people who have stood against "the call for [re]writing the history of Jordan" and applauded the intellectual activity that has made the history of Jordan a tangible reality,

> through Bilad al-Sham [Greater Syria] conferences and through the Hashemite documents that Al al-Bayt University publishes in addition to the university's supervision over a series of books related to Jordan's history. Already books on Amman and vicinity, Irbid and vicinity, and Salt and vicinity have been published. Besides, there is the series of Jordan-related history books that Al al-Bayt Foundation publishes. We believe that the product of the group of scholars and the academic institutions that contribute to this effort . . . are a sufficient answer to those who claim that Jordan is a country without history and to those who believe in disregarding geography as a drastic factor in political and economic relations as well as civilizational distinctness.[22]

(Al al-Bayt is another name for the Hashemites, meaning the House of the Prophet.)

This ongoing intellectual activity has been performed by both Jordanian scholars (some of them Transjordanian nationalists) and foreign scholars who have participated in international conferences related to the history of Jordan. One such conference was the "First International Conference on the History and Archaeology of Jordan," held at Christ Church College, Oxford, in March 1980. In his opening speech, Prince Hassan defined the conference as

the first intellectual awakening of the minds of over sixteen nationalities participating in a tribute to the history, not just of the Hashemite Kingdom, a sovereign state [for only] . . . sixty years, but of the territory of Jordan. . . . It is unfortunate that with the turmoil of events in today's world a country like my own does not have the opportunity of a pause, to take breath and recognize the achievements of the past in the task of identifying who we are, to whom we belong, and what our perspective our future will be.[23]

On the individual level, Youssef D. Ghawanmeh, a professor of Mamluke history at the Yarmuk University in Jordan, has written a number of books in this vein. From the title alone of one of them—*Al-Tarikh al-Hadari li-Sharq al-Urdun fi al-Asr al-Mamluki* (The Civilization History of Transjordan in the Mamluke Era [Fourteenth and Fifteenth Centuries])— we can guess that the book was written for nationalistic purposes.[24] We would expect to read The Civilization History of the Mamluke Era in Transjordan, rather than The Civilization History of Transjordan in the Mamluke Era, simply because there were no nation-states during the Middle Ages, nor was there an ethnically culturally distinct entity called Transjordan to which a distinct civilization could be attributed. Today's Transjordan was then part of a broader Arab-Islamic cultural block. In one part of the book, al-Ghawanmeh presents scores of names of people who excelled in jurisprudence and other religious branches of knowledge in the cities where Islamic civilization flourished—Damascus, Cairo, Jerusalem, Mecca, and Aleppo, where most of them settled. His point is that they originally came from Transjordanian towns and villages. In another section, al-Ghawanmeh talks about the art of woodcarving in a village in northern Jordan. He points to geometrically carved drawings on the surface of wooden pots made in that village and asserts that these ornamentations reflect the influence of the mosaic art so familiar from the Byzantine era. He then adds, "Undoubtedly the Jordanian artist has mastered this inherited craft in which his forebears had excelled."[25] What al-Ghawanmeh is suggesting, of course, is that Transjordanians have their roots deep in history as a settled people with a continuous civilization.

Along the same lines, Khaled al-Keraki, who was the chief of the royal court from 1992 until 1996), said, in a lecture entitled "Al-Shakhsiya

al-Wataniya Li-Dawla al-Urduniya" [The National Identity of the Jordanian State]" and given at the War College in Amman in December 1994,
that "Mousa Bin Nusseir, the conqueror of Andalusia, came from a tribe
that lived in Jordan at that time." (Bin Nusseir was a prominent Arab
leader who conquered North Africa and Andalusia in the late seventh and
early eighth centuries A.D.).[26]

Jordan is not unusual in its efforts to infuse its land and people with a
sense of historical continuity in order to strengthen the foundations of
territorial nationalism. Every Arab state has done and continues to do the
same. According to Amatzia Baram,

> Ever since their creation, all Arab nation-states generated particularized sym-
> bols and rites. Their national flags, for example, even though they sometimes
> closely resembled each other, were nevertheless unique to each state. The vari-
> ous royal houses and republican regimes each introduced their own national
> anniversaries and holidays.[27]

Moreover, some Arab states have engaged actively in promoting linkages
between the present and the pre-Islamic past in their countries as a source
of national "self-assertion." Egypt, in the 1920s, was the first to link its
Pharaonic past and its modern era. Lebanon's Baalbek, Iraq's Babylon,
Syria's Bosra, Tunisia's Carthage, Algeria's Timgad, and Jordan's Jerash
have become centers for annual cultural events. According to Baram, "thus,
to replace the Dome of the Rock and al-Aqsa as symbols of Jordanian-
Palestinian identity and unity, the Hashemites had to resort to East Bank
landmarks, most conspicuously to Petra and Jerash."[28]

Whether or not al-Ghawanmeh and others who have made or are making similar attempts will succeed in dispelling the impression of the artificiality of Transjordan remains uncertain. However, despite the exaggerated claims that have been made for Jordan's status as a historical entity,
contemporary Jordan is by no means artificial but is instead a strong state
with well-established modern institutions.

THE LACK OF A NATIONAL MYTH

The lack of a national myth based on a master narrative woven from national heroes, glorious victories, and prominent national achievements over
the years is another aspect of the predicament faced by Transjordanian
nationalism. Transjordanian nationalism was deprived of a liberating or
unifying content because Transjordanians did not fight for their independence. There were no national heroes, no martyrs, and no heroic stories

from which nationalism usually draws in writing its master narrative. Even today's Transjordanian cities were not known in Islamic history to be centers of scholarship like Damascus, Aleppo, Baghdad, Basra, Cairo, Jerusalem, and Mecca were. There were Transjordanian heroes who defended East Jerusalem and its approaches in 1948, but the short time between their heroic defense and its fall at the hands of Israel in 1967 was not sufficient for this episode to ferment into a national myth. The Hashemite-led Great Arab Revolt, under whose banner most Transjordanians fought the Ottoman Turks on their territory and which brought the Hashemites from the Hejaz to the Fertile Crescent (Iraq and Greater Syria), also cannot fill the need for a myth, since the myth of a pan-Arab movement and the myth needed by a territorial nationalist movement are different, if not mutually exclusive. Besides, the Great Arab Revolt failed to attain one of its major goals—Arab unity under a Hashemite rule in al-Sharq al-Arabi (Arab East).

By process of elimination, one possibility is left for Transjordanian nationalists with which they might weave a Transjordanian national narrative: the fedayeen episode in Jordan (1968–71), starting with the battle of al-Karama and ending with the expulsion of the fedayeen. At first glance this makes sense, because according to conventional wisdom among Transjordanian nationalists, al-Karama symbolizes a glorious battle against the Israeli attempt to occupy part of the country, while the expulsion of the fedayeen symbolizes the victory over a rival national movement that was perceived to have tried to take over and dominate the country. After all, the fedayeen episode was a major factor in awakening the dormant Transjordanian nationalism.

Yet this option is not completely sound. As to the battle of al-Karama, the credit for its glory is contested by the fedayeen. As to victory over the fedayeen, it is dangerous to make it a Transjordanian national myth while 50 percent of the population is of Palestinian origin. Transjordanian nationalists thus tend to be content with what al-Karama and the expulsion of the fedayeen did in awakening Transjordanian nationalism, but they do not, for good reasons, wish to make them the core of their national narrative.

The predicament, then, persists. It has been eloquently articulated by Transjordanian columnist Khaled al-Kassasbeh: "[Trans]jordan lacks a [Trans]jordanian symbolic figure, as it lacks ancient [Trans]jordanian monuments since the Roman amphitheater [in Amman] and the columns of Jerash, as we all know, are not [Trans]jordanian monuments [since they belong to another civilization]. . . . What makes us distinct are our *mansaf* [the Transjordanian national dish], *al-midraqa* [women's robe], and the songs of Abdo Mousa [a gifted gypsy singer of folkloric Transjordanian songs]."[29]

Sarcastic as they sound, al-Kasasbeh's remarks touch on two aspects of the missing myth—national heroes and pride-inspiring national accomplishments. What is surprising is his disregard of Wasfi al-Tal as the prominent national symbol, since al-Tal has been revered by Transjordanians as the hero who saved Jordanian identity by expelling the fedayeen in 1971, paying with his life. Could this oversight occur because al-Tal was from the north of Jordan and al-Kasasbeh is from the south? As a southerner, can he not psychologically accept a national hero from a different district? Or could it be that al-Tal was a controversial political figure within Transjordanian elite circles? Or is it because it is embarrassing to pinpoint a national symbol other than the monarch, who should be the real national symbol in a monarchy? Or is it because the time that has elapsed since his assassination in 1971 has not been long enough to develop the legendary halo that a national hero needs to become a symbol? No matter what the reason, Transjordanian nationalists have not yet unanimously agreed on a national symbol.

Still, the difficulties that have thus far impeded a spontaneous consensus on a national symbol other than the king himself have not prevented ultranationalists from highlighting other signs and symbols. They have been indirectly helped by the government's post–Rabat Resolution (1974) policy of emphasizing the distinct Jordanian character of certain symbols. The government-controlled media, especially Jordan TV, plays a major role in this effort. In addition to the established media policy that preceded the communal rupture, which focused on the king's image as the head of the larger Jordanian family (Transjordanians and Palestinian-Jordanians) and on the army units on parade or in action, now shots of historical sites in Jordan, such as Petra, Jerash, and Amman's amphitheater, as well as film clips of Transjordanian folk dancing and singing, have become daily presentations. The men's red-checkered head cover has become a symbol of Transjordanianness, while the men's blue-checkered head cover has become a symbol of Palestinianness. Such symbols under normal circumstances indicated not divisiveness but diversity; they were always taken as a sign of identity, without additional emphasis placed on it. After all, communal diversity has always been one of Jordan's salient traits.

But as of the early 1970s, the Palestinians began to be stereotyped. Transjordanians started to refer to Palestinian-Jordanians as *Baljik* (Belgians). The term was used first among Transjordanians in reference to Palestinian-Jordanians, but it gradually came to be used in front of Palestinian-Jordanians in a light-spirited manner. In the beginning, Palestinian-Jordanians did not feel insulted by this stereotyping. They were even flattered by it, understanding it as an implicit recognition of their sophistication. "Belgians" are a sophisticated European people in comparison with Arab Jordanians. But when the term persisted alongside discriminating practices against them, Palestinian-Jordanians began to resent it; they realized then that the term *Baljik* implied that they did not belong to Jordan and that this justified the discrimination. In attempting to discover the source of this odd term for Palestinian-Jordanians, I heard a myriad of interpretations ranging from the most insulting to the most flattering. I believe, though, that *Baljik* is just a label for the Transjordanian nationalists' definition of "the other"—namely, the Palestinian-Jordanian.

THE DEMOGRAPHIC ISSUE

The large number of Palestinian-Jordanians in Jordan is the most tangible and serious aspect of the predicament faced by Transjordanian nationalists. Since 1967, two censuses have been conducted, one in 1979 and one in 1994. On both occasions the government has refrained from publishing the breakdown of Palestinian-Jordanians and Transjordanians. The assumed Palestinian majority in Jordan was used by the Israeli proponents of *al-Watan al-Badil* in the 1970s and 1980s to make the claim that Palestinians "already have a state"—that is, Jordan—so they didn't need to create another one in the occupied territories. Since the 1970s, Jordanian officials and Transjordanian nationalists have been bent on denying the Palestinian majority in order to undermine *al-Watan al-Badil*. Tareq al-Tal puts it this way:

> Transjordanianists dispute the evidence of a Palestinian majority on the East Bank. Many assert instead that such sources as an unpublished study of internal migration conducted in parallel with the 1979 census, and the information collected by the Civil Affairs Department in the mid 1980s, showed that at most 40 percent of East Bank residents were of Palestinian origin at the time of disengagement from the West Bank in 1988. Transjordanianists argue that the

number of returnees from Kuwait in 1990–91 was overestimated for the purpose of obtaining emergency aid, and assert that the percentage of Palestinians in Jordan is now 45 percent.[30]

Mousa quotes a statement by Prime Minister Majali published in a Jordanian daily:

> It is absolutely incorrect to say that there is a Palestinian majority in Jordan. It lacks evidence, figures, and statistics. . . . When the first Palestinian emigration occurred (1948), we and the Arabs inflated the number of refugees . . . for purely political and propaganda purposes. . . . Since then an accurate census for those refugees has not been conducted. . . . We had intended to attract the attention to the tragedy. . . . We Arabs tend always to exaggerate.[31]

Clearly, the issue of the number of Palestinian-Jordanians in Jordan is so worrying that these two nationalists essentially accused the government of lying about the figure.

Valerie Yorke, who writes on Middle Eastern affairs, looked into this issue during the many trips she has made to Jordan. In April 1988, a few months before the disengagement decision, she published an article in *Middle East International* entitled "Jordan Is Not Palestine: The Demographic Factor." She writes, "According to well-informed senior members of Jordan's political elite, it is the Transjordanians . . . who have constituted a majority in the kingdom since the loss of the West Bank to Israel in 1967."[32] Proceeding from this premise, Yorke wonders why the Hashemites have not spoken out and why the Jordanians have not called for the publication of the figures that they claim exist. She says that a public disclosure would deal simultaneous blows against the "Jordan is Palestine" argument and in favor of Jordan's security and Palestinian rights. Her answers to her own questions again are based on Transjordanian sources who argued that the regime had a strong interest in preserving the sentiment among Transjordanians that they were outnumbered because this helped weld them to the throne. If the idea of Palestinian predominance had been allowed to recede, then more Transjordanians would have pushed for free elections. She adds that "the Palestinian majority idea adds weight to the Hashemites' openly declared sense of responsibility for the fate of the Palestinians and helps justify Jordan's involvement in the search for a West Bank solution."[33]

Yorke's interpretation of why a disclosure of the large number of Transjordanians had not occurred was proved wrong soon after the publication of her article. In July 1988, the king made his decision to disengage from the West Bank, and in November 1989 general elections in

Jordan were conducted. Why would the Transjordanians, who dominate security and government, enact an election law that ignored the principle of proportionate representation if the Palestinians were a minority? Nevertheless, the real percentage of Palestinian-Jordanians in Jordan is still a highly classified secret.

AGGRESSIVE MANIFESTATIONS OF TRANSJORDANIAN NATIONALISM

Since 1971, Transjordanian nationalism has been marked by an aggressive attitude toward Palestinian-Jordanians. This aggressiveness has been made possible by the following facts and perceptions:

- The threatened Transjordanian identity is linked with the land—that is, with the East Bank from which it derives its name. To Transjordanians, the East Bank has become a purely Transjordanian possession as much as the West Bank has become a purely Palestinian possession after the disengagement decision of 1988. Thus the Palestinians on the East Bank have become foreign residents who could be asked or ordered to leave the country by Transjordanians. The latter, from their own perspective, hold the high moral ground.

- The *muhajirin-ansar* dichotomy connotes that Transjordanians are the hosts and Palestinian-Jordanians the guests. The connotation of the Palestinian guest is that he is a stranger whose long visit has become irritating.

- The continued existence of thirteen Palestinian refugee camps spread over the north and center of the country is a continuous reminder of the peculiar nature of the Palestinian presence in Jordan, a presence that was supposed to be temporary and has now continued for too long.

- The faltering peace process on the Israeli-Palestinian front fuels Transjordanian concern with *al-Watan al-Badil*.

- The relatively submissive Palestinian-Jordanian reaction to the government's discriminatory practices and the failure of Parliament and the political parties to protest these practices clearly and strongly have encouraged Transjordanian nationalists to sustain their aggressive approach, sometimes with a derogatory attitude.

In the political discourse of Transjordanian nationalists not part of the government, these facts and perceptions have engendered the following themes:

- *Palestinians are alien and disloyal:* "We want those who choose to stay on *our* Jordanian territory, irrespective of their origins, to be *loyal* to this country."[34]
- *Palestinians are not at home in Jordan:* "The Palestinian-Jordanian who chooses Jordan as his homeland will *not be hurt* in al-Hussein's homeland, *the Jordanians' homeland*."[35]
- *Palestinians are a burden on Jordanians:* "Any visitor to Amman, Jordan's capital, soon realizes that the city suffers from a shortage in drinking water. . . . Why? Because of the population surplus resulting from the *Palestinian debacle* of which Jordan alone, or rather the Jordanian people alone, took the brunt."[36]
- *Palestinians are rejected by Transjordanians:* After King Hussein's instruction to the government to issue five-year passports to Palestinian-Jordanians, Transjordanian nationalists protested the decision. A Jordanian weekly reported the affair, writing that the Jordanian National Movement intended to publish a document signed by one million Transjordanians expressing their opposition to giving Jordanian passports to the Palestinians. The leaders of the movement believed that "this document is meant to reflect Transjordanians' position in a drastic manner. They also believe that this document is the Transjordanians' answer to the opinion polls that show that Jordanians and Palestinians are for unity."[37]

Above all, the nightmare of *al-Watan al-Badil* itself implies the potential complicity of Palestinian-Jordanians with Israel by the sheer fact that they are the bridgehead for the Palestinian substitute homeland, thus lending "credibility" to the Transjordanian proposition of Palestinian-Jordanian disloyalty. Obviously, hammering on disloyalty, implicitly or explicitly, is needed to highlight the theme of conspiracy—an essential ingredient for any ethnic-based or religious-based discrimination.

In this atmosphere, Palestinian-Jordanians become oversensitive to such exclusionary innuendoes. Ali al-Fazza', a Transjordanian nationalist poet, wrote a poem entitled *Marhala* (A Phase), which was published in a volume issued by the Ministry of Culture. In the poem, al-Fazza' says,

It is time for the Fatherland to recognize two groups:
One has stolen his sword and pants
While the other has accepted to starve in order to feed him;
Hence there are two fronts on the two ends of the compass,
He who claims that he can reconcile them or equate them . . . is a hypocrite.

O Fatherland! Rise and say your word:
Which of the two do you bless?
Those who took the country as a homeland
Or those who view it as a farm![38]

Although the two groups to which the poet refers might be the rich and the poor as much as it might be the Transjordanians and Palestinian-Jordanians, Palestinian-Jordanians have taken the poem as a communal insult, believing the poet to have cast them as the thief of "sword and pants" from the self-denying Transjordanians.

Interestingly enough, Transjordanian nationalists cloak their stark exclusionary attitude in the assertion that they are motivated by nothing more than the desire to preserve the Palestinian identity as the antithesis to Zionism.

The official discourse, in contrast, is imbued with suggestive themes about Jordan as the gallant brother who, despite his limited resources, has generously accorded the Palestinian brethren refuge three times in the last fifty years (1948, 1967, 1990–91). The implication is that the Palestinians have been a burden on Jordan for a long time, a sin for which they are collectively responsible, and consequently they should be grateful for the Jordanians' generosity. Transjordanian nationalists have taken this message to mean that Palestinian-Jordanians should not be Jordanian citizens, while Palestinian-Jordanians have started to feel that they are indeed guilty and that they should keep silent or atone for their sins. The risk here is huge, for when the government treats a domestic community as a different nationality, in the long run that community becomes exactly that, which is a recipe for conflict.

Still, there are Palestinian-Jordanian responses to the writings of Transjordanian nationalists, and these responses usually appeal to legal premises and to the principles of the Great Arab Revolt (a broader framework that conceptually accommodates Transjordanians and Palestinians). One such response came from Taher al-Masri, former prime minister, to al-Majali's lecture on the "Issue of Identity and Dual Loyalty." Al-Masri writes:

That group [Palestinian-Jordanians] acquired their Jordanian nationality in accordance with law and by the concord of all parties [Transjordanians and Palestinians] in the wake of the unification of the two banks, which came in conformity with the principles of the Great Arab Revolt as a step toward the broader Arab unity. A contract was reached by the East Bank and West Bank by which the latter came under Jordanian sovereignty and became an integral part of the territory of the Hashemite Kingdom of Jordan. Its inhabitants became Jordanian citizens. When the West Bank was occupied by Israel, that happened without their willingness or consent.[39]

Unlike al-Masri, Anees al-Qassem, a Palestinian-Jordanian lawyer, invokes history: "Let's establish at the outset that the Palestinian existence in Jordan was not a Palestinian choice. . . . It was dictated by international events. . . . And let's concur again that the Palestinian existence in Jordan was a Jordanian choice that Jordan made voluntarily."[40]

Unfortunately, the younger generation of both Palestinian-Jordanians and Transjordanians are not aware of the essential realities that were discussed in chapter 3 because they are not taught them in school. Even the majority of Palestinian-Jordanians have internalized the new version of recent history instilled in them through the mass media and have behaved accordingly. Transjordanians in general have forgotten, or perhaps are unaware, that both the displaced of 1967 and the returnees from Kuwait were Jordanians. As for the younger generation of Transjordanians, they are utterly ignorant of the fact that it was King Abdullah, motivated by his pan-Arab goals, who planned for and succeeded in expanding the kingdom westward and that he could not unify the West Bank with his kingdom without making the Palestinian inhabitants Jordanian citizens. To these young Transjordanian nationalists, Palestinian-Jordanians are no more than unwelcome guests whose departure is overdue.

Motivated by concern for the stability of the country and surprised at the silence of the members of Parliament regarding this widening crack in the national unity, I was curious to identify their positions as well as the positions of others who are involved in public life. In August 1995, I interviewed a group of deputies of the Islamic Action Front (IAF) and a pan-Arabist. I chose these deputies for my interview because they represent cross-communal ideologies. Neither Islamist nor pan-Arabist principles tolerate discriminating attitudes or practices, especially by fellow Muslims or Arabs toward their peers. I asked the deputies separately ten questions; their answers are given in table 4 (see pp. 262–263).

The answers of the Islamists and pan-Arabist deputies are almost congruent. They agree that there is discrimination, that it is unconstitutional, and that it should be stopped. But they also admit that they cannot raise the issue specifically for general debate in Parliament because it is a sensitive one with the government and Transjordanian nationalists who are influential in public life. They try to float it by using "injustice," in the case of Islamists, and by talking about "discrimination on a district basis," in the case of the pan-Arabist.

A similar position could be detected from a statement issued and distributed in Amman in March 1996 by twelve political parties of all political stripes except those that advocated Palestinian exclusion from Transjordan's political life. They highlighted the following: "We are all Jordanians to build and defend an Arab democratic Jordan, and we are all Palestinians to restore the national Palestinian and Arab legitimate rights, including Jerusalem, and we are all Arabs to build Arab solidarity and unity." They also condemned any call for the division of "our people" and emphasized the essential nature of national unity. They stressed that equality among all Jordanians is the right of every Jordanian. The statement demanded that the executive and legislative authorities "reconsider all measures and practices that are conducive to giving preference to certain citizens over others and to enact a legislation that would guarantee justice to all citizens and would put an end to any preferential treatment that does not emanate from respect for efficiency, justice, and equality."[41]

It is noteworthy that the political parties, like the deputies, avoid using the term *discrimination*. Instead, deputies used the term *injustice*, while the parties use the phrase *preferential treatment*. Although this usage may seem evasive, I see in these comments a healthy sign—namely, that a sizable portion of political activists from the Transjordanian and Palestinian-Jordanian elite still believe in "Jordanianness," or in the pan-Jordanian identity, and expect that soon it will once again prevail while Transjordanianness recedes and perhaps even vanishes. These activists seem to believe that raising the issue of discrimination serves to deepen the communal rupture rather than to erase Transjordanianness.

Table 4. Discrimination against Palestinian-Jordanians?—Attitudes among Some Members of Parliament

Questions	Answers: IAF Deputies	Answers: Pan-Arab Deputy
Do you agree that the state looks divided on a politically bicommunal basis?	There are two types of imbalanced treatment: (a) at the level of Jordanian versus Palestinian; and (b) at the level of Islamist versus non-Islamist.	Yes.
If yes, do you think that this situation has been the product of a deliberate policy or has it occurred by accident?	Not by accident.	It is the product of a deliberate policy. The government support for territorially oriented parties attests to that.
If by deliberate policy, do you think that this policy is constitutional?	Unconstitutional. (A former Transjordanian Islamist deputy interrupted to say, "The disengagement decision is the big sedition. Transjordanians say that it is 'impossible' to accept the fact that Palestinian-Jordanians have a state in the West Bank and at the same time seek to be our partner here.")	No.
If unconstitutional, do you believe that it is the deputy's duty to raise this issue?	Yes.	I don't know. But as for me, I have raised the issue of the passports in the committee on civil liberties.

If yes, have you ever raised the issue in Parliament?	We have never raised the issue of discrimination against Palestinian-Jordanians because of the sensitivity of the issue. We raise instead the issue of injustice. (A Transjordanian deputy added that discrimination is not against Palestinian-Jordanians only but also against Transjordanians from certain districts and parties.)	The Islamists and myself did, but in the context of general debate over discrimination against certain districts. We avoid talking about discrimination against Palestinian-Jordanians because of the sensitivity of the issue.
Does your constituency put pressure on you to raise the issue?	Yes. Not only Palestinians but also Jordanians.	Yes. I receive complaints by mail.
Do you think that the issue is too sensitive to be raised?	Yes, because raising the issue will cause a communal sedition. If we raise it we shall escalate the tension. The escalation is seditious.	Yes.
Is the Palestinian constituency aware of discrimination practices?	Yes.	Yes.
Do you think this imbalance could be straightened up?	Yes.	Yes.
If yes, how?	By statements and by giving advice to the decision makers.	By increasing awareness among the public through the political parties, clubs, and symposia. Besides, the king's instructions will eliminate the problem.

Conclusions

Throughout its existence, Jordan has been affected by the Palestinian factor (the human dimension and the political identity). Until the unification of the West and East Banks in 1950, the Palestinian factor was exogenous and was confined mainly to Emir-King Abdullah's differences over the future of Palestine with the grand mufti, the leader of the Palestinian national movement. Unification brought the Palestinian factor "inside the house," both as a demographic reality (Palestinians came to account for two-thirds of the Jordanian population) and as a political force (in the 1960s, for example, Palestinians placed pressure on the Jordanian regime to embrace Nasser's policies toward the West and Israel). The establishment of the PLO in 1964 by an Arab League resolution signaled "the existence of an independent Palestinian nationalist movement"[1] and significantly increased the influence of the Palestinian factor on Jordan's political life. The 1967 war and the occupation of the West Bank by Israel then added momentum to the Transjordanian-Palestinian dynamic.

During the fedayeen episode of 1968–71, the Palestinian factor affected the Jordanian domestic scene adversely, precipitating a rupture between the Palestinian and Transjordanian communities. Among other consequences, this breach led to a largely de-Palestinianized public sector and the introduction of an electoral law that effectively consigned the Palestinian-Jordanians to the status of a political minority. On the regional and international scenes, the Palestinian factor has become the pivot around which Jordan's foreign policy revolved. Even after the 1988 disengagement decision, which ostensibly made the Palestinian presence in Jordan a purely demographic issue, the Palestinian factor has continued to exert significant influence on Jordan's foreign policy, and it is likely to continue to do so until the Palestinian refugee problem is solved.

The main factor that enabled Jordan to survive so many dangerous political episodes and threats to its security, though, has been the statesmanship shown by King Hussein. Another reason, less visible than the king's statesmanship but nonetheless a constant factor in contributing to Jordan's national security, is the country's regional role.

"Jordan's role" or "Jordan's regional role" is one of the most commonly cited concepts in Jordan's political discourse. It has reached such a level of political currency that it has become a rubric in the country's political lexicon.

The recurring references to Jordan's regional role, whatever their context, betray a deep-seated sense of dependence and insecurity. This is because Jordan's regional role has provided its citizens with reassurance about the country's future, a modicum of national relevance, and perhaps a guarantee that Jordan will continue to exist as an independent state. These are genuine needs, which Jordanians feel due to their awareness of the meager resources of the country, which is surrounded by larger and more powerful states.

On October 26, 1994, the day Jordan and Israel signed their peace treaty, President Clinton, who attended the ceremony, addressed the Jordanian Parliament in Amman during a special session:

> You have nurtured a growing partnership between Your Majesty and all Jordanian citizens. Your nation's commitment to pluralism has been matched by a remarkable generosity of spirit, for you have opened your doors to millions of your Arab brethren. And they have come here, year after year, seeking refuge in your nation. And here they have found a true home. In return, they have enriched your economy and culture.
>
> My country, a nation of immigrants from every area of this world, respects your openness and your understanding that diversity is a challenge but it can be a source of strength. America's commitment to Jordan is as strong tonight as it was when Your Majesty traveled to the United States for the first time thirty-five years ago and met President Dwight Eisenhower, the first of eight presidents you have known. The President and Your Majesty discussed the great threat that communism then posed to America and to the Arab World.[2]

In this excerpt of his address, President Clinton suggested a new regional role for Jordan: the incorporation of Palestinian refugees in the country. By reaffirming the American commitment to Jordan, he was suggesting the reward for Jordan's prospective role. In view of the rise of Transjordanian nationalism, which is based on the exclusion of Palestinian-Jordanians, the president's statement should have provoked an adverse nationalist reaction. Surprisingly enough, there was no immediate response. Yet, not surprisingly, the response came eighteen months later, when Benjamin Netanyahu, the Likud leader, was elected to Israel's prime minister's office. Netanyahu's election platform was a precise reflection of the position that the former Likud prime minister Shamir carried to the Madrid Conference of October 1991—namely, "no to the land-for-peace formula, no to sharing Jerusalem as a capital for Israel and Palestine, and no to the Palestinian state." Such a platform, which also called for the expansion of Jewish settlements, was obviously bound to generate concern about the future of the peace process, not only among the Palestinians but also among a good portion of the Israelis and the Arabs. Jordanians—particularly Transjordanian nationalists—were scared. To them, "no to the Palestinian state" meant Israel's return to the "Jordan is Palestine" formula. With Netanyahu's election on a Likud platform, the general assessment was that Jordan was back to square one, but with one difference: Jordan and Israel could now talk to each other.

This combination of latent tension and the availability of an open channel for public dialogue between Jordan and Israel is in many ways a new situation. Until the Madrid Conference, this combination existed, but only for a very limited group at a very high level and in a very limited way. Now the situation is quite different: dialogue is conducted on every level between governments, institutions, individuals, and so on. It may be precisely this combination of tension generated by a rightist Israeli prime minister and of dialogue made possible by a peace treaty that has set off the public debate in Jordan over the future of Jordan's regional role.

While the election of a right-wing Israeli prime minister sparked a public debate over Jordan's regional role, the Jordanian-Israeli peace treaty of October 1994 has determined the course of the debate, which has taken three different directions: Transjordanian nationalist, pan-Arabist, and internationalist.

The first direction is that of the Transjordanian nationalists, whose major concern, after the separation of the West Bank (Palestine) from Jordan based on the DOP and the Jordanian-Israeli peace treaty, is to exclude Jordanians of Palestinian origin from Jordan. To the Transjordanian nationalists, this exclusion can be achieved either by demoting

Palestinian-Jordanians to alien residents or by waiting for them to leave the country for Palestinian territory—either the prospective Palestinian state or Israel proper after it complies with UN Resolution 194, which gives Palestinian refugees the right of repatriation or compensation.

One of Jordan's regional roles for more than four decades has been connected with the Palestinian question. The assumption of power in Israel by the Likud (which opposes the establishment of a Palestinian state and is determined to maintain its control over the West Bank) has clouded the peace process with uncertainty. This could mean only one thing: the continued presence of the Palestinians in Jordan. To the Transjordanian nationalists, this is a nightmare.

Simply because they are aware of the intimate relationship between Jordan's regional role and the country's survival, most Jordanians cannot evade the ongoing debate. The Transjordanian nationalists feel that they must take the lead in this debate, building their case—namely, that Jordan is for the Transjordanians and that the Palestinians in Jordan should return to Palestine—before others can establish a strong case for the continued presence of the Palestinians in Jordan. One of the most articulate advocates of this strain of Transjordanian nationalism is Fahad al-Fanek. In a recently published article entitled "Jordan: A Stable State and an Entrenched System," al-Fanek explains that only an artificial entity seeks to justify its existence by relying on a role that serves the interests of others whose power can make a difference in the well-being of such an entity.[3] Since Jordan, according to him, possesses all the ingredients necessary for its survival in its own right, its role should not be the fulfillment of others' needs. On the contrary, al-Fanek argues, Jordan can become a model for democracy and a center of excellence in higher education and health services. Furthermore, Jordan can act as an intellectual center in the region.[4] It is obvious that al-Fanek supports the notion of the regional role but sees that role in a new way. In fact, he tries to appeal to Jordanian national pride to attain his political goal, the nonabsorption of the Palestinians—this, he maintains, would represent the "fulfillment of others' need."

Another direction is being emphasized by Transjordanian pan-Arabists, who view the country's regional role in an Arab context. On June 18, 1996, the Jordanian daily *al-Dustour* published a report on a symposium that had been held in Amman the day before. The press account alludes to a paper entitled "Jordan's Political Identity and Its Arab and Islamic Relations," presented by Mazen al-Saket, a Transjordanian Arab nationalist. Al-Saket states, according to the Jordanian daily, that there is no doubt that Jordan's role in a political settlement, especially in regard to the Palestinian question, is essential due to the special geographic and demographic relations that bind Jordan with Palestine. Nevertheless, he argues, Jordan's role with regard to this particular issue and any other that might arise should be governed by the fact that Jordan is an integral part of an Arab nation that has its own attitudes, rights, interests, and common goals. Jordan's regional role, therefore, should be determined by its membership in this Arab nation. Al-Saket further contends that any regional role for Jordan that is not in congruence with its special status as part of the Arab nation is necessarily an inferior one and cannot be central. In fact, such a role would lead to security risks and economic constraints.[5]

The third direction is the internationalist one, which derives from a realistic understanding of world politics. This view is naturally popular among Jordan's ruling elite, who are more exposed to international dynamics, more familiar with post–Cold War interdependence, more aware of the country's needs and limitations, and more pragmatic than their fellow activists (the exclusive nationalists and the pan-Arabists). Between 1990, as Jordan's regional role was shaken to its roots, when it failed to join the American-led multinational coalition during the second Gulf War, and 1994, when Jordan concluded a peace treaty with Israel, the Jordanian ruling elite refrained from identifying a new regional role for Jordan. The conclusion of the peace treaty made it possible for this ruling elite to come up with a definition of the new regional role, but they still chose not to. In fact, they did not feel that they had to put into words their vision of this role. Rather, they assumed that Jordan's peace treaty with Israel, which is based on the concept of complementarity rather than parity (in contrast to the Egyptian-Israeli peace treaty), can speak for Jordan's new regional role. But Netanyahu's election as prime minister of Israel has raised fears in the United States, in Israel itself, and among the Jordanian ruling elite that the peace process might collapse. It is this fear that has prompted the Jordanian government to shift from an implicit, low-profile definition of its new regional role to an explicit announcement.

The clearest and most candid definition so far of this newly conceived regional role was articulated in Washington, D.C., by the then Jordanian minister of information, Marwan al-Mu'asher. In a talk he gave at the Washington Institute for Near East Policy on June 14, 1996, al-Mu'asher said:

> Jordan's peace with Israel is based on a strategic decision to develop a new atmosphere of peace in the region based on cooperation and interdependence. . . . The U.S. needs to raise the level of political and economic support toward

Jordan to a new plateau. . . . If the Jordan model is successful, it will serve U.S. interests of peace and security in the region. . . . Jordan is well positioned to play a prominent role in efforts to end the Arab-Israeli conflict.[6]

The fact that this official definition of Jordan's regional role was made in Washington is most telling. This public definition was meant to put to rest any fears that might have arisen after Netanyahu's election as to how far Jordan will go in implementing the Jordanian-Israeli peace treaty's principle of complementarity. Al-Mu'asher emphasized that peace with Israel is a strategic decision for Jordan.

He also broke down the definition of Jordan's regional role into its fundamental components. First, he said that Jordan will present itself as the model for cooperation and interdependence to develop a new atmosphere of peace in the region. Jordan, he stressed, is well positioned to play such a prominent role. Second, he pointed to U.S. interests that will be served by this role. As for Jordan's reward for doing so, the minister was quite candid: "The U.S. needs to raise the level of political and economic support toward Jordan to a new plateau." What al-Mu'asher failed to specify, though, was whether the conceived "Jordanian role," in addition to normalizing relations with Israel, will encompass the permanent absorption of the Palestinian refugees into Jordan.

In December 1996, addressing a meeting in Amman held as a follow-up to a conference in New York where donors had pledged approximately one-third of the United Nations Relief and Works Agency's budget of $352 million, Prince Hassan of Jordan remarked:

> In the case of Jordan, I think, the question of raising the specter of further social distress is a red flag . . . certainly in the instance of the occupied territories. We can only hope and pray that the ongoing impasse of the peace process will be resolved, but clearly the dangers of transfer [of Palestinians] . . . from the territories elsewhere do exist. . . . Once again let me go back to nondiscriminatory moves toward social productivity. We cannot talk about employment and underemployment in the context of Jordan and distinguish [between Jordanians and Palestinians]. We are talking about economic improvement across the board, we are talking about infrastructure across the board.[7]

Prince Hassan's statement implies that Jordan is ready to assimilate in a principled manner the Palestinian refugees who are now in Jordan, provided the funds allocated for such a program are used to develop Jordan as a whole. This notion is compatible with Jordan's prospective regional role. Comments about the Palestinian refugees made by the secretary general of al-Ahd party, which was very close to the government, are consistent with Prince Hassan's statement.[8] Prince Hassan and Transjordan's ruling elite stick to three principles to govern the Palestinian-refugee assimilation. The three principles are put in the form of three "yes's": yes to the right of return; yes to compensation; yes to the national unity.

As this book has shown, the Transjordanian-Palestinian dynamic has always operated within the triangular interaction of Jordan, Israel, and the Palestinians. The origins of this triangular relationship, which for eight decades has been marked by continuous political rivalry and intermittent violence, can be traced back to the colonial map of the region after World War I, which gave the British a mandate over Palestine and Transjordan. Jordanians, Palestinians, and Israelis have become like three people locked in one room with only two seats. One of the three—the Palestinians—has been left without a seat. And until the third secures his own seat, the adverse interaction among the three is bound to continue.

Theoretically, there are two ways to put an end to this conflict: either to eliminate or negate one of the three, or to build another seat in the same space. Over seventy years, the first option has been tried with each of the trio. In 1948, the Arabs tried to eliminate Israel, but failed. From 1968 to 1970, the fedayeen episode in Jordan amounted to an attempt to eliminate Jordan, but that too failed. Between 1967 and 1993, Israel tried to eliminate the Palestinians as a distinct people, but failed.

In 1950, King Abdullah approached the issue constructively. By uniting the West Bank and the East Bank, he tried to amalgamate Jordan and Palestine into one. However, the Gaza Strip remained under Egyptian administration, a fact which made it a hotbed for Palestinian nationalism. Abdullah's attempt was first disrupted by the establishment of the PLO in 1964, and then terminated by the Arab summit in Rabat in 1974.

The failure of attempts to eliminate one of the three or to amalgamate two of them has left us with just one option—namely, to build a seat for the Palestinians by creating a Palestinian state in the West Bank and Gaza Strip.

It is ironic to note that the small Jewish community of 1920 is today a prosperous, strong state, and that the Jordanian tribal community of 1920 is today also a state with well-established institutions, but that the Palestinian community, the largest of the three in the 1920s and the only one that then possessed a discernible sense of nationhood, is still struggling to achieve statehood. More than half of the Palestinians are still refugees. Although King Hussein's disengagement decision of 1988 removed one obstacle to the Palestinians' ascent to statehood, Israel is still reluctant to do its share.

Still, the fact remains that no member of the triangular relationship, whether acting alone or in tandem, has been able to obliterate or negate another. Palestinian nationhood is as much a reality today as are the State of Jordan and the State of Israel. The lesson from the eight-decade tragic experience is surely that the three of them are destined to be locked in a symbiotic relationship, one that instead of generating mutual discord might be formalized to serve their individual and collective interests.

The presence of Palestinians in Israel and Jordan as well as in the area controlled by the Palestinian Authority; the dependence of all three territories on common resources, most notably water; the short distances between their population centers and tourist attractions—all these factors have produced competition and conflict, yet they could be turned into sources of mutual benefit if the three peoples so choose. The Jordanian-Israeli peace treaty is a step in the right direction; indeed, it has projected economic interdependence between the two signatories, which has begun to materialize. But to realize and sustain interdependence, the third actor in the triangular interaction must be involved on an equal footing with the other two. This means the creation of a full-fledged Palestinian state, not merely an autonomous Palestinian entity. Independence is the essential prerequisite to interdependence. The promotion of interdependence, furthermore, requires regionwide peace—hence the significance of achieving a comprehensive peace and of establishing an array of supranational structures that will sustain and solidify that peace.

For a long time, conventional wisdom has regarded the creation of a Palestinian state as a security risk to both Israel and Jordan, since such a state is expected to be a hotbed for irredentism. This expectation, however, seems misguided. I would argue that a Palestinian state would serve as a stabilizing factor. During fifty years of hope and patience mingled with struggle and suppression, the vast majority of the Palestinians in the diaspora have transformed their major national goal from the liberation of Mandatory Palestine into the establishment of a Palestinian state on the West Bank and Gaza Strip. Their hope is to secure a national home where Palestinian identity will be embodied and recognized and where Palestinians can always find refuge. To a large extent, the Palestinian objective is similar to that of the Jews before the establishment of the State of Israel.

With the establishment of a Palestinian state, the sentimental component of Palestinian nationalism will be largely satisfied, which should leave the majority of Palestinians in the diaspora free to decide their futures based on nonsentimental considerations. For many Palestinians, economic considerations will probably dictate whether they leave the country in which they are already living and working and where their children have been born and are being raised. Palestine is likely to offer a more comfortable life only to those Palestinian refugees in Lebanon, where it is very difficult to obtain work permits, and to a small percentage of Palestinians resident in Syria and Jordan. Once the Palestinian state has been established, the international community should be prepared to address the process of resolving the refugee issue within the framework of UN Resolution 194, which gives each refugee the right to choose between returning to Palestine and receiving financial compensation.

Sharing, as a value and a guiding principle—or rather, the lack of sharing—lies at the heart of the Arab-Israeli conflict. It was the failure of Palestinians to recognize the need to share Mandatory Palestine with the Jewish community that made the 1948 war, and it was the Arab failure to recognize the need to share the region with another nationality that made the 1967 war. On the other side, it was Israel's refusal to give back to the Palestinians their remaining share of Mandatory Palestine (the West Bank and the Gaza Strip) after the 1967 war that led to the Israeli invasion of Lebanon in June 1982 and to the *intifada*.

With its sweeping victory over the Arab states in 1967, Israel threw off its besieged mood—a mood that had led it to seek accommodation with its Arab neighbors, as in its attempts to reach a peace treaty with King Abdullah in the early 1950s—and instead donned a spirit of triumphalism. This new attitude, which disdained compromise and expected the vanquished to capitulate, caused Israel's leadership to underestimate the significance of Egypt's acceptance of Security Council Resolution 242—Nasser's Egypt had accepted the existence of another nationality in the midst of the Arab nation. In other words, Israel failed to appreciate that Egypt and Jordan had relinquished their "no sharing" position. This failure brought on the 1973 war. Among other things, Israel's triumphalist mood stimulated expansionist tendencies within some Israeli parties and groups—hence Israel's settlements in the Sinai, the Golan Heights, the West Bank, and the Gaza Strip and the annexation of Arab Jerusalem; hence also the general Israeli perception of the Palestinians on the West Bank and in Gaza as a burden to be removed and of the PLO as an obstacle to be bypassed.

It took Jordan and Egypt nineteen years (until 1967), Syria twenty-five years (until 1973), and the Palestinians forty years (until 1988) to accept the need to share. In total, it took them five wars to change their positions and turn the key in the locked door of Arab-Israeli peace. It took Israel twenty-five years before it was prepared to try the same key in Israeli-Palestinian relations. Prime Minister Rabin was the first Israeli leader to recognize the Palestinians as a peace partner to be approached rather than as an obstacle to be bypassed. The DOP attests to that. Partnership in the Israeli-Palestinian case implies sharing. This simple yet essential fact makes Rabin, who tried to reverse the prevailing trend in his country, a real statesman. By the same token, it makes of his assassination a great loss both to his own people and to the Palestinians and the peace process in general. Rabin brought the Israeli political scales back into balance when he forsook the strident tones of triumphalism in favor of the conciliatory principle of sharing. Unfortunately, Rabin paid with his life for the principle of sharing before it could stand on steady legs.

Among other things, peace means pulling down barriers between peoples, communities, and states. In Jordan, King Hussein acknowledged sharing and pluralism as the keys to intercommunal harmony. Sadly, however, domestic barriers between Palestinian-Jordanians and Transjordanians have been rising over the past twenty-five years. These barriers are not yet so high as to create internal polarization and conflict, but they are high enough to cause concern about the peace process. Almost 2 million Palestinians have been Jordanian citizens since the two banks were unified in 1950; another twenty-two thousand Palestinians came to Jordan after they were displaced from the Gaza Strip in the wake of the 1967 war, although they were not given citizenship. In view of the prevailing political and economic considerations, few Palestinian-Jordanians are likely to give up their Jordanian citizenship or residency in Jordan if and when a Palestinian state is established. By conferring citizenship on the Palestinian refugees in 1950, Jordan has already gone halfway toward absorbing them into its society, although their representatives have continued publicly to reject the refugees' settlement. This rejection, especially in the last decade, has been more a matter of emphasizing the refugees' rights than of rejecting a permanent settlement. Full integration will occur only when the Israeli-Palestinian peace track comes to fruition—that is, when agreement is reached on final status issues and a Palestinian state is established. One of these issues involves giving the refugees the choice between compensation and return, in compliance with UN Resolution 194. Most of the refugees in Jordan appear to be interested in compensation. Their major concern, as I discovered when I discussed the matter with some of their representatives in the summer of 1995, is whether they or their host state will be the party to be compensated. The second half of the process of integrating the refugees into Jordanian society thus requires the contribution of the international community. Large amounts of money are needed to compensate the displaced individuals and to finance government programs to close refugee camps and integrate the refugees.

Running counter to the trend toward integration is the attitude of radical Transjordanian nationalists who call for the exclusion of Palestinian-Jordanians—either physically by seeing them leave Jordan or politically by disfranchising them. Though such calls have thrown into question the long-held view that Jordan might serve as a model for other Arab states in absorbing the refugees, these calls so far do not seem to represent the Transjordanian mainstream. A survey conducted in September 1994 by the Center for Strategic Studies of Jordan University indicated that strong affinities still exist between Palestinian-Jordanians and Transjordanians. Among a nationwide sample, 64.9 percent of Transjordanians and 72.3 percent of Palestinian-Jordanians believed that the interaction between the two communities had molded them into one people. Interestingly, while the division of opinion among Palestinian-Jordanian opinion makers closely mirrored the opinions of Palestinian-Jordanians as a whole (65.2 percent of opinion makers considered the two groups to have been molded into one people), opinion makers in the Transjordanian community were significantly less likely than other Transjordanians to subscribe to this view (the figure for Transjordanian opinion makers was only 47.8 percent).[9] This finding is not surprising when we consider that a large section of the Transjordanian elite has been involved for more than two decades in encouraging exclusivist attitudes toward Palestinian-Jordanians. As historian Eric Hobsbawm has remarked, "official ideologies of states and movements are not guides to what is in the minds of even the most loyal citizens or supporters."[10] Because the findings of the opinion poll ran counter to what the radical Transjordanian nationalists claimed and promoted, the Center for Strategic Studies and its director were bitterly criticized (see chapter 11). The findings of the opinion poll, in essence, indicated that the "affinity and the political goals that this Palestinian identity has engendered in the past are tempered both by economic and personal security reasons," as Hillel Frisch of the Department of Political Science at Hebrew University has put it.[11]

When in the wake of the September showdown the ruling elite opted to side with Transjordanian nationalist sentiment rather than with the Jordanian people, they did so as a purely defensive response to the growing

Palestinian national movement spearheaded by the PLO. To the ruling elite, Palestinian-Jordanians as such were not an enemy to be subdued but a potential source of individual collaborators with the PLO to be closely watched and controlled. Transjordanization of the public sector was viewed more as a means of rewarding or appeasing Transjordanians than of discriminating against Palestinian-Jordanians.

Two events, however, prompted the Transjordanian elite to regard Transjordanians and Palestinian-Jordanians as two distinct communities: the 1974 Rabat Resolution and the formation of a Likud government in Israel in 1977. Thereafter, the ruling elite viewed Palestinian-Jordanians collectively as a potential bridgehead for *al-Watan al-Badil.* Transjordanization of the public sector developed in the late 1970s into de-Palestinianization—a process defended on the grounds that it constituted no more than an equitable division of labor, given Palestinian dominance of the private sector. The Transjordanian elite did not seem concerned about the long-term ramifications of this unwritten policy—namely, that it would aggravate and institutionalize the communal rupture. Nor did they expect that they would lose control of Transjordanian nationalism. The systematic official effort to promote and propagate Transjordan's national narrative domestically and internationally over the past twenty years has, however, resulted in the emergence of a radical Transjordanian nationalism. Proponents of this ideology range from those who urge the disenfranchisement of some or all Palestinian-Jordanians to those who call for Palestinian-Jordanians to leave Jordan and settle in territory controlled by the Palestinian Authority. The 1988 disengagement decision with the West Bank and the 1993 Oslo Declaration of Principles broadened the Transjordanian nationalists' platform. As noted in chapter 11, these radical nationalists feel confident enough to voice their opinions publicly.

Assuming that the peace process will run its course to a successful end and that the Jordanian government will decide to help solve the refugee problem by integrating those who choose not to exercise their right of return, will the government find its efforts to do so frustrated by Transjordanian radical nationalists? Before answering this question, we must underscore four aspects of Jordan's situation in light of the refugees. First, although an exclusionary attitude toward Palestinian refugees is by no means uncommon among Transjordanians, the fact remains that most (64.9 percent) Transjordanians regard Transjordanians and Palestinian-Jordanians as one. Second, Jordan is host to 41 percent (1.3 million) of the total number of Palestinian refugees. Third, if the refugee problem is not solved, there can be no comprehensive peace, and vice versa. Or as Donna E. Arzt, professor of international law at Syracuse University, has observed, "the refugee question is ultimately inseparable from the underlying cause of the decades-long conflict: the failure to accept the reality that Israelis and Palestinians, Arabs and Jews, live together in the same neighborhood. Thus, only when the burdens and benefits of peace are distributed in a regionally balanced fashion will all the parties come on board."[12] Fourth, the task of democratically integrating Palestinian refugees into Jordanian society as full citizens will provide Jordan with a significant regional role—a goal that Jordan always seeks.

In light of these four factors, my answer to the question of whether radical nationalists could derail or obstruct a government plan to integrate Palestinian refugees into Jordanian society is a qualified no. However, a number of conditions, both external and domestic, must be met to defuse the obstructive potential of these nationalists.

Externally, two conditions are of particular importance. First, regional peace agreements and other arrangements deriving from them should reflect the principle of sharing. Among other things, this means the establishment of a Palestinian state, shared sovereignty over Jerusalem (two capitals in an undivided city), equitable distribution of water and other natural resources, and joint security arrangements. It also means deciding "a mutually agreeable division of responsibility among all of the parties to the peace process" for the absorption of Palestinian refugees in the region.[13] The burden of that responsibility must be shared by Israel as well as by the Arab states, even though the number of Palestinian refugees who might be expected to move to Israel would be relatively small. Arzt, for example, has proposed a seven-year plan in which Israel would gradually absorb seventy-five thousand refugees.[14]

Second, the greatest possible number of supranational structures should be established in the region. Such structures—whether concerned with economic, cultural, political, environmental, or other issues—embody the principle of sharing, reflect and encourage interdependence, and are likely to dilute nationalistic tendencies.

Foremost among the domestic conditions necessary to defuse radical nationalism and allow Jordan to undertake its regional role is a reexamination by the Transjordanian ruling elite of its age-old conviction that the power base of the regime rests exclusively with the Transjordanian community. Before 1967, the elite viewed the cohesive Palestinian community on the West Bank as a threat to the unity of the kingdom—a threat that needed to be counterbalanced by an East Bank power base. But the situation today is very different, as evidenced by the existence both of a peace treaty between Jordan and Israel and of a declaration of principles signed by the leaders of Israel and the PLO.

Another important domestic condition is that the public sector be made as open to the two communities as the private sector is already. Since the late 1970s, the Transjordanian community has gradually come to enjoy a sort of political hegemony over the public sector. Such a situation does nothing to deter, and may even encourage, the expression of radical Transjordanian nationalism.

Charges of Palestinian-Jordanian disloyalty to the state of Jordan have become ludicrous, especially after the signing of the DOP. Equally ludicrous are arguments that Palestinian-Jordanians pose a threat to Jordanian identity—a threat that seems not to have existed before 1967, despite Palestinian-Jordanians accounting for two-thirds of the population. With the signing of the DOP—which is decidedly ambiguous regarding the issues of "refugees" and of "the Palestinian state"—even those who had clung to their Palestinian identity began to reconcile themselves to the fact that Jordan was their final home. As opinion polls reveal, most Palestinian-Jordanians and Transjordanians today regard one another as fellow Jordanians; most of the population, it may also be noted, were born after the September showdown, and attempts to keep that episode an open wound in the national psyche should cease.

Official promotion of Transjordanian nationalism, a campaign that has now been waged for more than twenty-five years, should be abandoned in favor of the message propounded before 1970—namely, that the Palestinian-Jordanians and the Transjordanians are both part of the same pan-Jordanian community. A sense of pan-Jordanian identity began to be forged in the 1950s, despite the fact that the Palestinians still cherished hopes of returning to an independent Palestine; in the aftermath of the DOP, which almost dispelled such hopes, the climate for promoting popular acceptance of such a pan-Jordanian character seems much more favorable.

Encouragingly, there are clear signs that the ruling elite has started to realize that its policy of making common cause with the Transjordanian community has gone a little too far. In a lecture at the International Affairs Council in Amman on September 7, 1996, Prince Hassan said,

> The rubric in our policy and public decisions should be the concentration on national unity, harmony among people, and the support for efficiencies and talent. The dichotomous discourse (hosts and guests, the dark and the white,

and other categorizations) is bound to deepen differences, consciously or un-consciously. A group of people who benefit [from this discourse] will emerge and will stimulate bigotry and will open wounds, paving the way for the en-emies of this country to jeopardize its unity and cohesiveness.[15]

The enduring guarantee of national unity in Jordan, after all, is the Hashemite royal family. As discussed in chapter 1, Hashemites are supracommunal, supratribal, supraregional, and suprasectarian. This *supra*-ism, so to speak, has been impaired by the "Transjordanization" policy insofar as the Hashemites have been perceived (no matter how er-roneously) as identifying with only half of the people of Jordan for the past two decades. Transjordanization has resulted in two casualties: the status of Palestinian-Jordanians (see chapter 10) and the status of Hashemitism. Hashemitism, in the final analysis, stands for the inherent quality of being above differences and subidentities within Jordanian soci-ety. A Hashemite is the ultimate arbitrator in his country and among his people. Therefore, Hashemitism is a rallying force, as it has proved to be four times in this century: during the Great Arab Revolt in 1916, in Jor-dan in 1921 and Iraq in 1922, and during the unification of the East and West Banks in 1950.

It is time for the Hashemite monarchy in Jordan to redress the current situation, a situation sustained by a policy whose primary rationale has vanished since the 1991 Madrid peace conference. Jordan can enhance its national security and secure a regional role through a comprehensive peace in which Palestinian-Jordanians are recognized as the second pillar (Transjordanians being the first) on which the State of Jordan rests. Simi-larly, the destabilizing excesses of Transjordanian nationalism can be curbed only if Palestinian-Jordanians are accepted as full partners.

It is not too late to accomplish this amalgamation of the two commu-nities. Palestinian-Jordanians and Transjordanians still view the king as a supracommunal monarch and as their ultimate arbitrator. The creation of a single pan-Jordanian identity under the Hashemites would stand as a grand national accomplishment, one that both current communities could regard with pride.

To fuse the two communities together, Jordan will have to employ a wide variety of means, both practical and symbolic. Further democracy, in which the rule of law prevails and basic liberties are protected, could cer-tainly be an important catalyst, for under democracy, cross-communal re-lations tend to flourish. But to make democracy do its job, the distribu-tion of parliamentary seats among the various districts should be made more proportionate to the demographic makeup of the country. Transjordanians understandably fear that such redistribution would see a major shift of political power toward the large Palestinian-Jordanian community. This fear could be allayed by reaching some agreement on the political status of those displaced by the 1967 war and resident since then in Jordan. There are a number of ways in which this issue could be resolved, but no matter what solution is reached, it should be a fair one—that is, a solution that does not impair the national economy or the economic interests and the political identity of the displaced.

Transjordanian willingness to see Jordan absorb substantial numbers of refugees will depend heavily on whether that process generates economic hardships or economic rewards. It may be noted that the radical wings of Transjordanian nationalism emerged during the economic stagnation of the mid 1980s. For the absorption process to proceed smoothly, the economic dividends of peace must be made available to the ordinary people of Jordan. Since the solution of the refugee problem is a concern to the international community as well as to Jordan, the donor community should focus on helping Jordan solve its economic and social problems, specifically unemployment and poverty. Absorption of the Palestinians should be accompanied by the creation of a better life for all, so that Transjordanians cease to view Palestinian-Jordanians as a burden and come instead to see them as a rewarding partner.

A similar sense of participating in "rewarding partnerships" should be encouraged at a higher level, too. As already noted, although the triangular interaction among Jordan, Israel, and the Palestinians has been characterized by hostility and violence, the potential exists for mutually beneficial cooperation on such matters as shared resources and economic development. High politics also offers an opportunity for institutionalized and ongoing cooperative interaction. The idea has already been raised of a Jordanian-Palestinian confederation that would cement mutual confidence and cooperation between Jordan and the prospective Palestinian state. King Hussein was the first to propose, in 1972, a federal relationship between Jordan and Palestine. In 1985, King Hussein and Chairman Arafat agreed on a confederal formula. Since then, a confederal and not a federal relationship has attracted much attention within the triangular context. Israel's Labor party, for example, has expressed its support for a Jordanian-Palestinian confederation. Transjordanian and Palestinian radical nationalists reject the notion, but overwhelming majorities of Jordanians and Palestinians support it. King Hussein's view was that confederal arrangements should not be rushed into and that discussion of the issue should be postponed until the Israeli-Palestinian peace track comes to fruition and a Palestinian state is established. Only then, when the two peoples can freely decide in a democratic manner, might the confederal formula become the framework for the future Palestinian-Jordanian relationship. For Jordan, first things first: Palestinian independence on Palestinian soil is the sine qua non of Palestinian national identity; then, interdependence and confederation can follow. As for Chairman Arafat, he is prepared to reach a confederal treaty with Jordan at any time. The PNC endorsed the idea of a confederal relationship between the two countries in 1988.

The confederal formula, which allows both Jordanians and Palestinians to maintain their identities, seems an ideal means of promoting mutual confidence and healing the rupture between Transjordanians and Palestinian-Jordanians. Confederation would make it possible for a large number of Palestinian-Jordanians to vote for a Palestinian Parliament while they are still residents of Jordan. Though each country would have its own head of state, the presidency of the confederation could alternate between the king of Jordan and the president of Palestine. (Should the king find such an arrangement unacceptable, the Hashemite supraregional monarch might assume the role of reigning head of the confederation.) Defense, economic affairs, and foreign affairs would be areas for joint planning and implementation. Other areas—such as water, tourism, environmental affairs, security, transportation, aviation, and energy—could be organized, supervised, and perhaps managed by councils that would include Israelis, Palestinians, and Jordanians. Just as the cornerstone in peacemaking is the establishment of a Palestinian state, the cornerstone in peace building is the transformation of the adverse triangular interaction into an integrative trilateral effort where cooperation and rewarding partnership replace hatred and conflict and where parity and comparability have a chance to grow.

Following such a course is certain to bring about changes in attitudes and even identities. As Eric Hobsbawm has observed, "national identification and what it is believed to imply can change and shift in time, even in the course of quite short periods."[16] This is not to suggest that this grand mission is easy to accomplish but is rather to emphasize that its potential outcome is worth the efforts and the sacrifices. Good intentions, political will, and unbinding resolve will make it possible. After all, during his forty-seven-year reign King Hussein transformed his country: Transjordan was conceived in the wake of World War I as a land link between two strategic lynchpins (Iraq and the Suez Canal), but today Jordan is itself a regional lynchpin in its own right.

Notes

1. THE ORIGINS OF PALESTINIAN AND TRANSJORDANIAN NATIONALISM

1. In the mid-nineteenth century, the competition among European powers to increase their influence in Palestine rose remarkably. Acting in the name of preserving the religious rights of the Christians in the Holy Land, each of the powers strove to support one or another of the local Christian churches that were themselves engaged in a fierce competition for greater influence. Thus, for example, Orthodox Russia competed with Catholic France, while Catholic Austria competed with Protestant Britain and Catholic France. Consuls representing these countries were appointed in Jerusalem, Jaffa, and Acre, where they maintained close contacts with the notables of the local congregations of the church supported by the consul's country.

2. See Rashid Khalidi, *Palestinian Identity* (New York: Columbia University Press, 1997), 150–153.

3. Yehoshua Porath, *The Emergence of the Palestinian Arab National Movement* (London: Cass, 1974), 6.

4. Ibid., 7.

5. Khalidi, *Palestinian Identity*, 151.

6. Ibid., 29.

7. Ali Mahafthah, *Al-Fikr al-Siyasi fi Filastin* [Political Thought in Palestine,1918–1948] (Amman: Markaz al-Kutub al-Urduni, 1989), 19.

8. Cited in ibid., 20.

9. Porath, *Emergence of the Palestinian Arab National Movement*, 29.

10. Shaul Mishall, *West Bank/East Bank* (New Haven, Conn.: Yale University Press, 1978), 4.

11. David Fromkin, *A Peace to End All Peace* (New York: Avon, 1990), 528.

12. Uriel Dann, *Studies in the History of Transjordan, 1920–49* (Boulder, Colo.: Westview Press, 1984), 18.

13. Fromkin, *A Peace to End All Peace*, 513.

14. Benedict Anderson, *Imagined Communities: Reflections on the Origins and Spread of Nationalism* (New York: Verso, 1991), 163–164.

15. Suleiman Mousa, *Tarikh al-Urdun al-Siyasi* [The Political History of Jordan]: *1900–59*, 2d ed. (Amman: Maktabat al-Muhtasib, 1996), 106–109.

16. Abdullah ibn al-Hussein, *Al-Athar al-Kamilah Lil-Malik Abdullah* [The Complete Works of King Abdullah] (Beirut: al-Dar al-Mutahida lil-Nashr, 1979), 161.

17. Anne Sinai and Allen Pollack, *The Hashemite Kingdom of Jordan and the West Bank: A Handbook* (New York: American Academic Association for Peace in the Middle East, 1977), 39.

18. Dann, *Studies in the History of Transjordan*, 11.

19. Peter Gubser, *Politics and Change in al-Karak, Jordan: A Study of a Small Arab Town and Its District* (London: Oxford University Press, 1973), 102.

20. Naseer Aruri, *Jordan: A Study in Political Development, 1921–65* (The Hague: Nijhoff, 1972), 5.

21. Ernst Gellner, *Nations and Nationalism* (Ithaca, N.Y.: Cornell University Press, 1983), 15.

2. THE STRUGGLE OVER PALESTINE

1. On November 2, 1917, British foreign secretary Arthur J. Balfour issued a statement that declared, "His Majesty's government view with favor the establishment in Palestine of a national home for the Jewish people, and will use their best endeavors to facilitate the achievement of this object, it being clearly understood that nothing shall be done which may prejudice the civil and religious rights of existing non-Jewish communities in Palestine, or the rights and political status enjoyed by the Jews in any other country." This statement, which became known as the Balfour Declaration, was endorsed by Britain's allies at the San Remo Conference of April 1920 and incorporated in the terms of the mandate over Palestine in July 1922.

2. A. Konikoff, *Transjordan: An Economic Survey* (Jerusalem: Economic Research Institute of the Jewish Agency for Palestine, 1946), 94.

3. The Supreme Muslim Council was created in 1922 by the British government in Palestine as part of an effort to conciliate Arab antagonism to Jewish immigration. The council, without government control, was to administer al-Awqaf (the Muslim trust) and to appoint and dismiss the judges and officers of the *shari'a* (Islamic law) courts.

4. Walter Laqueur and Barry Rubin, eds., *The Israel-Arab Reader: A Documentary History of the Middle East Conflict* (New York: Facts on File, 1985), 84.

5. Al-Hai'a al-Arabiya al-Ulia was set up by the council of the Arab League on June 19, 1946. It was distinct from al-Lajna al-Arabiya al-Ulia, which was set up with the mufti as its president to supervise and guide the Palestinian general strike in 1936, which developed into a rebellion against the British mandate authorities and the Jewish community. In English, the two bodies have the same name—the Higher Arab Committee (HAC).

6. Avi Shlaim, *Collusion across the Jordan: King Abdullah, the Zionist Movement, and the Partition of Palestine* (New York: Columbia University Press, 1988), 130–131.

7. After fleeing Palestine in 1939, the mufti had settled in Iraq until 1941; then he escaped to Germany, where he stayed until the end of the war. During his years of exile, he maintained his leadership and influence in Palestinian politics.

8. Zvi Elpeleg, *Grand Mufti*, trans. Mustafa Kabaha (Acre, Israel: Mu'assassat al-Ansar Publications, 1989), 140.

9. Shlaim, *Collusion*, 167.

10. Aref el-Aref, *Nakbet Filastin wa al-Firdaws al-Mafqud* [The Debacle of Palestine and the Lost Paradise], vol. 3 (Beirut: Dar al-Huda, 1956), 707.

11. Ibid., 878.

12. Shlaim, *Collusion*, 412.

3. UNIFICATION OF THE TWO BANKS

1. Jordanian Parliament, *Official Gazette*, June 2, 1949.

2. Ibid.

3. Shlaim, *Collusion*, 435.

4. Department of State, "Policy of the United States with Respect to Jordan," 611.8514-1750 (issued in Washington, D.C., April 17, 1950).

5. Robert Satloff, *From Abdullah to Hussein: Jordan in Transition* (New York: Oxford University Press, 1994), 66, 77.

6. Suleiman Mousa, *Tarikh al-Urdun Fi al-Qarn al-Ishrin, 1958–95* [Jordan's History in the Twentieth Century], vol. 2 (Amman: Maktabet al-Muhtasib, 1996), 510.

7. John Bagot Glubb, *A Soldier with the Arabs* (London: Hodder and Stoughton, 1957), 237–274.

8. Satloff, *From Abdullah to Hussein*, 61.

9. Aruri, *Jordan*, 93.

10. Dispatch 785.00/9-2051, Amman, September 20, 1951.

11. Satloff, *From Abdullah to Hussein*, 43.

12. Telegram 78.0017-3151, Amman, July 31, 1951.

13. Department of State, "Policy of the United States with Respect to Jordan."

14. Chargé d'affaires in Jordan (Fritzlan) to the Department of State, Dispatch 110.15MCG/3-2951, Amman, March 29, 1951.

15. Department of State, Central Files, 785.5-MSP/2-1857.

16. Cited in Satloff, *From Abdullah to Hussein*, 10.

17. Mishall, *West Bank/East Bank*, 43.

4. KING HUSSEIN

1. I use the "semi-liberal" term instead of "liberal" as opposite to "conservative" because the nonconservative parties in the 1950s and 1960s had no clear position on democracy and civil and human rights. Their main focus was on regional and international political issues.

2. Satloff, *From Abdullah to Hussein,* 76.

3. Glubb, *A Soldier with the Arabs,* 245–246.

4. Satloff, *From Abdullah to Hussein,* 82.

5. Aruri, *Jordan,* 93.

6. Ibid., 101.

7. Glubb, *A Soldier with the Arabs,* 250–251.

8. Aruri, *Jordan,* 120.

9. Satloff, *From Abdullah to Hussein,* 123.

10. Aruri, *Jordan,* 135–136.

11. Ibid., 131.

12. Ibid., 139.

13. Kamal S. Salibi, *A Modern History of Jordan* (London: I. B. Tauris, 1993), 206.

14. Ibid., 195.

15. Article 51 states: "Nothing in the present Charter shall impair the inherent right of individual or collective self-defense if an armed attack occurs against a Member of the United Nations, until the Security Council has taken measures necessary to maintain international peace and security. Measures taken by Members in the exercise of this right of self-defense shall be immediately reported to the Security Council and shall not in any way affect the authority and responsibility of the Security Council under the present Charter to take at any time such action as it deems necessary in order to maintain or restore international peace and security."

16. Aruri, *Jordan,* 172.

17. King Hussein, *Uneasy Lies the Head: An Autobiography of H.M. King Hussein of Jordan* (London: Heinemann, 1962), 75.

18. This information is based on a personal conversation with Wasfi al-Tal in April 1967.

19. Aruri, *Jordan,* 170.

20. Salibi, *Modern History of Jordan,* 205.

21. Hazem Nusseibeh, *Tarikh al-Urdun al-Siyasi al-Mu'asir* [Contemporary Political History of Jordan], *1952–67,* vol. 2 (Amman: Committee of Jordan History, 1990), 106.

22. Ibid., 156.

5. THE SEEDS OF THE PALESTINIAN ENTITY AND THE RISE OF THE NATIONAL PALESTINIAN LEADERSHIP

1. The Israeli military operation "Grapes of Wrath" lasted from April 11 until April 26, 1996, when a cease-fire agreement was reached. The operation resulted in the deaths of 150 Lebanese, mostly civilians, and in the destruction of sizable portions of Lebanese infrastructure. The Arab world was at the peak of its anger when the PNC adopted its resolution.

2. Arab League Resolution 17, 2nd Ordinary Session, 12th meeting, December 4, 1945.

3. Arab League Resolution 1909, 40th Ordinary Session, 2nd meeting, September 19, 1963.

4. Moshe Shemesh, *The Palestinian Entity, 1959–74: Arab Politics and the PLO* (London: Cass, 1988), 33.

5. Omar Massalha, *Towards the Long-Promised Peace* (London: Saqi Books, 1994), 156.

6. Ibid.

7. Mishall, *East Bank/West Bank,* 109.

8. Ibid.

9. Ibid., 114.

10. Massalha, *Towards the Long-Promised Peace,* 163.

11. Cited in Karl W. Deutsch and William J. Foltz, eds., *Nation Building* (New York: Atherton Press, 1966), 10.

12. Herbert C. Kelman, "Nationalism, Patriotism, and National Identity: Social-Psychological Dimensions," in D. Bartal and E. Staub, eds., *Patriotism in the Lives of Individuals and Nations* (Chicago: Nelson Hall, 1997), 173.

13. Ibid.

14. Ibid.

6. THE INTERACTION BETWEEN JORDAN (THE STATE) AND THE PALESTINIAN ENTITY (THE ORGANIZATIONS)

1. Salibi, *Modern History of Jordan,* 212.

2. Mousa, *Tarikh al-Urdun,* 102.

3. Asher Susser, *On Both Banks of the Jordan: A Political Biography of Wasfi al-Tal* (London: Cass, 1994), 80.

4. Mousa, *Tarikh al-Urdun,* 78.

5. Shemesh, *Palestinian Entity,* 45.

6. Mousa, *Tarikh al-Urdun,* 78.

7. Abu Iyad (Salah Khalaf), *Filastini bila Hawiya* [A Palestinian without Identity] (Jerusalem: Manshurat al-Maktab al-Filastini lil-Khidmat al-Sanafiya, n.d.), 78–79.

8. Mousa, *Tarikh al-Urdun,* 82.

9. Susser, *On Both Banks of the Jordan,* 80–81.

10. Mousa, *Tarikh al-Urdun,* 103–104.

11. Shemesh, *Palestinian Entity,* 71.

12. Mousa, *Tarikh al-Urdun,* 97.

13. Ibid., 110.

14. Author's interview with Raji Sahyun (one of Shuqairi's aides, especially in the field of information at that time), Washington, D.C., June 1996.

15. Mousa, *Tarikh al-Urdun,* 109.

16. Shemesh, *Palestinian Entity,* 73–74.

17. Salibi, *Modern History of Jordan,* 215.

18. Mousa, *Tarikh al-Urdun,* 102.

19. Shemesh, *Palestinian Entity*, 74.

20. *Khamsa wa Ishrun Aman min al-Tarikh* [Twenty-Five Years of History], vol. 2 (London: Sharikat Samir Mutawi' lil-Nashr wa al-Alagat al-Ama, 1979), 435–438.

21. Mousa, *Tarikh al-Urdun*, 112.

22. Ibid., 114.

23. Abu Iyad, *Filastini bila Huwiya*, 82.

24. Mousa, *Tarikh al-Urdun*, 130.

25. Susser, *On Both Banks of the Jordan*, 116.

7. THE 1967 WAR

1. *Al-Watha'iq al-Urduniya* [Jordanian Documents] (Amman: Press and Publication Department, 1967), 54.

2. *Al-Watha'iq al-Urduniya*, 1967, 42.

3. Shemesh, *Palestinian Entity*, 128.

4. *Al-Watha'iq al-Urduniya*, 1967, 58–59.

5. Ibid., 7.

6. Ibid., 121.

7. Ibid., 308.

8. Mousa, *Tarikh al-Urdun*, 208.

9. *Al-Watha'iq al-Urduniya*, 1967, 58.

10. Ibid., 63.

11. Mousa, *Tarikh al-Urdun*, 226.

12. Shemesh, *Palestinian Entity*, 128.

13. *Al-Watha'iq al-Urduniya*, 1967, 97.

14. Ibid., 122–124.

15. Ibid., 274.

16. Vick Vance and Pierre Lauer, *Al-Malik Hussein: Harbuna maᶜa Isra'il* [King Hussein: Our War with Israel] (Beirut: Dar al-Nahar lil-Nashr, 1968), 115.

17. *Al-Watha'iq al-Urduniya*, 1967, 88.

18. Yehuda Lukacs, *Documents on the Israeli-Palestinian Conflict: 1967–83* (London: Cambridge University Press, 1984), 17.

19. *Al-Watha'iq al-Urduniya*, 1967, 103–109.

20. Mousa, *Tarikh al-Urdun*, 230–231.

21. Vance and Lauer, *Al-Malik Hussein*, 95.

22. *Al-Watha'iq al-Urduniya*, 1967, 98.

23. Salibi, *Modern History of Jordan*, 222.

24. *Al-Watha'iq al-Urduniya*, 1967, 202–203.

25. Ibid., 211–212.

26. Lukacs, *Documents on the Israeli-Palestinian Conflict*, 213; emphasis added.

27. Ibid.

28. Shemesh, *Palestinian Entity*, 90–91.

29. Mousa, *Tarikh al-Urdun*, 235.

30. Vance and Lauer, *Al-Malik Hussein*, 96.

8. FROM CONSENSUS TO CONTENTION

1. Abu Iyad, *Filastini bila Hawiya*, 102.

2. *Al-Watha'iq al-Urduniya*, 1970, 235.

3. Herbert Kelman, "The Palestinianization of the Arab-Israeli Conflict," *Jerusalem Quarterly* 46 (spring 1988).

4. Abu Iyad, *Filastini bila Hawiya*, 96.

5. Ibid., 99.

6. Ibid.

7. Helena Cobban, *The Palestine Liberation Organization: People, Power, and Politics* (Cambridge: Cambridge University Press, 1984), 34.

8. Mousa, *Tarikh al-Urdun*, 249–250.

9. *Al-Watha'iq al-Urduniya*, 1968, 46.

10. Cobban, *Palestine Liberation Organization*, 35.

11. Hisham Sharabi, *Palestinian Guerrillas: Their Credibility and Effectiveness*, Supplementary Papers, Center for Strategic and International Studies, Georgetown University (Washington, D.C.: Center for Strategic and International Studies, 1970), 3–4.

12. Cobban, *Palestine Liberation Organization*, 42.

13. Mousa, *Tarikh al-Urdun*, 365.

14. Shemesh, *Palestinian Entity*, 99.

15. Alan Hart, *Arafat: A Political Biography* (Bloomington: Indiana University Press, 1988), 314.

16. Ibid., 315.

17. Cobban, *Palestine Liberation Organization*, 48–49.

18. Sharabi, *Palestinian Guerrillas*, 26–27.

19. Hart, *Arafat*, 330.

20. William B. Quandt, *Decade of Decisions: American Policy toward the Arab-Israeli Conflict* (Berkeley: University of California Press, 1977), 63–64.

21. Ibid.

22. Ibid., 65.

23. Ibid., 66.

24. *Al-Watha'iq al-Urduniya*, 1968, 153–154.

25. Mousa, *Tarikh al-Urdun*, 252.

9. THE BATTLE FOR JORDAN

1. *Al-Watha'iq al-Urduniya*, 1968, 46.

2. Mousa, *Tarikh al-Urdun*, 253.

3. Abu Iyad, *Filastini bila Hawiya*, 105–106, 108.

4. Mousa, *Tarikh al-Urdun*, 258–59.

5. *Al-Watha'iq al-Urduniya*, 1969, 448.

6. *The Observer*, December 15, 1968, 1.

7. Frank Giles, *Sunday Times*, January 19, 1969.

8. *Al-Watha'iq al-Urduniya*, 1969, 274.

9. Mousa, *Tarikh al-Urdun*, 304.

10. *Al-Watha'iq al-Urduniya*, 1969, 255.

11. Abu Iyad, *Filastini bila Hawiya*, 136–137.

12. *Al-Watha'iq al-Urduniya*, 1970, 102–103.

13. Quandt, *Decade of Decisions*, 110.

14. Mousa, *Tarikh al-Urdun*, 319–320.

15. Abu Iyad, *Filastini bila Hawiya*, 136–137.

16. Mousa, *Tarikh al-Urdun*, 323.

17. Paul Lalor (lecturer in contemporary Arabic studies at Edinburgh University), "Black September, White September" (paper presented at a symposium sponsored by the Centre d'Études et de Recherches sur le Moyen-Orient Contemporain, Paris, June 24–25, 1997).

18. Reuters dispatch, Amman, September 22, 1970.

19. Mousa, *Tarikh al-Urdun*, 334

20. Quandt, *Decade of Decisions*, 113.

21. Ibid., 115.

22. Ibid., 117.

23. Mousa, *Tarikh al-Urdun*, 350.

24. Abu Iyad, *Filastini bila Hawiya*, 155.

25. Ibid., 155–156.

26. *Al-Watha'iq al-Urduniya*, 1968, 257.

27. Susser, *On Both Banks of the Jordan*, 175.

28. Mousa, *Tarikh al-Urdun*, 375.

29. Shemesh, *Palestinian Entity*, 147.

10. THE DYNAMICS OF RETROGRESSION

1. Marwan al-Saket, "Mutafiqun Am Mukhtalifun" [Agreed or Disagreed], *al-Hadath* (a Jordanian weekly), December 6, 1995, 9.

2. Oraib Rantawi, "Qira'a Fi al-Bu^cd al-Dakhili Lil-Alaqa Al-Urduniyya al-Filastiniya" [Reading the Domestic Component of the Jordanian-Palestinian Relationship], *al-Dustour* (a Jordanian daily), October 3, 1995, 27.

3. U.S. Department of State, *Country Reports on Human Rights Practices for 1995: Jordan*, a report submitted to the Committee on Foreign Relations, U.S. Senate, and the Committee on International Relations, U.S. House of Representatives, by the Department of State, April 1996, 1203.

4. Salibi, *Modern History of Jordan*, 246–247.

5. Abu Iyad, *Filastini bila Hawiya*, 131.

6. King Hussein, opening speech, first conference of the Jordanian National Union, Amman, November 25, 1971, *Al-Majmuᶜa al-Kamila Li-Khutab Jalalat al-Malik Hussein, 1952–1985* [The Complete Collection of H.M. King Hussein's Speeches, 1952–1985] (Amman: Ministry of Information, 1986), 341.

7. Author's interview with Fahad al-Fanek, Amman, August 31, 1995.

8. Arthur Day, *East Bank/West Bank* (New York: Council on Foreign Relations, 1986), 56.

9. Salibi, *Modern History of Jordan*, 251.

10. King Hussein, *Al-Majmuᶜa al-Kamila Li-Khutab Jalalat al-Malik Hussein*, address to the nation, March 15, 1972, 363–364.

11. Ibid., 362.

12. Salibi, *Modern History of Jordan*, 251.

13. Ibid.

14. Shemesh, *Palestinian Entity*, 230.

15. William B. Quandt, *Peace Process* (Washington, D.C.: Brookings Institute and University of California Press, 1993), 299.

16. Adam Garfinkle, *Israel and Jordan in the Shadow of War* (New York: St. Martin's Press, 1992), 91.

17. Shemesh, *Palestinian Entity*, 266.

18. Salibi, *Modern History of Jordan*, 257.

19. King Hussein, *Al-Majmuᶜa al-Kamila Li-Khutab Jalalat al-Malik Hussein*, address to the nation, November 30, 1974, 497.

20. Early in the seventh century A.D., Prophet Muhammad emigrated with his followers *(muhajirin)* from his hometown of Mecca to Medina in order to escape increasing persecution by the infidels. The people of Medina *(ansar)* welcomed the prophet, and most of them embraced Islam. Both *muhajirin* and *ansar* formed the first Islamic state in history and the base from which Islam spread.

21. Garfinkle, *Israel and Jordan*, 101.

22. Shemesh, *Palestinian Entity*, 232–333.

23. "Al-Shakhsiya al-Wataniya lil-Dawla al-Urduniya" [The National Identity of the State of Jordan], *al-Ra'i* (a Jordanian daily), December 15, 1994, 8.

24. Author's interview with Ibrahim Bakir, Amman, July 27, 1995.

25. *International Financial Statistics Yearbook*, vol. 48, *1995* (Washington, D.C.: International Monetary Fund, 1995), 474–475.

26. Lukacs, *Documents on the Israeli-Palestinian Conflict*, 23.

27. Yehuda Lukacs, *Israel, Jordan, and the Peace Process* (Syracuse: Syracuse University Press, 1997), 156.

28. Mousa, *Tarikh al-Urdun*, 466.

29. Lukacs, *Israel, Jordan, and the Peace Process*, 158.

30. Salibi, *Modern History of Jordan*, 262.

31. Lukacs, *Documents on the Israeli-Palestinian Conflict*, 243.

32. George Shultz, *Turmoil and Triumph: My Years as Secretary of State* (New York: Macmillan, 1993), 444.

33. Ibid., 454.

34. Ibid., 437.

35. Lukacs, *Israel, Jordan, and the Peace Process*, 166.

36. Shaul Mishal and Reuben Aharoni, *Speaking Stones* (Syracuse, N.Y.: Syracuse University Press), 70.

37. *King Hussein's Address to the Nation, July 31, 1988* (Amman: International Press Office, Royal Hashemite Court).

38. Interview with al-Majali, *al-Sharq al-Awsat* (Arabic daily published in London), April 10, 1995.

39. *Al-Mithaq al-Watani* [The National Charter] (Amman: Press Department, Government of Jordan, 1990), 49–50.

40. Laurie A. Brand, "Palestinians and Jordanians: A Crisis of Identity," *Journal of Palestine Studies* 24, no. 4 (summer 1995): 36.

41. Mousa, *Tarikh al-Urdun*, 589.

42. Lukacs, *Israel, Jordan, and the Peace Process*, 196.

43. *Summary of the Most Significant Results from the Opinion Polls Conducted on Current Relations between Palestinian-Jordanians and Transjordanians* (Amman: Center for Strategic Studies, Jordan University, 1995).

11. TRANSJORDANIAN NATIONALISM

1. George Tarabishi, *Al-Dawla al Qutriya wa al-Nazariya al-Qawmiya* [The Nation-State and National Theory] (Beirut: Dar al-Tali^ca wa al-lil Tab^ca wa al-Nashr, 1982), 20.

2. E. J. Hobsbawm, *Nations and Nationalism since 1780* (Cambridge: Cambridge University Press, 1990), 10.

3. Brand, *A Crisis of Identity*, 52.

4. "Al-Huwiya al-Wataniya wa Izdiwajiyat al-Wala'" [National Identity and Dual Loyalty], *al-Ra'i*, January 21, 1997, 6.

5. Interview with Abdul-Hadi al-Majali, Amman, February 1996.

6. "Al-Huwiya al-Wataniya wa Izdiwajiyat al-Wala, '" 6

7. Author's interview with al-Majali.

8. Dale F. Eickelman, "Being Bedouin: Nomads and Tribes in the Arab Social Imagination," in *Changing Nomads in a Changing World*, ed. Joseph Ginat and Anatoly Khorzanov (Brighton, Great Britain: Sussex University Press, 1997), 39–50.

9. Andrew Shryock, *Nationalism and the Genealogical Imagination* (Los Angeles: University of California Press, 1997), 311.

10. Ibid., 326.

11. Dr. al-Abbadi, "Jawaz Muba^c, Watan Muda^c" [A Sold Passport, a Lost Homeland], *al-Bilad* (a Jordanian weekly), November 1, 1995, 8.

12. Interview with al-Abbadi, *al-Hadath,* November 1, 1995, 5.

13. Salibi, *Modern History of Jordan,* 20.

14. Shryock, *Nationalism and the Genealogical Imagination,* 316–317.

15. Author's interview with Nahedh Hattar, Paris, June 23, 1997.

16. Tareq al-Tal, statement at a workshop organized by the Centre d'Études et de Recherches sur le Moyen Orient Contemporain (CERMOC), Amman, February 1996.

17. Ibid.

18. Ibid.

19. Benedict Anderson, *Imagined Communities,* rev. ed. (London: Verso, 1991), 101.

20. Shryock, *Nationalism and the Genealogical Imagination,* 316.

21. Kelman, "Nationalism, Patriotism, and National Identity," 171.

22. Bilal al-Tal, *al-Dustour,* February 4, 1997, 26.

23. Adnan Hadidi, ed., *Studies in the History and Archaeology of Jordan* (Amman: Director of Antiquities, 1982), 11.

24. Youssef Darwish Ghawanmeh, *Al-Tarikh al-Hadari li Sharq al-Urdun fi al-Asr al Mamluki* [The Civilization History of Transjordan in the Mamluke Era], 2d ed. (Amman: Dar al-Fikr lil-Nashr wa al-Tawazi^c, 1982), 117.

25. Ibid.

26. "Al-Shakhsiya al-Wataniya lil-Dawla al-Urduniya" [The National Identity of the State of Jordan], *al-Ra'i,* December 15, 1994, 8.

27. Amatzia Baram, "Territorial Nationalism in the Middle East," *Middle Eastern Studies* 26, no. 4 (October 1990): 428.

28. Ibid., 441.

29. Khaled al-Kassasbeh, "Al-Bahth An al-Ashia' al-Urduniya" [The Search for Jordan's Symbols], *al-Hadath,* May 29, 1996, 2.

30. Al-Tal, statement at CERMOC workshop.

31. Mousa, *Tarikh al-Urdun,* 379.

32. Valerie Yorke, "Jordan Is Not Palestine: The Demographic Factor," *Middle East International,* April 16, 1988, 16–17.

33. Ibid.

34. Abdulhadi al-Majali (the secretary general of al-Ahd party), *al-Ra'i,* February 1, 1997, 27.

35. Ibid.

36. Muhammad Said al-Juneidi, "La Lil Khiyar al-Urduni" [No to the Jordanian Option]," *al-Arab al-Alamiya* (a London-based Arab newspaper), February 17, 1997, 2.

37. "Al-Haraka al-Wataniya al-Urduniya Tuᶜalan Rafdaha Isdar Jawazat: Fidraliya wa Qunfidraliya" [The Jordanian National Movement Declares Its Rejection of Issuing Passports: Federation and Confederation], *al-Hadath,* November 1, 1995, 5.

38. Ali al-Fazza', *Al-A'mal Asshi'riyya* [Poetic Works] (Amman: Ministry of Culture, Manshurat al-Thaqafa, 1996), 14–15.

39. Taher al-Masri, "Rad Ala Muhadarat al-Amin al-Am li Hizb al-Ahd" [Response to the Lecture of the Secretary General of al-Ahd Party], *al-Ra'i*, January 27, 1997.

40. Anis al-Qassem, "Al-Difatan Wahid bil-nas al-Dustur" [The Two Banks Are One People by Constitution], *al-Aswaq* (a Jordanian daily), February 12, 1997, 1.

41. *Bayan ila al-Sha'b al-Urduni Sadir an al-Ahzab al-Urduniya al-Muwaqaᶜa Alayh bi-Sha'n al-Wahda al-Wataniya al-Urduniya* [A Statement Addressed to the Jordanian People by the Jordanian Parties That Are the Signatories of the Statement Concerning Jordanian National Unity], March 16, 1996.

CONCLUSIONS

1. Raad al-Kadiri, "The Palestinian Factor in Jordanian Foreign Policy: 1967–88," *Nationalism, Minorities, and Diasporas: Identities and Rights in the Middle East* (London: Tauris Academic Studies, 1996), 68.

2. President Clinton's address to Jordanian Parliament, October 26, 1994 (as distributed by the U.S. Information Agency and printed in Jordan's daily newspapers).

3. Fahad al-Fanek, "Jordan: A Stable and an Entrenched System," *El-Sharara* 4, no. 51 (June 15–30, 1996): 12.

4. Ibid.

5. "Nadwat al-Mithaq al-Watani" [The Symposium on the National Charter], *al-Dustour*, June 18, 1996, 6.

6. Marwan al-Mu'asher, *Jordan and the Peace Process*, Washington Institute for Near East Policy Special Policy Forum report no. 96 (Washington, D.C.: Washington Institute for Near East Policy, 1996).

7. "Jordan Cautions against Cuts in Refugee Services," *Jordan Times* (Jordanian English-language daily), December 13, 1996, 1.

8. Author's interview with al-Majali.

9. Jordan University, *Istitla' lil-Ra'i Hawl al-Alaqa al-Urduniya al Filastiniya* [Opinion Survey Regarding the Jordanian-Palestinian Relationship] (Markaz al-Dirasat al-Stratijiya, al Jamia'a al Urduniyya [Center for Strategic Studies, Jordan University], Amman, February 1995), table 3.

10. Hobsbawm, *Nations and Nationalism since 1780*, 11.

11. Hillel Frisch, "Ethnicity, Territorial Integrity, and Regional Order: Palestinian Identity in Jordan and Israel," *Journal of Peace and Research* 34, no. 3 (1997): 259.

12. Donna E. Arzt, *Refugees into Citizens* (New York: Council on Foreign Relations, 1997), 83–84.

13. Ibid., 83.

14. Ibid., 85, 90.

15. *Al-Ra'i*, September 8, 1997.

16. Hobsbawm, *Nations and Nationalism since 1780*, 11.

Index

Adnan Abu-Odeh was a senator in the Jordanian National Assembly from 1998 until March 1999, when he was appointed political adviser to King Abdullah II. He had previously served as Jordan's permanent representative to the United Nations, minister of information, chief of the Royal Court, and political adviser to King Hussein. He is a fellow at the Center for International Affairs at Harvard University and was a Senior Fellow at the United States Institute of Peace in 1995–96. He is a former fellow at the Woodrow Wilson International Center for Scholars and is a member of the Arab Thought Forum (Amman). He is also a member of the CSIS International Consultative Group on the Middle East. Abu-Odeh is the author of several English-language articles on the Middle East peace process, including "Two Capitals in an Undivided Jerusalem" in *Foreign Affairs* (spring 1992) and "Bridging the Gap of Peace in the Middle East" in the *Journal of Palestine Studies*.

JENNINGS RANDOLPH PROGRAM FOR INTERNATIONAL PEACE

This book is a fine example of the work produced by senior fellows in the Jennings Randolph fellowship program of the United States Institute of Peace. As part of the statute establishing the Institute, Congress envisioned a program that would appoint "scholars and leaders of peace from the United States and abroad to pursue scholarly inquiry and other appropriate forms of communication on international peace and conflict resolution." The program was named after Senator Jennings Randolph of West Virginia, whose efforts over four decades helped to establish the Institute.

Since 1987, the Jennings Randolph Program has played a key role in the Institute's efforts to build a national center of research, dialogue, and education on critical problems of conflict and peace. More than a hundred senior fellows from some thirty nations have carried out projects on the sources and nature of violent international conflict and the ways such conflict can be peacefully managed or resolved. Fellows come from a wide variety of academic and other professional backgrounds. They conduct research at the Institute and participate in the Institute's outreach activities to policymakers, the academic community, and the American public.

Each year approximately fifteen senior fellows are in residence at the Institute. Fellowship recipients are selected by the Institute's board of directors in a competitive process. For further information on the program, or to receive an application form, please contact the program staff at (202) 457-1700.

Joseph Klaits
Director

Jordanians, Palestinians, and the Hashemite Kingdom

This book is set in Galliard; the display types are Matrix and Kabel. Kenneth Allen designed the book's cover, and Joan Engelhardt and Day Dosch designed the interior. Pages were made up by Day Dosch. Nancy Palmer-Jones edited the text. The index was prepared by Susan Nedrow. The book's editor was Nigel Quinney.